Lynda Weinman's | Hands

Includes CD-ROM with Exercise Files

Acrobat® 5
H·O·T ™
Hands-On Training

lynda.com/books

By Garrick Chow
developed with **Lynda Weinman**

Acrobat 5 | H·O·T
Hands-On Training

By Garrick Chow
developed with Lynda Weinman

lynda.com/books | Peachpit Press
1249 Eighth Street • Berkeley, CA • 94710
800.283.9444 • 510.524.2178 •
510.524.2221 (fax)
http://www.lynda.com/books
http://www.peachpit.com

lynda.com/books is published
in association with Peachpit Press,
a division of Pearson Education
Copyright ©2003 by lynda.com

ISBN: 0-321-11275-X

0 9 8 7 6 5 4 3 2 1

Printed and bound in the
United States of America

H•O•T | Credits

Original Design: Ali Karp, Alink Newmedia *(alink@earthlink.net)*

lynda.com Director, Publications: Garo Green *(garo@lynda.com)*

Peachpit Project Manager: Suzie Lowey

Peachpit Copyeditors: Jennifer Ashley, Darren Meiss

Peachpit Proofreaders: Leslie Ayers, Darren Meiss

Peachpit Production: Myrna Vladic

Peachpit Compositors: Rick Gordon, Emerald Valley Graphics; Deborah Roberti, Espresso Graphics

Beta Testers: Steve Perry, Lisa Brenneis, and Mark Siler

Cover Illustration: Bruce Heavin *(bruce@stink.com)*

Exercise Graphics: Dominique Sillett

Indexer: Steve Rath

H•O•T | Colophon

The original design for Acrobat 5 H•O•T was sketched on paper. The layout was heavily influenced by online communication—merging a traditional book format with a modern Web aesthetic.

The text in Acrobat 5 H•O•T was set in Akzidenz Grotesk from Adobe and Triplex from Emigré. The cover illustration was painted in Adobe Photoshop 6.0 and Adobe Illustrator 9.0.

This book was created using QuarkXPress 4.1, Adobe Photoshop 6.0, and Microsoft Office 2001 on a Macintosh G4, running MacOS 9. It was printed on 50 lb. Utopia Book at Von Hoffmann, Owensville, Missouri.

Dedication

To my parents:

For supporting me in the paths I've followed,
and for providing guidance along the way.

Acrobat 5 | H•O•T _____ **Table of Contents**

Introduction

H•O•T

Acrobat 5

A Note from Lynda Weinman

Lots of people "use" Acrobat, but few people understand or use all its features. Garrick Chow has done a tremendous job of making this program come alive through thoughtful and educational tutorials. As a teacher at our training facility in Ojai, California, Garrick has long impressed us with his warmth, humor, intellect, and caring nature. As we worked on this book together, I was consistently impressed with how well it was turning out. In the process of developing the title, I got the unexpected benefit of becoming much more proficient in Acrobat than I ever expected. Our motto—read the book, follow the exercises, and you will know the product—has certainly proved true for me!

In my opinion, most people buy computer books in order to learn, yet it is amazing how few of these books are actually written by teachers. I take pride in the fact that this book was written by an experienced teacher who is familiar with training students in this subject matter. In this book, you will find carefully developed lessons and exercises to help you learn Acrobat 5—one of the most needed software packages on the planet!

This book is targeted toward beginning- to intermediate-level Acrobat users who are looking to become proficient in all of Acrobat's key features. The premise of the hands-on exercise approach is to get you up to speed quickly in Acrobat while actively working through the book's lessons. It's one thing to read about a product and another experience entirely to try the product and get measurable results. We have received countless testimonials that praise this book series, and it is our goal to make sure it remains true for all of the titles we take on!

Many exercise-based books take a paint-by-numbers approach to teaching. While this approach works, it's often difficult to figure out how to apply those lessons to a real-world situation, or to understand why or when you would use the technique again. What sets this book apart is that the lessons contain lots of background information and insights into each given subject, which are designed to help you understand the process as well as the exercise.

At times, pictures are worth a lot more than words. When necessary, we have also included short QuickTime movies to show any process that's difficult to explain with words. These files are located on the **H•O•T CD-ROM** inside a folder called **movies**. It's our style to approach teaching from many different angles, since we know that some people are visual learners, others like to read, and still others like to get out there and try things. This book combines a lot of teaching approaches so you can learn Acrobat 5 as thoroughly as you want to.

This book didn't set out to cover every single aspect of Acrobat. The manual, and many other reference books are great for that! What we saw missing from the bookshelves was a process-oriented tutorial that taught readers core principles, techniques, and tips in a hands-on training format.

We welcome your comments at **acro5hot@lynda.com**. Please visit our Web site at **http://www.lynda.com**. The support URL for this book is **http://www.lynda.com/products/books/acro5hot/**.

It's Garrick's and my hope that this book will raise your skills in creating and using PDFs. If it does, we will have accomplished the job we set out to do!

—Lynda Weinman

> **NOTE | About lynda.com/books and lynda.com**
>
> **lynda.com/books** is dedicated to helping Web designers and developers understand tools and design principles. **lynda.com** offers hands-on workshops, training seminars, conferences, on-site training, training videos, training CDs, and "expert tips" for Web design and development. To learn more about our training programs, books, and products, be sure to give our site a visit at **http://www.lynda.com**.

About the Author

Garrick Chow is an Adobe Certified Expert in Acrobat 5. In addition to Acrobat 5 Hands-On-Training, he has also authored *Learning Acrobat 5*, a self-paced study program on CD-ROM available through **lynda.com**. Garrick has been instructing students in Acrobat since version 3, and it remains as one of his favorite applications to teach. In addition to his classes at **lynda.com** in Ojai, California, he also trains on-site at private corporations and state and federal agencies across the country.

When he isn't traveling, Garrick lives in Harrisburg, Pennsylvania, where he teaches Web design courses and works as a freelance Web consultant. In his other life, Garrick plays bass in the indie-rock band The Jellybricks (**www.thejellybricks.com**). He can often be found in the band's van, working on his laptop with a blanket over his head.

Gratuitous Photos of the Author

Garrick recording tracks for his band's next album while simultaneously contemplating the next chapter in his book.

Garrick prepares to launch the Space Shuttle from his home command console.

Acknowledgments

My deepest thanks and appreciation to:

Lynda Weinman, for giving this former student of yours the amazing opportunity to teach in your class-rooms and represent your school around the country. Thank you for having the faith in me to write this book and for your encouragement, support, and guidance along the way

Garo Green, for being the grizzled veteran (and I'm a month older than you!) I knew I could turn to for advice and 24-hour support.

Maggie Bachleda, for giving me my first teaching job and for introducing me to Acrobat way back when. Thanks to both you and **Kevin Cagno** for your valuable real-world insights into Acrobat.

Domenique Sillett, for all of your wonderful work designing exercise files. Turning my clumsy sketches into files that people would actually appreciate is no small feat. I shudder to think of what some of these exercises would have looked like without you.

Dan Klain, **Dave Clipper**, **Jay Nelson**, and **Matt Chroust** for your generous contributions of content and/or server space. You've helped to take this book's interactivity to a higher level.

My **beta testers**, **Lisa Brennis**, **Mark Siler**, and **Steve Perry**. You guys kept me honest and made sure I didn't cut any corners. Your suggestions, corrections, and tips made this a better book than I could have hoped for.

My bandmates **Larry Kennedy**, **Bryce Connor**, and **Tom Kristich** for being understanding, or at least tolerant, of my frequent trips out of state. And when it comes to being stuck in a van with three guys for days on end, I'm glad it's with you guys.

And **Leigh Ann Berry**, for editing my first drafts and making me look like a better writer than I really am. Your support and encouragement made a world of difference. I couldn't have written this book without you.

How to Use This Book

Please read this section—it contains important information that's going to help you as you use this book. The chart below outlines the information we cover:

Acrobat 5 H•O•T
Information in this section:
The Formatting in This Book
About Operating System Differences and Screenshots
Macintosh and Windows Interface Screen Captures
A Note to Windows Users
Making Exercise Files Editable on Windows Systems
Making File Extensions Visible on Windows Systems
Acrobat System Requirements
What's on the CD-ROM?

The Formatting in This Book

This book has several components, including step-by-step exercises, commentary, notes, tips, warnings, and movies. Step-by-step exercises are numbered, and file names and command keys are shown in bold so they pop out more easily. Captions and commentary are in italicized text: *This is a caption.* File names/folders, command keys, and menu commands are bolded: **images** folder, **Ctrl+Click**, and **File > Open**. Code is in a monospace font: `<html></html>`. URLs are in bold: **http://www.lynda.com**.

About Operating System Differences and Screenshots

At the time of publication of this book, Acrobat is supported by more than half a dozen operating systems. Windows 95, 98, 2000, ME, NT, and XP as well as Mac OS 8.6, 9.x, and X can all run Acrobat 5. Fortunately, Acrobat's differences between operating systems are minor, with the greatest variations occurring between Windows and Macintosh platforms. Because Acrobat has a larger user base in Windows operating systems, screenshots in this book were taken in Windows XP Professional, using the Classic Appearance theme that more closely resembles earlier Windows versions. Differences between Acrobat on Windows and Macintosh have been noted at the necessary locations throughout the book, and screenshots have been provided in Mac OS 9.x or X, as the situation warranted.

A Note to Windows Users

This section contains essential information about making your exercise folders editable and making file extensions visible.

Making Exercise Files Editable on Windows Systems

By default, when you copy files from a CD-ROM to your Windows 95/98/2000/XP hard drive, they are set to read-only (write protected). This will cause a problem with the exercise files, because you will need to write over some of them.

1. Copy the chapter folder from the **H•O•T CD-ROM** to your hard drive.

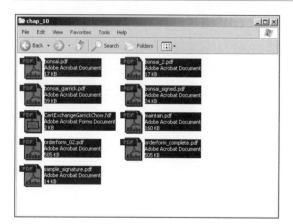

2. Open the chapter folder and press **CTRL+A** to select the folder's entire contents.

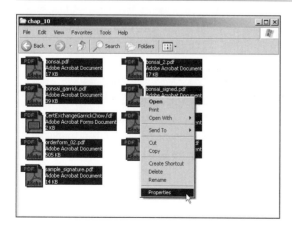

3. Right-click on one of the selected items and choose **Properties**.

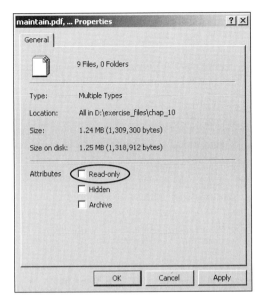

4. In the Properties window, uncheck **Read-only**. If **Archive** is selected, uncheck it as well. This will change the setting for all of the selected files.

5. Click **OK**.

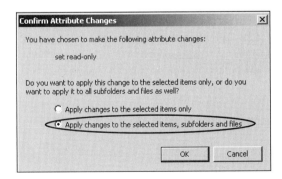

6. If there are other folders inside the chapter folder, Windows 2000 and XP users have the option of selecting **Apply changes to this folder, subfolder, and files** to make the contents of all folders editable. Users of earlier Windows systems, will have to open each subfolder and follow steps 2 through 5 above.

Making File Extensions Visible on Windows Systems

In this section, you'll see two different examples of how to turn on file extensions for Windows 98 and Windows 2000/XP. By default, Windows 98/2000 users cannot see file extensions, such as **.gif**, **.jpg**, or **.html**. Fortunately you can change this setting!

Windows 98 Users:

1. Double-click on the **My Computer** icon on your desktop. **Note:** If you (or someone else) have changed the name, it will not say **My Computer**.

2. Select **View > Folder Options**. This opens the **Folder Options** dialog box.

3. Click on the **View** tab at the top. This opens the **View** options screen so you can change the view settings for Windows 98.

4. Uncheck the **Hide file extensions for known file types** checkbox. This makes all of the file extensions visible.

Windows 2000/XP Users:

1. Double-click on the **My Computer** icon on your desktop. **Note:** If you (or someone else) have changed the name, it will not say **My Computer**.

2. Select **Tools > Folder Options**. This opens the **Folder Options** dialog box.

3. Click on the **View** tab at the top. This opens the **View** options screen so you can change the view settings for Windows 2000.

4. Make sure there is no checkmark next to the **Hide file extensions for known file types** option. This makes all of the file extensions visible.

Acrobat System Requirements

This book requires that you use either a Macintosh operating system (Power Macintosh running System 8.6 or later) or Windows 95, Windows 98, Windows 2000, Windows NT 4.0, or Windows XP. Some features of Acrobat are not yet fully compatible or available on Mac OS X, and have been noted throughout the book. You also will need a color monitor capable of at least 800 × 600 resolution and a CD-ROM drive. We suggest that you have at least 64 MB of RAM in your system, so that you can open Acrobat and a Web browser at the same time, which will be necessary for certain exercises. More RAM than that is even better, especially on Macintosh computers, which do not dynamically allocate RAM, as Windows does. Although Mac OS X does dynamically allocate RAM, more is always better. Here's a little chart that cites Adobe's RAM requirements, along with our recommendations:

Acrobat System Requirements		
	Acrobat Requires	**We Recommend**
Mac	32 MB	64 MB
Windows 95/98/NT/2000/XP	32 MB	64 MB

What's on the CD-ROM?

Exercise Files and the H•O•T CD-ROM

Your course files are located inside a folder called **exercise_files** on the **H•O•T CD-ROM**. These files are divided into chapter folders, and you will be instructed to copy the chapter folders to your hard drive during many of the exercises. Unfortunately, when files originate from a CD-ROM, the Windows operating system defaults to making them write-protected, meaning that you cannot alter them. You will need to alter them to follow the exercises, so please read "A Note to Windows Users" for instructions on how to convert them to read-and-write formatting.

Files on the CD-ROM

Unlike other books from the H•O•T series that included trial versions of software, there is no trial version of Adobe Acrobat available, so you will need to purchase and install the full version before beginning the exercises in this book. We also strongly recommend that you install the upgrade to Acrobat 5.05, which offers many improvements to Acrobat. The upgrade is included on the **H•O•T CD-ROM**. The **H•O•T CD-ROM** also contains installers for:

• Acrobat Reader 5.05

• The Make Accessible plug-in for Windows (used in Chapter 15)

• The Paper Capture plug-in for Windows (used in Chapter 13)

1.

Background

Before you begin reading the rest of this book, take a few moments to read through this chapter, which covers some fundamental points about Acrobat and the PDF format. There's nothing technical in this chapter, but it should help define the PDF format and clear up any confusion you might have about the different Acrobat products available. After you've familiarized yourself with some basic terms and concepts, you'll then be able to jump right into the exercises.

no exercise files

Acrobat 5 H•O•T

Why Write a Book About Acrobat?

When I first began telling my friends that I was writing a book on Adobe Acrobat, the most common response was usually something like, "What do you need to write a whole book for? Isn't Acrobat just for looking at documents?" I would then launch into my well-rehearsed speech about how they were thinking about *Acrobat Reader* and not the full version of Acrobat. My so-called friends would then respond with, "Oh. But what do you need to write a whole book for?"

To me, that annoying little question is exactly why Acrobat deserves to have an entire book devoted to its features. It is true that most people's exposure to Adobe Acrobat comes via Acrobat Reader, the free program through which anyone can view PDF (**P**ortable **D**ocument **F**ormat) files. But where do these PDFs come from? And once a PDF has been created, what else can be done with it other than immediately sending it out into the world?

Adobe Acrobat 5 offers a rich set of features that have been refined over the course of its previous releases. It also includes many new features that can help you enhance and—to use a technical phrase—add some pizzazz to your documents.

It's my hope that this book will replace "What do you need Acrobat for?" with "How the heck did you make your document do that?"

Acrobat and PDF

Adobe Acrobat and the Portable Document Format (PDF) were developed out of a need for a universal file format that could be opened on any computer regardless of platform or operating system. The PDF format allows you to create accurate versions of your documents for the purpose of electronic distribution. With Acrobat installed on your computer, you can create PDF files from any application that has a print function, and remain confident that your users will see the document exactly as you intended it to be viewed. PDF files preserve a document's layout, formatting, fonts, colors, and graphics, and can be opened and accurately printed by anyone who has Acrobat or the free Acrobat Reader installed on his or her computer.

As its name implies, Acrobat Reader allows you to view a PDF document. It does not, however, allow you to edit or create PDFs. Acrobat Reader is available via free download from Adobe's Web site (**www.adobe.com**), but is often pre-installed on most computer systems. Also, many software manufacturers now publish their user manuals in PDF format and include Acrobat Reader on their installation CDs.

Acrobat, on the other hand, is the name of the full-featured application that not only allows the viewing of PDFs, but also contains the necessary components to create and edit PDFs. The differences between Acrobat and Acrobat Reader will be discussed further in Chapter 2, *"Interface."*

The Acrobat Family

With the increasing popularity of the PDF format, Adobe has developed several applications that bear the Acrobat name. Having so many programs named Acrobat Something has created a bit of confusion for some people. To make matters worse, the main Acrobat application itself actually consists of other applications that bear the Acrobat moniker. Here's a brief listing of what's currently available:

Acrobat 5

This is the main program. It contains everything you need to create, edit, and view PDF files. Throughout the rest of the book, whenever the word **Acrobat** appears by itself, it refers to this application. Other applications will be referred to by their full names, such as Acrobat Reader or Acrobat Capture.

Acrobat Distiller

When you install Acrobat, it also installs Acrobat Distiller, an application whose sole purpose is to create PDFs. Acrobat Distiller is one of the components of the main Acrobat program; it is not available separately. Chapter 12, *"Acrobat Distiller,"* is devoted entirely to Distiller.

Acrobat Reader

A free application used only for viewing PDF documents. Reader is not capable of creating or editing PDFs. Users of Acrobat Reader can view and print PDFs as well as fill out and submit PDF forms, but Acrobat Reader cannot save a partially completed form to be completed at a later time. Acrobat Reader is available for Mac OS, Windows, Unix, Palm OS, and several other platforms, making PDF a truly universal format.

Acrobat Approval

An application for filling out and saving PDF forms. Acrobat Approval is ideal for businesses whose employees need to fill out and save PDF forms, but do not need the more expensive, full featured Acrobat.

Acrobat Capture

A specialized application for scanning large volumes of paper documents and converting them to PDF.

Acrobat Distiller Server

An application that specializes in converting PostScript files to PDF over a network.

Acrobat Messenger

An application used for automatically scanning paper documents, converting them to PDF, and then sending them electronically via e-mail, Web, or fax.

These are most, but not all, of the products currently available in the Acrobat family. This book, however, covers only Acrobat 5 and Acrobat Reader, the two most mainstream Acrobat applications. Additional information on other Acrobat products can be found at Adobe's Web site (**http://www.adobe.com/ acrofamily/familyprod**).

About This Book

This book is intended for beginning and intermediate users of Adobe Acrobat 5. It covers the features that will be most useful for people using Acrobat to create PDFs for electronic distribution via the World Wide Web, local network, or on CD-ROM. This book does not cover the preparation of PDFs for use in prepress or professional printing scenarios. For an excellent source of information on this advanced topic, pick up a copy of **Real World PDF with Adobe Acrobat 5** by Anita Dennis (Peachpit Press).

Although this book is intended to be read in sequential order, you can also skip ahead or around as needed. The exercises in each chapter do not rely on having completed exercises in prior chapters, although I will occasionally refer to techniques covered in previous lessons. For example, the bulk of the book's chapters cover working with previously-created PDFs, but if you want to skip ahead to learn how to create PDFs from scratch, you can jump ahead to Chapter 12, "Acrobat Distiller."

As you progress through this book, you'll learn about the many PDF-enhancing features Acrobat offers. You'll soon find that you can do far more with your PDFs than simply creating them and posting them online. You can add bookmarks, create links, generate form fields, and add security to your documents. Each of these functions and more are covered in detail throughout the book.

Screenshots for this book were taken in Windows XP Professional. Fortunately, Acrobat is fairly consistent across Windows and Macintosh operating systems. In the few areas where the versions of Acrobat differ, screenshots from either Mac OS 9 or OS X have been included. In fact, this book is so packed with screenshots that if you flip through the pages fast enough, it looks like you're watching a movie. Well, not really, but speaking of movies, the **H•O•T CD-ROM** includes several movies that demonstrate certain exercises that might be confusing or difficult to understand on paper.

Upgrading to Acrobat 5.05

If you haven't done so already, please upgrade your copy of Acrobat 5 to version 5.05 before beginning the exercises in this book. For Windows users, the 5.05 upgrade offers increased stability and adds support for Windows XP and better integration with Office XP. For Macintosh users, the 5.05 upgrade offers increased stability and installs PDFMaker, a macro for creating PDFs from Microsoft Office 98/2001. The upgrade also makes Acrobat run natively in Mac OS X (although Distiller still needs to open in Classic mode). You can download the 5.05 upgrade from **http://ww.adobe.com/ products/acrobat/update.html**.

2.

Interface

The Acrobat 5 Main Window	The Status Bar
The Toolbar	Viewing Tools	Basic Tools	Navigation Tools
View History Tools	Expanding Toolbar Buttons
Undocking Toolbars	The Navigation Pane

no exercise files

Acrobat 5 H•O•T

This chapter will expand your knowledge of the Acrobat 5 interface and will help you learn some efficient ways to navigate in your documents. Its focus is on the main interface areas and the purposes they serve.

If you've worked with other Adobe applications, you might discover that you are in new interface territory here. That's because the Acrobat interface is quite different from the interfaces of other Adobe applications. Most Adobe applications are designed for creating artistic media, such as images in Photoshop, illustrations in Illustrator, Web sites in GoLive, and so on. Acrobat is different because you don't have access to paintbrushes, pens, and other creative tools for creating new media. Instead, Acrobat is designed to bring together many different types of media into a single and accessible Portable Document Format (PDF) file. Once a document has been saved in this format, anyone with the free Acrobat Reader application can read and print it, regardless of the applications originally used to create the source files.

Acrobat and Acrobat Reader

Acrobat and Acrobat Reader are virtually identical in terms of navigational interface; therefore the information in this chapter applies to either version. Adobe's free Acrobat Reader, which is included on the **H•O•T CD-ROM** and can also be downloaded from Adobe's Web site, is a **PDF viewer** and does not offer any true editing capabilities. If you want to create new PDF documents, generate bookmarks and thumbnails, create forms, move pages, or otherwise alter your PDF documents, you must use the full Acrobat application. We'll be exploring Acrobat's authoring tools throughout the rest of the book, but for now we'll concentrate on the navigation tools that Acrobat and Acrobat Reader have in common. To help you with this task, this chapter will review the main Acrobat 5 interface areas: the status bar, the toolbar, and the Navigation pane.

The Acrobat 5 Main Window

The **main window** of Acrobat and Acrobat Reader contains everything that has to do with your PDF document. The PDF is displayed in the **Document pane**. The rest of the window contains the various tools and displays used to work with the PDF. In the full Acrobat application, the main window contains the tools necessary to view, alter, or enhance a PDF document.

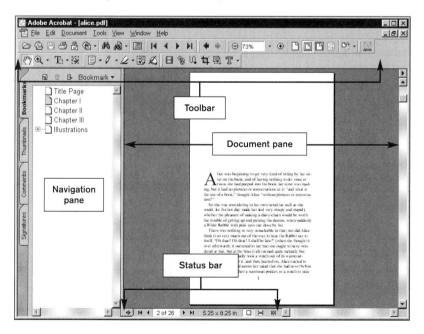

The Adobe Acrobat interface consists of four main components: the toolbar, Navigation pane, Document pane, and status bar.

The Acrobat 5 Reader Main Window

The Acrobat Reader main window is almost the same as the Acrobat main window, but it contains only the tools needed to view and navigate the document.

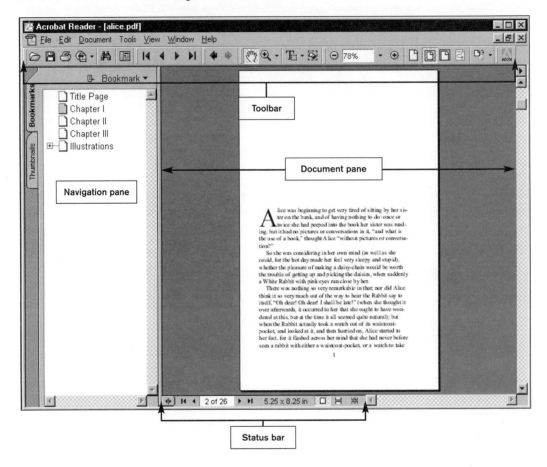

Acrobat Reader lacks any tools that allow you to edit or alter the PDF. Otherwise, its interface is nearly identical to that of Acrobat.

NOTE | Customizable Toolbars

In Acrobat 5 and Acrobat Reader 5, Adobe has introduced customizable toolbars, so the locations of the tools in the toolbar on your screen might vary from the screen shots in this chapter. We'll discuss how to customize the toolbar later in this chapter.

The Status Bar

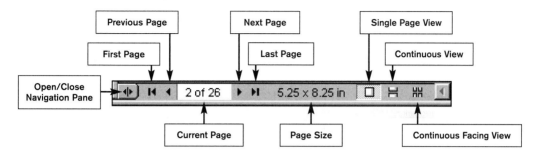

The **status bar** is located in the lower left corner of the document pane. It can be used to page through your document and to view information such as the currently displayed page and the dimensions of the printed page.

The left side of the status bar contains the page navigation features, including buttons for navigating among the pages and information on the current page and the page size. The chart below lists the names and descriptions of these features.

Page Navigation Features on the Status Bar	
Button	**Description**
First Page	Takes you to the beginning of the document.
Previous Page	Takes you to the page that immediately precedes the current page.
Next Page	Takes you to the page immediately following the current page.
Last Page	Jumps to the end of the document.
Current Page	Tells you what page is currently being displayed onscreen. You can click inside this box, enter a new page number, and press Enter/Return to jump to that page. This can be a quick way to jump around in a large file.
Page Size	Indicates the print size of the document, but doesn't reflect the document's onscreen size (magnification size). The page size is just for display and can't be changed from within the status bar.
Open/Close Navigation Pane	Believe it or not, this button opens and closes the Navigation pane.

On the right side of the status bar are three buttons that control the **page display view**. You can choose among **Single Page**, **Continuous**, or **Continuous Facing** views. Often the default view will be Single Page view, which, as its name implies, allows you to view the document one page at a time. Scrolling through the document will snap each page into view individually. Scrolling while in **Continuous** or **Continuous Facing** view will display the pages end to end.

As with most applications, you can also navigate the document by clicking and dragging the scrollbox. The effect of dragging the scrollbox will vary depending on the page view you're in.

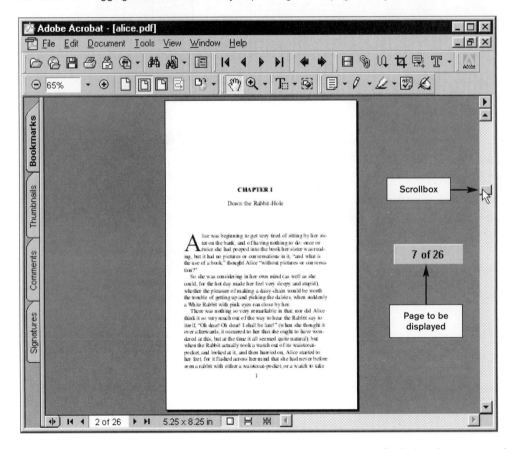

If you drag the scrollbox in Single Page view, a page indicator appears displaying the page number that will be displayed when you release the mouse button. This can very helpful when you have to jump quickly between pages in a large document.

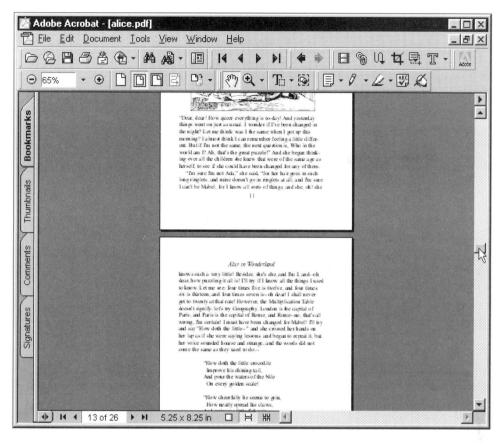

Dragging the scrollbox in Continuous or Continuous Facing view produces the same effect as clicking the scrollbar arrows: You'll see the document scrolling onscreen in end-to-end fashion.

The Toolbar

The **toolbar** is located at the top of your Document pane and consists of a number of small buttons that give you access to the various tools. In Acrobat, the buttons are arranged in seven categories: File, Basic, Viewing, Navigation, View History, Editing, and Commenting. Acrobat Reader lacks the Editing and Commenting categories. As you'll see later, each of these categories is actually a separate toolbar that can be displayed or hidden or dragged to another part of the screen. We'll cover the File, Commenting, and Editing toolbars later in this book; here we'll concentrate on the tools for viewing and navigating in your documents.

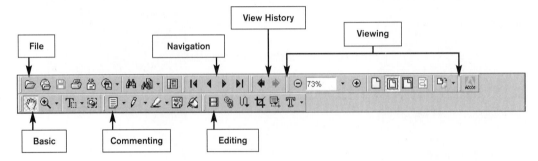

The Acrobat toolbar consists of a collection of small buttons that give you quick access to the most commonly used options.

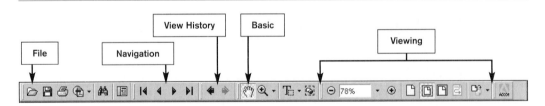

The Acrobat Reader toolbar gives you several options for navigating through a PDF document but no tools for altering or editing the document.

Viewing Tools

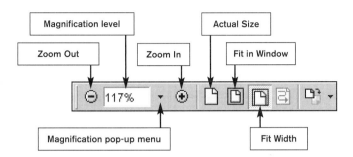

The **Viewing toolbar** controls the view of your document. The buttons on this toolbar affect only the appearance of your document onscreen, not the printed document. No matter how much you adjust the magnification of the document, its page size remains at its original setting. You can, however, use these buttons to make the PDF easier to read onscreen. The Viewing toolbar allows you to adjust your document's magnification in several ways.

The **Zoom Out button** lets you reduce the magnification view of the document. The smallest magnification available is 8.33%, which is very useful if you're using Acrobat to make billboards.

The **Zoom In button** lets you increase the magnification view of the document. The largest magnification available is 1600%, almost large enough to read the fine print in car dealership ads.

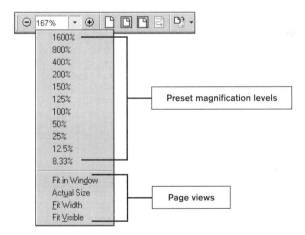

You can also use the **Magnification pop-up menu** to select from some preset magnification levels. The inherent problem with these percentage sizes, however, is that they will vary from monitor to monitor; for example, 150% on a monitor displaying 1024 x 768 resolution will look much smaller than 150% on a monitor displaying 800 x 600 resolution. The most useful magnification settings are the **page views** found at the bottom of the menu.

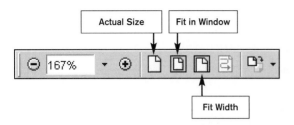

Because Actual Size, Fit in Window, and Fit Width are such common selections, they're also represented in button form in the Viewing toolbar. (Fit Visible is available only on the Magnification menu.) Take a moment to learn the icon for each button—it will save you time in the long run.

The following chart describes the page view options on the Viewing toolbar.

Page View Options on the Viewing Toolbar	
Button	**Description**
Actual Size	The equivalent of choosing 100%. Because of differences in monitor resolutions, 100% will not necessarily match the page size indicated in the status bar. Acrobat treats PDFs as 72-pixel-per-inch images, so at Actual Size each pixel on the page is represented by one pixel on the screen.
Fit in Window	Resizes the document so that it fits entirely within the document window, no matter what size the window happens to be, even when you resize it.
Fit Width	Displays the entire width of the document, allowing you to read the page without having to scroll from left to right. When you reach the bottom of the viewable area, you can scroll down to continue reading—an action we're all accustomed to from using word processors and Web browsers.
Fit Visible	Sometimes Fit Visible looks a lot like Fit Width. The difference is that while Fit Width fits the entire width of the page into the window, Fit Visible ignores empty regions, such as the margins on the page, and magnifies the width of the page's content.

TIP | Scrolling and View Settings

Sometimes trying to view the bottom of a page in Fit Width view can be frustrating. If you scroll down to the very bottom of the page you're currently on, you might click one too many times and end up seeing the top of the next page. This problem is a result of viewing the page in Single Page view. If you switch to Continuous view, you'll have a much easier time scrolling through your document.

Basic Tools

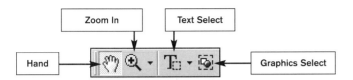

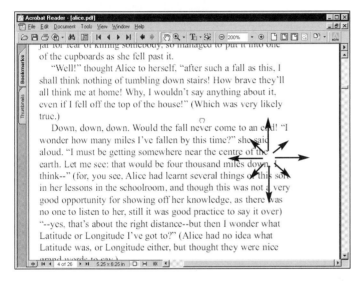

The Hand tool can be used to adjust the position of the page, in any direction, within the Document pane. This can be helpful when you are zoomed in on a document and need to see another portion of the page.

The **Basic toolbar** contains some of the tools you'll use most frequently in Acrobat. When you are navigating through your PDF documents, you'll most likely be using the **Hand tool** as your primary tool. The Hand tool allows you to drag a page when less than 100% of the page is visible. In Fit in Window view, you can see the whole page, so you can't drag it around the screen. In Fit Width, you can drag up and down, but not left and right, because you can already see the entire width of the page. The only time dragging is available when the whole page is visible is when you're in Continuous or Continuous Facing view.

 MOVIE | toolbar.mov

To view a movie of how the toolbar works, open toolbar.mov from the movie folder on the H•O•T CD-ROM.

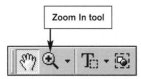

Zoom In tool

Next to the Hand tool, you'll find the **Zoom In tool**. The Zoom In tool behaves in much the same way as similar tools do in other programs, such as Adobe Photoshop or Illustrator.

When this tool is selected, you can use one of two methods to enlarge the image on the page. If you click directly on the image, the page magnification will increase with each click, based on preset magnification levels. A quicker technique, however, is to use the Zoom In tool to draw a rectangular selection, or **marquee**, around the portion of the image that you're interested in. This will enlarge the selected area to the largest possible size to fit within the Document pane.

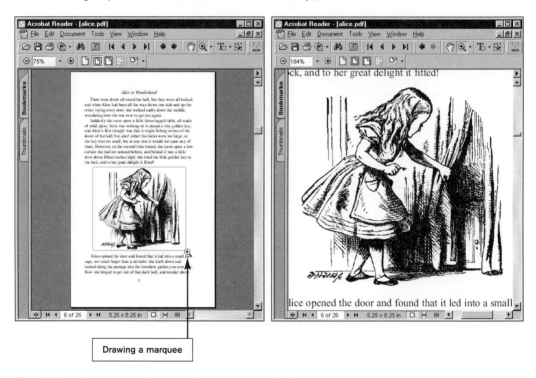

Drawing a marquee

To quickly enlarge a specific area of the page, use the Zoom In tool to drag a marquee around the area. The selected area will enlarge to fit the Document pane.

TIP | Dragging a Marquee with the Zoom In Tool

Use the "+" symbol in the Zoom In tool as the center point to draw the corners of your marquee. Keep in mind that Acrobat enlarges selections to their maximum proportional size. So if you accidentally draw a tiny selection area, your page will most likely zoom to 1600%. If that happens, just click the Fit in Window button to return your view to a more reasonable size and try again.

To reduce the magnification level of the document, you can select the **Zoom Out tool** by clicking the **More Tools button** next to the Zoom In tool. Realistically, though, the results of clicking with the Zoom Out tool can be unpredictable, so it's usually better to click the Fit in Window button to see the entire page and get your bearings.

TIP | Keyboard Shortcuts for the Power User

Using keyboard shortcuts can really save you a lot of time. Some keyboard shortcuts allow you to select a tool temporarily, while you're holding down the keys. For example, if you want to magnify any area of your document, hold down **Ctrl+spacebar** (Windows) or **Cmd+spacebar** (Mac) to access the Zoom In tool temporarily. Holding **Ctrl+spacebar+Alt** (Windows) or **Cmd+spacebar+Opt** (Mac) will give you the Zoom Out tool. (In Windows, make sure you press the keyboard keys in the specified order.) Lastly, you can always temporarily access the Hand tool by holding down the **spacebar**. Releasing the keys returns you to the tool you were using previously.

Navigation Tools

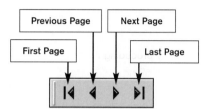

The **Navigation toolbar** performs exactly the same functions as the buttons that appear in the status bar. It contains the **First Page**, **Previous Page**, **Next Page**, and **Last Page** buttons, only in a slightly larger, easier-to-click form. If you have trouble clicking the buttons in the status bar, keep in mind that the Navigation toolbar is available for you.

View History Tools

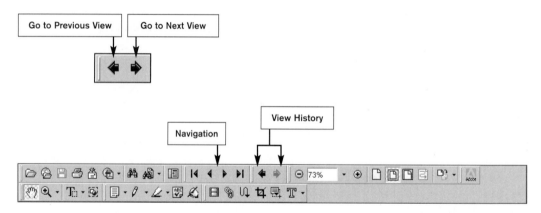

Be sure not to confuse the Navigation toolbar with the **View History toolbar**. The two buttons on the View History toolbar, **Go to Previous View** and **Go to Next View**, are comparable to the Back and Forward buttons you find in Web browsers.

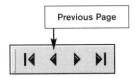

Unlike the Previous Page button, which takes you to the page immediately preceding the current one, the Go to Previous View button allows you backtrack through your viewing of the document. It remembers not only the order in which you've been viewing the pages but also at what magnification level and page view (Single Page, Continuous, or Continuous Facing). You can backtrack up to 64 steps (32 if you're using the Acrobat plug-in in a Web browser). The Go to Previous View button really starts to come in handy when you're doing things like setting up links and bookmarks, which you'll learn how to do in Chapter 3, "*Creating Links*," and Chapter 5, "*Bookmarks*." Go to Previous View also remembers if you've been jumping between separate documents, so it can be used when you want to open a PDF that you closed by accident.

NOTE | Quick Navigation

You can also select First Page, Next Page, Previous Page, Last Page, Go to Previous View, and Go To Next View from the Document menu in the menu bar. Similarly, all the various available views are found on the View menu in the menu bar. You'll probably find that clicking the buttons in the toolbar and status bar is more convenient when navigating through your documents, but the Document and View menus will play an important role when you want to set a particular view for your end user to see. We'll explore these menus in later chapters, when we discuss form and page actions.

Expanding Toolbar Buttons

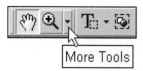

Just like the Zoom In/Zoom Out tool, some tools on the toolbar are not displayed and are hidden within their toolbar. A More Tools symbol next to a tool indicates that there are additional tools hidden within that tool. Clicking the More Tools button allows you to select the hidden tools.

To place all of the tools within a given set on the toolbar, you can choose **Expand This Button**.

Once a set of tools has been expanded, click on the **Collapse button** to hide the tools again.

Undocking Toolbars

Acrobat 5 allows you to customize and "tear off" the various tool groups located in the main toolbar. This lets you customize the Acrobat workspace so it better meets your needs. It is especially useful if you have limited screen space available.

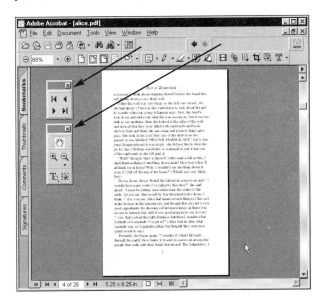

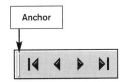

Clicking the **anchor** of any tool group will allow you to drag that tool group to any location within the toolbar. Dragging a tool group out of the main toolbar turns that group into its own floating toolbar. You can combine toolbars by dragging one floating toolbar on top of another.

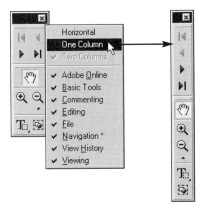

By right-clicking (Windows) or Ctrl-clicking (Mac) a floating toolbar, you can choose different configurations for the toolbar to further customize your workspace.

Redocking Toolbars

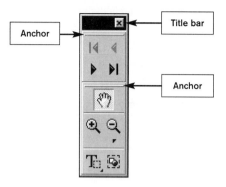

Once you've undocked a toolbar, you'll probably begin to wonder how to get the thing back to its original position. The trick is to make sure you're grabbing the toolbar by the anchor and not by the title bar. Grab the toolbar by the anchor and drag it over the main toolbar. When you release the mouse button, it will snap back into place with the other toolbar elements.

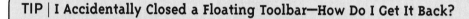

TIP | I Accidentally Closed a Floating Toolbar—How Do I Get It Back?

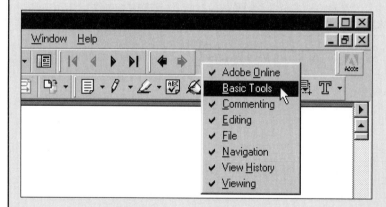

If you close a floating toolbar by mistake, you can get it back by right-clicking (Windows) or Ctrl-clicking (Mac) the main toolbar and choosing the missing toolbar from the resulting contextual menu. Additionally, all the toolbars are listed under Window > Toolbars.

Toolbar Keyboard Shortcuts

Most of the tools on the Acrobat toolbar have corresponding keyboard equivalents that will activate the tool. For example, pressing **H** selects the Hand tool. Pressing **Z** selects the currently displayed Zoom tool. Pressing **Shift+Z** toggles between the two Zoom tools. To find out if a tool has a keyboard shortcut, just roll the mouse over the tool and view the tool tip that appears. The following chart lists some of the more commonly used and helpful keyboard shortcuts.

Handy Keyboard Shortcuts		
Toolbar Button	**Windows Shortcut**	**Mac Shortcut**
Actual Size	Ctrl+1	Cmd+1
Fit in Window	Ctrl+0	Cmd+0
Fit Width	Ctrl+2	Cmd+2
Fit Visible	Ctrl+3	Cmd+3
First Page	Ctrl+Shift+Page Up Ctrl+Shift+Up Arrow	Opt+Shift+Page Up Opt+Shift+Up Arrow
Next Page	Down Arrow Right Arrow Page Down	Down Arrow Right Arrow Page Down
Previous Page	Up Arrow Left Arrow Page Up	Up Arrow Left Arrow Page Up
Last Page	Ctrl+Shift+Page Down Ctrl+Shift+Down Arrow	Opt+Shift+Page Down Option+Shift+Down Arrow
Go to Previous View	Alt+Left Arrow	Cmd+Left Arrow
Go to Next View	Alt+Right Arrow	Cmd+Right Arrow

The Navigation Pane

Another way to navigate PDF documents is through **bookmarks** and **thumbnails**, which are located in the **Navigation pane**. You can adjust the size of the Navigation pane by dragging the border between the Navigation pane and the Document pane or by dragging the **Open/Close Navigation Pane button**.

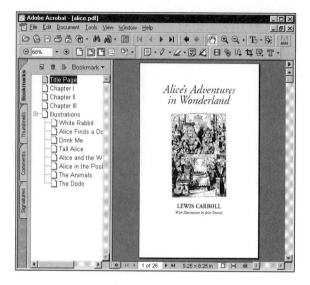

You can display or hide the bookmarks for a document by clicking the **Bookmarks tab**. Bookmarks allow you to move quickly between sections of a document. Acrobat does not generate bookmarks automatically; they have to be created intentionally. You will learn how to create and edit bookmarks in Chapter 5, "*Bookmarks*."

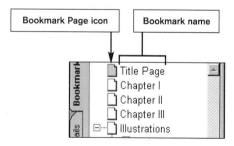

To keep Acrobat from thinking that you want to rename the bookmark, it's better to click on the Page icon, rather than on the bookmark name.

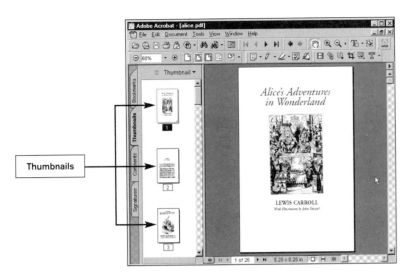

Thumbnails

Acrobat automatically generates thumbnails when you click the **Thumbnails tab**. Thumbnails are minia-
ture versions of each page of the PDF and can be used to navigate in the document. When you click
on the thumbnail for a page, Acrobat takes you to the corresponding page. In Acrobat (but not Reader),
you can also use the thumbnails to move, add, or delete pages from the PDF. You'll learn how to do
this in Chapter 6, "*Modifying PDFs.*"

If you scroll quickly through the Thumbnails pane, you'll notice that the thumbnails briefly appear as
gray rectangles before Acrobat renders the images. On slower computers, the process of generating
thumbnails on the fly can get tedious, especially when you're using thumbnails to reorganize your document. Fortunately, you can have Acrobat embed thumbnails into the document for you. You will learn
how to create and edit thumbnails in Chapter 6, "*Altering PDF Documents.*"

*Whew! As you might have noticed, there are many redundant ways of navigating around the Acrobat
interface. As you continue to work with Acrobat and Acrobat Reader, you'll start to figure out which
methods work best for certain situations. Now that you've familiarized yourself with the interface, let's
dive into Acrobat and starting making your documents interactive.*

3.

Working with Links

| Using Links | Creating Links | Creating More Links |

| Editing Links | Linking to a Web Page |

| Automatically Creating Web Links |

| Changing the Appearance of Web Links |

| Cross-Document Linking |

| Setting Link Destinations |

chap_03

Acrobat 5
H•O•T CD-ROM

One of the most powerful features of Acrobat is its ability to create links within PDF documents. Links give your audience the ability to quickly move to specific sections of a document, much like links on a Web page. With a single click the user can move to any point in the document. This function is especially useful when you are trying to navigate large documents, such as software manuals. But the power does not stop there! Links can also be used to link multiple PDF documents together or to point to pages on the Web, right from within the PDF file. Links are very cool, and very important to master.

In this chapter you'll learn how to use, create, and edit links in a PDF document. You will also learn how to create links that take you to pages on the Web. Finally, you will learn how to link multiple PDF documents together to create a cohesive browsing experience for your audience. In Chapter 14, *"Creating PDFs from Popular Applications,"* I will show you methods of creating links automatically from other applications such as Microsoft Word and Adobe InDesign, but in this chapter you'll be creating links manually, which, as you'll see, gives you a lot of control over their appearances and actions.

I. _____Using Links

Navigating large documents can be a pain. Have you ever tried to scroll through a 50+ page Microsoft Word document? It can be frustrating and time consuming. The PDF format offers relief from this problem through its ability to create links to specific portions of your documents. Links make it easy to jump from page to page in a large document.

In this exercise, you will learn to use links. Later in this chapter, you will learn to create them.

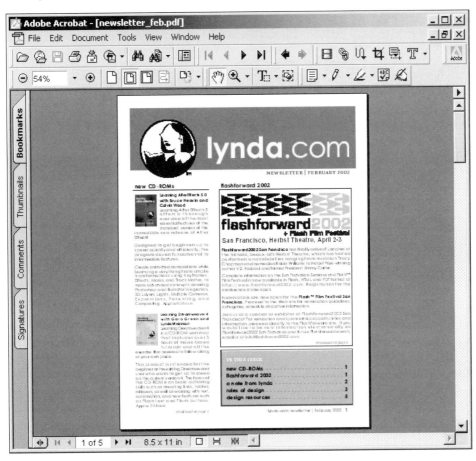

1. Open the **newsletter_feb.pdf** file from the **chap_03** folder on the **H•O•T CD-ROM**. This file contains a sample newsletter that has been created for this exercise.

2. Click the **Fit Width** button to increase the document's legibility, and then scroll to the bottom of **page 1**.

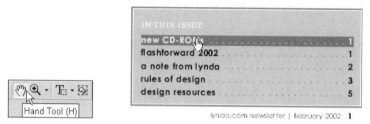

3. If it's not already active, select the **Hand** tool and place the cursor over the words **new CD-ROMs**, in the lower-right corner. Notice that the cursor turns into a pointing finger. Like on an HTML page, this means you are over a link. Click the link.

Once the link is clicked, you are taken to the beginning of the new CD-ROMs *article. The view has also been magnified to focus your attention on this article.*

Learning Dreamweaver 4 with Garo Green and Lynda Weinman
Learning Dreamweaver 4 is a CD-ROM workshop that includes over 3 hours of movie-based tutorials and all the exercise files needed to follow along at your own pace.

This product is intended for the beginner or the existing Dreamweaver user who wants to get up to speed on the current version 4. The focus of this CD-ROM is on basic authoring skills such as creating links, tables, rollovers, as well as working with text, automation, and new features such as Flash text and Flash buttons.
Approx 3.5 hours

continued on page 2

4. Scroll to the bottom of the page. Move your cursor over the words **continued on page 2**. This is another link. Click the link to jump to **page 2**. Pretty quick, huh?

Go to Previous View

5. Click the **Go to Previous View** button until you return to your original view of the table of contents. This is a useful button that always returns you to your previous view, much like the Back button in a Web browser window.

2. ——————————Creating Links

You'll now complete the table of contents by creating links for the remaining listings.

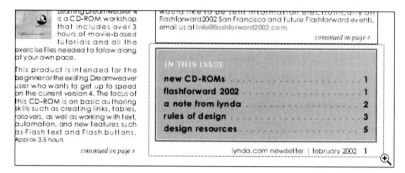

1. Select the **Zoom In** tool and draw a marquee around the table of contents area. This action will magnify the area around your selection and make it easier for you to draw your links.

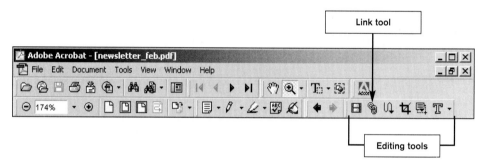

2. Select the **Link** tool from the toolbar. The Link tool is part of the **Editing** tool group and is used to create links in your PDF documents. Your cursor will change into a crosshair.

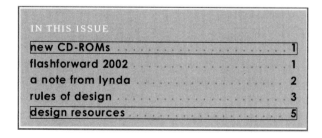

Notice that selecting the Link tool reveals any links that are already in the document. Links are displayed with a thin border around them, which makes them easily identifiable in your PDF documents.

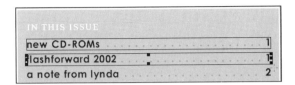

3. Use the cursor to draw a rectangle around the **flashforward 2002** listing in the table of contents. As soon as you release your mouse button, the **Link Properties** dialog box will appear. If you didn't draw the hotspot quite right, don't worry; you can always go back and fix it later.

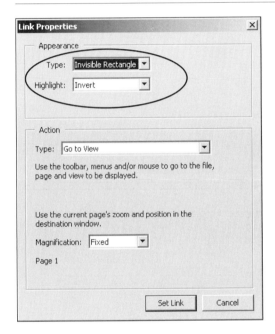

4. In the **Appearance** section of the **Link Properties** dialog box, choose **Invisible Rectangle** as the **Type** option. An invisible rectangle means that the end user will not see any sort of border around the link area. If you chose **Visible Rectangle**, your links would appear with a colored border around them, which could be visually distracting and is not what we want in this case.

5. For the **Highlight** option, choose **Invert**. The highlight determines the appearance of the link area when the user clicks on the link. See the note that follows for more information.

Once you have defined your link's appearance you need to choose a Link Action. A Link Action defines what the link will do when a user clicks on it. The default choice is Go to View, which just happens to be the one you want in this case. Go to View simply means that you want this link to take the user to a particular view of this or any other PDF document.

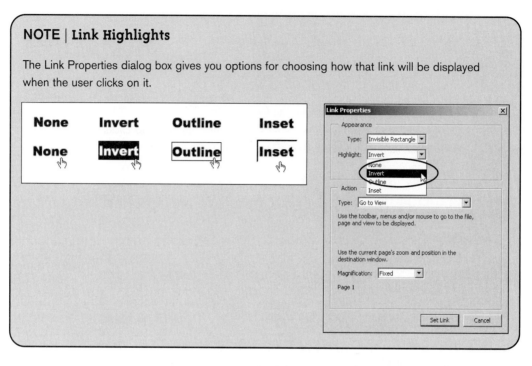

NOTE | Link Highlights

The Link Properties dialog box gives you options for choosing how that link will be displayed when the user clicks on it.

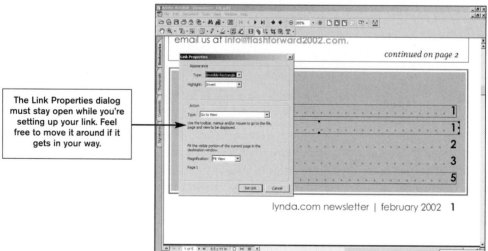

The Link Properties dialog must stay open while you're setting up your link. Feel free to move it around if it gets in your way.

This is the point where the linking process might appear a little strange. With most applications, you usually can't work with your document if there's a window open on top of it. However, when setting up your links in Acrobat, the Link Properties dialog box must remain open while you find the page that you want to link to.

6. If necessary, move the Link Properties dialog box off to the side of the screen. Click the **Fit in Window** button so that you can see the entire page. This will make it easier for you to set up the link. The article you want to link to happens to be here on page 1. At first glance, it might seem strange to link to an article that's on the same page as the table of contents, but because all of the listings in the table of contents will eventually be linked, we want to remain consistent and make sure we have a proper link set up here.

The next step is to decide how you want this article to appear when the user clicks on the link in the table of contents. Most likely, you want the article to appear at a legible size so that the user may immediately begin reading it.

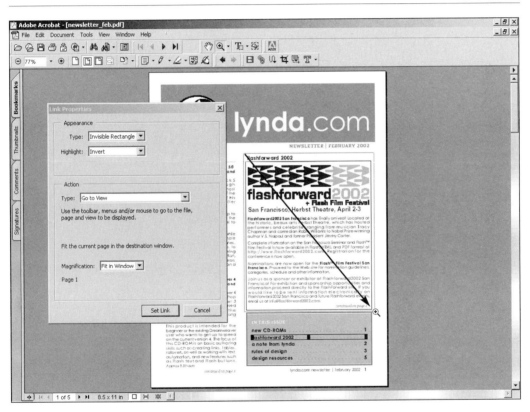

7. Select the **Zoom In** tool from the toolbar and draw a marquee around the entire **flashforward** article to magnify it. This action will cause the flashforward article to be magnified onscreen, just as you want it to appear when the user clicks on the link.

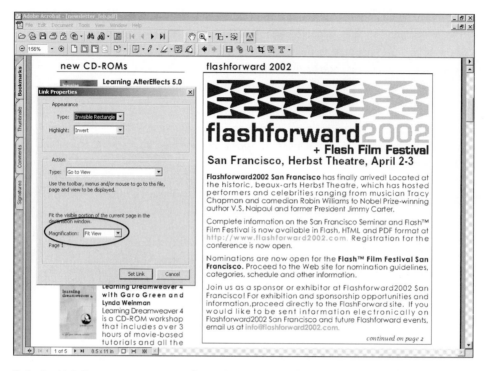

8. In the **Link Properties** dialog box (which is still open), **Magnification** will be set to **Fit View**. Fit View ensures that when the user clicks on this link, Acrobat will size the linked area so that everything that you're seeing onscreen right now will be visible, no matter what size their document window happens to be.

9. Click the **Set Link** button. Your link is created and you are returned to the view of the table of contents.

10. Select the **Hand** tool and click the **flashforward 2002** link to test it.

11. Click the **Go to Previous View** button to return to the table of contents.

12. Make your document window smaller and click on the link again. Notice that the link destination has also become smaller to fit the entire area within the window.

13. Resize your window to its original size and return to the magnified view of the table of contents.

14. Save the document and leave it open for the next exercise.

Link Magnifications

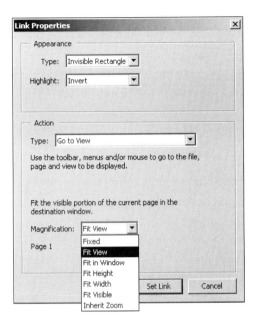

The Magnification settings in the Link Properties dialog box can be a bit confusing when you begin creating links in Acrobat. The chart below will help demystify some of the different magnification settings.

Link Properties Magnification Settings	
Magnification Setting	**Result**
Fixed	Displays the link destination area at current magnification level and position.
Fit View	Fits the area of the page that was visible when the link was created into the document window. Will vary in different document window sizes.
Fit in Window	Displays the entire linked page within the document window.
Fit Height	Displays the entire height of the linked page.
Fit Width	Displays the entire width of the top of the linked page.
Fit Visible	Similar to Fit Width, but will ignore empty regions of the page such as margins.
Inherit Zoom	Displays the linked area at the same magnification level that was selected when the user clicked on the link.

3. ——————————Creating More Links

This exercise will give you more practice creating links within a PDF document. You will learn how to use some of the magnification settings in the Link Properties dialog box more effectively and gain some necessary practice to build your linking skills.

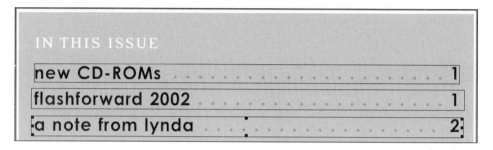

1. Select the **Link** tool and draw a marquee around the words **a note from lynda**.

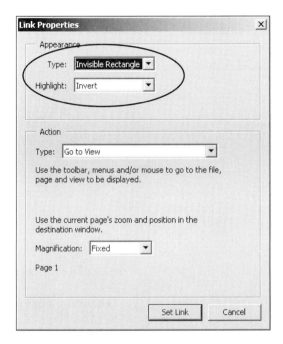

2. In the **Link Properties** dialog box, your previous setting of **Invisible Rectangle** should still be there; if it isn't, select **Invisible Rectangle**.

3. Keeping the Link Properties dialog box open, use the **scrollbar** to go to **page 2** of the document.

4. Click the **Fit in Window** button. **Tip:** Clicking the **Fit in Window** button is not an essential part of the linking process; it's just a quick way of getting the scope of the entire page when you're looking for a specific area.

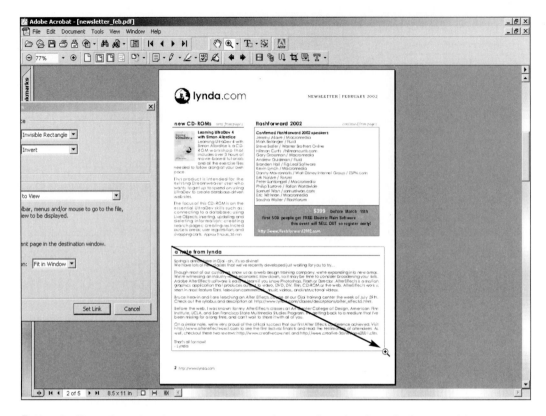

5. Use the **Zoom In** tool to draw a marquee around **a note from Lynda** at the bottom of the page.

6. Make sure that **Magnification** in the Link Properties dialog box is set to **Fit View**, and click **Set Link**.

7. Select the **Hand** tool and click the new link to test it.

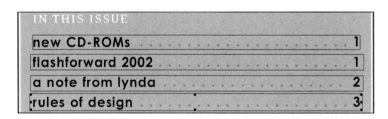

8. Click the **Go to Previous View** button to return to the table of contents, and use the **Link** tool to draw a link area around the words **rules of design**.

9. Scroll to **page 3** (or click the **Next Page** button twice).

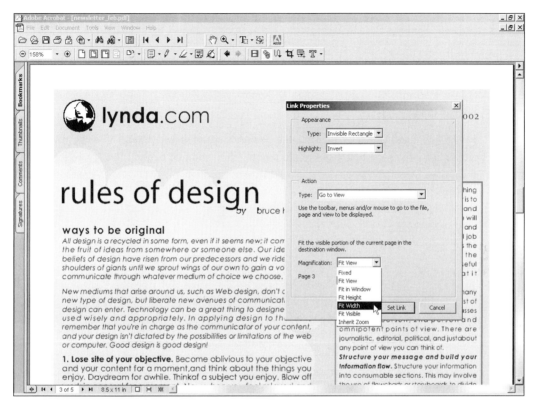

10. Instead of zooming into a specific area this time, choose **Fit Width** from the **Magnification** pop-up menu in the **Link Properties** dialog box. Fit Width is an appropriate setting here because this article and its sidebar take up the entire page. You're setting the magnification to a level that will make it easy for the user to begin reading the article immediately after clicking the link.

---

11. Click **Set Link**. This will create the link at the current magnification level.

---

12. Select the **Hand** tool and click the link to test it.

---

13. Click the **Go to Previous View** button to return to the table of contents. Save the document and leave it open for the next exercise.

MOVIE | createlinks.mov

To learn more about creating links, check out **createlinks.mov** located in the **movies** folder on the Acrobat 5 **H•O•T CD-ROM**.

4. _____Editing Links

In Acrobat, editing links is just as easy as creating them; Acrobat makes editing links a painless process. In this exercise, you'll fix the incorrect **design resources** link in the table of contents. Knowing how to edit broken links is an important part of the linking process within Acrobat; it is something you will inevitably have to face.

1. With the **Hand** tool selected, click the **design resources** link. Instead of taking you to the proper article on page 5, it takes you to **a note from lynda** on page 2. This link was created incorrectly. Oops! You'll be fixing it in the following steps.

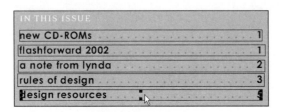

2. Select the **Link** tool and double-click on the **design resources** link area to open up its **Link Properties** dialog box.

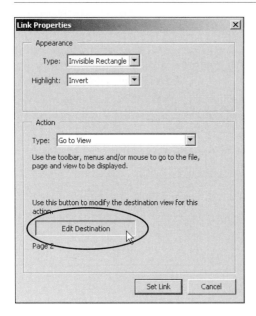

3. In the **Link Properties** dialog box, click the **Edit Destination** button. Now all you have to do is find the correct article in the document.

4. With the Link Properties dialog box open, click the **Fit in Window** button and scroll down to **page 5**.

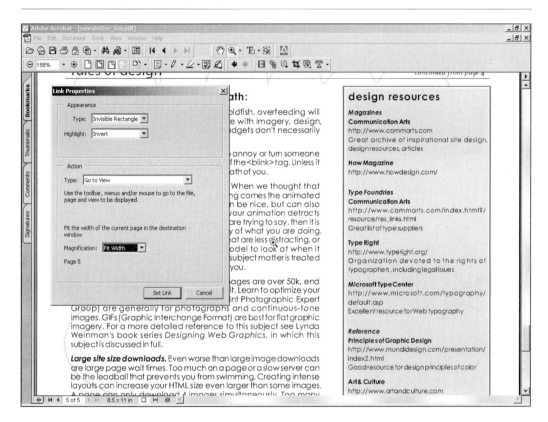

5. In the Link Properties dialog box, select **Fit Width** for the **Magnification** setting.

6. Click **Set Link**. This will correct the link. That's it! Editing a link is no more difficult than creating one.

7. Save the file and keep it open for the next exercise.

NOTE | Creating Easy Text Links

IN THIS ISSUE	
new CD-ROMs	1
flashforward 2002	1
a note from lynda	2
rules of design	3
design resources	5

Unless you have the steady hand of a brain surgeon, the link boxes you drew most likely vary slightly in size. In the example above, it's not a big a deal because the boxes are invisible to the end user. As long as you don't draw your link hotspots extremely poorly, or overlap the hotspots, your users shouldn't run into any problems. However, there may come a time when you need to have perfectly shaped links. (**Note:** This technique is for creating new links, not to edit existing ones.)

With the **Link** tool selected, hold down the **Ctrl** (Windows) or **Option** (Mac) key. The link cursor will turn into an I-beam cursor, allowing you to select the text you want to link. When you release the mouse button, you'll have a perfectly sized link box around the text.

Unfortunately, this trick only works for turning text into links. If you're creating links around images, it's up to you and your steady hand.

5. ——————————Linking to a Web Page

As mentioned earlier, you're not limited to creating links only within your PDF document. For example, you might want to link to a Web site. Rather than relying on users copying Web addresses from the PDF and entering them into their browsers, you can create links over a Web address (also known as a URL) that take the users directly to the Web page (assuming they are connected to the Internet when viewing your PDF). Adding Web links is a great way to enhance your PDF and to draw more visitors to your Web sites.

1. Go to **page 2** of the **newsletter_feb.pdf** document and click the **Fit Width** button in the toolbar.

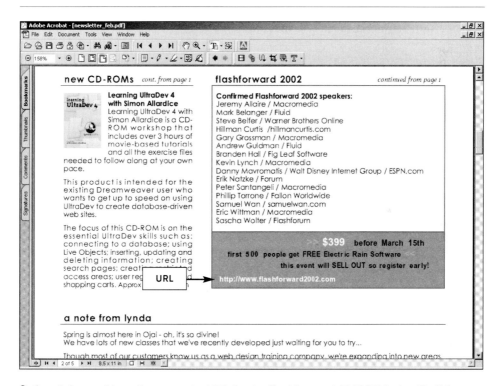

2. Scroll down a bit until you see the URL for the **flashforward 2002** Web site. You'll be creating a link for this address, but before you do, you're going to select the text on the page and copy it. This will save you from having to type in the address and will prevent any potential typos that would result in a broken link.

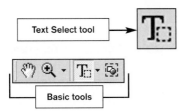

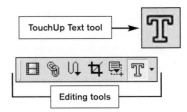

To select the address, you'll use the Text Select tool, which is located in the Basic tool group. Don't confuse this with the TouchUp Text tool, which is located in the Editing tool group. Although the TouchUp Text tool could also be used, in this case you'll want to stick with the Text Select tool whenever possible because, unlike the TouchUp Text tool, the Text Select tool does not allow you to edit text. You don't want to risk accidentally altering the URL on the PDF. (You'll see more on the TouchUp Text tool in Chapter 6, "Modifying PDFs.")

>> **$399** before March 15th
first 500 people get FREE Electric Rain Software <<
this event will SELL OUT so register early!

http://www.flashforward2002.com

3. Select the **Text Select** tool and highlight the entire URL: **http://www.flashforward2002.com**.

4. Choose **Edit > Copy** from the menu bar, or press **Ctrl+C** (Windows) or **Cmd+C** (Mac).

5. Click anywhere in the blank margin on the right to deselect the text.

6. Select the **Link** tool and draw a link area around **http://www.flashforward2002.com**.

7. In the **Appearance** section of the Link Properties dialog box, choose **Invisible Rectangle** from the **Type** pop-up menu.

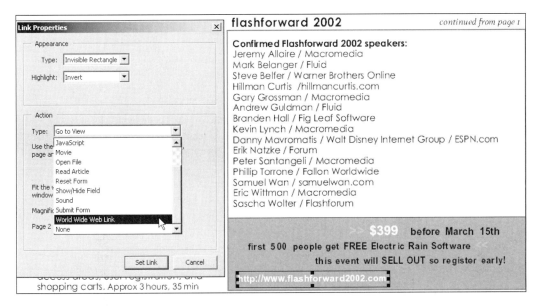

8. In the **Action** section of the dialog box, choose **World Wide Web Link** from the **Type** pop-up menu. This selection tells Acrobat that you want to go to a Web address rather than somewhere within the document.

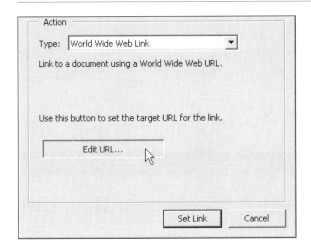

9. Click the **Edit URL** button. (**Note:** This option is available only when you have the **Type** set to **World Wide Web Link**.)

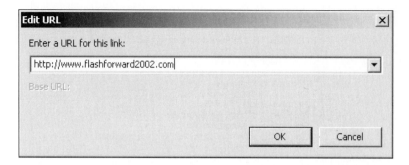

10. Choose **Edit > Paste** to paste the copied address into the URL field, and then click **OK**. (On some Windows systems, you might have to right-click in the URL field and choose **Paste**, rather than using the menu command). As you can see, copying the URL directly from the page was much easier than retyping the entire URL.

11. Click **Set Link**.

To test your link, as you'll do next, you must be connected to the Internet.

12. Select the **Hand** tool and click on the **flashforward2002** URL.

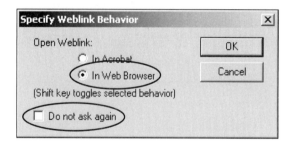

A dialog box will appear, asking if you want to open the page in your Web browser or in Acrobat. If you choose to open the page in Acrobat, Acrobat will access the page over the Internet, convert it to a PDF, and then display it in the document window. In this case, however, we want to go directly to the Web page through our browser.

13. In the Specify Weblink Behavior dialog box, select **In Web Browser** and uncheck **Do not ask again**, if it's checked.

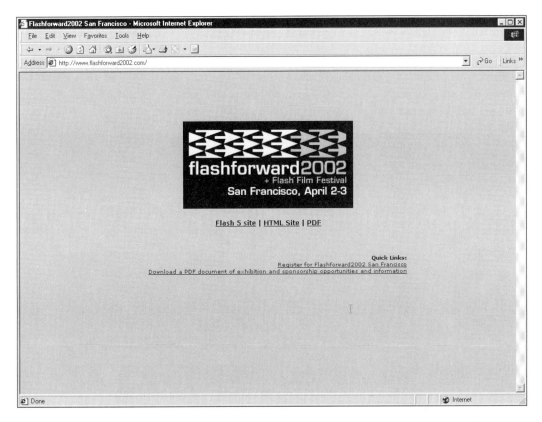

14. Click **OK**. Your default Web browser will open and take you to the **flashforward** Web site.

15. Close your browser and return to Acrobat.

16. Save the file and keep it open for the next exercise.

TIP | Hey, I Didn't See That Dialog Box You Mentioned

If you don't get the dialog box asking you to choose between opening the Web link in Acrobat or in your browser, someone (possibly you) has previously clicked **Do not ask again**. Fix this by choosing **Edit > Preferences > Web Capture**.

In the Web Capture Preferences dialog box, click **Reset Warning Dialog Boxes to Default**, and then click **OK**. Voila! (That's French for "Your dialog boxes have been reset.")

6. ―――――――**Automatically Creating Web Links**

Now that you know how to create Web links manually, let's take a look at a powerful and little-known feature of Acrobat that lets you create Web links automatically. (Sure, you could have done this instead of the last exercise, but then you wouldn't appreciate this one as much.) In this exercise, you will learn how to generate links automatically using the URLs in your PDF document.

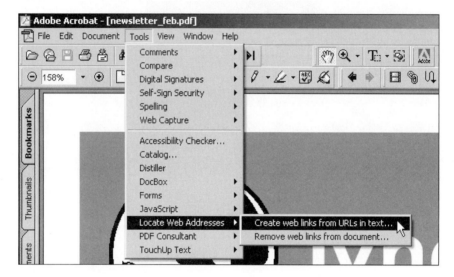

1. Select **Tools > Locate Web Addresses > Create web links from URLs in text**. This action will open the **Create Web Links** dialog box.

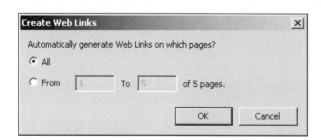

2. In the Create Web Links dialog box, choose **All** and click **OK**.

Acrobat will hunt through the document, find all the Web addresses, and convert them into Web links. An important point to note is that Acrobat will only find the Web addresses that begin with http:// *; it won't recognize partial Web addresses such as* lynda.com *or* www.lynda.com. *So, if you want to use this feature, make sure you have complete URLs, including the* http:// *header.*

After a few moments Acrobat will let you know how many Web addresses it found.

3. Click **OK** and select the **Link** tool from the toolbar to reveal the new links.

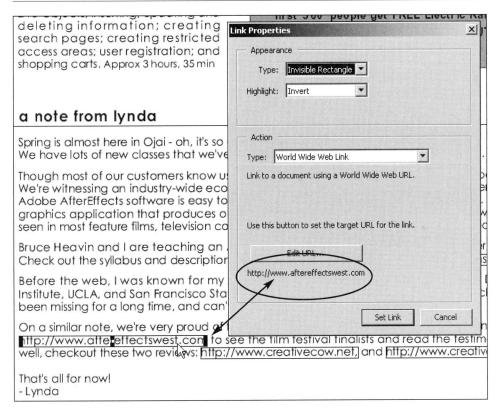

4. Scroll down to **page 2**. Notice the links that were created near the bottom of the page. To see if Acrobat created the links properly, double-click on the link over **http://www.aftereffectswest.com**. The Web address is listed at the bottom of the **Link Properties** dialog box and reflects the correct URL.

5. Click **Cancel** to close Link Properties. Scroll down to **page 5**.

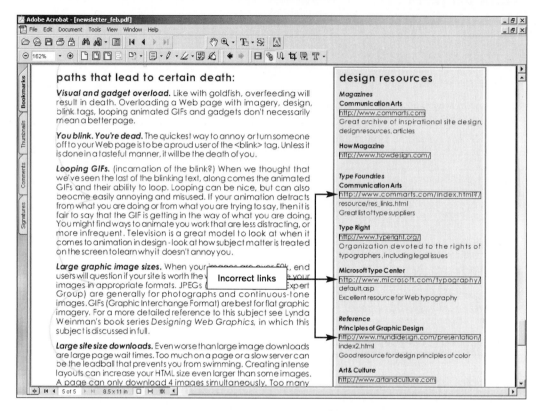

Acrobat has also detected and created Web links here, but some of them were created incorrectly. Unfortunately, Acrobat cannot recognize entire URLs when they wrap from one line to the next. Under the design resources section of this page, Acrobat was unable to create links properly for Communication Arts, Microsoft Type Center, and Principles of Graphic Design.

To fix these links, you'll not only have to resize them to cover the entire addresses, you'll also have to manually correct the URLs in the Link Properties dialog box. See? It's a good thing you did that previous lesson after all.

Type Foundries
Communication Arts
http://www.commarts.com/index.html?/
resource/res_links.html
Great list of type suppliers

6. With the **Link** tool, select the link under the words **Communication Arts** (under **Type Foundries**) by single-clicking it. Place your cursor over the black handle on the bottom center and drag it down until the link area encompasses the next line.

7. Double-click on the link area to open the **Link Properties** dialog box.

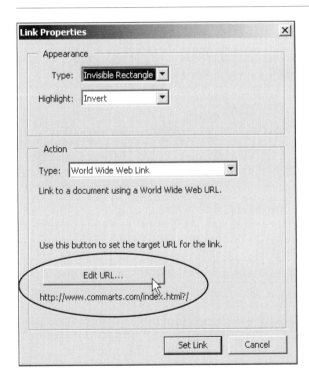

8. The Web address here is incomplete because Acrobat didn't recognize the second line of the URL. Click **Edit URL**.

9. Place the cursor after the partial address and type **resource/res_links.html** to complete the URL, and then click **OK**.

10. Click **Set Link**. The link has been corrected.

11. Resize the link areas under **Microsoft Type Center** and **Principles of Graphic Design** to cover their entire respective URLs. Use the table below to complete their addresses.

Address Correction Information for Exercise 6	
Incomplete Address	**Complete Address**
http://www.microsoft.com/typography/	http://www.microsoft.com/typography/**default.asp**
http://www.mundidesign.com/presentation/	http://www.mundidesign.com/presentation/**index2.html**

12. Save the file when you're done and keep it open for the next exercise.

7. —————————Changing the Appearance of Web Links

By now you're probably thinking, "Okay, so I can create links to the Web from my PDFs, but how is anyone going to know the links exist unless they roll their mouse over them? The linked text looks just like all the other text in the document." And you're right.

To make the links stand out, we could change them to Visible Rectangles, but that would most likely have an adverse effect on the appearance of the document; you don't want your pages covered with dozens of tiny rectangles. Instead, we'll take a tip from standard Web design practices and change the color of our linked text.

1. Scroll to **page 2** and find the link for **After Effects West** in Lynda's note.

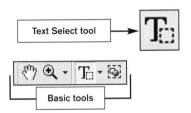

2. Choose the **Text Select** tool from the menu bar.

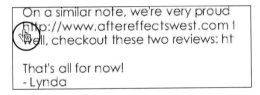

3. Place the cursor over the text **http://www.aftereffectswest.com**. Notice that the cursor turns into the pointing finger icon, indicating that clicking will take you to the Web. The presence of the link over this text makes it very difficult to select the text itself. This time you'll use the **TouchUp Text** tool to make your selection.

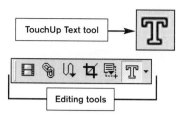

4. Select the **TouchUp Text** tool. The TouchUp Text tool ignores links on the page, allowing you to select text freely. It also lets you select individual characters, while the **Text Select** tool only selects entire words. Just be careful not to accidentally type anything on the keyboard while text is selected, or your text will be erased.

5. Highlight the text **http://www.aftereffectswest.com**.

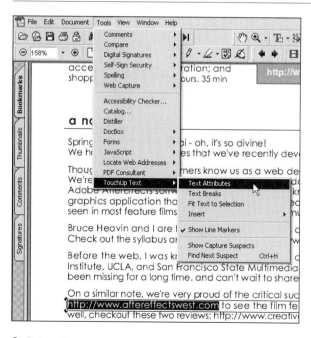

6. Select **Tools > TouchUp Text > Text Attributes**. This will open the **Text Attributes** dialog box.

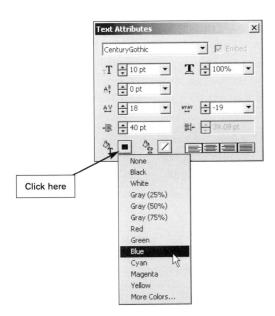

Click here

7. In the Text Attributes dialog box, click the black-colored rectangle in the lower-left corner and select **Blue** from the list of colors.

8. Close the Text Attributes dialog box and click in a blank area of the page to deselect the text. The text is now blue and looks much more like a link. You can practice this technique on the other links in the document if you like.

9. Save and close the file when you're done.

8._____**Cross-Document Linking**

Occasionally there will be times when you'll want to create links between PDF documents. For instance, suppose you have a PDF that contains references to sections of another PDF document. Instead of duplicating the same text in two documents, you could create direct links between the two documents without forcing the user to open and close files manually. In this exercise, you will learn to create this type of cross-document link.

1. Open the file **newsletter_02.pdf** from the **chap_03** folder on the **H•O•T CD-ROM**. This is a variation on the same PDF file you've been working with so far in this chapter.

2. Click the **Fit Width** button and go to **page 2**.

Notice the button in the flashforward 2002 *section that says* View the entire list of speakers. *Clicking on this area with the Hand tool has no effect. You'll add a link around this button to take the reader to a specific section of the* flashforward 2002 *PDF brochure.*

3. Select the **Link** tool and draw a link area around the **View the entire list of speakers** button.

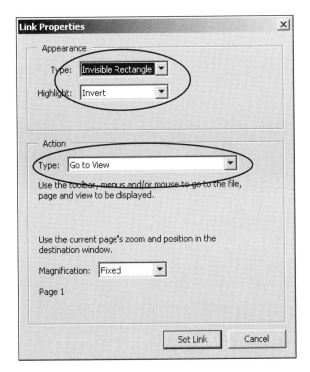

4. In the **Link Properties** dialog box, choose **Invisible Rectangle** from the **Type** pop-up menu in the **Appearance** section, and select a highlight style of your choice.

5. From the **Type** pop-up menu in the **Action** section, choose **Go to View**. **Note:** You could also choose **Open File** if you wanted to go to the first page of a new document, but we're linking to a specific area of the document, so **Go to View** is the appropriate choice here.

The process of linking to a separate document is nearly identical to linking within the same document; at this point you have to find the page in the other PDF document.

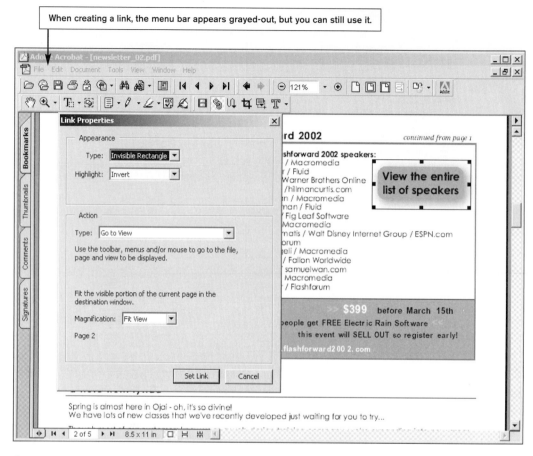

When creating a link, the menu bar appears grayed-out, but you can still use it.

6. Keeping the Link Properties dialog box open, choose **File > Open**. **Note:** In Windows, don't let that fact that the menu bar is grayed-out fool you. You can still make selections from it. Now, who would have guessed that?

7. Browse to the **chap_03** folder and open the **ff2002SF.pdf**.

8. Navigate to **page 17** of the **flashforward 2002** brochure PDF.

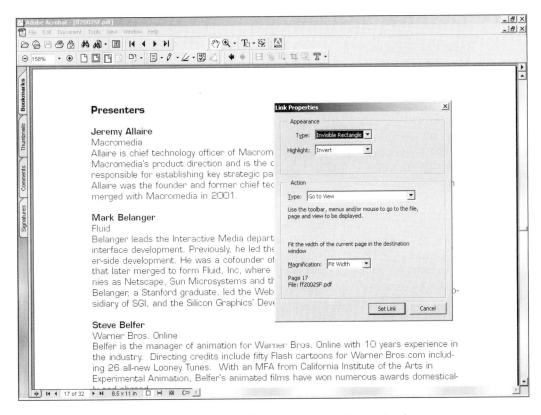

9. In the Link Properties dialog box, select **Fit Width** as the magnification level.

10. Click **Set Link**. You will be returned to the **newsletter_02.pdf** document.

11. Select the **Hand** tool and click your link to test it.

12. Choose **Document > Go to Previous View** to return to the newsletter.

13. Save and close the file.

WARNING | Don't Move Linked Files!

After you've created a cross-document link, you must keep the two documents in the same relative relationship to prevent breaking the link. Currently, **newsletter_02.pdf** and the **ff2002SF.pdf** are within the same folder (**chap_03**). If you were to move either of these to a new directory on your computer, the link between the two would no longer function. In order to maintain the link, you'd have to move both files together into the same directory. If you absolutely have to change their relationship, you'll have to go back and recreate the link.

Therefore, when distributing PDFs that contain cross-document links, you must maintain the relationship between the PDFs when copying them. If you are distributing your PDFs on a CD-ROM, be sure to copy the entire folder that contains all of your PDFs, in order to maintain the relationships between the documents.

Distributing PDFs from a Web site is slightly trickier. Because you can't create a link from a Web page to multiple documents, you'd have to create a link that allows the end user to download your collection of PDFs as a compressed archive such as a .sit or .zip file. Once the user decompresses the file, the PDFs will be in their proper relative locations.

TIP | Setting Cross-Document Preferences

When you click on a cross-document link, it's a default action of Acrobat to close the current document when it opens the new one. You can always get back to the original document by clicking the **Go to Previous View** button, but there are times when you might want both documents to be open simultaneously.

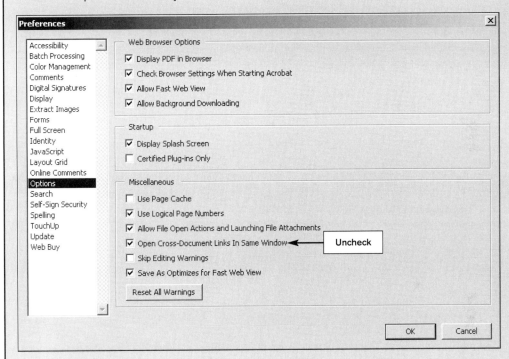

If you prefer to have new documents open in a separate window, choose **Edit > Preferences > General** (Mac OS X: **Acrobat > Preferences > General**). Select the **Options** category on the left and uncheck **Open Cross-Document Links In Same Window**. Keep in mind that this only sets the preferences for your own copy of Acrobat; it won't affect the end user's preferences at all.

9. ——————Setting Link Destinations

When you set up cross-document links, you can link to a specific page of the document. But what happens if you delete a page from the destination document after you've set up the link? In the previous exercise, you linked to page 17 of the **flashforward** PDF. If you decide that you no longer need the first page of the document and delete it, page 17 becomes page16 and the link is broken.

To avoid this problem you have the option of linking to a **destination** rather than a page. A destination is a link to specific content that Acrobat can track, no matter how many pages are deleted or added. Linking to a destination is preferred over linking to a page if you suspect that the document you're linking to might change later. In this exercise, you'll learn to create a destination, delete a page, and test that the destination link still works.

1. Open **ff2002SF.pdf** from the **chap_03** folder.

2. Go to **page 17** and click the **Fit Width** button.

3. Choose **Window > Destinations** from the menu bar. This will open the **Destinations** palette.

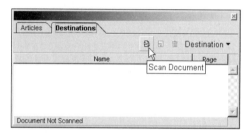

4. Click the **Scan Document** button in the Destinations palette. Before you can create a new destination, you must scan the document for any existing destinations first. Currently, there are no other destinations within this document. You are next going to create a new destination.

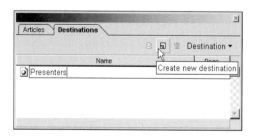

5. Click the **Create new destination** button. Name the new destination **Presenters** and press **Enter**. You've now created a destination. The next step is to create a link to it.

6. Choose **Window > newsletter_02.pdf** to switch back to the newsletter PDF. (If you've closed the file, choose **File > Open** to open **newsletter_02.pdf**.)

7. Go to **page 2** of the **newsletter_02.pdf**, select the **Link** tool, and double-click the link around **View the entire list of speakers**.

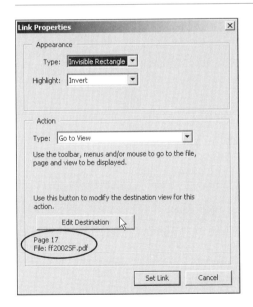

Notice that the link near the bottom of the Link Properties dialog box is currently pointing to page 17 of the ff2002SF.pdf *document.*

8. Click **Edit Destination**.

9. Choose **Window > ff2002SF** to switch back to the **flashforward** document.

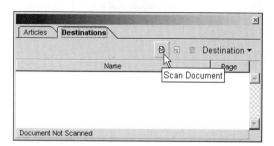

10. In the Destinations palette, click the **Scan Document** button to locate the destination that you previously created.

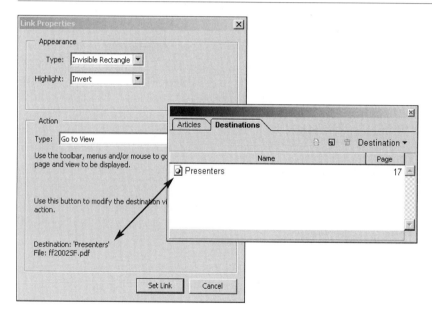

11. Double-click **Presenters** to link to it. The Link Properties dialog box now shows that you're linking to **Destination: 'Presenters'**.

12. Click **Set Link**. You are returned to the newsletter document.

13. Close the Destinations palette.

14. Select the **Hand** tool and click the link to test it. You should be taken to the list of presenters again.

Next, you'll learn how to delete a page in order to test whether the destination link feature works after a page is deleted from the ff2002sf.pdf *file.*

15. In the **ff2002SF.pdf** document, choose **Document > Delete Pages**.

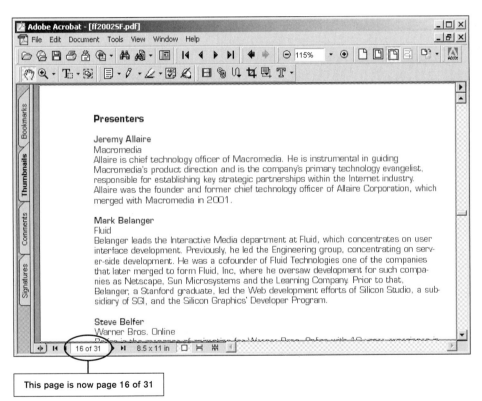

This page is now page 16 of 31

16. In the Delete Pages dialog box, enter from **1** to **1 of 32** and click **OK**. Click **Yes** when Acrobat asks you if you're sure you want to delete the page. Because we've deleted a page from the document, page 17 has become page 16. Save **ff2002SF.pdf** and close it.

17. Open **newsletter_02.pdf** once more and click the **View the entire list of speakers** link on page 2.

Acrobat opens ff2002SF.pdf *and takes you to the list of presenters on page 16. Notice that you are now on page 16, not page 17 as before. It's working like a charm!*

18. Save and close all files.

The Link Properties Dialog Box

On the next page you'll find a handy chart that describes actions you can do from the Link Properties dialog box below.

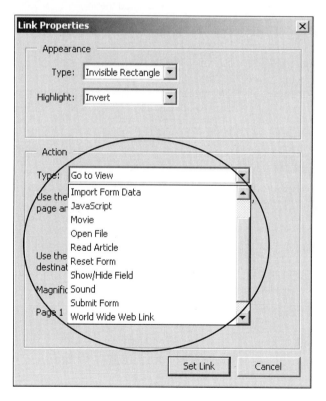

Actions in the Link Properties Dialog Box	
Type of Action	**Action It Performs**
Go to View	Used to jump to a particular view of a document.
Import Form Data	Imports data into a PDF form.
JavaScript	Runs a specified JavaScript.
Movie	Runs a QuickTime or AVI movie that's been inserted into the PDF page.
Open File	Opens a specified file, PDF or non-PDF. (For non-PDFs the user must have the native application that created the file.)
Read Article	Links to an article thread (see Chapter 4, *"Creating Articles"*).
Reset Form	Resets form fields to their original states.
Show/Hide Field	Used to display or hide a selected form field.
Sound	Link area will play a sound when clicked.
Submit Form	Submits form data to a specific location.
World Wide Web Link	Links to Web addresses.
None	Makes the link area inactive.

At this point, you should have a pretty good idea of the capabilities of links. You will be applying what you've learned in this chapter to several other exercises as you continue through the book. You've no doubt noticed that there are several actions other than Go to View and World Wide Web Link in the Link Properties dialog box. I'll be covering some of them in later chapters.

4.

Creating and Editing Articles

| Reading Article Threads | Creating Article Threads |
| Editing Article Threads | Setting Magnification Preferences |

chap_04

Acrobat 5
H•O•T CD-ROM

Imagine that you're reading an article in a PDF newsletter. At the foot of the column is a line that reads: "Continued on page 35." In an actual printed publication, all you would have to do is turn to page 35 and continue reading. In a PDF document, however, you have to decide whether you want to scroll there, type the page number in the status bar, or just click forward through the document. Once you arrive at page 35 you'll still have to find where the story continues and magnify the text before you can continue reading. If the story jumps to another page once more, you must begin the whole process again. Sometimes, even reading a multiple-column article on a single page can be a challenge, requiring you to scroll down to the bottom of one column and then back up to read the top of the next, which can definitely disrupt the flow of an article.

To avoid all this jumping around you can use Acrobat's Article tool to connect all the article pieces together into a "thread." The end user now only has to click on an article area to start reading. It doesn't matter how many columns or pages the article may span; all the user has to do is keep clicking the mouse button to advance through the text.

Unfortunately, the Article tool is one of the least familiar functions in Acrobat, both to PDF authors and PDF users. Even if you know how to use the Article tool to create articles within your PDF, there's no guarantee that the end user will know how to recognize or read the article thread you've created. At the end of the chapter, I'll address some methods of educating your audience, but first let's introduce you to the Article tool.

I. _____Reading Article Threads

The **Article tool** is unique to Acrobat. No other document-viewing application provides a similar tool, and users new to Acrobat may find themselves unfamiliar with how to use it to read or create articles. Before learning to create your articles, it's important to see a threaded article in action to understand how it is used to facilitate navigation. The point of using the Article tool is to provide a method for the user to be able to quickly follow the flow of an article through a document without having to resort to scrolling. That's exactly what you are going to do in this exercise.

NOTE | Hand Tool Icons

The following chart explains each of the different Hand tool icons you might encounter while navigating through an article thread. It's a good idea to review this chart, because you always want to know what the other hand is doing.

Article Navigation Icons	
Symbol	**Meaning**
	You are hovering over an article box. Clicking will enter you into the article thread.
	You are in an article thread and there is more content below. Clicking will take you to the next part of the article thread.
	Access this icon by pressing the **Shift** key. Clicking allows you to backtrack through the article.
	Access this icon by press **Ctrl** (Windows) or **Option** (Mac). Clicking will take you back to the beginning of the article thread.
	You have reached the end of the article. Clicking will exit the article and return you to the page where you first entered the article thread.

---

1. Open the file **news_0202.pdf** from the **chap_04** folder of the **H•O•T CD-ROM**. This file is a newsletter that contains several articles.

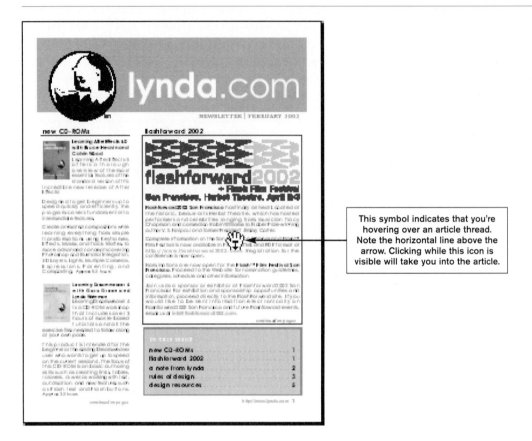

This symbol indicates that you're hovering over an article thread. Note the horizontal line above the arrow. Clicking while this icon is visible will take you into the article.

2. Click the **Hand** tool, and place it over the **flashforward 2002** article on the first page. Notice that an arrow and a horizontal line appear within the Hand tool icon. This indicates that the mouse is positioned over an article thread.

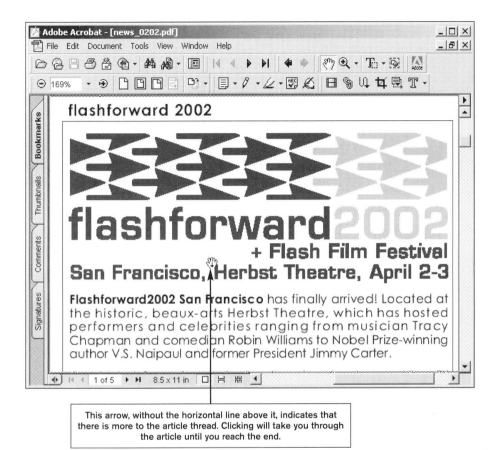

This arrow, without the horizontal line above it, indicates that there is more to the article thread. Clicking will take you through the article until you reach the end.

3. Click on the **flashforward** article thread. The **flashforward** article magnifies to fill the screen. The Hand tool now contains just the downward-pointing arrow; it no longer shows a horizontal line at the top of the arrow. This indicates that you have entered the article thread and that there is more to the article than what is currently shown onscreen.

4. Click the mouse to display the next section of the article. Notice that you jump down to **page 2**, where the article thread continues.

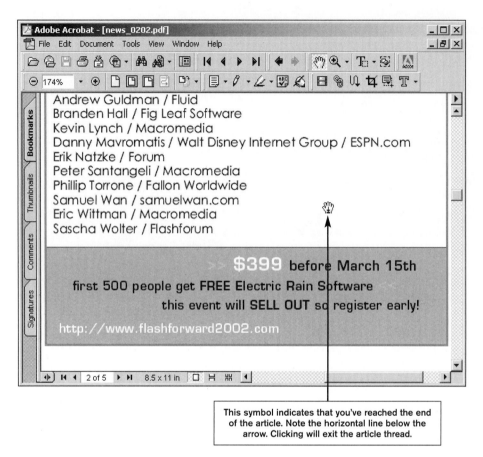

This symbol indicates that you've reached the end of the article. Note the horizontal line below the arrow. Clicking will exit the article thread.

5. Continue clicking the mouse to move through the rest of the article thread. When you have reached the end of the article thread, a horizontal line appears under the arrow in the Hand tool, indicating you're at the last piece of the article thread.

6. Click once more to exit the article thread. You will be returned to your original view of the document before you entered the article.

7. Close **news_0202.pdf**. If Acrobat prompts you, don't save any changes to the document.

2. ——————Creating Article Threads

When viewing an article thread, the article does not have to flow from page 1 to page 2 and so on. With a properly created article thread, the text will seamlessly flow from one section to the next and, in most cases, the users won't even need to know which page they are on. This is very useful for layouts that don't always flow from one page to the next, such as newspapers.

In this exercise, you will use the **Article** tool to create your own article thread that navigates through a multipage newsletter.

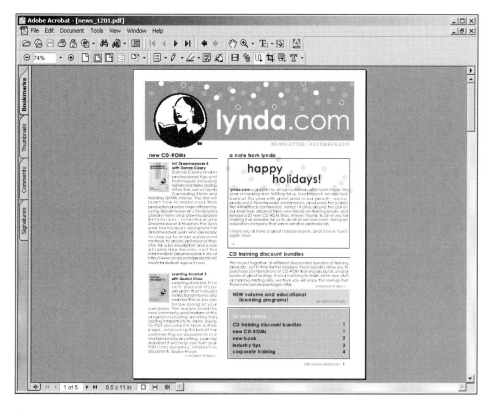

1. Open the **news_1201.pdf** file from the **chap_04** folder.

2. Using the **scrollbar**, navigate to **page 3** of 5.

The article on Web-safe color begins on page 3 and ends on page 5. In order to read this article, the user will have to magnify the first column, scroll down while reading it, scroll back up to read the top of the next column, scroll down, and then continue on the next page. That's enough to make the reader pass out. Adding an article thread here will greatly simplify this process for the user.

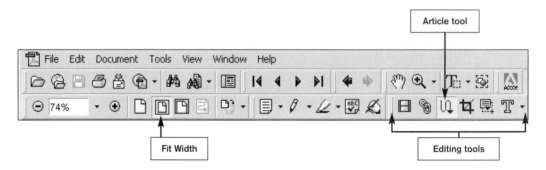

Articles are created with the Article tool, which is located in the toolbar among the Editing tools.

3. Select the **Article** tool from the toolbar. Your cursor will become a crosshair. **Note:** Viewing the document in **Fit in Window** view will make the next steps much easier to follow.

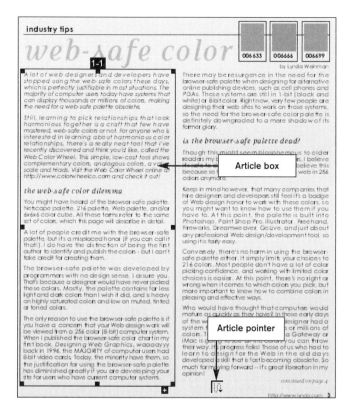

Article box

Article pointer

After you draw a box around the text, your cursor will turn into an Article pointer, which lets you define more areas for this article.

4. Using the Article tool, draw a box around the first column of text on the page. When you release the mouse, an **article box** will appear. Don't worry if you didn't draw the box quite to your liking, you can go back to adjust it later. **Warning:** Don't click anywhere else once you've finished. If you click, you might accidentally draw another article box, which is not a big problem, but it is an annoyance nonetheless. If you do draw another box by accident, see the tip on deleting article boxes at the end of this exercise.

The number 1-1 *has appeared at the top of the article box you've drawn. The first* 1 *indicates this is the first article in this document. The second* 1 *indicates this is the first section of the first article. When you create the next article section, it will display* 1-2 *because it is the second section of the first article.*

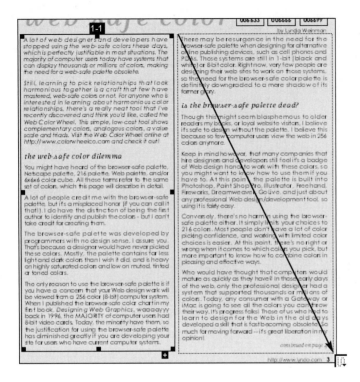

5. Using the **Article pointer**, draw a box around the second column on the page. When you release the mouse, the article box will read **1-2** at the top, indicating that this is the second piece of the first article thread in the document.

The next piece of the article appears on page 4.

---

6. Use the **scrollbar** or the **Next Page** button to move to page 4. **Warning:** Do not type **4** in the status bar area to go to the next page. This will break the article thread.

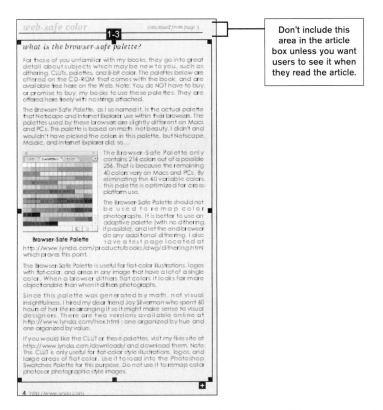

Don't include this area in the article box unless you want users to see it when they read the article.

7. Using the **Article pointer**, draw an article box around the column on the left. Don't include the column's heading when drawing the box. This will make the article flow better when the reader is moving through it.

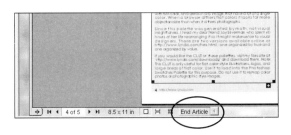

8. You've reached the end of the article. In the status bar, click **End Article** to end this thread. This action will close the article thread and open the **Article Properties** dialog box.

Occasionally the End Article button will not be visible, usually as a result of switching tools while creating an article thread. If the End Article button is missing, just select the Hand tool from the toolbar to close the article thread.

9. In the **Article Properties** dialog box that appears, enter **web-safe color** as the **Title**, **lynda wein-man** as the **Author**, and **web-safe palette**, and **color** as **keywords**. Once you have entered the infor-mation, click **OK**.

You aren't required to enter any information in these fields to complete your article, but at the very least you should always have a title. Adding information for the Subject, Author, and Keywords fields makes the article easier to search. Also, case-sensitivity is not an issue, so you can keep everything lowercase if you like. Searching PDFs is covered later in Chapter 9, "Indexing and Searching PDFs."

10. Select the **Hand** tool from the toolbar and test your article by clicking in the first column on page 3.

11. When you're done testing the article thread, save and close the document.

TIP | Deleting Article Boxes

If there's an article box on your document that you want to delete, simply click it with the **Article** tool and press the **Delete** key on your keyboard.

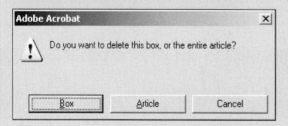

You will be presented with this dialog box asking whether you want to delete just the box or the entire article. Click **Box** to delete just the selected article box, leaving the rest of the article intact. If you wish to remove the entire article thread from the document, click **Article**.

3. ——————————Editing Article Threads

As you create more and more article threads, there will be times when you'll need to go back and edit some of them. Editing can include everything from resizing an article box to adding more boxes to the article thread. This exercise will show you how to perform some of these editing tasks.

1. Open the **news_0202.pdf** file from the **chap_04** folder. This file contains a finished article thread that you will learn to edit.

2. Go to **page 3** and select the **Article** tool to reveal the **article box** on this page (box **3-1**). Notice that the article box does not cover all of the text in the column.

Any time you want to edit or create an article box, you must first select the Article tool.

3. With the **Article** tool selected, click within the article box once to select it. When the article box is properly selected, you will see eight block resizing **handles** (squares) inside the article border.

4. Place the crosshair cursor over the lower-right-hand **handle**. The cursor will become a diagonal double-headed arrow.

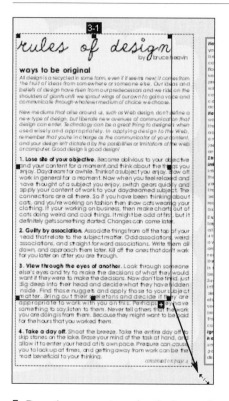

5. Drag the **corner** to resize the box and cover the entire column. That's all there is to resizing article boxes.

When creating article threads, wait until you've closed the article thread before attempting to resize any of its article boxes. One wrong click could break an active article thread, forcing you to start all over again. See the tip in the last exercise on deleting article boxes for information on how to remove an entire article thread.

6. Go to **page 4** of 5.

Notice here that an article box is missing in the center column. Box 3-2 appears over the left column; box 3-3 appears over the right column, but there is no article box over the center column. The following steps show you how to add another article box to the existing thread.

7. With the **Article** tool, click once inside box **3-2** to select it.

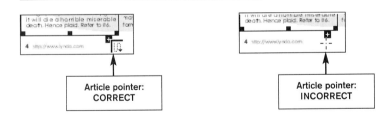

Article pointer:
CORRECT

Article pointer:
INCORRECT

8. Place your cursor over the (**+**) sign at the bottom of the **3-2** article box and click once. Make sure the cursor becomes the **Article pointer** before you click. The **End Article** button will appear in the status bar if you click correctly.

If you click incorrectly, Acrobat assumes that you're trying to create a new article thread and provides this helpful message. Just click OK *and try again.*

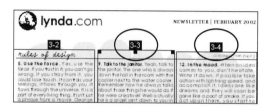

9. Using the **Article pointer**, drag a box around the middle column on the page. The middle box now becomes box **3-3** and the next one has become **3-4**.

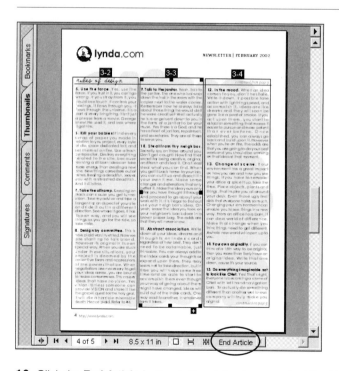

10. Click the **End Article** button in the status bar, or select the **Hand** tool to exit the article thread.

11. Test the article by selecting the **Hand** tool and clicking on the first column of page 4. Continue clicking to follow the article thread to the end.

12. Save the document and keep it open for the next exercise.

TIP | Other Ideas for Using the Article Tool

Bear in mind that the Article tool does not necessarily have to be used on just a single article thread. For example, if you had a PDF book that included summaries at the end of each chapter, you could connect them all with the Article tool, naming the article thread, **Chapter Summaries**. The user could then access and read all the chapter summaries at once by choosing **Window > Articles** and clicking the **Chapter Summaries** article thread. The Article tool is an excellent means of connecting separate areas within a PDF document.

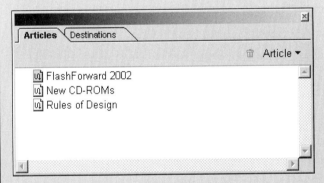

You can view a listing of all the articles in a PDF by choosing **Window > Articles**. Double-clicking any of the article titles will take you into that article.

4.————————Setting Magnification Preferences

By default, Acrobat will enlarge an article thread to its largest possible width within a document pane. In some cases, especially when boxes are small, the text can be enlarged too much. Too much enlargement can limit the amount of text displayed on the screen and make navigation more difficult. There is good news, however; you can limit the level of magnification used to display the article threads.

In this exercise, you will learn how to limit the magnification level of the article threads in your PDF documents to make the text more readable.

Hmm, do you think there are any new CD-ROMs available? This article has been enlarged waaaay too much.

1. The **news_0202.pdf** file should still be open from the previous exercise. Go to **page 1** and click the first column on the left with the **Hand** tool. Because of the narrow width of the column, this article has been enlarged to a very high percentage.

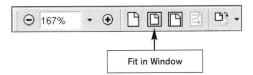

Fit in Window

2. Click the **Fit in Window** button to reduce the magnification.

3. Select **Edit > Preferences > General** (Mac OS X: **Acrobat > Preferences > General**) or press **Ctrl+K** (Windows) or **Cmd+K** (Mac).

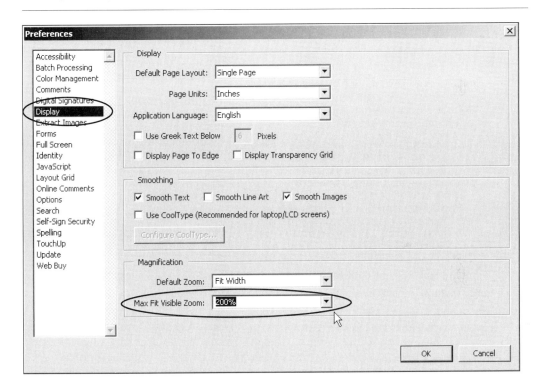

4. From the list on the left, choose **Display**.

5. In the **Magnification** category near the bottom of the dialog box, change the **Max Fit Visible Zoom** to **200%**. This reduces the maximum magnification limit. (You might have to experiment with your magnification settings for your own system.)

6. Click **OK**.

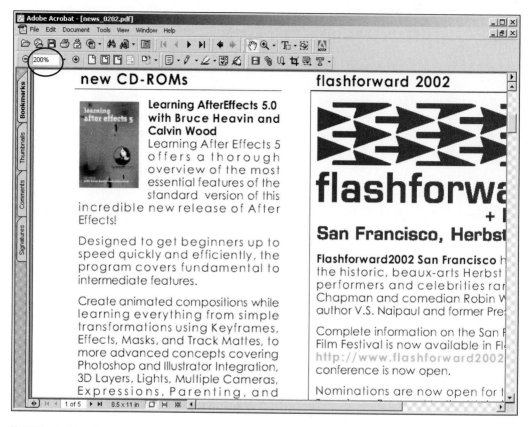

7. With the **Hand** tool, click the **Go to Previous View** button then click the **new CD-ROMS** article again. Notice that the magnification setting jumps to 200%. You no longer have to stand back from the monitor to read the text. **Note:** The preferences you just set are for your copy of Acrobat only. Each user will have to set his or her own preferences. See the note below for more information.

NOTE | Educating Your Audience

In Chapter 3, "*Working with Links*," you learned how to insert link areas into your PDF documents. Most users are able to instantly recognize the presence of a link when the mouse cursor turns into a pointing finger. The pointing finger is a navigational icon that most people are familiar with from surfing the Web, and usually requires no further explanation.

The same cannot be said for the various icons associated with the Article tool. Now that you've spent all this time inserting article threads into your document, how do you teach your end users to navigate them (other than encouraging them to purchase a copy of **Acrobat 5 H•O•T**)? If you plan to use the Article tool within a PDF, it's helpful to insert a page that addresses such topics as how to navigate the PDF, how to set display preferences, and any other issues specific to the document. The **help.pdf** inside the **chap_04** folder is an example of this type of help page.

As you can see, the Article tool is an excellent means of helping your readers through your PDF documents. It's unfortunate that the Article tool is not used very often. Used in combination with links and bookmarks, article threads greatly increase the interactivity and ease-of-use of your documents. So, the next time you're staring at one of your PDFs wondering how to make it more interesting and easily accessible, use your imagination and think of ways to use the Article tool to enhance your document.

5.

Bookmarks

| Creating Bookmarks | Nesting Bookmarks |
| Automatically Naming Bookmarks |
| Setting Document Open Options |

chap_05

Acrobat 5
H•O•T CD-ROM

In Chapter 2, "*Interface*," you saw how the Bookmarks panel could be used to navigate your documents. In this chapter you'll learn how to create bookmarks.

At first glance, bookmarks appear to be very similar to links. Many users might wonder why you include both links and bookmarks in your PDF document. Indeed, bookmarks and links share many similar features. When clicked, both take the user to specific areas within the document. Both can be assigned such actions as opening files, linking to the Internet, or playing multimedia content. However, while links are created within the document itself and can only be accessed from the pages on which they reside, bookmarks reside in the Navigation pane. The significance of the Navigation pane is that it is always available, no matter which page is currently visible. Ideally, an interactive PDF document should contain both links and bookmarks to important content.

Additionally, bookmarks have the capability to be nested, allowing them to be easily expanded and collapsed. This feature gives bookmarks greater functionality than simple links, and allows the user to quickly access locations and content that you have deemed important.

In this chapter you'll look at several methods of creating bookmarks manually. In Chapter 14, *"Exporting PDFs from Popular Applications,"* you'll learn how to create bookmarks automatically from such authoring applications as InDesign and Word.

I. ——————Creating Bookmarks

Bookmarks help readers easily navigate their way through PDF documents. By simply clicking a book-mark, the reader is taken to specific content in the PDF document. This interactivity enhances the reader's experience and makes reading and searching large documents easy. In this exercise, you'll be setting up bookmarks that allow the reader to navigate to specific areas of your PDF document.

1. Copy the **chap_05** from the **H•O•T CD-ROM** to your hard drive.

2. Open the **alice.pdf** file from the **chap_05** folder.

2. Click the **Bookmarks** tab to open the **Navigation** pane.

3. Click the **Fit in Window** button to ensure that the entire page is visible.

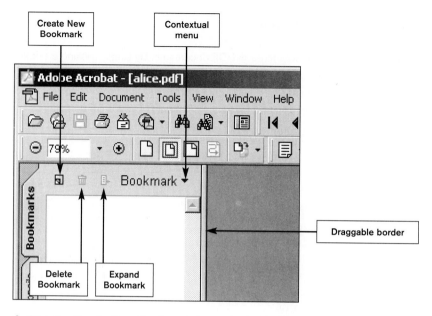

4. Click the **Create New Bookmark** button in the **Bookmarks** panel. A new, untitled bookmark appears in the Navigation pane. **Note:** If you don't see the **Create New Bookmark** button, expand the width of the Navigation pane until the button appears.

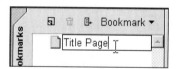

5. Type **Title Page** for the bookmark name.

Whenever you create a new bookmark, it is immediately associated with the current page view.

TIP | Alternate Methods for Creating New Bookmarks

Acrobat allows you to create new bookmarks using several different methods. You can click the **Create New Bookmark** button, as in the exercise. Or, you can choose **Bookmark > New Bookmark** from the contextual menu (see the figure above), use the keyboard command **Ctrl+B** (Windows) or **Cmd+B** (Mac), or **right-click** (Windows) or **Ctrl-click** (Mac) anywhere in the Bookmarks tab and choose **New Bookmark**. You do not have to remember all of these different methods—choose one that you like and remember that one.

6. To test your new bookmark, scroll forward a few pages and then click the **Title Page** bookmark. You will be returned to the title page.

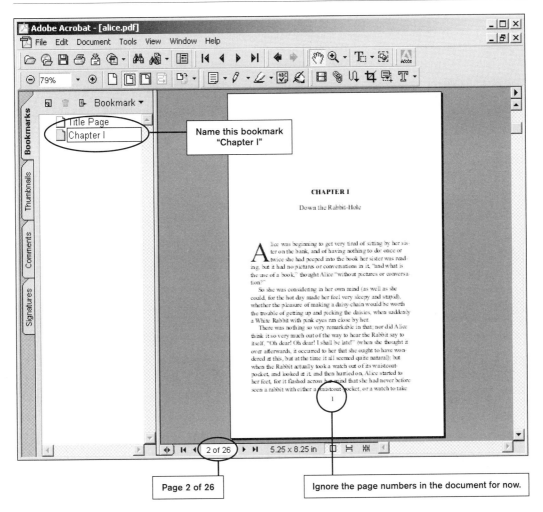

Name this bookmark "Chapter I"

Page 2 of 26

Ignore the page numbers in the document for now.

7. Go to **page 2** of 26. Click the **Create New Bookmark** button and name it **Chapter I**. (Note that I am using capital I, which is Roman numeral 1.)

Also, be sure that you are viewing page 2 of 26 in the status bar. Because you are using a title page, a discrepancy will exist between the page numbers on the document and the page numbers in the status bar. You will learn how to correct this in Chapter 6, *"Modifying PDFs,"* but for now all page references refer to the status bar page numbers.

8. Go to **page 10** of 26. Click the **Create New Bookmark** button and name it **Chapter II**.

9. Go to **page 18** of 26, create a new bookmark, and name it **Chapter III**.

10. Scroll forward a few more pages, and click each bookmark. You should be taken to each of those pages. Pretty easy, huh?

11. Click the **Title Page** bookmark to return to the beginning of the document.

Your goal so far has been to create bookmarks that quickly move the user to different chapters and allow them to view the entire page they are taken to. Next, you'll create bookmarks that will quickly jump to the illustrations in the book. For this exercise, it would be nice for the user to be able view the illustrations in as large a size as possible. The various preset magnification levels (Fit in Window, Fit Width, etc.) won't be very useful, so you will use the Zoom tool instead to quickly enlarge each image.

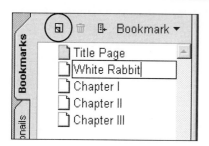

12. Click the **Create New Bookmark** button and name the bookmark **White Rabbit**. The new bookmark appears directly beneath the Title Page bookmark. (Each time a new bookmark is created, it always appears beneath the currently selected bookmark.) You will move the White Rabbit bookmark to the bottom of the list.

Bookmark icon

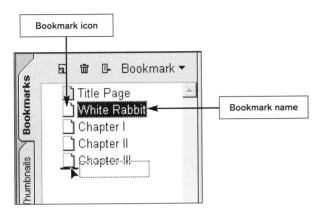

Bookmark name

13. Click and drag the **Page** icon for the **White Rabbit** bookmark down the list until a solid line appears under the Chapter III bookmark. Release the mouse button. (Be sure that the line appears under the Page icon for the Chapter III bookmark. If you drag too far, you'll see a **no** icon, which is a circle with a line through it. Also, ensure that you drag the icon below the Chapter III icon and *not* the text. Placing the White Rabbit icon below the Chapter III text will cause the White Rabbit bookmark to be placed as a subset of Chapter III.)

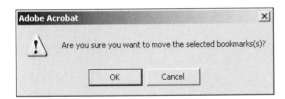

14. Confirm that you want to move the bookmark.

The bookmark is now in a more logical location, but it's pointing to the wrong destination. When a bookmark is created, it is immediately associated with the page and magnification level that's currently displayed in the document window. Because the title page was visible when you created the bookmark, the bookmark currently points here. To fix a bookmark, you must first select the bookmark and then navigate to the proper destination.

15. Click the **White Rabbit** bookmark to select it.

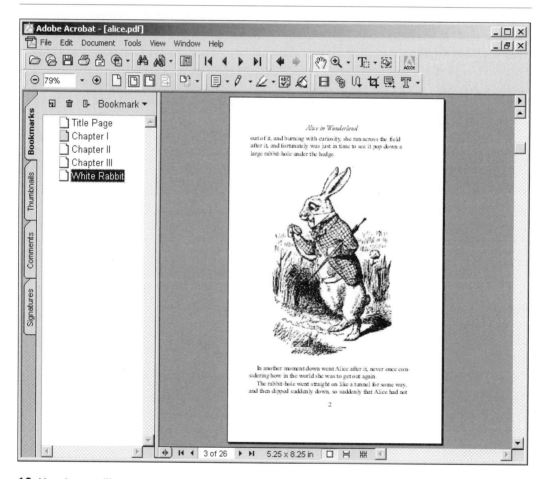

16. Use the **scrollbar** to go to **page 3** of 26.

17. Select the **Zoom** tool from the toolbar and draw a selection marquee around the illustration, as in the above figure. The point is to set the image at its largest possible size for easy onscreen viewing. You could also use the other magnification tools, but the Zoom tool is usually the most convenient tool for quickly enlarging a specific area of your page.

18. Select the **Hand** tool. You can use the Hand tool to grab the image onscreen and adjust its positioning if necessary. Click and drag the image to position it exactly as you would want it to appear for the end user, when they select the White Rabbit bookmark.

Now that you have the image set exactly the way you want it, you can fix the White Rabbit bookmark.

The bookmark is selected.   The bookmark is not selected.

Before continuing to the next step, ensure that the White Rabbit bookmark is still selected. If it's not selected, return to step 15 and start again. If it is selected, don't click it again; otherwise it will take you right back to the title page and you'll have to go back to step 15 and start again. You can recognize a selected bookmark when its name is either highlighted or outlined with a dotted line.

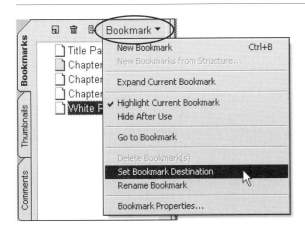

19. With the **White Rabbit** bookmark selected in the Bookmarks panel, click the **Bookmark** contextual menu and choose **Set Bookmark Destination**.

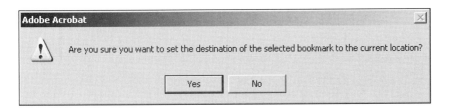

A dialog box will appear asking you to confirm the destination. Click **Yes**.

It's a little more time consuming to create your bookmarks first and then modify their destinations. In most cases, you'll want to set up your destination first, and then create your bookmark as you did when you created the bookmarks for the Title Page, and Chapters I, II, and III.

curtain she had not noticed before, and behind it was a little door about fifteen inches high: she tried the little golden key in the lock, and to her great delight it fitted!

Alice opened the door and found that it led into a small passage, not much larger than a rat-hole: she knelt down and

20. Scroll to **page 6** of 26 and enlarge the illustration using the **Zoom** tool and the **Hand** tool.

21. Click the **Create New Bookmark** button and name the bookmark **Alice Finds a Door**.

22. Using the chart below, create bookmarks for the images listed on each page. **Tip:** To get your bearings each time, go to the specified page and click **Fit in Window**. This will help you much more easily find and magnify the illustrations.

Bookmarks for Exercise I	
Bookmark Name	**Acrobat Page Number**
Drink Me	7 of 26
Tall Alice	10 of 26
Alice and the White Rabbit	12 of 26
Alice in the Pool of Tears	15 of 26
Alice and the Mouse	16 of 26
The Animals	19 of 26
The Dodo	22 of 26

23. When you are finished, save your work and leave this file open for the next exercise.

2. ———————Nesting Bookmarks

As you can see, your bookmark list is getting longer and longer. To make it easier for the end user to navigate the bookmark structure, it's a good idea to create **nested** bookmarks within the Bookmarks tab.

Nested bookmarks let you create a hierarchal structure for your bookmarks so that a long list of bookmarks can be more easily managed. In this exercise, you will learn how to create nested bookmarks.

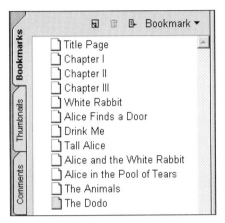

1. Click in a blank area beneath your bookmark list to deselect any bookmarks. Don't worry if the Page icon next to a bookmark is still gray. As long as the bookmark name isn't highlighted or outlined, it's not selected. **Tip:** A bookmark with a gray icon indicates that the bookmark is associated with the page that is currently visible.

2. Click the **Create New Bookmark** button and name the new bookmark **Illustrations**. This bookmark will act as a heading for the illustration bookmarks. In the next steps, you will nest the bookmarks to the illustrations within this bookmark.

Title Page
Chapter I
Chapter II
Chapter III
White Rabbit
Alice Finds a Door
Drink Me
Tall Alice
Alice and the White Rabbit
Alice in the Pool of Tears
The Animals
The Dodo
Illustrations

3. Click and drag the icon for the **Illustrations** bookmark upward until a black line appears between the Chapter III and White Rabbit icons, and then release the mouse button. A dialog box will appear asking you to confirm your change. Click **OK**.

You will now nest all of the illustration bookmarks under the new heading.

4. Click the **icon** for the **White Rabbit** bookmark (not its name).

Title Page
Chapter I
Chapter II
Chapter III
Illustrations
White Rabbit
Alice Finds a Door
Drink Me
Tall Alice
Alice and the White Rabbit
Alice in the Pool of Tears
The Animals
The Dodo

5. Press the **Shift** key and click the **Dodo** icon to select it plus all the bookmarks in between it and **White Rabbit**.

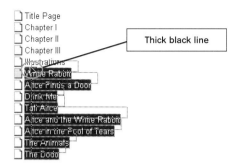

6. Click and drag the **White Rabbit** icon up and to the right. Make sure that the black line appears under the first letters of Illustrations, not under its Page icon.

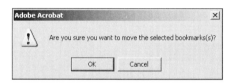

7. A dialog box will appear asking you to confirm your changes. Click **OK**.

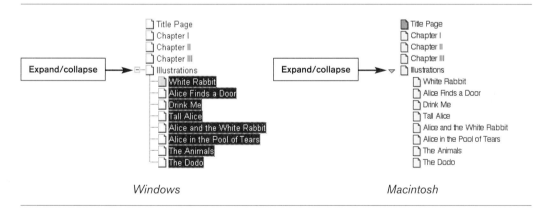

Windows   *Macintosh*

You have now nested the bookmarks. You can collapse and expand the nest list by clicking on the toggle button by the Illustrations bookmark: (+) Windows, (▽) Mac.

Okay, you're doing great. But there is a small problem. The Illustrations bookmark is still pointing to a specific page. If you click the Illustrations bookmark, you'll notice that it still takes you to the page view that you were viewing when you created the bookmark. In the steps that follow, you will set the Illustrations bookmark so that it acts as a heading, and does not take the user anywhere when clicked. You will also alter its appearance to draw attention to the fact that this bookmark is different from the others.

8. Click the **Illustrations** bookmark to select it. You will jump to whatever page you happened to be on when you created the bookmark. (It does not matter which page; soon this bookmark will not be jumping you anywhere at all.)

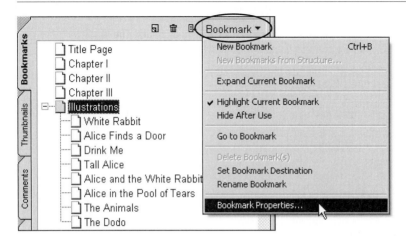

9. From the **Bookmark** contextual menu, choose **Bookmark Properties**.

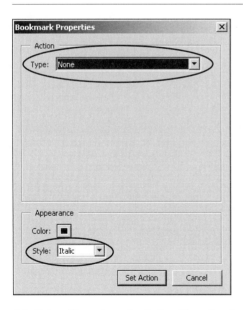

10. Select **None** from the **Action Type** list. As with links, bookmarks have several action types that you can set. In this case, you will remove all actions from the Illustrations bookmark, because you want it to be only a heading.

11. In the **Appearance** area, choose **Italic** as the **Style**. This setting will change the appearance of the bookmark just enough that the reader will know something is different about it.

12. Click **Set Action**.

13. Click any bookmark in your list and then click the **Illustrations** bookmark. The Illustrations bookmark now acts as the heading for the nested bookmark list, but does not perform any action itself.

14. Choose **File > Save** and close **alice.pdf**.

The ability to change the color and style of bookmarks is new to Acrobat 5. When you italicized the Illustrations bookmark, you provided a helpful visual indication that it is different from the rest of the bookmarks. You can also assign other actions to bookmarks such as opening a file or linking to the Internet. If you create a bookmark that links to the Internet (by selecting the World Wide Web Link action), you could also change the bookmark's color to blue to indicate that it is an external link. You'll be exploring other bookmark actions in later chapters.

3. ————————Automatically Naming Bookmarks

It is possible that, when you are creating bookmarks, the name you want to use for a bookmark also appears as text in the body of the document. If this is the case, creating bookmarks becomes even easier. As you're about to see, Acrobat will automatically use any selected text as the name for your bookmark when you create it.

1. Open **newsletter_feb.pdf** located in the **chap_05** folder.

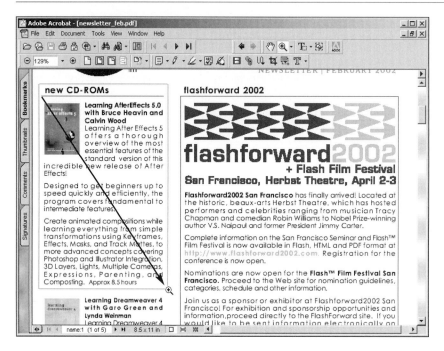

2. Use the **Zoom** tool to magnify the paragraph under **new CD-ROMs** entitled **Learning AfterEffects 5.0 with Bruce Heavin and Calvin Wood.**

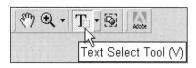

3. From the **toolbar**, choose the **Text Select** tool.

4. Highlight the text **Learning AfterEffects 5.0**.

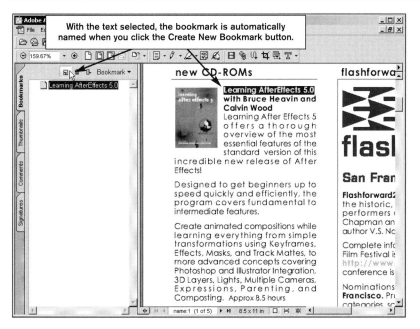

5. In the **Bookmarks** panel, click the **Create New Bookmark** button. A new bookmark appears with the title already in place. Pretty cool! Try a few more of these on your own.

Important note: *This technique won't work if you right-click or Ctrl+click the Bookmarks tab to create your bookmarks. You must use the Create New Bookmark button, the Bookmark menu, or the keyboard command to create your bookmarks.*

6. Save your changes and keep this file open for the next exercise.

TIP | Power User Keyboard Commands

Use one hand to highlight your text, and use the other hand to create bookmarks with the keyboard command **Ctrl+B** (Windows) or **Cmd+B** (Mac).

4. ————————**Setting Document Open Options**

For all the many things that bookmarks are capable of, they do no good if the end user does not know that they exist. Fortunately, you can set up your PDF documents to open in specific views. In this exercise, you will set the options for the document to open in Fit in Window view with the Bookmarks panel open.

1. From the menu bar, choose **File > Document Properties > Open Options**.

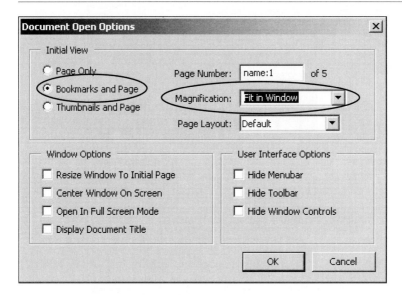

2. In the **Document Open Options** dialog box, select **Bookmarks and Page** under **Initial View**. For **Magnification**, choose **Fit in Window**.

3. Click **OK**.

Now you will test the open options you've set.

4. Save and close **newsletter_feb.pdf**.

5. Open **newsletter_feb.pdf**.

The document opens in Fit in Window view with the Bookmarks panel open.

6. Close the file.

Like links, bookmarks play a vital role in making your documents interactive. Although you may have already created links within your PDF file, bookmarks provide yet another way to quickly acces content. In this chapter you've acquired a basic understanding of how bookmarks work. Later you'll be covering more advanced features of bookmarks, such as linking to Web pages and activating multimedia content.

6.

Modifying PDFs

| Inserting PDF Documents |
| Deleting, Moving, Cropping, and Rotating |
| Extracting Pages | Renumbering Pages |
| Touching Up PDFs | Embedding Thumbnails |

chap_06

Acrobat 5
H•O•T CD-ROM

Perhaps one of the most misunderstood aspects of Acrobat is that it is not a content creation tool. Many users are under the impression that you can just fire up Acrobat and start creating the content of PDFs from scratch. But if you look under Acrobat's File menu, you won't find a New command. All the documents you work with in Acrobat must be created in other programs. This means that you will not find the typical editing features such as those available in Microsoft Word that are designed to create new content.

Still, there are plenty of times when you will need to modify a PDF document that you created or one you imported from somewhere else. PDFs can be edited from within Acrobat to some degree, but you don't have nearly the amount of control over content that you have with real document creation programs.

In this chapter you'll learn just how much you can alter PDFs using Acrobat. You'll run through some exercises teaching you how to insert, move, delete, and crop pages, and you'll also get a chance to work with Acrobat's limited text and object editing capabilities. By the end of this chapter, you will have an understanding of what editing tools are available from within Acrobat 5, and how to use them.

I. _____Inserting PDF Documents

There may be times when you'll want to or need to add additional pages to a PDF document; for example, you might have a chart or a graph you need to add to a business report.

Acrobat gives you two methods for inserting additional pages into existing PDF documents. You can use the **Insert Pages** feature, or you can use **thumbnails** to drag new pages into your document. The Insert Pages method inserts entire PDFs into your existing PDF document, while the thumbnails method allows you to insert specific pages into your PDF. You will learn both methods in the following exercise. **Note:** In order for new pages to be inserted into a PDF, the new pages must already be PDF documents. You cannot insert any other type of file into an existing PDF document.

Inserting New Pages Using the Document Menu

1. Copy the **chap_06** folder from the **H•O•T CD-ROM** to your hard drive.

2. Open the file **alice.pdf** from the **chap_06** folder. This document contains the first three chapters of **Alice's Adventures in Wonderland**. The first page is currently a title page. You're going to add a cover page to this document.

3. From the menu bar, choose **Document > Insert Pages**.

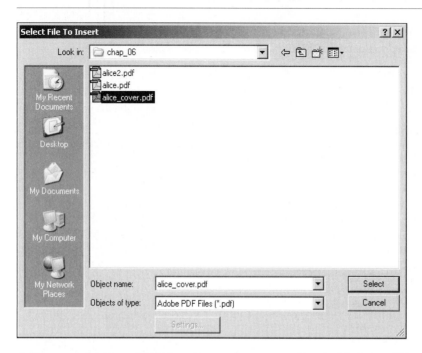

4. Browse to the **chap_06 folder**, choose **alice_cover.pdf** and click **Select**. This will open the **Insert Pages** dialog box, which lets you specify where the file is to be inserted.

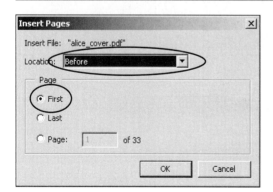

5. From the **Location** pop-up menu, select **Before** and click the **First** radio button. Click **OK**. This action will tell Acrobat to insert the file you selected before the first page of the PDF document. And because this is the cover page, what a great place to put it!

First Page button

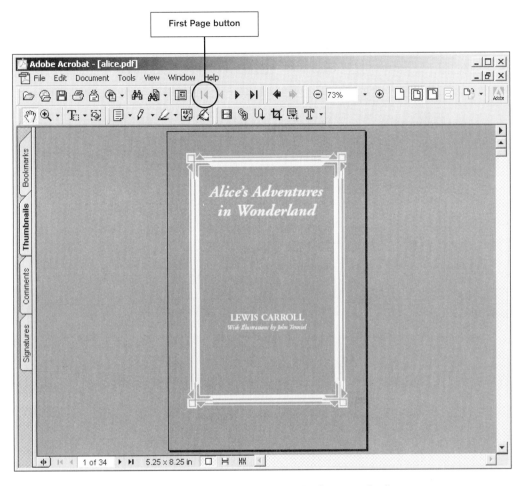

The First Page button is available on every page except the first one. Go figure.

6. Click the **First Page** button to jump to the first page of the document and view the cover page you just inserted. It's important to note here that when you inserted this page, Acrobat merely copied the contents of **alice_cover.pdf** into **alice.pdf**; leaving the **alice_cover.pdf** unchanged.

7. Save the changes you made to this document. Do not close this file–you will need it for the next exercise.

The Document > Insert Pages menu command should really be called Document > Insert PDF, because when you choose this command, you have no choice but to insert the entire contents of the new PDF into the current document. If you want to insert only a few pages from a different document, you can use the thumbnails method, which is covered next.

Inserting New Pages Using Thumbnails

In the first part of this exercise, you learned how to insert a PDF document into an existing one. There may be times when you only want to insert specific pages of one PDF document into another PDF document. In this case, you cannot use the **Insert Pages** command you just learned. The only way to insert individual pages of one PDF document into another is by using **thumbnails**.

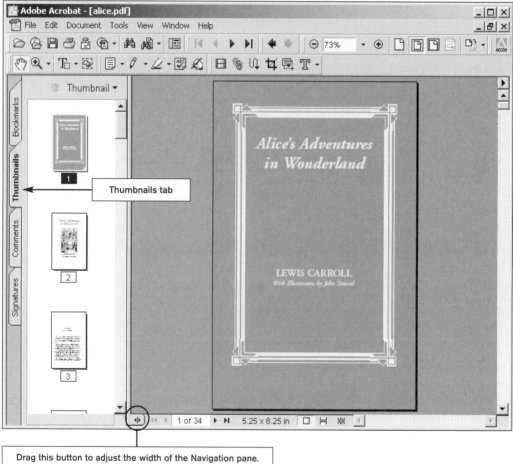

1. If **alice.pdf** is not open, open it now. Click the **Thumbnails** tab on the left side of the window to open the **Thumbnails** panel in the **Navigation** pane. If you see more than one column of thumbnails, drag the **Navigation pane** button to the left until you see just one column. The Thumbnails panel displays small images of each page in the PDF document, providing a nice page preview and offering a quick way to jump between pages.

NOTE | Where'd My Thumbnails Go?

If you don't have a Thumbnails tab in your Navigation pane (or are missing any other tab for that matter), chances are you or someone else using your computer made the Thumbnails panel a floating palette and then closed it.

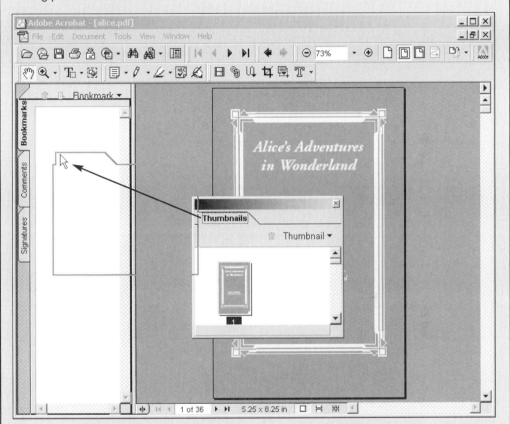

To get it back, choose **Window > Thumbnails**. The Thumbnails panel will appear as a floating palette that you can then drag into the Navigation pane to re-dock it. The next time you open Acrobat, that Thumbnails panel will be docked in the appropriate location.

2. Keep this **alice.pdf** file open and open **alice2.pdf** from the **chap_06** folder. The file from the **chap_06** folder is a slightly different version of the **alice.pdf** document—it contains a different cover page and a table of contents page. You will move both of these pages into **alice.pdf**.

3. Click the **Thumbnails** tab to view **alice2.pdf**'s thumbnails, again making sure that you only see one column of thumbnails (in this exercise, one column is easier to manage). You might notice that the page 3 thumbnail looks different from the rest. Don't worry about that right now; you'll tackle this issue in the next exercise.

In order to copy pages using thumbnails, you need to see both documents at once.

4. Choose **Window > Tile > Vertically**. This action will nicely tile both windows, making it much easier to move pages from one document to another. Next you'll use the thumbnails to copy the cover page and table of contents into **alice.pdf**.

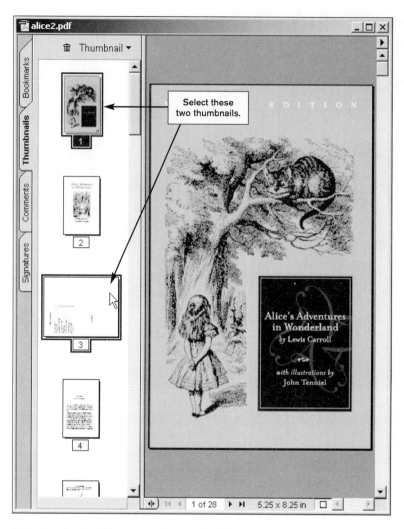

5. In **alice2.pdf**, click once on the thumbnail for the **cover page** to select it. Then **Ctrl+click** (Windows) or **Cmd+click** (Mac) on the thumbnail for **page 3** so that both pages are selected. A border will appear around the selected thumbnails.

6. Click and hold either of the selected thumbnails and drag it toward the **Thumbnails** panel in **alice.pdf**. When you reach the Thumbnails panel, a line will appear. Keep dragging until the line appears between the thumbnails for pages 1 and 2. This thin line indicates where the page(s) will be inserted. Release the mouse button. The two pages will be copied into **alice.pdf**.

7. Close only **alice2.pdf**—don't save any changes. Keep **alice.pdf** open and maximize its window to fill your screen again.

You've just learned two methods of adding additional pages into an existing PDF. Remember that the Document > Insert Pages menu command will insert the entire contents of a PDF document into your current document, while moving thumbnails allows you to insert only selected pages. Next you'll continue to use the thumbnails to further modify your document.

 MOVIE | newthumb.mov

To see this exercise in action, check out **newthumb.mov** located in the **movies** folder on the **Acrobat 5 H•O•T CD-ROM**.

2. —————————Deleting, Moving, Cropping, and Rotating

At this point, you've added two cover pages and a weirdly shaped table of contents page to the **alice.pdf** document. This exercise will teach you how to **delete**, **move**, **crop**, and **rotate** pages. These commands are all found under the **Document** menu in the menu bar.

1. With the **alice.pdf** file still open, choose **Document > Delete Pages**. This action will open the **Delete Pages** dialog box.

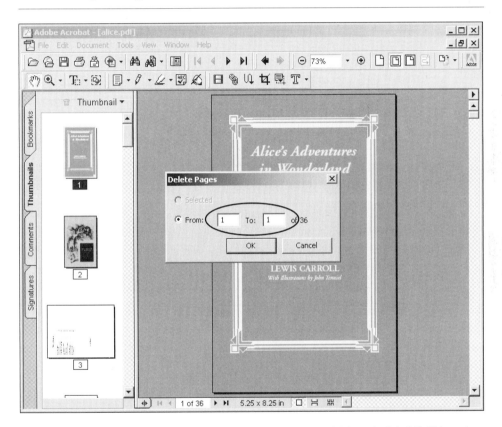

2. Click the **From** radio button, choose to delete from **1** to **1** of 36, and click **OK**. This action will remove the bright red cover page from the PDF. It does not matter what page you are viewing when you choose to delete a page, but the information you enter in the **Delete Pages** dialog box is very important.

3. When Acrobat asks you to confirm that you want to delete page 1, click **Yes**. (Macintosh users using OS X should click **OK**.)

I should also point out that you could have clicked the thumbnail for page 1 and pressed the Delete key to delete the page. Thumbnails are a very useful tool for modifying, moving, or deleting pages. To select multiple pages at once, you can use the Ctrl (Windows) or Cmd (Mac) key and click the thumbnails for each page you want to select. If you wish to select a range of consecutive pages, click the thumbnail for the first page in the sequence, hold down the Shift key, and then click the last thumbnail in the sequence. All the pages between and including the two thumbnails you clicked will be selected. At this point, you can move or delete all the selected pages.

WARNING | Delete Cannot Be Undone

Be careful when you delete pages in Acrobat. If you choose to delete a page, you cannot select Edit > Undo to bring the page back. Your only option is to close the file and be sure to *not* save the changes; choose Don't Save when asked to save your changes. So when you decide to delete a page, make sure you really want it gone.

Next, you'll move the table of contents page between the title page and Chapter 1. This is extremely easy to do with thumbnails—all you have to do is drag a page's thumbnail to wherever you want to move it.

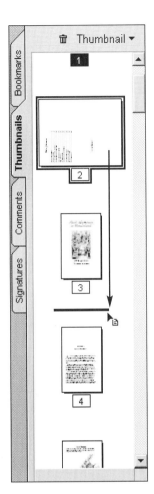

4. In the **Thumbnails** panel, click the thumbnail for **page 2** and drag it down until the line appears between the thumbnails for pages 3 and 4. Release the mouse button. The page has been moved.

Now that the page has been moved, you'll fix it so that it looks more like the rest of the document.

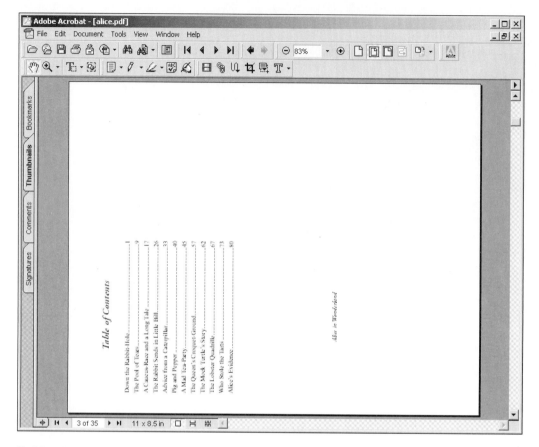

5. Click the **page 3** thumbnail to select it and then click the **Thumbnails** tab to close the **Navigation** pane. Closing the Navigation pane enables you to more easily see the rest of the page.

There are two things wrong with this page. It's oriented incorrectly, and its dimensions are different from those in the rest of the document. You will correct both of these issues next.

6. Select **Document > Rotate Pages**. The **Rotate Pages** dialog box opens.

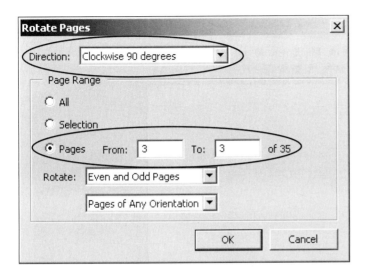

7. Set the **Direction** to **Clockwise 90 degrees** and set the **Page Range** to rotate from pages **3** to **3** of 35. Click **OK**.

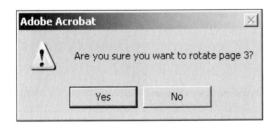

8. Click **Yes** when Acrobat asks if you're sure you want to rotate the page.

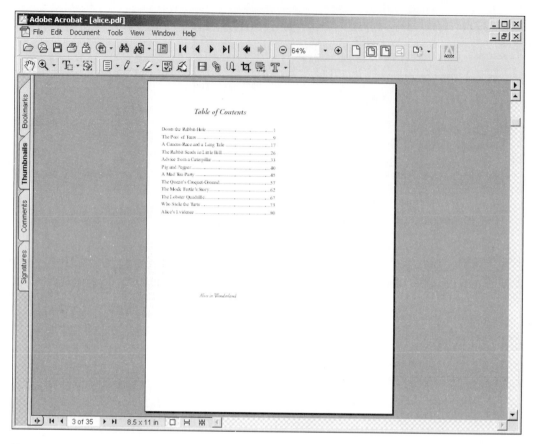

The page rotates to the proper orientation. Now you'll crop the page so that it matches the rest of the document.

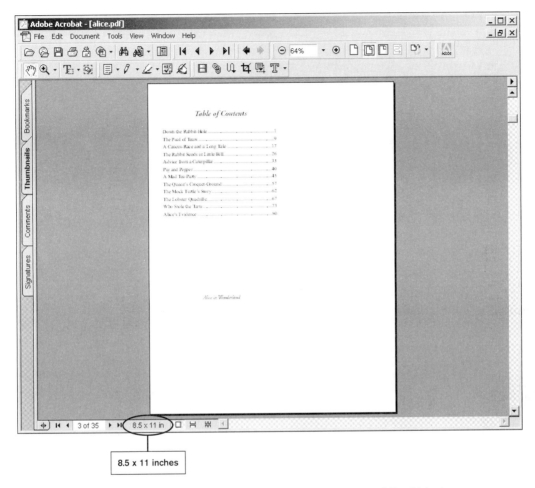

8.5 x 11 inches

9. Look at the **status bar** and notice that the dimensions of this page are **8.5 x 11 inches**.

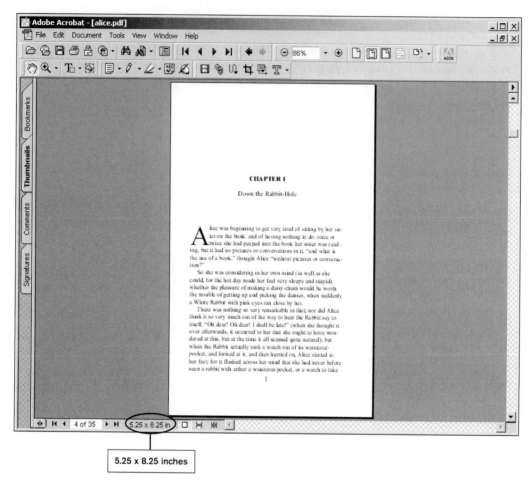

5.25 x 8.25 inches

10. Scroll forward a few pages, and you'll see that the pages in the rest of the document are **5.25 x 8.25 inches**.

11. Scroll back to **page 3**. You're going to crop page 3 to **5.25 x 8.25 inches**.

12. Select **Document > Crop Pages**. This selection will open the **Crop Pages** dialog box.

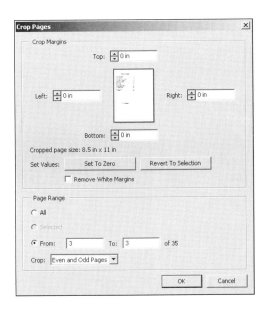

In the Crop Pages dialog box you can determine which pages you want to crop and how you want to crop them. Because the content of the page is located in the upper-left corner of the page, you'll only need to crop the right and bottom sides of the page.

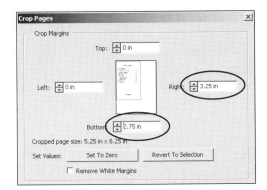

13. In the **Right** field enter **3.25** and press the **Tab** key. In the **Bottom** field, enter **2.75**. Notice that the red border around image in the center has moved to reflect the new crop marks. The **Cropped Page Size** display now reads **5.25 in x 8.25 in**.

Of course, I'm not always going to be there to do the math for you, so the next time you need to crop a page, get your trusty calculator (or do it in your head) and determine how much you need to crop from each margin. Alternatively, you could just click the up/down arrows in each box and adjust the crop lines until the Cropped Page Size indicator displays the proper dimensions.

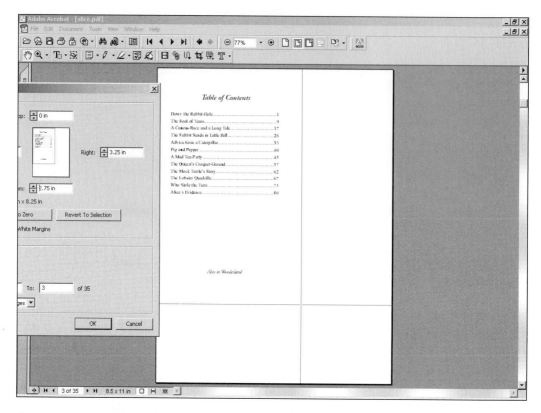

If you move the Crop Pages dialog box off to the side, you'll see thin dashed lines on the page itself, representing the new crop marks. This orientation can give you a better sense of how the page will look when you crop it.

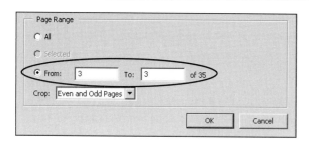

14. Make sure the **Page Range** is set to crop page **3** to **3** of 35 and click **OK**.

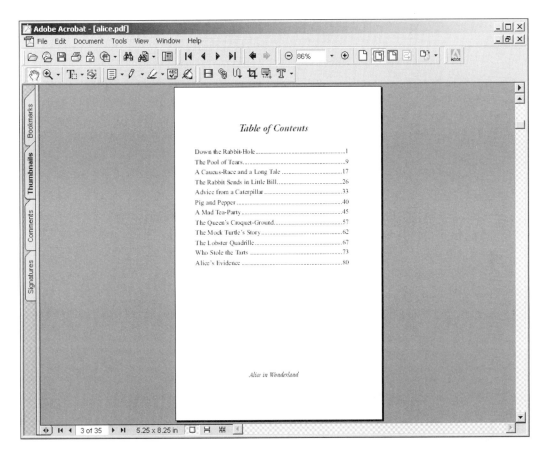

The page has been cropped to match the dimensions of rest of the document.

15. Save this file and keep it open for the next exercise.

3. _____**Extracting Pages**

In the last exercise, you learned how to delete pages from your PDF document. But what if you want to remove specific pages from your PDF but not delete them entirely? Acrobat's **Extract Pages** command works perfectly in such situations. This feature lets you pull pages from a PDF document and save them elsewhere, a great way to remove pages and save them for use later. And my mom always said, "Don't throw away pages you might need later!" Okay, not really, but this is still a cool feature.

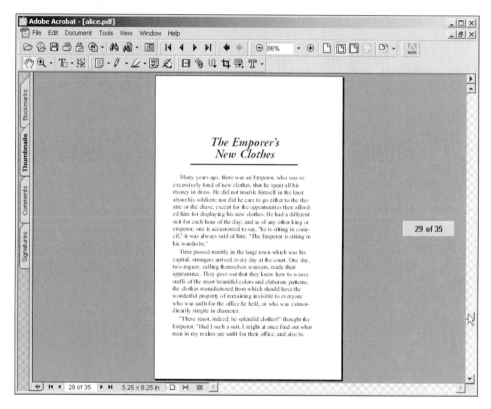

1. With the **alice.pdf** file still open, scroll to **page 29** of 35. Oops! Someone stuck a different story in here. **The Emporer's New Clothes** occupies pages 29 through 35. The story doesn't belong here, but you might want to use it some other time. So rather than deleting it, you're going to extract it. When you extract pages from a PDF document, you take specific content from an exisitng PDF and turn the content into a separate file.

2. Select **Document > Extract Pages**. This will open the **Extract Pages** dialog box.

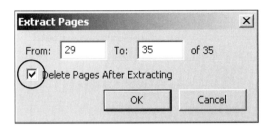

3. In the **From** field enter **29**. In the **To** field enter **35**. Check the **Delete Pages After Extracting** checkbox. Checking this option means that the pages will be removed from the current document. If you left it unchecked, the pages would remain in the current document and would additionally be extracted into a new document. Click **OK**.

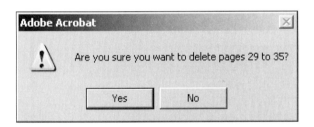

4. Click **Yes** when you are asked to confirm that you want to delete pages 29 to 35. Remember that although you're deleting them from the **alice.pdf** document, they'll end up as a separate document.

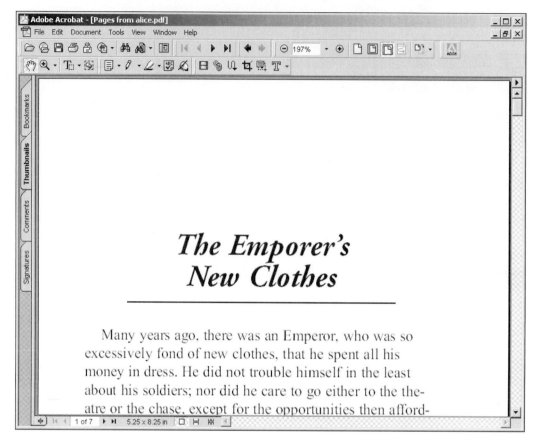

You're now looking at a 7-page document that's been extracted from the alice.pdf file. Notice the title bar says [Pages from alice.pdf]. You need to save this file if you want to keep it.

---

5. Save this file as **emperor.pdf** in the **chap_06** folder. You can close **emperor.pdf**.

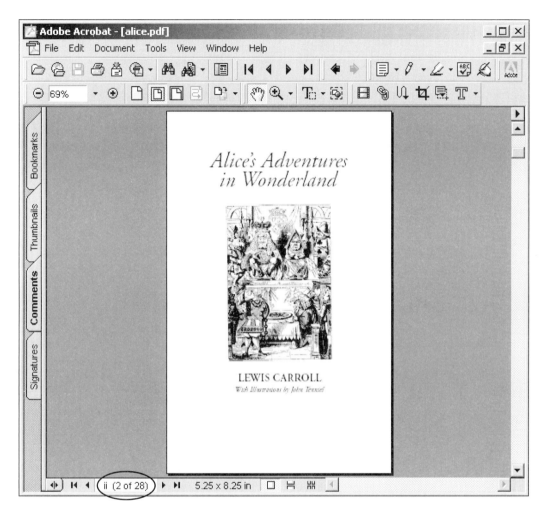

You should be seeing alice.pdf again. It's now a 28-page document.

6. Save the changes to **alice.pdf** and keep it open for the next exercise.

Extracting pages can be very useful. Imagine you have a PDF of a 30-page travel brochure that contains a map. If you needed to e-mail just the map to a friend, you could extract it from the PDF (without checking Delete Pages After Extracting) and you'd have a small single-page PDF to e-mail, with no damage to the original brochure.

TIP | Extracting Images

New to Acrobat 5 is the ability to extract images from your PDF. This great little feature can really come in handy if you have a PDF containing an image you want to use on a Web page or publication, but you have no access to the original image. To extract images from a PDF choose File > Export > Extract Images As. From there you can choose whether you want your images saved as JPG, PNG, or TIF files. Acrobat will ask where you want to save the files. You have no choice but to extract all of the images in the PDF, so if there are a lot of images, your best bet is to create a new folder in which to collect the images. After the images have been extracted, you can look through the folder to find the images you want to keep and discard the rest.

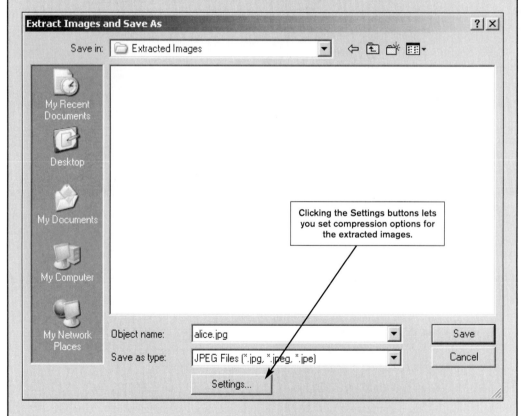

Clicking the Settings buttons lets you set compression options for the extracted images.

Of course, this means that anyone with a copy of Acrobat 5 can extract images from your PDFs. If you want to prevent unauthorized image copying, see Chapter 10, "*Document Security.*"

4. _____Renumbering Pages

If you look carefully, you'll notice that the page numbers in your status bar don't match the page numbers in the document itself. This is because the cover page, title page, and table of contents page in the **alice.pdf** document don't contain page numbers. Even though Acrobat starts counting the pages on page 1, the document doesn't display a page 1 until the fourth page. This can be very confusing for the user trying to read the PDF document, because the reported page count doesn't match the numbering system found in the document.

In this exercise you'll change Acrobat's numbering system so that it matches the numbering of the document.

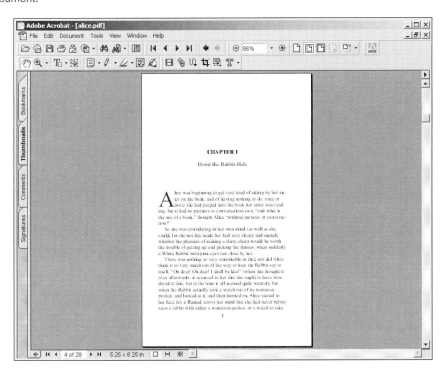

1. With the **alice.pdf** file stilll open, scroll to **page 4** of 28. This is the first page of Chapter 1. According to the document, this page is page 1, because, traditionally, cover pages, title pages, and table of contents pages aren't considered part of the body of a publication. So although the document says this is page 1, the Acrobat status bar indicates that the page is page 4.

There's no easy way to change the page numbers in the document, so instead you'll change the way Acrobat counts the pages and you'll renumber the first three pages. The most common convention is to use lowercase roman numerals to number pages preceding the main body of text.

2. Select **Document > Number Pages**. The **Page Numbering** dialog box will open. This dialog box controls the way the page numbering is handled.

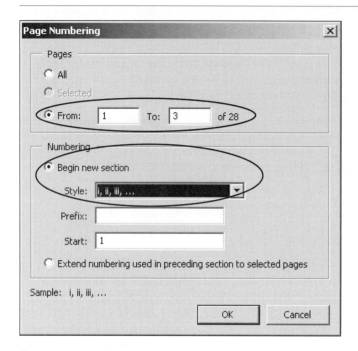

3. In the **Pages** area of the dialog box, click the **From** radio button and enter **1** to **3** to indicate that you want to renumber the first three pages. In the **Numbering** section, click the **Begin new section** radio button and choose lowercase roman numerals as the **Style**. (These look like a bunch of lower-case i's. What were those Romans thinking?) Click **OK**.

It is important to point out that you are not changing the numbers on the actual pages. Instead, you're changing what is displayed in the Acrobat status bar. Note also that you can add a prefix, or start counting on a number other than one. Adding a prefix would be useful in the case of an appendix where you might want the pages numbered a.i, a.ii, a.iii, and so on.

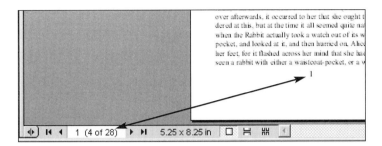

The number in the status bar has changed. It reads 1 (4 of 28). Acrobat now concedes that this is page 1, but under its breath it's muttering, "Yeah, but it's really page 4 of 28."

4. Scroll back a few pages and confirm that the first three pages of the document are represented by lowercase roman numerals in the status bar.

Your numbers now match up, which makes it much easier to reference a page when you're discussing a document with someone or writing a book in which you constantly need to refer readers to a particular page.

5. Save the **alice.pdf** file and keep it open for the next exercise.

5. —————————Touching Up PDFs

Acrobat does not have the ability to generate content from nothing. Its real strength lies in its ability to enhance existing PDFs.

That said, there *are* ways to perform minor corrections or alterations to your PDF documents. For example, what would you do if you found a spelling error in the PDF document? One possibility is to delete the PDF, fix the spelling error in the original application, and then generate a new PDF. This would be ideal if you were getting paid by the hour. Otherwise, there is an easier way to handle this problem. In cases in which only a small correction is needed, you can use one of Acrobat's touch-up tools. As you'll see, Acrobat is not made to perform large editing tasks.

In this lesson, you'll work with the **TouchUp Text** tool and the **TouchUp Object** tool to see exactly which content Acrobat will and will not let you change.

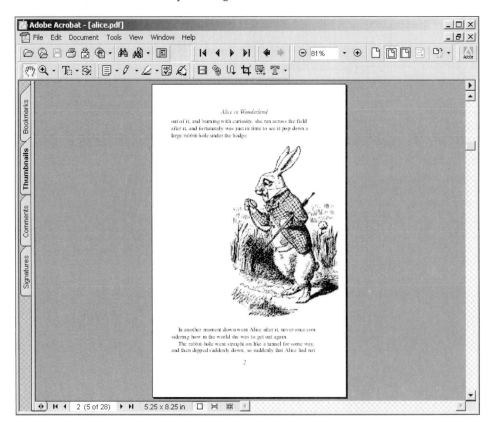

1. Go to **page 2** (5 of 28) of the **alice.pdf** file.

2. Click the **Fit Width** button in the toolbar to enlarge the page.

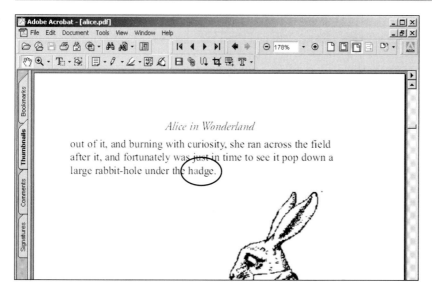

Notice that "hedge" is misspelled as "hadge" at the end of the paragraph at the top of the page. You will use the TouchUp Text tool to fix this.

Note: *You can only correct text if the font used to create the text has been embedded into the PDF document, or if the specified font is installed on your computer. If the font has not been embedded, it will not be available for Acrobat to use and you won't be able to fix the misspelling. Embedding fonts is covered in Chapter 13,* "Creating PDFs within Acrobat." *This particular file uses Times New Roman, which is installed on just about every computer.*

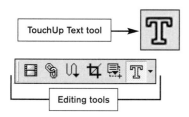

3. From the toolbar, select the **TouchUp Text** tool. You previously used this tool in Chapter 3, "*Creating Links*," to copy text. Here you will use it to correct misspelled text.

> *Alice in Wonderland*
>
> out of it, and burning with curiosity, she ran across the field
> after it, and fortunately was just in time to see it pop down a
> large rabbit-hole under the ha|dge.

4. Click on the word **hadge** at the end of the first paragraph. A box is drawn around the entire line of text, which is the default action of the **TouchUp Text** tool. The box indicates what Acrobat sees as editible on that line.

Note that the box does not appear around all the text at the top of the page. In fact, it's impossible to use the TouchUp Text tool to select more than one line at a time. This is why you can't use Acrobat to alter large sections of text; Acrobat doesn't recognize paragraphs, wrapping text, or line breaks.

> *Alice in Wonderland*
>
> out of it, and burning with curiosity, she ran across the field
> after it, and fortunately was just in time to see it pop down a
> large rabbit-hole under the h█dge.

> *Alice in Wonderland*
>
> out of it, and burning with curiosity, she ran across the field
> after it, and fortunately was just in time to see it pop down a
> large rabbit-hole under the he|dge.

5. Highlight just the letter **a** in **hadge** and press the **e** key on the keyboard. After a moment, the **e** appears and the spelling has been corrected. Acrobat automatically uses the font of the surrounding text. Click in the blank area of a margin to deselect the text box.

In addition to touching up text, you can also touch up the position of objects in your PDF using the TouchUp Object tool. Notice on this page that the image of the White Rabbit is off to the right side of the page. You will use the TouchUp Object tool to move the image to the center of the page.

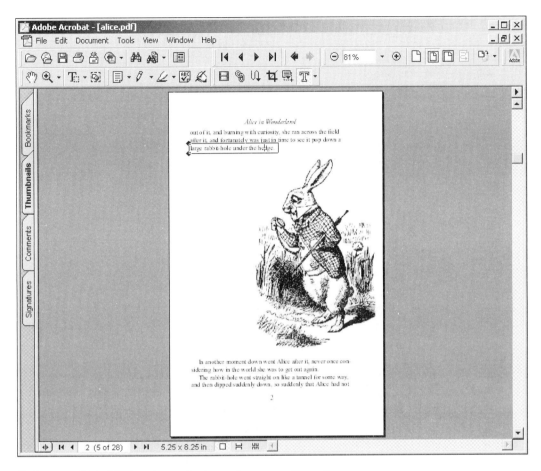

6. Click the **Fit in Window** button in the toolbar to see the entire page.

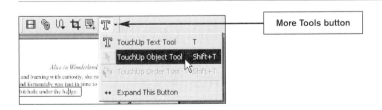

More Tools button

7. Click the **More Tools** small arrow button next to the **TouchUp Text** tool to access the **TouchUp Object** tool. If you are a keyboard person, you can also use the **Shift+T** keyboard shortcut, but make sure your text from the previous step has been deselected. Otherwise, you'll have the word "htdge," which isn't a word at all.

8. With the **TouchUp Object** tool active, click once on the image of the White Rabbit. A border will appear around the image.

Alice in Wonderland

out of it, and burning with curiosity, she ran across the field after it, and fortunately was just in time to see it pop down a large rabbit-hole under the hedge.

In another moment down went Alice after it, never once considering how in the world she was to get out again.

The rabbit-hole went straight on like a tunnel for some way, and then dipped suddenly down, so suddenly that Alice had not

2

9. Click on the image and drag it to the left and do your best to center it on the page. Acrobat offers no image aligment tools, so you'll have to eyeball this one.

10. Click in the blank area of a margin to deselect the image. Save the file and keep it open for the next exercise.

6. ———————Embedding Thumbnails

In this chapter you've learned to use thumbnails as a means of navigating and adding pages to your PDFs. If you like this feature and think you might use it a lot, you might want to embed your thumbnails into your PDF while you work with it.

Acrobat automatically generates thumbnails when the Thumbnails panel is opened. If you scroll quickly through the Thumbnails panel, you'll notice that the thumbnails briefly appear as gray rectangles before the thumbnails themselves appear. On slower computers, the process of generating thumbnails on the fly can get tedious, especially when you're using thumbnails to reorganize your document like you did in this chapter. Having Acrobat embed thumbnails into the document allows you to work faster.

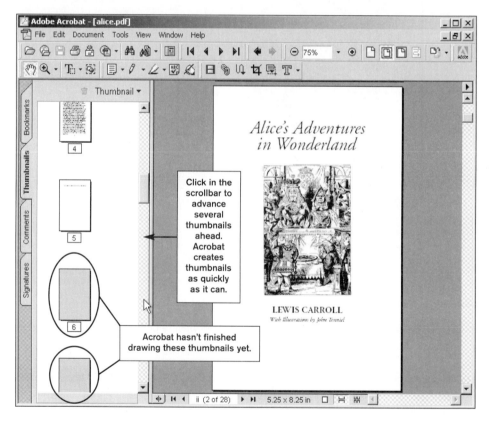

1. Click the **Thumbnails** tab to open the **Navigation** pane, and scroll through the thumbnails. Notice the gray rectangles that appear. (On some systems you may have to release the mouse button occasionally to allow the thumbnails to render. If you're on a particularly fast computer and aren't seeing the flashes of gray, you should go buy a slower computer! Just kidding. Try clicking in the scrollbar to see the thumbnails).

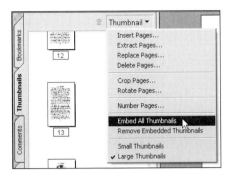
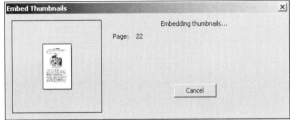

2. From the **Thumbnail** contextual menu in the **Thumbnails** panel, choose **Embed All Thumbnails**. Acrobat will display a dialog box indicating that it's creating the thumbnails. (Don't blink or you'll miss it.)

3. Scroll through the document's thumbnails again. Notice that you no longer see flashes of gray before the thumbnails appear. This is an important feature, especially if you're working on a relatively slow computer. Having the thumbnails embedded will eliminate the need to wait for Acrobat to create an image of each thumbnail every time you scroll through the list.

The Thumbnail contextual menu also contains all the commands found under the Document menu that were covered in this chapter. Additionally, you have the option of choosing large or small thumbnails for the most convenient viewing.

NOTE | Un-embedding Thumbnails

Both Acrobat and Acrobat Reader will automatically generate the on-the-fly thumbnails, but Reader does not have the capability of embedding thumbnails into the PDF document. If you want your audience to have the use of embedded thumbnails, you must generate them in Acrobat. But take note that each thumbnail adds approximately 3KB of file size to your document. You may find that you prefer to embed the thumbnails while working with your document, and then remove them before distributing the PDF to save file size. If you wish to "un-embed" the thumbnails after you've finished working with your document, choose **Remove Embedded Thumbnails** from the **Thumbnail** contextual menu.

Congrats, you've made it to the end of another chapter. For a program that has no content creation capability, Acrobat can sure do a lot in terms of altering existing PDFs. Maybe not as much as you would sometimes like, but you'll probably find yourself using the features covered in this chapter frequently to fix PDFs created by others. After all, not everyone can be as savvy as you and get their PDFs exactly right every time.

7.

Commenting

| Viewing Comments | Adding a Comment |
| Highlighting Text | Attaching Files | Stamp Tool |
| Exporting/Importing Comments |
| Summarizing Comments |

chap_07

Acrobat 5
H•O•T CD-ROM

Acrobat can play an important role in situations in which many people might need to review a document. Using Acrobat's commenting tools, reviewers can mark up PDF versions of the document electronically, without ever printing out the pages. Acrobat's commenting tools mimic almost every sort of way a reviewer might make a note by hand: with a pencil, Post-It note, rubber stamp, etc. Also, because Acrobat embeds fonts and images into PDFs, only one file needs to be circulated, rather than multiple copies of page layout software, images, and fonts just to get reviewers to approve your document electronically. Perhaps most importantly, Acrobat's commenting tools allow reviewers to visually annotate and mark up a PDF without altering any original content, kind of like writing in the margins of a paper document.

In this chapter, you'll explore the various commenting tools that are available in Acrobat and apply them to a PDF. After you've made your comments, you'll learn how to compile multiple comments into a single, easy-to-use reference page. At the end of the chapter you'll play with Acrobat's online commenting tools. There is a lot to cover, so read on and get started.

I. _____Viewing Comments

Acrobat has a robust set of tools to help you when you are dealing with content that needs to be approved by another individual or team. **Comments** is the general term for all the types of annotations that you can create in a PDF. Each comment, except for the **Sound Attachment** tool and the **File Attachment** tool, has an associated **note window** in which you can write a text **note**, explaining why you've marked up the document in that particular location.

Once comments have been added to a document, they're pretty easy to spot on the page. Comments are easily identified by an icon, a graphic markup, or a text markup.

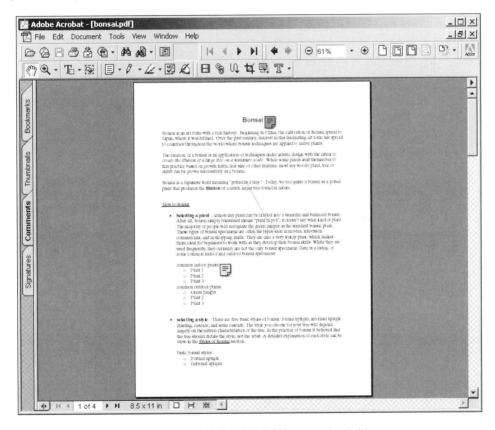

1. Copy the **chap_07** folder from the **H•O•T CD-ROM** to your hard drive.

2. Open **bonsai.pdf** from the **chap_07** folder. This file contains a draft of a document about bonsai trees that was originally created in Word and then converted to a PDF for distribution and review. The colored icons and the red line indicate the presence of comments in the document.

I would like to thank Matt Chroust of http://www.treebay.com for donating the bonsai images and text used in this example. If you are interested in learning more about bonsai, be sure to check out Matt's Web site!

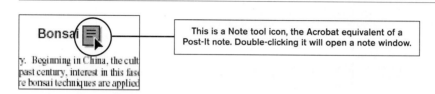

This is a Note tool icon, the Acrobat equivalent of a Post-It note. Double-clicking it will open a note window.

3. Place the cursor over the comment icon that appears at the top of page 1. This is a **note**, which is comparable to Post-It notes that you can place on paper documents. Whenever you place the mouse over a comment icon, the cursor will become a black arrowhead indicating that you can double-click on the comment for more information.

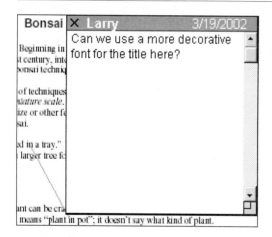

4. Double-click the icon to read the note. The note window opens, displaying the note text as well as the author's name and the date the note was created.

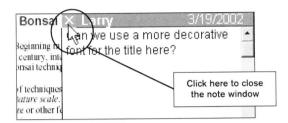

Click here to close the note window

5. After you've read the note, click the **Close** button to hide the note window.

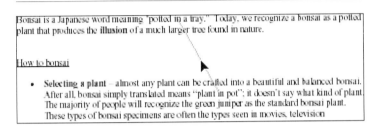

6. In the middle of the page, place your cursor on the red line. Instead of using a note in this case, the reviewer has used a **graphic markup** tool to draw attention to particular sections of the document. In this case, the reviewer has used the **Line** tool to draw a line between two definitions of a term that seem to be contradicting each other.

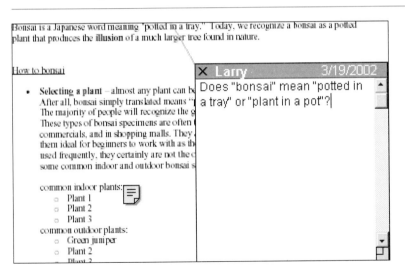

7. Mouse over the line, and when the cursor becomes a black arrowhead, double-click to read the associated note. The reviewer has noticed that there are conflicting definitions of "bonsai" on this page, and has drawn a line between the two instances.

8. Click the **Close** button to close this note.

You could continue this way throughout the document, double-clicking on each comment icon in the document to read the associated note, but there's another way to view the comments in the document.

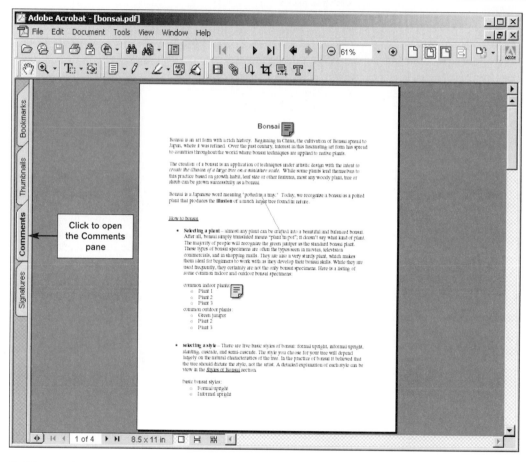

9. Click the **Comments** tab in the **Navigation** pane. The Comments pane lists all the comments in the document. This feature makes it very easy to locate and navigate between the various comments in a document, especially if the document is a large one.

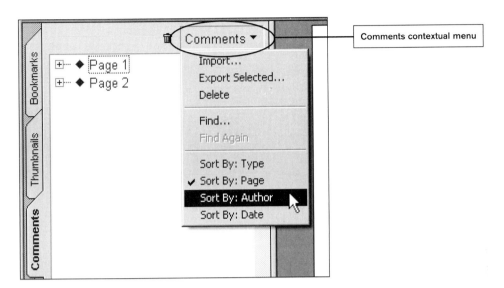

10. You can sort the comments list by **type**, **page**, **author**, or **date**. Click the **Comments** contextual menu and choose **Sort By: Author**. When you sort by author, the name of each person who made a comment is displayed along with their individual comments and an icon representing the type of comment that was made.

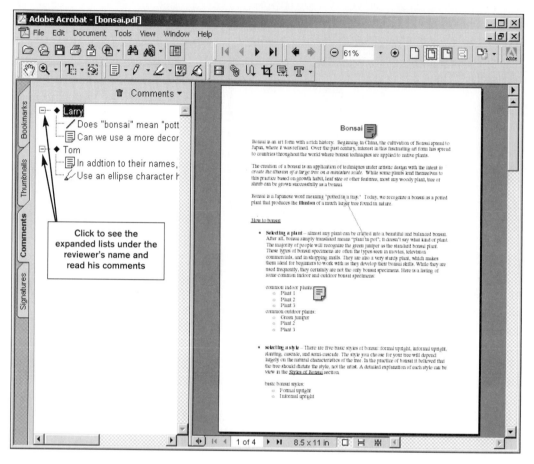

11. Click the **Collapse/Expand** buttons (the **minus** and **plus** symbols, respectively, if you're on a Windows machine; the little triangle icon if you're on a Mac) by the two names to read the comments.

You can click on a comment in the Comments pane to be taken automatically to its location within the document. Double-clicking the comment will open the associated note window. Double-clicking it while the associated note window is open will close the note window.

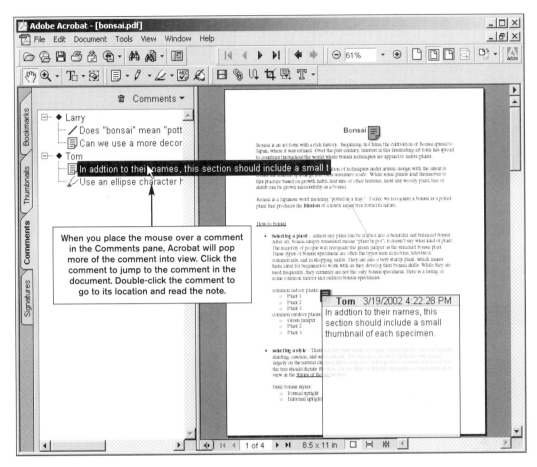

12. Double-click on the first comment listed under **Tom** that begins **In addition to....** The note window for that comment opens and you can read the comment.

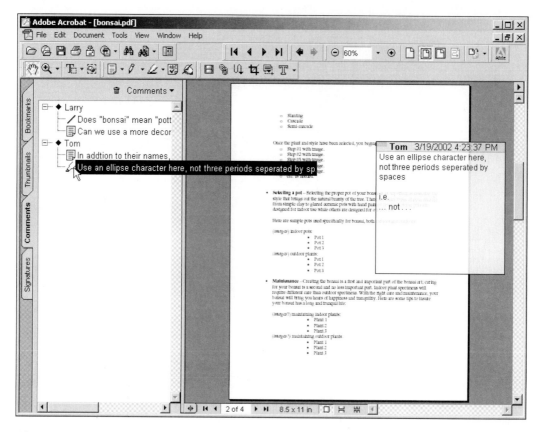

13. Close the note and double-click on the second comment under Tom's name in the **Comments** pane. You are taken to page 2 and the note is opened for you to read.

Notice that Tom and Larry have specific colors for their notes. This is not something Acrobat will implement automatically. Someone had to tell Tom and Larry that their respective colors are green and red, and they have kept this in mind when adding their comments by coloring their comments with their assigned colors. Assigning each reviewer a particular color for his or her comments makes the author of a comment discernible at a glance when examining the PDF. You will learn how to create and color comments in the next exercise.

14. Close Tom's note and return to **page 1**. Leave this file open for the next exercise.

NOTE | Adding Comments

The following sections of this chapter show you how to add your own comments with the most frequently used commenting tools. You will learn about the wide range of commenting tools that are available in Acrobat. The commenting tools are located in the toolbar and look like this.

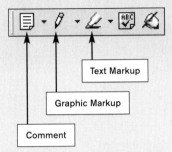

Text Markup

Graphic Markup

Comment

The tools are broken down into three sections: Comment tools, Graphic Markup tools, and Text Markup tools.

More Tools buttons

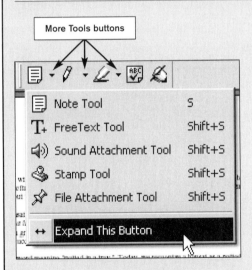

Clicking the More Tools button (marked with a down arrow) next to each section will reveal the tools associated with that category. You can select Expand This Button to view all the tools at once.

The chart below describes each tool category under the commenting tools.

Commenting Tools	
 From left to right: the **Note** tool, **Free Text** tool, **Sound Attachment** tool, **Stamp** tool, and **File Attachment** tool.	The **Comment** tools: These tools are used when you want to add a text or audio comments to the PDF. Each is represented by a specific icon when added to a document.
 The **Pencil** tool, **Square** tool, **Circle** tool, and **Line** tool.	The **Graphic Markup** tools: These tools allow you to mark up your documents visually by drawing lines and shapes, much as you would traditionally do on paper with a pencil or pen. You can associate a note with any graphic markup that you draw.
 The **Highlight** tool, **Strikeout** tool, and **Underline** tool.	The **Text Markup** tools: These are also visual markup tools; however, these tools only allow you to mark up text.

2. _____Adding a Comment

In this exercise, you'll add your own comments to the **bonsai.pdf** document.

1. Make sure you're on **page 1**, and select the **Note** tool.

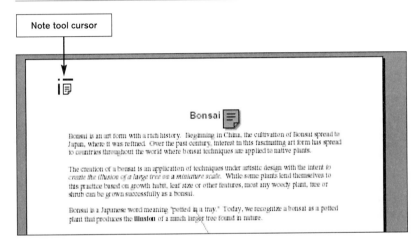

Note tool cursor

2. When you move your cursor into your document, it turns into the **Note tool cursor**. All you have to do is click wherever you want the note to appear. Click in the upper-left corner of page 1.

Note: A single click places a new comment onto the page. As you continue through this chapter, you might click somewhere by accident and place a comment where you don't want one. If this happens, just click the comment's icon to select it and press the Delete key on your keyboard. If you want to keep a note, but have put it in the wrong place, you can click and drag the icon to move it wherever you like.

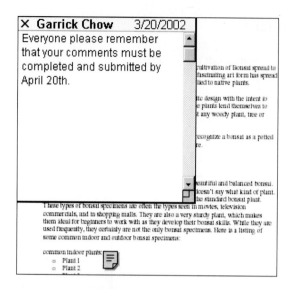

3. In the **note window** that appears, type **Everyone please remember that your comments must be completed and submitted by April 20th.** Don't worry if your name is wrong or doesn't appear in the title bar of the note window. You'll fix this shortly.

After creating a note or graphical markup, you should always add text to explain why you added the comment. All comments that you add to your document can be explained further or elaborated on by using the comment's note window.

---

4. When you've finished typing the note, click the **Close** box in the upper-left corner to close the note window. Notice that your note has been added to the **Comments** pane in the Navigation pane and a small note icon appears in the upper-left corner of the document window.

In the next few steps you'll examine the properties of the note. Each commenting tool has properties that can be customized to change the color, appearance, or author of the note.

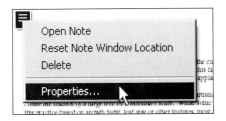

5. Right-click (Windows) or Ctrl+click (Mac) the note icon and choose **Properties** from the contextual menu.

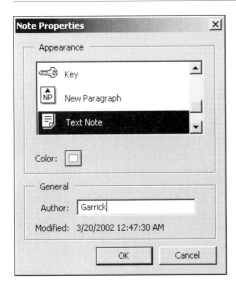

In the Note Properties dialog box, you can choose an alternate icon for the note. You can also select a color for the note icon, and you can change the name of the author if necessary.

6. Click the **Color** button and pick a color for your note. In the **Author** field, type your first name to indicate that you created this note, and then click **OK**.

7. Select the **Hand** tool from the toolbar and click in a blank area of the page to deselect the note and view its new color. Acrobat will now make all your subsequent comment note icons this color, so you won't have to change the properties of each note you create.

When you first created the note, the name that appeared in the title bar of the note window was generated by Acrobat from your computer's login information. This name may or may not be the name you want to use on your comments. To avoid having to retype your name each time you create a note, you will change a setting in your preferences.

8. From the menu bar, choose **Edit > Preferences > General** (Mac OS X: Choose **Acrobat > Preferences > General**).

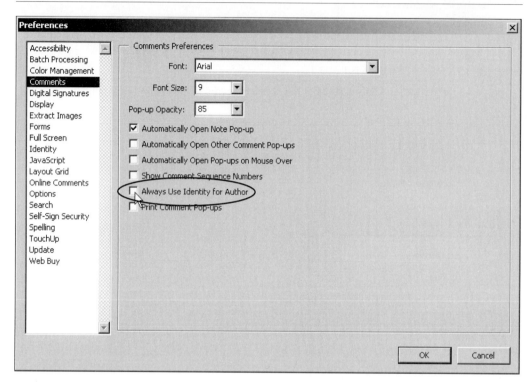

9. Select the **Comments** category from the left side of the **Preferences** window and uncheck **Always Use Identity for Author**.

The Comments preferences let you change the appearance of note text by selecting a different font, font size, and pop-up opacity. Just keep in mind that this will only change the settings on your copy of Acrobat. Note text will appear to other users based on their own preference settings. The content of the note and the name on the note, however, will always remain the same.

10. Click **OK**. Now you won't have to worry about changing the name in the note window every time you add a new note. Instead, Acrobat will remember the name you used in the last note you created and use that as the name for each note you create from now on.

11. Save the changes to this file and leave it open for the next exercise.

3. ——————Highlighting Text

Another set of very useful tools for commenting on documents are the **Text Markup** tools. Rather than simply putting a note near the text, the Text Markup tools allow you to call attention to specific text by highlighting it with a color, underlining it, or striking it out, rather than simply putting a note near the text. In this exercise you will learn how to use the **Highlight** tool and modify its properties.

> Once the plant and style have been selected, you begin by...
> - Step #1 with image.
> - Step #2 with image.
> - Step #3 with image.
> - Step #4 with image.
> - Step #5 with image.
> - etc. as needed.
>
> • **Selecting a pot** – Selecting the proper pot of your bonsai is as important as selecting style that brings out the natural beauty of the tree. There are many types of pots, rang from simple clay to glazed ceramic pots with hand painted detailing. Some pots are designed for indoor use while others are designed for outdoor use.

1. Go to **page 2** of the document and locate the section **Selecting a pot**. The text here reads, **Selecting the proper pot of your bonsai....** It should read *for* **your bonsai**. You'll add a comment here to make sure someone corrects this.

2. Select the **Highlight** tool from the **commenting** toolbar.

ɔt – Selecting the proper pot of your bonsai is as important as se
ɲgs out the natural beauty of the tree. Ther⫿re many types of po
ɔlay to glazed ceramic pots with hand painted detailing. Some po
indoor use while others are designed for outdoor use.

3. Click and drag over the text **proper pot of your bonsai**. When you release the mouse, the text will be highlighted, just like a real highlighter on paper. Neato. Unlike a real highlighter, though, you can add a note here explaining why you highlighted the text.

the proper pot of your bonsai is a
ural beauty of the tree. There are
ceramic pots with hand painted d
ɯ others are designed for outdoor

4. Place your cursor over the highlighted text and double-click to open the **note window**.

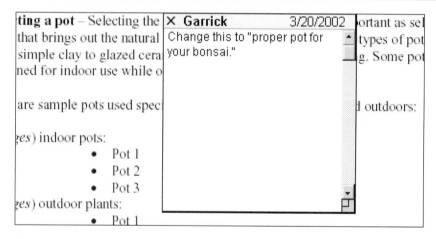

5. By default Acrobat copies the highlighted text into the note window. Delete it and type **Change this to proper pot for your bonsai**. Close the note window when you're done.

If the highlight color is too dark to allow the user to read the text behind it, or if you simply want to change the color of the highlight, right-click (Windows) or Ctrl+click (Mac) to select its properties and change the color.

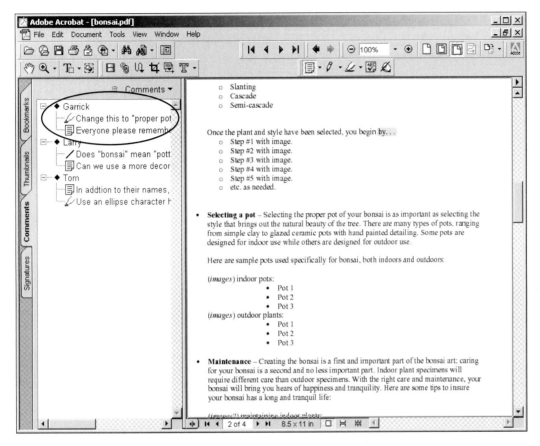

You've now added two comments to this document. If you look in the Comments pane, you'll notice that Acrobat is keeping track of your notes under your name.

6. Save the changes to this file and leave it open for the next exercise.

4. ——————————Attaching Files

Sometimes notes aren't enough to say what you need to express. This is where the **File Attachment** tool can be handy. This tool is very useful if you want to send a copy of a relevant file along with your comments. In this exercise you'll attach a PDF of a previously completed bonsai document so the person laying out the current document will have an example to reference.

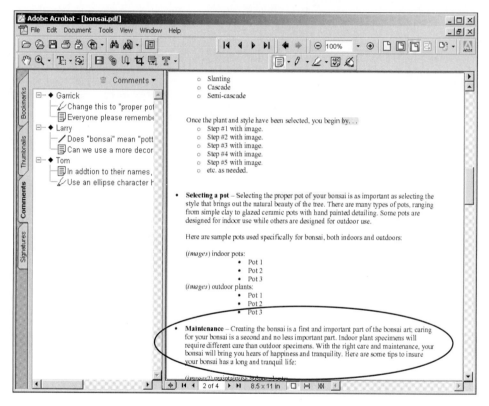

1. Go to **page 2** of **bonsai.pdf** and locate the section called **Maintenance**. Suppose you already have a completed document devoted to the maintenance of bonsai, which you believe makes this section redundant. You'll use the **File Attachment** tool to embed the maintenance document into this PDF, and you'll also leave a note asking the author to remove the maintenance section from the current file.

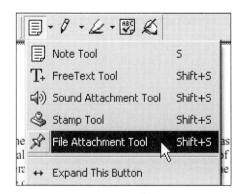

2. Select the **File Attachment** tool from the **Comment** tools section of the **commenting** toolbar. Your cursor turns into a pushpin icon.

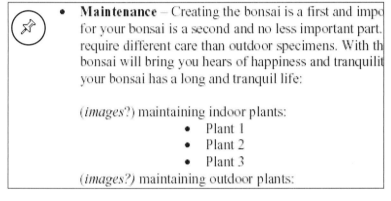

3. Place the cursor and click in the margin to the left of **Maintenance**. You will be prompted to select a file to attach. Browse to the **chap_07** folder and select the file **maintain.pdf**. This will open the **File Attachment Properties** dialog box.

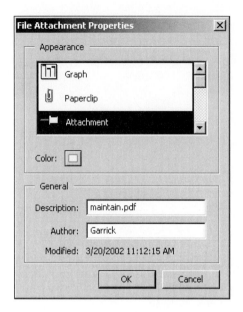

4. You don't have to change anything here, so just click **OK**.

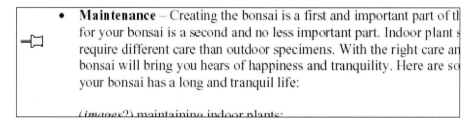

The pushpin icon now appears in the margin indicating that you've attached the maintain.pdf file. The great thing here is that you still only need to send one file, bonsai.pdf, back to the document's author. The file maintain.pdf is completely embedded within bonsai.pdf. And this works with any type of file! You can attach a Word document, a Photoshop document, or whatever. The only stipulation is that the people receiving the attached file must have the appropriate application on their computers to open it.

To view an attached file, all you have to do is double-click it.

5. Place the mouse over the pushpin icon and double-click.

6. You may see a warning informing you that file attachments may contain macros and viruses and that you should only open files from people you can trust. You can trust me. Click **Open**.

Naturally, maintain.pdf opens in Acrobat. (If this had been a Word attachment, Word would have opened the file.) Now that this file is attached, the author of bonsai.pdf will have an example of a completed page layout to reference.

7. Close **maintain.pdf**. You should be looking at **bonsai.pdf** again.

Unfortunately, the file attachment tool doesn't have a note window associated with it. As you just saw, double-clicking on the pushpin icon opens the attached file and not the note window, so you'll have to add a separate note if you want to explain why you attached the file.

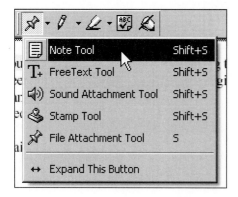

8. Select the **Note** tool from the **Comments** section of the **commenting** toolbar.

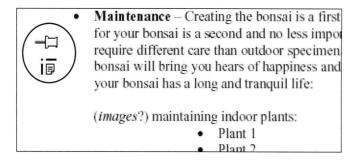

9. Click to add your note directly beneath the file attachment icon on the page.

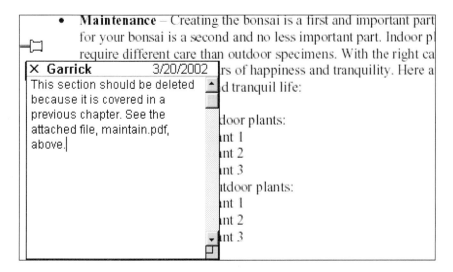

10. In the note window, type **This section should be deleted because it is covered in a previous chapter. See the attached file, maintain.pdf, above.**

---

11. Close the note window after you finish typing.

Note: Because maintain.pdf is embedded in bonsai.pdf, you'll have to open bonsai.pdf every time you want to look at maintain.pdf. To extract maintain.pdf, right-click (Windows) or Ctrl+click (Mac) on the file attachment icon and choose Save Embedded File to Disk.

---

12. Save the changes you made and leave this file open for the next exercise.

---

5. ——————————The Stamp Tool

The **Stamp** tool is a quick way of stamping a document much like you would on paper. Acrobat comes with a whole bunch of stamps for you to use. In this exercise, you will get a chance to work with the Stamp tool. Unlike with a real rubber stamp, though, you can add a note elaborating on why you stamped the document.

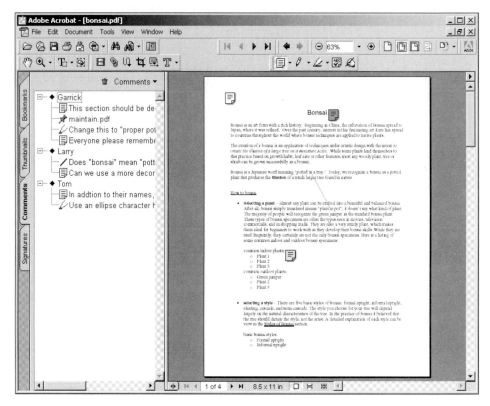

1. Go to **page 1** of the document and click the **Fit in Window** button to view the entire page.

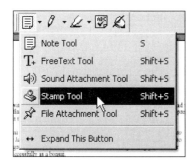

2. Select the **Stamp** tool from the **Comments** section of the **commenting** toolbar.

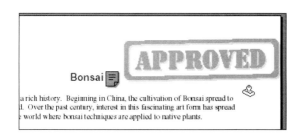

3. Place the **Stamp** cursor in the upper-right corner of page 1 and click. A default stamp will appear.
Note: If you or someone at your computer has previously used the Stamp tool, you might not see the "Approved" stamp. That's okay; you'll be changing it in a moment anyway.

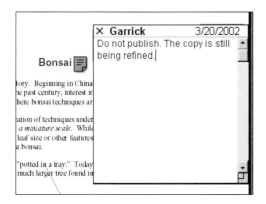

4. Double-click on the stamp to open the note window, and type **Do not publish. The copy is still being refined**. Close the note window when you're done.

Based on what you've just typed, the current stamp, Approved, is obviously not the appropriate stamp to use in this case. Fortunately, Acrobat comes with a variety of stamps for you to choose from.

5. Right-click (Windows) or Ctrl+click (Mac) the stamp icon and select **Properties** from the contextual menu.

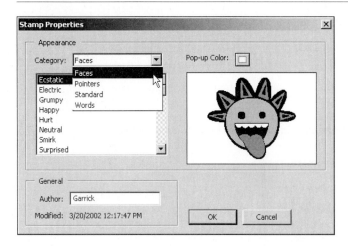

In the Stamp Properties window, you can choose from four categories: Faces, Pointers, Standard, and Words. Each category contains several stamps. Take a moment to explore the various stamps that are available.

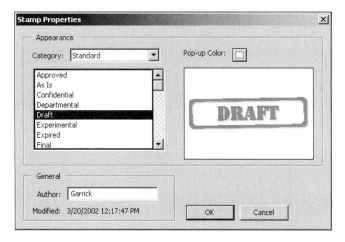

6. After you've finished browsing the various stamps, choose the **Standard** category and select the stamp **Draft**. (Yeah, I know, how boring). Click **OK**.

Note: Unfortunately, you can't alter the color of the stamps easily. The Pop-up Color button that appears in the upper-right corner of the Stamp Properties window only changes the color of the stamp's note window.

7. The stamp has changed to **Draft**. Select the **Hand** tool from the toolbar and click any blank area of the page to deselect the stamp.

8. Save the file and keep it open for the next lesson.

NOTE | Add Your Own Audio Commentary

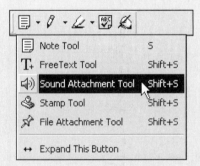

So you feel the note windows aren't expressing the level of urgency you need to get across for your comments? Well then say it! Located with the **Comment** tools in the **commenting** toolbar, you'll find the **Sound Attachment** tool. Just select it, click on your page, and click the **Record** button to record your comment. All you need to do is make sure you have a microphone connected to your computer (duh). Acrobat will embed the sound file directly into the PDF, so there's no need to attach a separate file. Anyone who clicks on the **Sound Attachment** icon will hear your lovely voice explaining the necessary changes to the document.

6. ——————Exporting/Importing Comments

In a real-world situation, you probably won't have multiple reviewers commenting on a single PDF document; each person will most likely have his or her own copy. Depending on how many people are reviewing a document, you could end up with a dozen or so copies of a PDF, each with a different set of comments on it. Fortunately, Acrobat allows you to export comments from PDFs to import into a single document.

In this exercise, you'll export comments from one PDF file and import them into another. This is a great feature when you have comments from multiple sources.

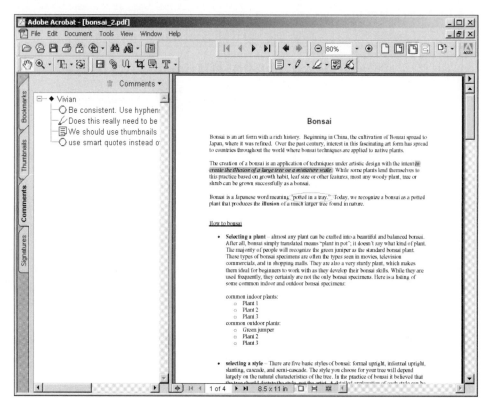

1. With **bonsai.pdf** open, open **bonsai_2.pdf** located in the **chap_07** folder. This file is a different copy of the bonsai document and contains someone else's comments.

2. Click the **Comments** tab to open it in the **Navigation** pane. Click the **Comments** contextual menu and choose **Sort By: Author**. This copy of the bonsai document contains four comments from one reviewer. Take a moment to read the comments and mentally note the location of each one in the document.

You can imagine how tedious it would be to sort through multiple copies of the same document while trying to make changes to the original. By exporting the comments from bonsai_2.pdf and importing them into bonsai.pdf you can collect all the comments into a master document. This is a big time saver and it's very easy to do.

3. Select **File > Export > Comments**. This will open the **Export Comments** dialog box.

4. In the **Export Comments** dialog box, name the file **vivian.fdf** and save it in the **chap_07** folder, then click **Save**. On Mac, make sure you keep the **.fdf** extension in the name. On Windows, the extension will be added if you don't type it yourself.

FDF stands for Form Data Format. Basically, you've exported just the necessary data that keeps track of the comments' contents and location. You'll encounter the FDF format again in Chapter 8, "Forms."

5. Close **bonsai_2.pdf**. Choose not to save changes if Acrobat prompts you. Next you'll import the **vivian.fdf** comment data into the **bonsai.pdf** master document.

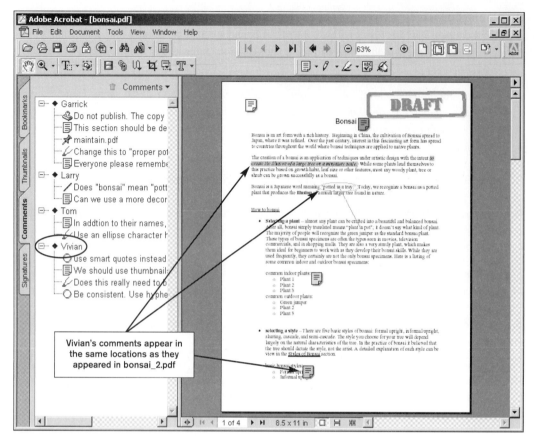

Vivian's comments appear in the same locations as they appeared in bonsai_2.pdf

6. In the **bonsai.pdf** master document, choose **File > Import > Comments** from the menu bar. This will open the **Import Comments** dialog box. Browse to the **chap_07** folder and select **vivian.fdf**. Vivian's comments are imported into the document. Notice that they appear in the same locations and in the same color as they were in the previous document. She's also been added to the **Comments** pane. Very cool!

7. Save the changes you've made to this file and leave it open for the next exercise.

Note: Importing comments will only work properly if both documents are identical. Acrobat tracks the location of each comment relative to the page it's on. If you move or delete pages before importing everyone's comments, be ready for some incorrectly placed notes.

7. _____Summarizing Comments

Now that you've imported the comments, you have a master document that contains all the changes that need to be reviewed. While it's certainly easier to manage one document than a dozen documents, it's still not easy to decipher so many comments while trying to edit the original document.

In this exercise you'll use Acrobat's **Summarize** command, which summarizes all of a document's comments onto a brand-new PDF—perfect for printing out and using as a reference while you edit your original document.

1. From the menu bar choose **Tools > Comments > Summarize**. This will open the **Summarize Comments** dialog box.

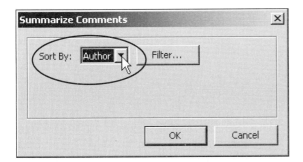

2. For the **Sort By:** option, choose **Author** and click **OK**. Note that you can also choose to sort by **Page, Date**, and **Type** as well—just like you did in the **Comments** pane in the **Navigation** pane.

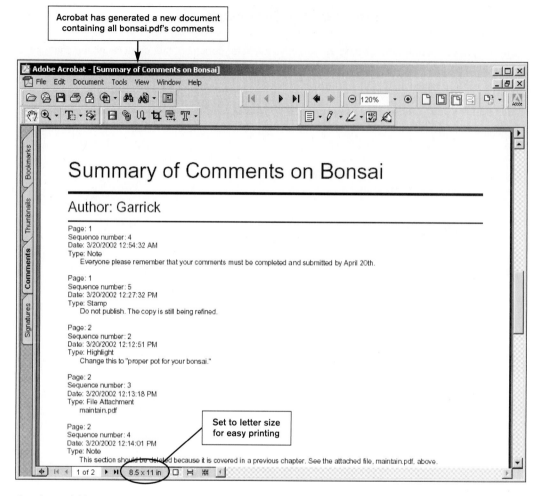

Acrobat quickly generates a new 2-page document, listing all the comments from bonsai.pdf, arranged by author.

3. Take a moment to scroll through and view the summary pages. Note in the **status bar** that the dimensions of the page are **8.5 × 11**, perfect for printing on letter-size paper. You could print this document and use it as a checklist for reviewing the original document.

4. Because this is a new document, it needs to be saved. Save the file inside the **chap_07** folder as **summary.pdf**.

5. Close **summary.pdf** once it's been saved. Make sure **bonsai.pdf** is still open for the next step.

TIP | Filtering Comments

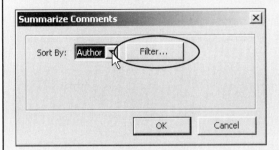

You probably noticed that the **Summarize Comments** dialog box had a **Filter** button. Clicking the **Filter** button opens the **Filter Comments** dialog box that lets you further sort the comments before generating the summary pages.

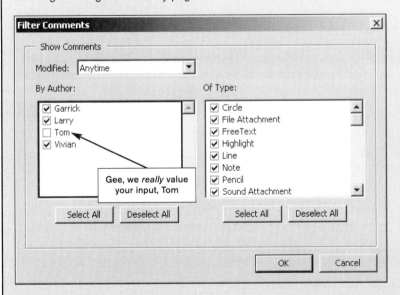

You have the option of filtering comments by when they were created, by author, or by their type. This is very useful, for instance, if you want someone in the review group to feel as though his opinion matters when it really doesn't. Allow him to make his comments and filter them out later so you won't have to waste valuable time reading them.

In the following steps you're going to insert summary.pdf at the end of bonsai.pdf so that you only have to manage one PDF file. You learned to insert pages in Chapter 6, "Modifying PDFs," so you get a bonus review here.

6. Select **Document > Insert Pages**. Browse to the **chap_07** folder and select the **summary.pdf** file you just saved.

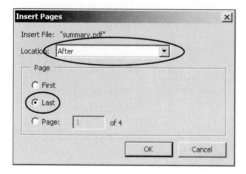

7. In the **Insert Pages** dialog box that appears, set the **Location:** option to **After** and click the **Last** radio button. Click **OK**. You now have a 6-page document, with the last two pages being the summary of comments.

And if you think that's great (you're a bigger geek than I am), take a look at one last little trick to make your life easier.

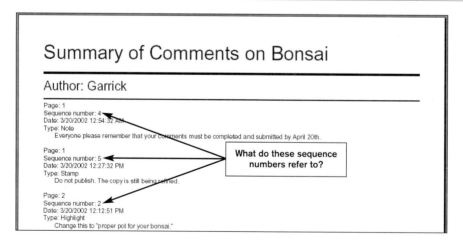

8. Scroll to **page 5**. Notice that each comment is assigned a sequence number. This number is based on the chronological order in which comments were added to each page. This can be very helpful when you are trying to match comments from the summary sheet to the actual document.

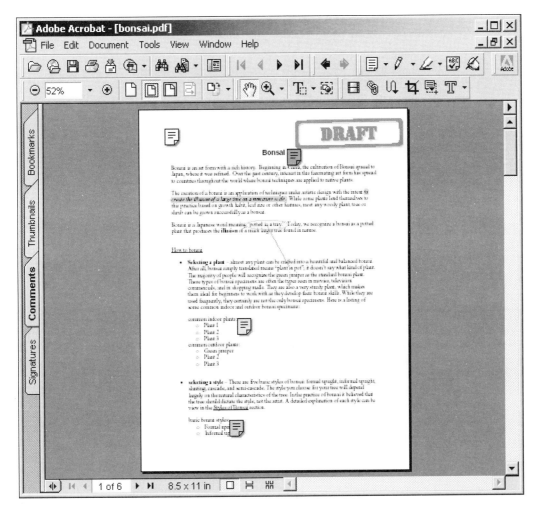

9. Scroll to **page 1**. The problem is that there's really no way to tell in what order the comments were created by just looking at the page.

10. Choose **Edit > Preferences > General**. This will open the **Preferences** dialog box.

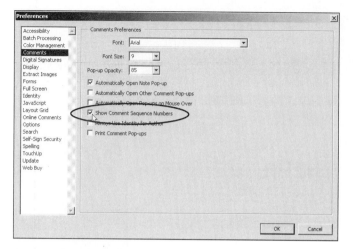

11. The **Comments** category should still be selected from the previous exercise, but if not, select it, and check **Show Comment Sequence Numbers**. Click **OK**.

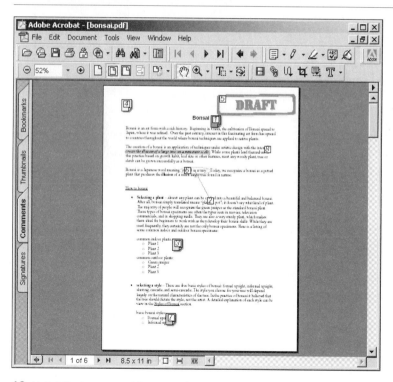

12. Voila! Each comment icon now has a sequence number associated with it so you can easily find the comments referenced on the summary pages.

13. If you wish to turn off the sequence numbers, choose **Edit > Preferences > General** and uncheck **Show Comment Sequence Numbers**.

14. Save the changes you made to the **bonsai.pdf** and close it; you won't need it for the rest of the chapter.

Resetting Note Window Locations

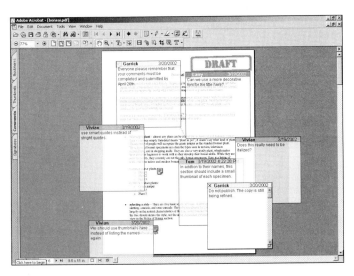

As your document begins to accumulate comment after comment, you may find that screen real estate starts getting crowded, especially as you move note windows around to read other comments that may be hidden underneath them. One remedy would be to close each note window when you've finished reading it. But every now and then you may find you have so many note windows open that you no longer remember which note window is associated with which comment icon, making it pretty difficult to know what part of the document a comment refers to. This sort of thing can drive you nuts.

To regain your sanity, right-click (Windows) or Ctrl+click (Mac) on the title bar of a stray note window and choose **Reset Note Window Location**. The note window will snap back into place over its parent icon, and your screen will look nice and neat again.

TIP | Online Commenting

In some cases you might find yourself in a situation in which you need everyone's comments quickly collected in a master PDF document, with little time to spare for distributing multiple copies of the PDF. If your organization or company has a network and/or access to the Web, you can use Acrobat's **online commenting** feature.

Online commenting allows you to share a single copy of a PDF on a Web server that is accessed through a Web browser, rather than directly through Acrobat. All you need to do is to place the PDF on a server where it's accessible to everyone in the review group. Then, each reviewer opens the preferences for his or her copy of Acrobat (**Edit > Preferences > General**).

Note: Because Max OS X does not support viewing PDFs directly in a Web browser, online commenting can only be accomplished through Mac OS 9 or earlier. To use this feature on a Mac, boot the computer into OS 9 or earlier.

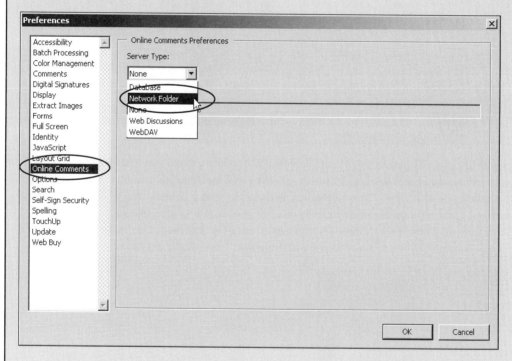

In **Preferences**, select the **Online Comments** category. Remember that everyone reviewing your document must do this as well, so make sure you or your network administrator provides each reviewer with the proper **Server Type** and the address for the **Server Settings**.

continues on next page

TIP | Online Commenting *continued*

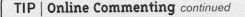

When you open a PDF in your Web browser, the Acrobat plug-in provides you with the tools for online commenting in addition to the usual set of toolbars.

After the preferences have been set, you can quit Acrobat and open your Web browser. From your Web browser, enter the address where the PDF is located. The Acrobat plug-in will load and the PDF will be displayed in your browser along with the full set of Acrobat tools. In addition to the regular tools, you'll find a set of tools for managing comments online.

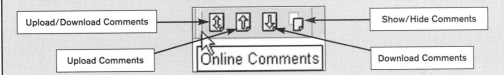

These **Online Comments** tools allow everyone to comment on the single PDF residing on the server. You can click the **Upload/Download Comments** button to place your comments on the server while downloading all other comments so that you can see each reviewer's notes right away. Best of all, Acrobat automatically creates a separate folder for each reviewer containing the FDF file for that reviewer's comments. Acrobat places these folders on the same server that's hosting the PDF file, so once all the reviews are in, you can import the FDF files into a master document, just like you did in the previous exercise.

As you've seen in this chapter, Acrobat offers a nice suite of commenting tools. As is the case with many things, for everything to flow smoothly, each reviewer must have a copy of the full Acrobat application and must know how to use the commenting tools properly.

Well, another chapter under your belt. You deserve a break and a fresh cup of coffee. If you don't drink coffee, have some water. Hydration is important.

8.

Forms

Filling Out a PDF Form	Inserting Form Fields
Formatting Text Fields	Form Field Calculations
Form Buttons	Sending Form Data Over the Web

chap_08

Acrobat 5
H•O•T CD-ROM

Acrobat's ability to maintain the look and feel of original documents is one of the main reasons so many companies and organizations have adopted the PDF standard. This ability to accurately replicate original documents is why the IRS has chosen to use the PDF format to distribute tax forms on the Web. Someone who downloads a form from **www.irs.gov** and prints it out ends up with the exact same document as someone who goes to the local post office and picks up an original copy of the form.

But it's possible to make your forms even easier for your end users to complete. Rather than requiring them to print out the form in order to fill it out, you can use Acrobat's Form tool to place form fields in your document, enabling the user to fill out the form onscreen. This chapter walks you through the process of creating form fields and implementing submit features. Once you get the basics down, you'll find that making your forms interactive isn't any more time consuming than converting them to HTML with a Web page editing program.

I. —————————Filling Out a PDF Form

In this exercise, you'll examine two versions of the same form and observe the differences between a regular PDF form and one that has been occupied with form fields. This exercise will guide you through the various things forms can do in Acrobat.

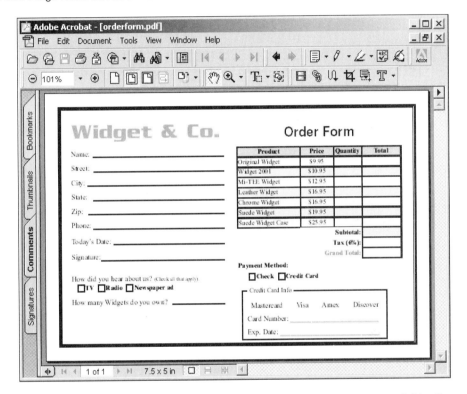

1. Copy the files from the **chap_08** folder on the **H·O·T CD-ROM** to your hard drive if you have not already done so.

2. Open the file **orderform.pdf** from the **chap_08** folder on your hard drive. This form was originally created in QuarkXpress and then converted to PDF for electronic distribution. You'll learn how to work with QuarkXpress and Acrobat in Chapter 14, "*Creating PDFs from Popular Applications.*"

3. Click around the form with the **Hand** tool. Notice that there are no areas that will let you enter any of your own data. The end user will have to print this form and fill it out by hand.

4. Keep **orderform.pdf** open. Open the file **orderform_complete.pdf** from the **chap_08** folder. This is the same form, except that this version has been populated with form fields so the end user can complete it onscreen rather than having to print it out. And because the form can be completed onscreen, you now have the option of submitting the form via e-mail or a Web server.

5. Place the **Hand** tool in the area next to **Name** in the upper-left corner. The cursor turns into an I-beam cursor, indicating that you can type here. Click in this area and type your name.

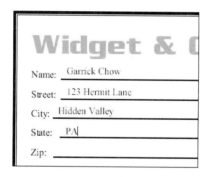

6. Continue filling out your address information for **Street**, **City**, and **State**. You can either click in each field to type, or move from field to field by pressing the **Tab** key on your keyboard.

Note that the Name, Street, City, and State fields have unrestricted entry privileges, meaning that Acrobat will accept pretty much anything you type into them. The next three fields, Zip, Phone, and Date, have been formatted to accept only certain types of entries.

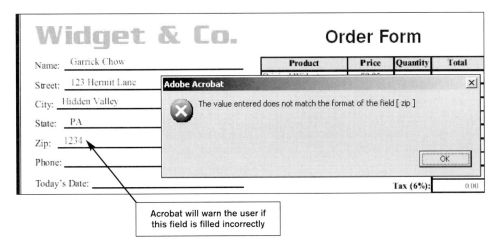

Acrobat will warn the user if
this field is filled incorrectly

7. Click in the **Zip** field and type only the first four digits of your Zip Code. Press **Enter**. Acrobat gives you a warning message indicating that your entry doesn't fulfill the requirements of this field. This field has been formatted to accept exactly 5 numbers. Filling in fewer than 5 numbers results in the warning dialog box shown above. Click **OK** and type your full 5-digit Zip Code. Notice that you are unable to type more than five digits into this field, or to enter letters or special characters. You'll learn how to set this type of format in the next exercise.

Phone: 5551234567 ⟶ Phone: (555) 123-4567

8. Click in the **Phone** field and type your phone number, including the area code, without any hyphens, parentheses, or other markings—just type 10 digits. When you press **Enter**, Acrobat automatically formats the phone number.

Today's Date: July 4, 2002 ⟶ Today's Date: 7/4/02

9. In the **Date** field, type today's date in the form of the full month, day, and year (e.g., July 4, 2002). When you press **Enter**, the date is automatically reformatted to contain slashes. This is a convenient way to keep all your forms consistent with one another: No matter how various users enter the date information, it will always be submitted in the same format.

You're not limited to just text fields when adding form fields to your documents. Acrobat's Form tool can provide an interface for virtually any type of object that appears on a form.

10. Under the **How did you hear about us?** section, click in the boxes next to **TV**, **Radio**, and **Newspaper ad**. These are **check boxes**, which allow you to choose any combination of the three selections.

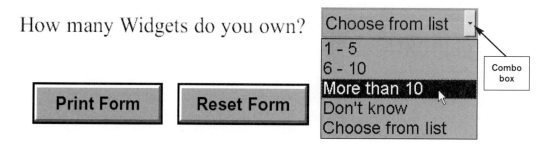

11. In the **Payment Method** area, click in the boxes next to **Check** and then **Credit Card**. While these boxes look identical to the check boxes in the last step, the boxes under Payment Method are in fact **radio buttons**, which allow the user to select only one answer out of the available choices.

12. In the section that asks **How many Widgets do you own?** a **combo box** has been created. **Combo box** is Acrobat's term for a pop-up menu. Clicking the combo box in this example allows you to select from **1-5, 6-10, More than 10**, or **Don't Know**. Choose one to try out the combo box.

Order Form

Product	Price	Quantity	Total
Original Widget	$9.95		0.00
Widget 2001	$10.95		0.00
Mi-TEE Widget	$12.95		0.00
Leather Widget	$16.95		0.00
Chrome Widget	$16.95		0.00
Suede Widget	$19.95		0.00
Suede Widget Case	$25.95		0.00
		Subtotal:	0.00
		Tax (6%):	0.00
		Grand Total:	$0.00

Look at the order area of the form next. If this form had been created without any Form fields, the person filling out the form would have to calculate the total of each line, the subtotal, the tax, and the grand total. Anyone with a calculator should be able to do this, but you always run the risk of human error. In this form, not only have form fields been provided for the end users to enter the quantities they wish to purchase, but the form has also been set up to automatically calculate the proper values for each field.

Product	Price	Quantity	Total
Original Widget	$9.95	3	29.85
Widget 2001	$10.95		0.00

13. In the first line of the order section, enter a quantity of **3** for the Original Widget and press **Enter**. Instantly, Acrobat calculates the total of that line.

Product	Price	Quantity	Total
Original Widget	$9.95	3	29.85
Widget 2001	$10.95		0.00
Mi-TEE Widget	$12.95	4	51.80
Leather Widget	$16.95		0.00
Chrome Widget	$16.95		0.00
Suede Widget	$19.95		0.00
Suede Widget Case	$25.95	1	25.95
		Subtotal:	107.60
		Tax (6%):	6.46
		Grand Total:	$114.06

14. Continue entering quantities for the other products. Notice that the **Subtotal**, **Tax**, and **Grand Total** fields are constantly updated; there's no need to fill them out manually. In fact, you can't even click in those fields to change the numbers. They've been set up as **read only**, a trick you'll learn in exercise 6.

Print Form	Reset Form

Finally, notice that two buttons have been added to the lower-left corner of this form. Clicking on Print Form will open the printer dialog box and allow you to print out the completed form. Reset Form will clear all of the form fields and return the form to the way it was when you first opened it. Although these two buttons aren't necessary, they certainly make things easier for the end user.

---

15. Close **orderform_complete.pdf** without saving any changes. Next you'll learn how to set up these form fields yourself.

---

2. ————————Inserting Form Fields

When adding form fields to a PDF, you should first determine which type of form field is best suited to the question that's being asked. It's your decision whether to use a text field, combo box, check box, radio button, etc. A chart describing the functions of each type of form element is at the end of exercise 3. Just remember that all form fields are created with the Form tool. In this exercise, you will learn how to add your own form elements to a PDF document.

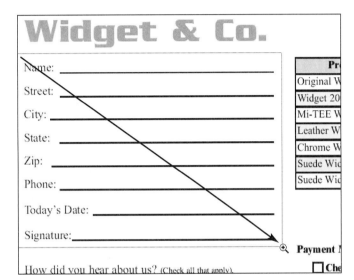

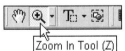

1. Select the **Zoom** tool and draw a marquee around the address area in **orderform.pdf** to enlarge it onscreen. This will make it easier to add text fields to the address area of the form.

2. Select the **Form** tool from the **Editing** tool group in the Toolbar.

3. Draw a form area above the line next to **Name**, making it the same length as the line itself.

Tip: When drawing a form area, keep in mind that you can always edit the size of the field after you've set up the field's other properties. Just draw an approximate size for the field if you're not quite sure how tall or wide to make it. After you've set the field properties and tested the field, you can go back to adjust its size if necessary.

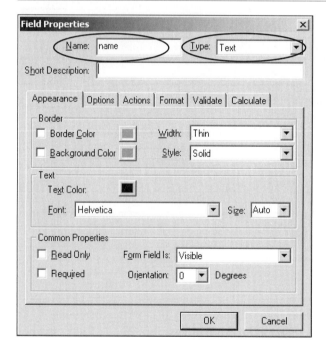

4. In the **Field Properties** dialog box, name the field **name** and select **Text** for the **Type** of field. In this case, text is the best choice of field because it allows the user to type into this area.

NOTE | Naming Form Fields

When naming your fields, there are a few factors to consider. With Acrobat, it's possible to submit a completed form over the Web or through e-mail, just like an HTML form on a Web page. If your form will only be used for printing and not for electronic submission, you can pretty much name your fields however you like. As a rule, though, you should avoid using capital letters, spaces, and special characters in the name. Although Acrobat will accept these characters, certain other factors make using special characters in your field name a risky choice. CGI, or **C**ommon **G**ateway Interface, is a protocol for sending information to and from a Web server. If you wanted, for example, to have completed form data sent to a database, it might require a CGI script to perform this operation. Scripts identify and locate individual fields by their names, and most CGI scripts are very specific about the types of field names they will accept.

If you're unsure whether you will be processing a form over the Web, to be safe, don't use capital letters, spaces, or any other special characters such as slashes or question marks (underscores are okay). You'll find more information on electronic submission at the end of this chapter.

CGI scripting falls outside of the scope of this book, but your Web host or company will most likely have people on staff who have access to CGI scripts that process your forms. Check with them before setting up your PDF form fields.

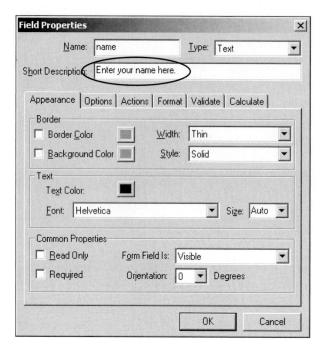

5. In the **Short Description** field of the **Field Properties** dialog box, type **Enter your name here**. This text will display when the user moves the cursor over the field. Although the short description is an optional field, using it improves your document's usability. Any text you enter into the Short Description field will appear whenever the user places the cursor over the field. The text you enter here can help explain to the user exactly what information needs to be entered into this field, so it's a good idea to enter a short description whenever appropriate.

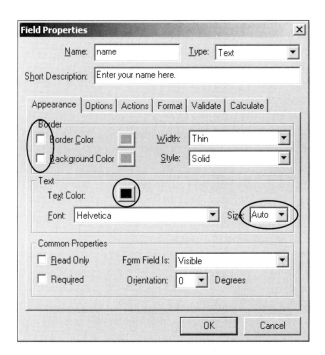

6. The Field Properties dialog box contains six tabs in which you can set different properties for the text field. Click the **Appearance** tab and make sure that **Border Color** and **Background Color** are unchecked. You don't need a border or background color here because there's already a line on the page indicating where the user is supposed to type. Make sure the **Text Color** is set to **black** and the **Size** is set to **Auto**. The Auto setting for text will resize text to automatically fit within the field.

7. Click **OK** to close the Field Properties dialog box. The **name** field appears in red because it is currently selected. Next you'll test the field.

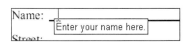

8. As long as you have the **Form** tool selected, Acrobat assumes that you either want to create or edit a form field. Select the **Hand** tool to test the field. The outline of the **name** field will disappear because you chose not to have a border or background color. Place the cursor over the **name** field. After a moment, the short description that you typed will appear in a small box next to the cursor.

Name:	Garrick Chow

Name:	Garrick Chow the more I type, the smaller the text gets.

9. Click in the field and type your name. You can also type some extra characters in this field to observe how the Auto text size resizes the text to fit in the field.

Tip: If your name is cut off or appears too high or low for your preference, you can use the Form tool to adjust the size and positioning of the field. Select the Form tool, click once on the field to select it, and use the handles to adjust the size. You can either drag the field to move it, or use the arrow keys on your keyboard.

10. Select the **Form** tool from the Toolbar. The **name** field becomes visible as soon as you select the Form tool. Draw a second field on the **Street** line.

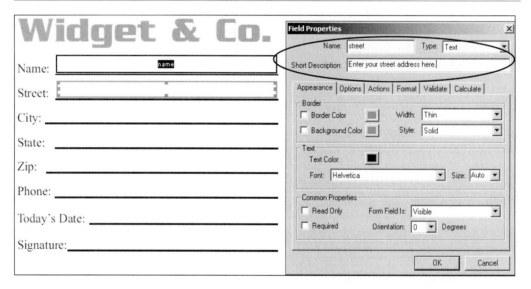

11. In the **Field Properties** dialog box, name this field **street** and type **Enter your street address here** as the **Short Description**. Acrobat remembers your previous settings in the **Appearance** tab, so border color and background color are still unchecked. Click **OK**.

Name:	Garrick Chow
Street:	123 Main Street
City:	

12. Select the **Hand** tool to test this field. Type your address in the new field.

Next you'll create fields for City, State, Zip, Phone, and Today's Date. Rather than drawing a new field each time, you're going to duplicate one of the fields you've already created. Not only is duplicating the field faster than creating new fields, but it also provides the added advantage of maintaining consistency in the size of your fields. This is especially important because you set the size of the text in the fields to Auto. The advantage of Auto text sizing is that you can be pretty sure that all of it will fit in the field. But the disadvantage is that text will be different sizes if you are inconsistent in drawing the heights of your fields. By duplicating fields, you can be sure that all of your fields are the same height.

To duplicate the form fields, you could copy and paste them, but pasting always inserts the field into the middle of your screen. Instead, you're going to use a keyboard and mouse combination to duplicate your fields. This can get a little tricky. See the movie forms.mov on the CD-ROM for more info.

13. With the **Form** tool selected, click once on the **street** field to select it. (It doesn't matter if you duplicate the **name** field or the **street** field—both are essentially the same.)

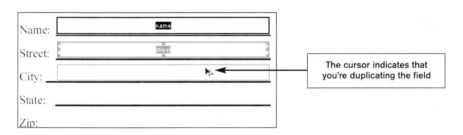

The cursor indicates that you're duplicating the field

14. Hold down the **Ctrl** (Windows) or **Option** (Mac) key and drag the **street** field down until it lines up with the City line. You'll know you're duplicating the field because the cursor will appear as black and white arrowheads. The most important part is that you **release the mouse button before you release the keyboard key**. If you release the keyboard key first, you'll have moved the field, not copied it. Don't you wish the manual told you things like this?

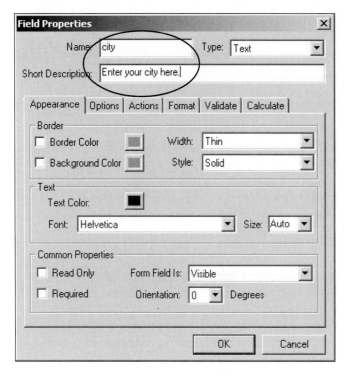

15. After successfully duplicating the **street** field, double-click it to open its **Field Properties** dialog box. Rename this field as **city** and change the **Short Description** appropriately. Everything else can remain the same. Click **OK** when you're done.

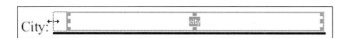

16. Since the **City** line is slightly longer than the **Street** line, you'll probably have to resize the **city** field a bit. Drag either the right or left side handle to resize the field to fit the line. Avoid dragging any of the corner handles because this may alter the height of the field.

Name:	name
Street:	street
City:	city
State:	state
Zip:	zip
Phone:	phone
Today's Date:	date

17. Using the keyboard command described in step 14, continue duplicating and resizing fields until you have the areas next to State, Zip, Phone, and Today's Date occupied. Name the fields just as you see them in the picture above. Remember to change the **Short Description** for each field.

18. Save the file and keep it open when you're done.

3. _____Formatting Text Fields

Now that you've created form fields for the address area of the order form, you'll format some of the fields to accept only certain types of information. Formatting fields can prevent the user from placing the wrong information in a field. This is really helpful when forms require specific information, such as telephone and Social Security numbers, etc.

1. With **orderform.pdf** still open from the previous exercise, double-click the **Zip** field with the **Form** tool.

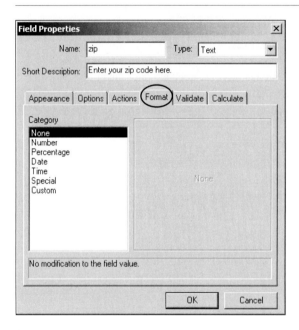

2. In the **Field Properties** dialog box, click the **Format** tab. The Format tab contains several categories for possible text input. The default category is None, which allows entries of any type to be entered. By choosing any other category, you specify exactly what can and can't go into that field. If you have ever used Microsoft Excel, this feature will look very familiar.

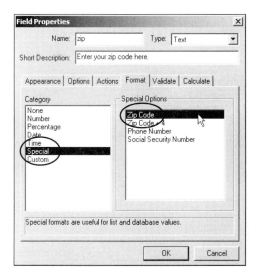

3. Choose **Special** as the **Category**. In **Special Options** choose **Zip Code**. This will set the **Zip** field so that it only accepts a 5-digit number. Click **OK**.

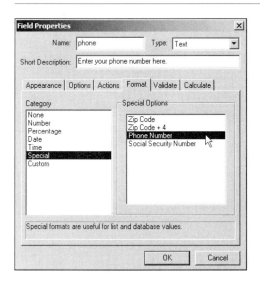

4. Double-click the **phone** field. Under the **Format** tab, choose **Special** as the category and select **Phone Number** under **Special Options**. This will set the field to accept either a 7- or 10-digit phone number. Click **OK**.

Next you'll specify a format for the date field. This will ensure that no matter how a user may enter the date, it will always be displayed in the format you prefer.

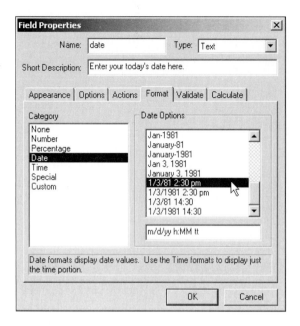

5. Double-click the **date** field. Under the **Format** tab, click **Date**. In the **Date Options** area you can choose from a large selection of formatting possibilities for the field. Select **1/3/1981 2:30pm**. This will display the date along with a time stamp. Click **OK**.

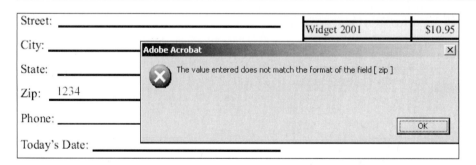

6. Select the **Hand** tool and enter numbers into the **Zip** and **Phone** fields. Notice that if you don't enter enough numbers for a proper Zip Code or phone number, Acrobat displays a warning dialog box. If you try to enter more than 5 digits for the Zip Code or more than 10 digits for the phone number, your computer just beeps, indicating that the field won't accept any more numbers.

7. Click the **date** field and try entering the date in several different ways such as **November 17, 2002** or **11/17/02** or **nov 17**. No matter how you enter the date, it will always be displayed as **11/17/02** along with the current time (taken from your computer's clock).

8. Save the file.

Text fields are some of the most involved fields to work with. There are lots of choices to make and many options from which to choose. Later on, you'll be using text fields to perform the calculations in the ordering area of the form. But first, in the next exercise you'll take a look at some other types of form fields.

NOTE | Form Field Types Chart

So far, you've added several text fields to the form. Selecting the proper type of field is critical to creating an effective form. This chart will introduce you to the different types of form fields and their uses. You'll get plenty of practice working with most of these fields throughout the rest of the chapter.

Form Field Types	
Type	**Function**
Text	Allows the user to input text and numeric data. Can be formatted to allow only certain types of input.
Button	Used when you want the user to click on an area to activate an action. Can also be used to display text or images.
Check Box	Used to present the user with a selection of choices. The user can select as many or as few of the choices as necessary.
Combo Box	A pull-down menu that allows you to present multiple choices or selections in a small amount of space.
List Box	Similar to a combo box, but presents choices in a scrolling box.
Radio Button	Similar to check boxes, but restricts the user to selecting only one of the possible choices.
Signature	Used to provide an area for the user to digitally sign the PDF. (See Chapter 10, "*Document Security*," for more information.)

4. ——————Check Boxes

Take a look at the **How did you hear about us?** section of the document. If this form were printed on paper, the user could simply check any combination of the three statements with a pen or pencil. But since you're preparing this form for onscreen delivery, you need to add form fields to enable your users to indicate their choices. In this exercise, you will learn how to add check boxes to your PDF form.

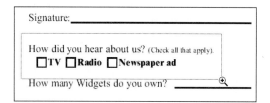

1. Locate the area in the lower-left corner of **orderform.pdf** that asks **How did you hear about us?** If necessary, use the **Zoom** tool to enlarge the area.

Because you want the user to be able to select any combination of the three choices, you'll insert check box form fields next to each selection.

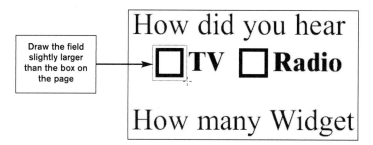

2. Select the **Form** tool and draw a form field over the box next to **TV**. Make the field slightly larger than the box that's on the page. A larger field will be easier for the user to click.

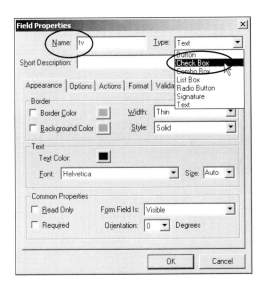

3. In **Field Properties**, name the field **tv** and choose **Check Box** as the type of field. After choosing Check Box, you'll notice that there are only three tabs available in the dialog box: **Appearance**, **Options**, and **Actions**.

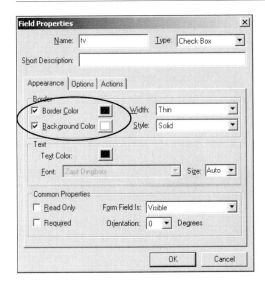

4. Under the **Appearance** tab, make sure **Border Color** is checked and set to black, and **Background Color** is checked and set to white. For **Width** choose **Thin**, and for **Style** choose **Solid**. You've now set the field to display as a white box with a thin black border that will cover up the one that's already on the form. The advantage here is that you'll have a larger, cleaner-looking field for the user to click.

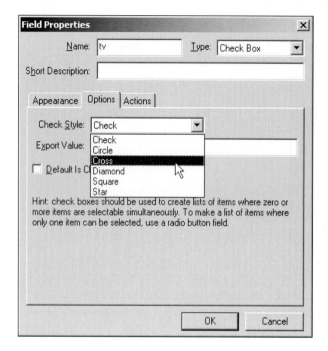

5. Click the **Options** tab. Here you can choose from six different check styles. Choose whichever one you prefer. The **yes** in the **Export Value** field means that if this form were submitted through a CGI script, the **tv** field would have a value of **Yes** if the end user checked it. Click **OK**.

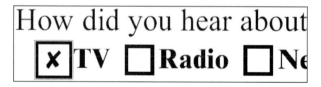

6. Select the **Hand** tool to test your field. Click the **TV** check box. Now you can see the result of drawing the field larger than the one that was on the form and adding a background and border color: a nicer-looking field that's large enough to easily click.

Since you've created the check box next to "tv" with all of the properties that you want the other check boxes to have, you'll simply duplicate the field twice.

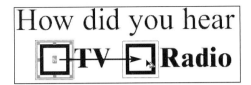

7. Select the **Form** tool and click the **TV** field once to select it. Hold **Ctrl** (Windows) or **Option** (Mac) and drag the field over the box next to **Radio**. Remember to release the mouse button before releasing the keyboard key. (If you're having a hard time with this dragging-to-duplicate thing, just select the field and choose **Edit > Copy** and then **Edit > Paste**. Then drag the copied field to the appropriate location.)

*Tip: While **Ctrl** or **Option** dragging a field to duplicate it, hold down the **Shift** key to keep your newly duplicated field in a straight line with the original field.*

8. Now drag a copy of the field over the box next to **Newspaper ad**. You should end up with three form fields called **tv**.

9. Double-click the field next to **Radio** and rename the field **radio**. Click **OK**.

10. Double-click the field next to **Newspaper ad** and rename the field **newspaper**. Click **OK**.

How did you hear about us? (Check all that apply).
[X]TV [X]Radio [X]Newspaper ad

11. Select the hand tool and test the check boxes. You should be able to select any combination of the three choices. Clicking a check box a second time deselects it.

12. Save the file and keep it open for the next exercise.

It's very important that all check box fields have unique names. If you had left all three named tv, the check boxes would have behaved more like radio buttons, allowing you to select only one choice.

5. ——————Radio Buttons

Radio buttons are used in situations where you only want the user to select one answer for a proposed question. For instance, smoking or non-smoking, male or female, coffee, tea, or decaf, and so on. In this exercise, you'll create two sets of radio buttons.

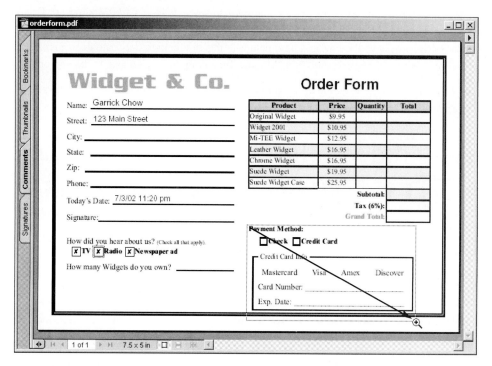

1. On the right side of the form, you'll find an area called **Payment Method**. Use the **Zoom** tool to enlarge that area on screen. (You may want to click the Fit in Window button first to see the entire page, and then zoom in on the Payment Method area.)

The boxes for Check and Credit Card look identical to the boxes that you just turned into check boxes. But radio buttons are the practical choice here because you want to restrict the user to choosing either Check or Credit Card, not both.

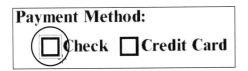

2. Select the **Form** tool and draw a form field around the box next to **Check** (again making it slightly larger than the one that's already there).

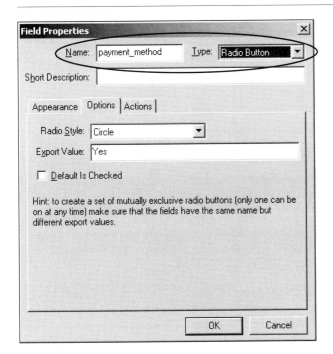

3. In the **Field Properties** dialog box, name the field **payment_method** and choose **Radio Button** as the **Type**.

Notice that you didn't name this field Check. When creating radio buttons, you must give all related buttons the exact same name. This is how Acrobat knows which radio buttons are supposed to work together. If you give the buttons different names, the user will be able to select more than one, which defeats the purpose of using radio buttons.

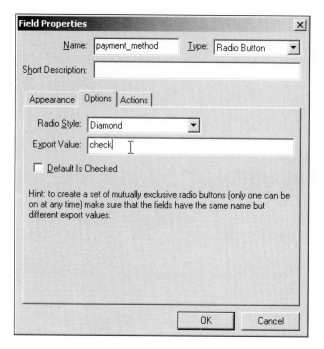

4. Under the **Options** tab, choose a **Radio Style** for the button. These are the same styles that were available for the check boxes. In the **Export Value** field, replace **Yes** with **check**. This will indicate to the CGI script that the user will be paying by check, not credit card. Click **OK**.

Next you'll duplicate this field over the Credit Card box.

5. Ctrl+click (Windows) or **Option+click** (Mac) drag the **payment_method** field to the right and place the duplicate field over the box next to **Credit Card**.

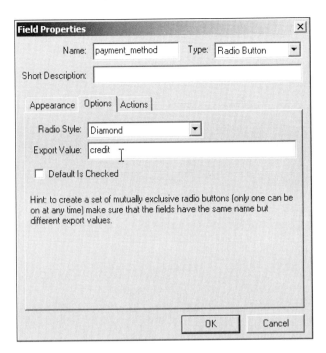

6. Double-click on the field you just created. You shouldn't change the name of the field because you want the two radio buttons to work together, but you should change the export value so a CGI script will be able to tell the difference between the two choices. Under the **Options** tab in **Field Properties**, change the **Export Value** from **check** to **credit** and click **OK**.

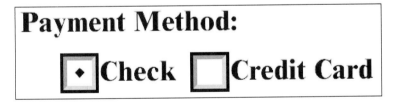

7. Select the **Hand** tool and test your radio buttons. You should only be able to select one choice at time. If you can select them both, select the Form tool and make sure both fields are named identically.

Below the payment method buttons you just created, you'll see the area for Credit Card Info. Here, the user must choose between MasterCard, Visa, American Express, or Discover. Again, you want the user to choose only one option from this selection, so you'll need to add radio buttons here. This time, however, there aren't any boxes around which to draw your form fields, so you'll have to freehand these.

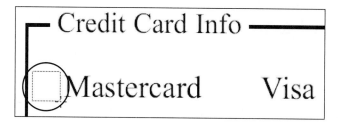

8. Select the **Form** tool and draw a small form field to the left of **MasterCard**.

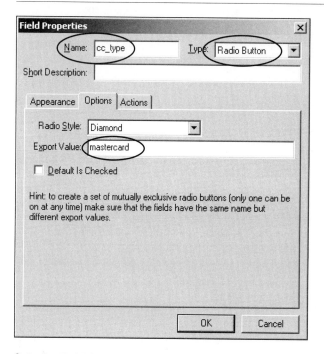

9. In the **Field Properties** window, make sure the **Type** is set to **Radio Button**, and name the field **cc_type** (as in credit card type. Remember that you want to pick a name that encompasses all of the radio button choices, not just the particular one you're working on). Under the **Options** tab, choose a **Radio Style** and type **mastercard** in the **Export Value** field. Click **OK**.

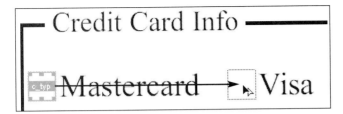

10. Ctrl (Windows) or **Option** (Mac) drag the **cc_type** radio button to make a duplicate next to **Visa**.

11. Double-click on the new radio button and change its **Export Value** to **visa**. Click **OK**.

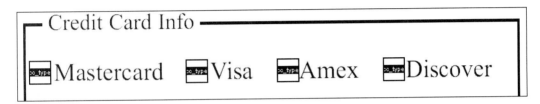

12. Create two more duplicates of the **cc_type** field (it doesn't matter which one you duplicate) and drag them next to **Amex** and **Discover**. Change their **Export Values** to **amex** and **discover**, respectively.

13. Select the **Hand** tool and test your radio buttons.

To complete the Credit Card Info section of this order form you'll need to add two text fields for the Card Number and Expiration Date. This should be a snap since you got so much practice with text fields when you created the address fields earlier.

14. Select the **Form** tool and draw a form field on the line next to **Card Number**.

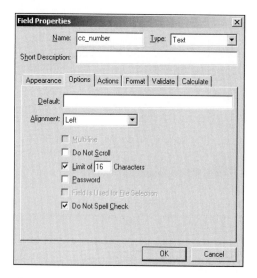

15. In **Field Properties**, name this field **cc_number** and change the **Type** to **Text**. Under the **Options** tab, click the check box next to **Limit of** and enter **16** to limit this field to accepting only 16 characters, which is the maximum for any credit card.

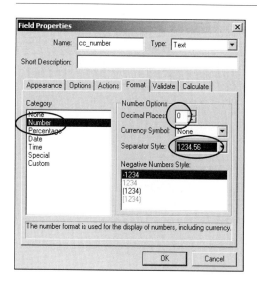

16. Click the **Format** tab and set the **Category** to **Number**. This will prevent the user from entering letters or special characters in this field. When you set the category to Number the field will display two decimal places whether you need them or not. Since you don't need decimal places for a credit card number, change **Decimal Places** to **0**. And because credit card numbers don't use commas or periods, choose **1234.56** from the menu next to **Separator Style**. Click **OK**.

Exp. Date:

17. Now draw a form field on the line next to **Exp. Date**.

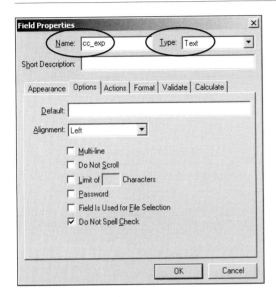

18. In **Field Properties**, name this field **cc_exp** and make sure its **Type** is set to **Text**. Since different credit cards have different ways of indicating their expiration dates, you'll just leave this field as a simple text field without any specific formatting. Click **OK**. Save the file and keep it open for the next exercise.

You'll learn about one more type of form field before you tackle the actual ordering area of this order form.

6. ——————————Combo Boxes

Continuing your tour of the various types of form fields, this exercise will introduce you to the **combo box**, which is Acrobat's term for a pop-up menu.

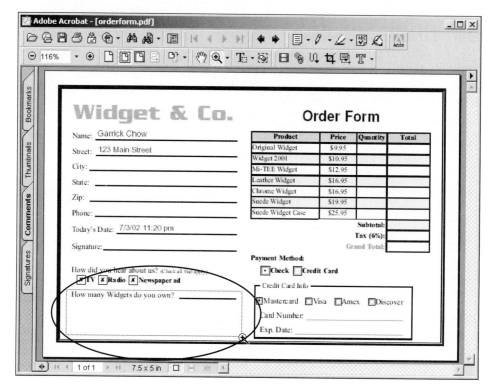

1. Click the **Fit in Window** button and then use the **Zoom** tool to enlarge the area in the lower-left corner that asks **How many Widgets do you own?** While you could just add a text field here and be done with it, for this exercise you'll use a combo box form field.

2. Select the **Form** tool and draw a field over the line next to **How many Widgets do you own?** Draw the field so that it covers the line on the page. Just like you did with the check boxes and radio buttons, you'll add a background color to this field, making the line unnecessary.

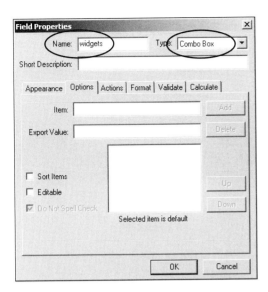

3. In **Field Properties**, name this field **widgets** and set the **Type** to **Combo Box**. To create the items for this menu, you'll add information under the **Options** tab.

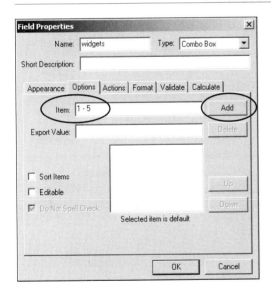

4. Click the **Options** tab. In the Item field, type, **1-5** and then click the **Add** button. This adds the item to the field at the bottom of the dialog box. If this form were to be submitted to a CGI script for processing, you would add an **Export Value** of **1-5** here as well, but for this exercise, you'll just bypass this step.

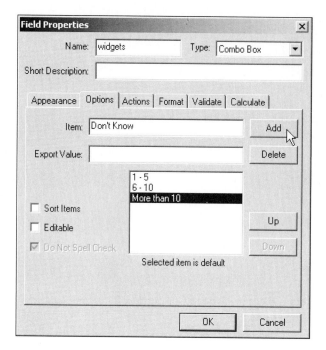

5. Now type **6-10** in the **Item** field and click **Add**. Following this same procedure, add the items **More than 10**, and **Don't Know**.

See where it says "Selected item is default" near the bottom of the dialog box? That means that whichever item is currently highlighted will be displayed in the combo box when the user first opens the PDF. Since you probably don't want to guess how many widgets a person might have, you'll add one more item to the combo box.

6. In the **Item** field, type **Choose from list** and click **Add**. **Choose from list** is now the selected item and is the default selection for the combo box. Next you'll move it up so that it appears at the top of the list.

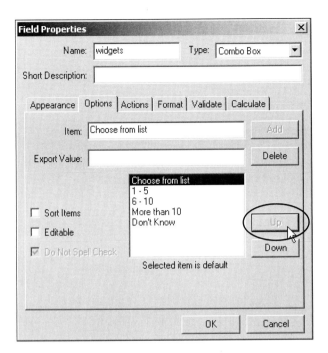

7. Click the **Up** button four times to move the selected item up the list. The **Up** and **Down** buttons are very useful for rearranging the items in your combo box.

Tip: *If you want to arrange your combo box items alphabetically, check "Sort Items" at the left of the dialog box. This is really useful when you have a combo listing all the states in the U.S.A.*

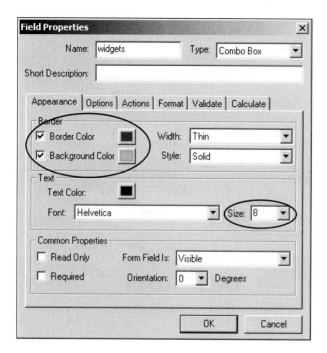

8. Click the **Appearance** tab and check **Border Color** and **Background Color**. Click the colored rectangles next to **Border Color** and **Background Color** and select some colors you prefer. Just remember that the text in the menu is going to be black, so pick a light background color that won't make the text disappear. Change the size of the text to **8**. (This is a relatively small form field, so you're choosing a text size that will fit within the boundaries of the field.) Click **OK** when you're done.

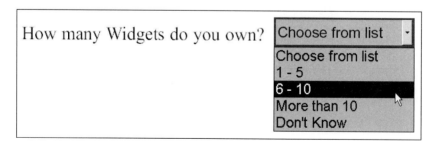

9. Select the **Hand** tool to test your combo box. Clicking on the combo box will pop open a menu displaying the choices you provided.

10. Save **orderform.pdf** and keep it open for the next exercise.

7. ——————————Form Field Calculations

Using what you've already learned, you could add text fields to the Quantity and Total columns of the form. In this exercise, not only will you add text fields to the order form, but you'll also enhance the form by having Acrobat perform all the necessary calculations. When you're through, the user will only have to enter the quantity for each item, and Acrobat will do the rest.

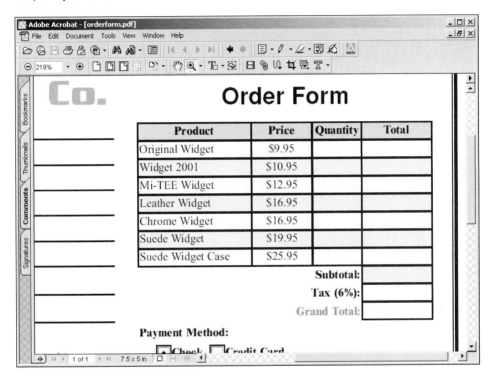

1. Use the **Zoom** tool to enlarge the **Order Form** section of the PDF.

Before you can perform any calculations, you have to create all the necessary form fields first. You need to create a text field for every cell in the form. You'll add text fields to the Quantity column first.

Price	Quantity	
$9.95		
$10.95		

2. Select the **Form** tool and draw a field in the first line of the **Quantity** column. Here's where the crosshair icon really comes in handy. Place the cursor so that it lines up with the upper-left-hand corner of the cell, and then draw your field down and to the right until it lines up with the lower-right-hand corner. Don't sweat it if you don't draw it quite right; just move on to the next step and adjust the size of the field later.

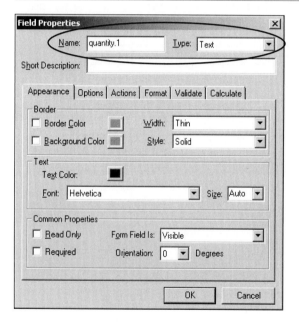

3. In **Field Properties**, name this field **quantity.1** and set the **Type** as **Text**. Make sure you include the dot (.) in the name of the field. As you'll soon see, naming fields in this fashion saves you a lot of work when the time comes to assign the calculation actions.

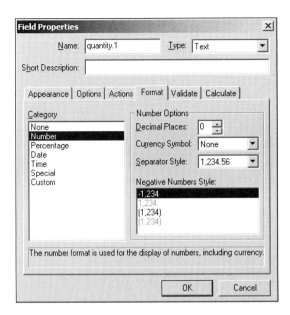

4. Click the **Format** tab. You want the user to enter only numbers for this field, so select **Number** under **Category**. Since you don't need any decimal places for quantities, set the **Decimal Places** to **0**.

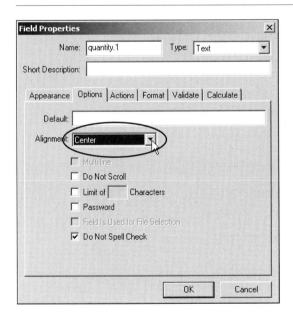

5. Click the **Options** tab and set the **Alignment** of the field to **Center**. This will keep the quantities centered within the cell.

6. Click the **Appearance** tab and make sure **Border Color** and **Background Color** are unchecked. Also confirm that the text **Size** is set to **Auto**. Click **OK**.

Price	Quantity	
$9.95	quantity_1	

7. Now you can readjust the size of the form field if you need to. Line up all the edges with the lines on the form. Take the time now to get it just right because you're going to be duplicating it six times.

NOTE | The Grid

So what's the deal? In this day and age of robotic dogs and electric socks, isn't there a way to make sure all of my form fields line up? Do I have to really have to size and align my fields by hand?

Well, kinda. Acrobat does have a **Grid** and **Snap to Grid** command under the **Tools** menu. Choosing **Tools > Grid** places blue grid lines on the screen. If you want your form fields to align themselves with the grid, you can choose **Tools > Snap to Grid** (you can choose **Snap to Grid** whether the grid is visible or not), and then drag the form fields to snap them to the grid. Unfortunately, you'll encounter few forms in which the cells in the form line up perfectly with the grid. You can change the grid spacing by going to **Edit > Preferences > General** and choosing **Layout Grid**, but more often than not you'll encounter forms that are too irregular to use the grid. In my opinion, you're better off drawing your fields freehand and taking the time to be precise. But hey, it can't hurt to turn on the grid just to see if it fits. You'll get a chance to work with the layout grid in Chapter 11, "*Creating an Interactive Multimedia Presentation.*"

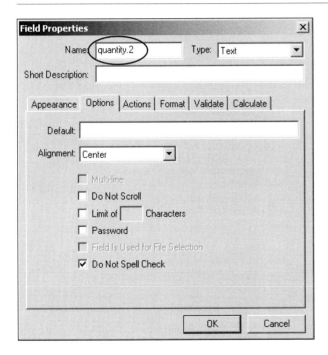

8. Click once on **quantity.1** to select it. **Ctrl+click** (Windows) or **Option+click** (Mac) on the field and drag a copy down to the next cell. Remember that you can add the **Shift** key while dragging to keep the field in the straight line, and remember to release the mouse button before releasing any of the keyboard keys. (If you're still having trouble with this concept, you can duplicate the field by choosing **Edit > Copy** and **Edit > Paste**. Then just drag the new field into the proper cell.) Additionally, you can use the arrow keys on the keyboard to nudge the field into place.

9. Double-click on the new field and rename it **quantity.2**. Since you duplicated the field, you don't have to change any of the other settings.

Price	Quantity	Total
$9.95	quantity.1	
$10.95	quantity.2	
$12.95	quantity.3	
$16.95	quantity.4	
$16.95	quantity.5	
$19.95	quantity.6	
$25.95	quantity.7	
	Subtotal:	

10. Continue duplicating the quantity field into the remaining cells. Rename each one by changing the number. Note that on some systems, you won't immediately see the new name reflected in the field. Don't be alarmed, just click once on the cell and the new name will appear.

11. Save the changes you just made. Phew. You sure don't want to do that work all over again.

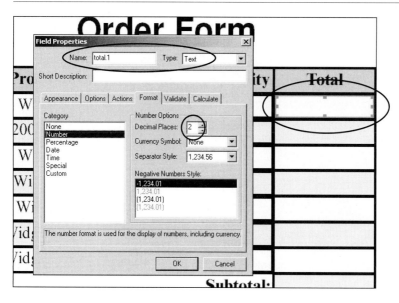

12. Use the **Form** tool to draw a form field inside the cell in the first row of the **Totals** column. In the **Field Properties** dialog box, name this field **total.1** and make sure its **Type** is set to **Text**. Under the **Format** tab, choose **Number** as the **Category**. Since this field will display the total cost of this row, set the **Decimal Places** to **2**.

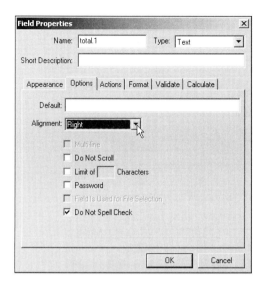

13. Under the **Options** tab, set the **Alignment** to **Right**. This will align the contents of the cell to the right and will make everything in the Totals column look nice and neat.

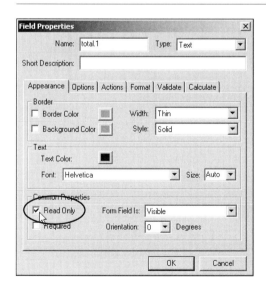

14. Next, click on the **Appearance** tab. Because the form will calculate the total of each row for the users, there is no need for them to click in the total fields to make changes. In the **Common Properties** section, check **Read Only**. This will prevent the end user from clicking in this field and changing any information in the field. This step is optional, but it makes the experience less confusing for your audience. Click **OK**.

15. Now that the first total field has been set up, you'll duplicate it. **Ctrl+click** (Windows) or **Option+click** (Mac) the **total.1** field and drag to duplicate it into the six remaining Total cells in the column. Be sure you don't duplicate it into the Subtotal, Tax, or Grand Total fields.

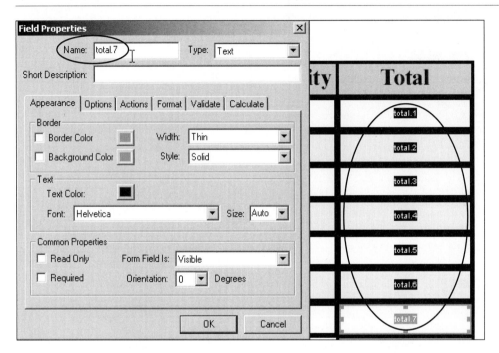

16. After you've duplicated the Total fields, double-click on each one and rename them as **total.2**, **total.3**, **total.4**—you see the pattern, right? When you are done, your screen should look like the one shown above. Save the file when you're done.

Before you can begin adding calculations to this form, you have to add one more column of fields.

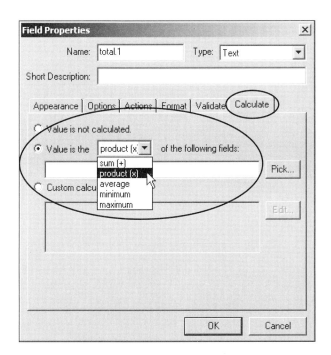

17. With the **Form** tool, double-click on **total.1** to open its **Field Properties**, and click the **Calculate** tab. This tab contains the options for your field calculations. The default setting is **Value is not calculated**. Click the radio button next to **Value is the**…. For this **total.1**, you need to calculate the price of the item multiplied by the quantity, so **product (x)** is the correct choice of operation here. But, you can't perform the calculation yet because you don't have a field that contains the price of the item. Doh! Even though prices are listed on the form, Acrobat can't work with them to perform calculations because the prices are not contained within form fields. **Acrobat can only calculate values contained in form fields**. Click **Cancel** to exit the **Field Properties** dialog box.

Even though the prices of each product are listed in the Price column for the user's benefit, you'll also need to add the prices into their own separate fields for Acrobat to use. Since the user doesn't need to see the prices on the form twice, you'll make these fields invisible to the end user.

Product	Price
1 Widget	$9.95

18. With the **Form** tool, draw a form field in the first cell of the **Price** column. You can relax a bit for this column—since the fields will be invisible, you don't have to be as precise when drawing them.

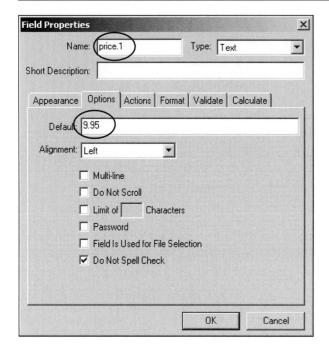

19. In the **Field Properties** dialog box, name this field, yep, you guessed it, **price.1**. Make sure its **Type** is set to **Text**. Under the **Options** tab, type **9.95** in the **Default** field. Text entered into the **Default** field will appear in the **Form** field when viewing the form. But since you don't need to have the price listed twice, you'll make this form field invisible.

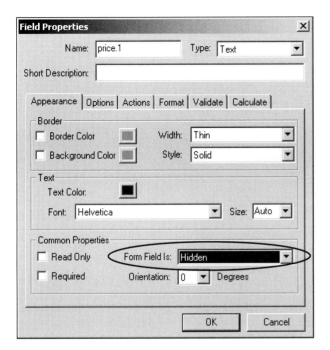

20. Click the **Appearance** tab. Under **Common Properties**, set the **Form Field Is** to **Hidden**. This will make the field invisible to the end user, but Acrobat will still be able to see it. Click **OK**.

Now you're ready to duplicate this field into the six remaining Price cells. As you did previously, you'll have to change the name for each field, but you'll also have to change the default text in each field because each item has a different price.

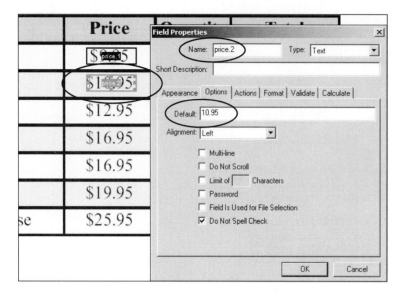

21. Ctrl+click (Windows) or **Option+click** (Mac) and drag **price.1** into the next cell to duplicate it. Double-click the new cell. Change its name to **price.2** and change the **Default** text to **10.95**. Click **OK**.

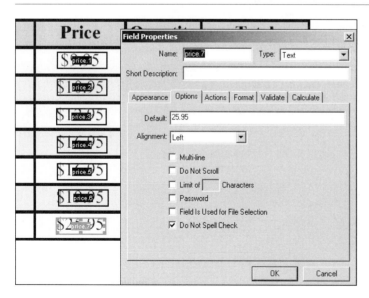

22. Duplicate the Price field into the remaining Price cells until each cell in the column has been occupied. Make sure you rename each field and change the price accordingly. To make things easier, use the chart on the next page as a reference.

Price Column Info	
Field Name	**Default Value**
price.1	9.95
price.2	10.95
price.3	12.95
price.4	16.95
price.5	16.95
price.6	19.95
price.7	25.95

23. Save the file when you're done.

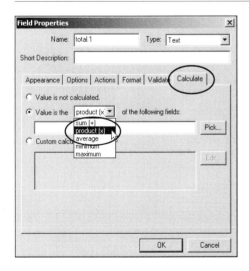

24. Double-click the **total.1** field with the **Form** tool. In **Field Properties**, click the **Calculate** tab and click the radio button next to **Value is the**…. Choose **product (x)** from the pop-up menu. For those of you who haven't had a math class in several years, a product is the result of multiplying two values together. Click the **Pick** button. This will open the **Select a Field** dialog box, which lists every single field you've created on this form so far.

Now you have to tell Acrobat which fields you want it to calculate. To arrive at the value for total.1, you have to multiply price.1 (the price of the product) by quantity.1 (the number of products ordered).

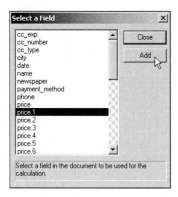

25. Single-click on **price.1** and click **Add** (Windows) or **Pick** (Mac). Then scroll down and click on **quantity.1** and click **Add** or **Pick**. Click the **Close** (Windows) or **Done** (Mac) button. (Since you're calculating a product, it doesn't matter in which order these items are selected.)

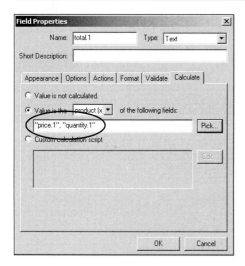

26. In the **Field Properties** window, **price.1** and **quantity.1** are both listed as part of the calculation. If your screen doesn't match the picture above (if, for example, you have extra fields listed), just delete the content of the field and click Pick to try again before moving onto the next step. When you've got it right, click **Close** or **Done** to return to **Field Properties** and click **OK**. **Note:** On Macs, the field names will not be enclosed in quotation marks.

Tip: When setting field calculations, you can type the field names into the field instead of clicking Pick if you know the exact names of the fields. This is risky though, because any typos will result in an incorrect calculation.

Now you'll test your calculation before moving on.

Product	Price	Quantity	Total
Original Widget	$9.95	3	29.85
Widget 2001	$10.95		
Mi-TEE Widget	$12.95		
Leather Widget	$16.95		
Chrome Widget	$16.95		
Suede Widget	$19.95		

Type 3 and press Enter. Acrobat automatically calculates the total.

27. Select the **Hand** tool. Click in the first cell of the **Quantity** column. Type **3** and press **Enter**. The total should be calculated as **29.85**. Pretty cool, huh?

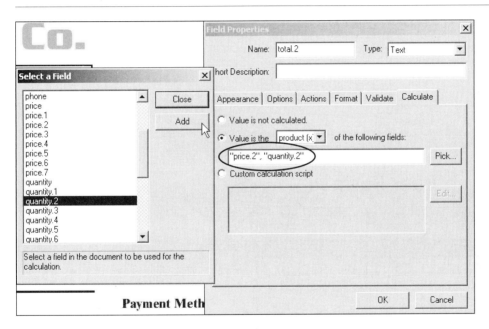

28. Select the **Form** tool and double-click on **total.2**. Under the **Calculate** tab, choose to calculate the **product (x)** of the selected fields, and click **Pick**. Single-click **price.2** and click **Add**. Single-click **quantity.2** and click **Add**. Click **Close** to return to **Field Properties** and click **OK**.

Instead of clicking a field and then clicking Add, you can just double-click on a field to add it to your calculation. Just be careful not to click more than twice or you may add the field more than once.

29. Set up the calculations for the five remaining Total cells. Remember to set the calculation to **product (x)** each time and to select the correct price and quantity fields. Use the chart below if you get stuck.

Total Field Calculations	
Total Field Name	**Fields to Calculate**
total.3	"price.3", "quantity.3"
total.4	"price.4", "quantity.4"
total.5	"price.5", "quantity.5"
total.6	"price.6", "quantity.6"
total.7	"price.7", "quantity.7"

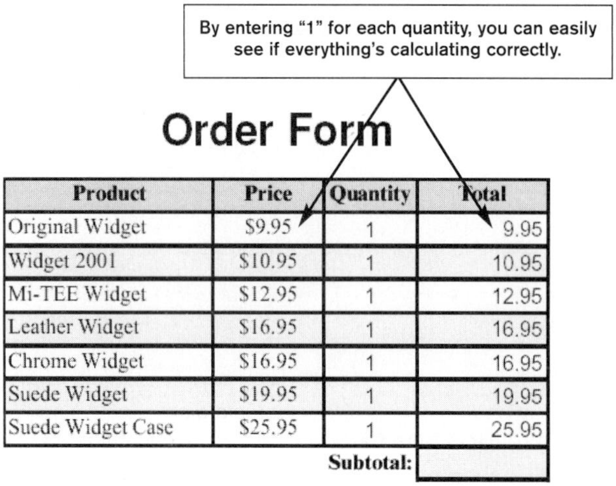

By entering "1" for each quantity, you can easily see if everything's calculating correctly.

Order Form

Product	Price	Quantity	Total
Original Widget	$9.95	1	9.95
Widget 2001	$10.95	1	10.95
Mi-TEE Widget	$12.95	1	12.95
Leather Widget	$16.95	1	16.95
Chrome Widget	$16.95	1	16.95
Suede Widget	$19.95	1	19.95
Suede Widget Case	$25.95	1	25.95
		Subtotal:	

30. After you finish entering the fields for calculation, select the **Hand** tool to test your calculations. The easiest way to make sure everything's calculating properly is to type a **1** in each quantity field. Go ahead and do that.

See? Even though price fields are hidden from view, Acrobat is still able to use them for calculations. Notice that you can't click in any of the Total fields because you set those to Read Only. Pretty spiffy.

Tip: If you find some incorrect totals, you'll find the problem in either the Total field or the Price field on that particular line. Use the Form tool to check them both.

31. Save the file.

You're almost done. Just a few more calculations to create.

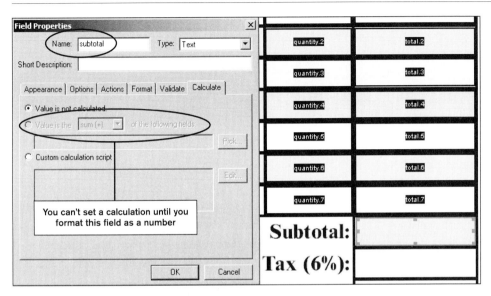

32. Select the **Form** tool and draw a field inside the cell next to **Subtotal**. In **Field Properties**, name this field **subtotal**. Notice that the choice to perform a calculation is grayed out. You must first format this field as a number before Acrobat will allow a calculation.

33. Click the **Format** tab and select **Number** as the **Category**. Return to the **Calculate** tab now and select **Value is the sum(+) of the following fields**. Click **Pick** to select the fields.

The value for the Subtotal is calculated by adding the values from all the Total fields. Now, you could click total.1, total.2, total.3, total.4, total.5, total.6, and total.7 in the Select a Field dialog box to arrive at the proper value. But because you named your fields with the "dot" naming convention, all you have to do is select the "parent" name of "total." That's exactly what you are going to do in the following steps.

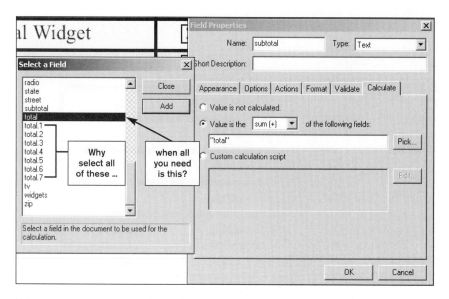

34. In the **Select a Field** dialog box, click **total** and click **Add** (Windows) or **Pick** (Mac). Click the **Close** (Windows) or **Done** (Mac) button. Now the Subtotal field will calculate the sum of all fields that begin with **total**. How cool is that!

---

35. Under the **Options** tab, set the alignment of the cell to Right. Click **OK**.

Product	Price	Quantity	Total
Original Widget	$9.95	1	9.95
Widget 2001	$10.95	1	10.95
Mi-TEE Widget	$12.95	1	12.95
Leather Widget	$16.95	1	16.95
Chrome Widget	$16.95	1	16.95
Suede Widget	$19.95	1	19.95
Suede Widget Case	$25.95	1	25.95
		Subtotal:	113.65
		Tax (6%):	
		Grand Total:	

36. Select the **Hand** tool to see the results. The Subtotal is already calculated.

As long as you include the dot in the name of a field, you'll be able to perform quick calculation like you did in the previous steps. What follows after the dot is not really important. Just use a name that you and anyone else who works with the form will be able to understand. For example, you could have named the fields total.line1, total.line2, total.line3, etc., or total.a, total.b, total.c, etc.

---

8. _____ Adding a Custom JavaScript Calculation

Next, you'll create a form field to calculate the 6% tax. One method of doing this would be to create a hidden field (like you did for the Price fields), give it a default value of 0.06 and then multiply it with the Subtotal to arrive at the tax. This would be a perfectly acceptable way of calculating the tax, but you already know how to do this and you want to learn a different method, right? Right.

For this section, you'll add a custom JavaScript to calculate the tax. JavaScript was created by Netscape Communications to enhance Web pages, and you will use this same language to perform a calculation here. Don't worry if you've never written any JavaScript. Everything you'll need to type will be provided here.

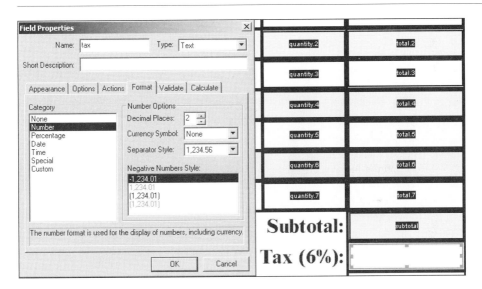

1. Use the **Form** tool to draw a field in the cell next to **Tax**. In **Field Properties**, name this field **tax**. Under the **Format** tab, set the **Category** to **Number**. Click the **Options** tab and set the **Alignment** to **Right**.

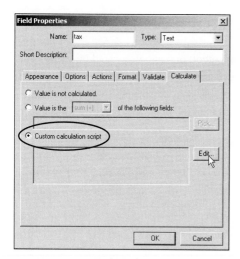

2. Under the **Calculate** tab, check the radio button next to **Custom calculation script**. Click **Edit** to add the script.

3. In the **JavaScript Edit** dialog box, type the following script exactly as it appears:

```
var a=this.getField("subtotal");
event.value=a.value*.06;
```

For you non-JavaScript writers, this script basically tells Acrobat to get the value in the field called subtotal *and multiply (*) it by .06. That's all there is to it. It's very important, though, that your* subtotal *field is spelled exactly the way the script asks for it (no capital letters) or else the calculation won't work. Click* OK *when you're done.*

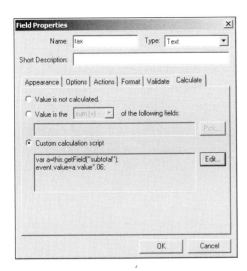

4. The script is now listed under the **Calculation** tab. Click **OK**.

Product	Price	Quantity	Total
Original Widget	$9.95	1	9.95
Widget 2001	$10.95	1	10.95
Mi-TEE Widget	$12.95	1	12.95
Leather Widget	$16.95	1	16.95
Chrome Widget	$16.95	1	16.95
Suede Widget	$19.95	1	19.95
Suede Widget Case	$25.95	1	25.95
		Subtotal:	113.65
		Tax (6%):	6.82
		Grand Total:	

5. Select the **Hand** tool to view your field. The tax has been calculated.

NOTE | Finding Custom JavaScripts

Acrobat's selection of calculation operations is pretty limited. As you've seen, you can select the basic math functions of sum, product, average, minimum, and maximum. But there's nothing for percentages or even subtraction. That's why it's sometimes necessary to add a custom JavaScript.

If you don't write JavaScript yourself, there are many resources on the Web from which you can copy scripts that have already been written. For example, **www.planetpdf.com** has a wealth of information and tutorials available. Just perform a search for JavaScript to see what's available.

You even have some scripts documented on your computer right now in the Acrobat Help PDF file that was installed with your copy of Acrobat. Choose **Help > Acrobat Help** to access it. Open the **Contents** bookmark and then open the **PDF Forms** bookmark. There you'll find a bookmark titled **Using Custom JavaScript in Forms**, which will take you to the section of the PDF that describes JavaScript. This section also provides some simple scripts for doing neat things like subtracting and dividing two values, or hiding a field until a condition is met.

If you really want to get into the nitty-gritty of JavaScripting, choose **Help > Acrobat JavaScript Guide**. But be warned, you're in for nearly 300 pages of JavaScript documentation. If you're like me (lazy), I prefer to find scripts that have already been written so I can just customize them and plug them into my PDFs.

9. _____Calculating the Grand Total

Woo-hoo! One more field to go! All you have to do is calculate the sum of the Subtotal and Tax fields, which is exactly what the following steps will teach you.

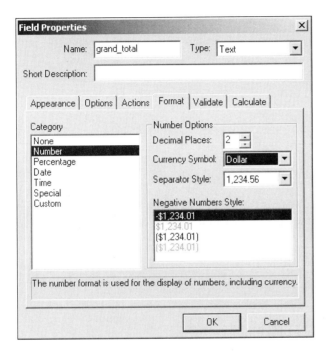

1. Use the **Form** tool to draw a field in the cell next to **Grand Total**. In **Field Properties**, name the field **grand_total**. Under the **Options** tab, set the **Alignment** to **Right**. Under the **Format** tab, set the **Category** to **Number**. Since this is the Grand Total, choose **Dollar** from the **Currency Symbol** menu to make it stand out a bit more.

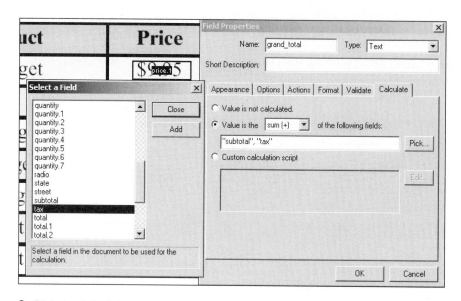

2. Click the **Calculate** tab. Choose **Value is the sum (+) of the following fields** and click **Pick**. In the **Select a Field** dialog box, click **subtotal** and click **Add** (Windows) or **Pick** (Mac). Click **tax** and click **Add** or **Pick** again. Click **Close** (Windows) or **Done** (Mac) to close the **Select a Field** dialog box. Click **OK** to close the **Field Properties** dialog box.

Product	Price	Quantity	Total
Original Widget	$9.95	1	9.95
Widget 2001	$10.95	1	10.95
Mi-TEE Widget	$12.95	1	12.95
Leather Widget	$16.95	1	16.95
Chrome Widget	$16.95	1	16.95
Suede Widget	$19.95	1	19.95
Suede Widget Case	$25.95	1	25.95
		Subtotal:	113.65
		Tax (6%):	6.82
		Grand Total:	$120.47

3. Select the **Hand** tool to view your completed masterpiece. Save the file and keep it open for the next exercise.

Phew! That was a really long set of exercises; you might want to get up and move around a little before moving on to the next exercise.

NOTE | Checking Field Calculation Order

In the calculations exercises, you created all of the calculations in the order in which Acrobat needs to run them. First, the total of each line is calculated, then the subtotal, then the tax, and finally the grand total. If, for some reason, you created the calculations out of order, you might end up with improper totals. If it ever seems like your numbers aren't adding up properly, select the **Form** tool and choose **Tools > Forms > Set Field Calculation Order**.

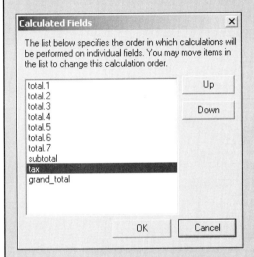

The **Calculated Fields** dialog box shows every calculation on the form in the order in which they're calculated. As you can see here, first the totals are calculated, then the subtotal, followed by the tax, and then the grand total is calculated last. If one of them is out of order, select it and click the **Up** or **Down** buttons to move it into its proper location. It's usually a good idea to check the calculation order even if you think everything's working properly, just to be sure.

NOTE | Resizing and Aligning Your Fields

If you had some trouble getting the all the fields in the order form to be the same size, or if they're not lined up as perfectly as you like, you can use Acrobat's **Size** and **Align** commands found under the **Tools** menu. I'll use the Quantity column as an example here.

1. Make sure the **quantity.1** field is sized and positioned exactly as you want it to appear. This will be the field on which you will base the appearance of the rest of the fields in this column, sometimes referred to as the **anchor** field. The anchor field will always be the first field you click on.

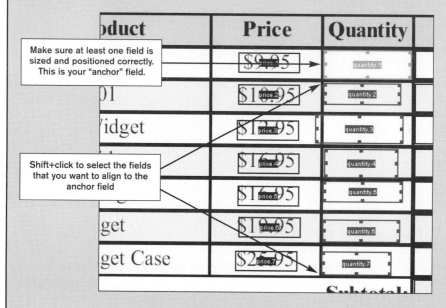

2. Use the **Form** tool and click on **quantity.1**. With **quantity.1** selected, hold down the **Shift** key and click the six remaining quantity fields to select them all. They'll be outlined in blue while **quantity.1** (the anchor field) will remain red.

3. Choose **Tools > Forms > Fields > Size > Both** to size all of the blue fields to match the anchor field.

4. Choose **Tools > Forms > Fields > Align > Horizontally** to align all of the blue fields with anchor field.

At this point, you can click anywhere off the fields to deselect them. You still may have to click individual fields to position them perfectly in their cells, but you can use the arrow keys on your keyboard to do that quickly.

IO. _____Form Buttons

Using the Form tool to create buttons is one of Acrobat's most useful features. Buttons are different from other form fields because rather than providing a space to enter information or to make a selection, buttons are usually used to perform an action such as printing or resetting a form. In this exercise you'll create two buttons to do just that.

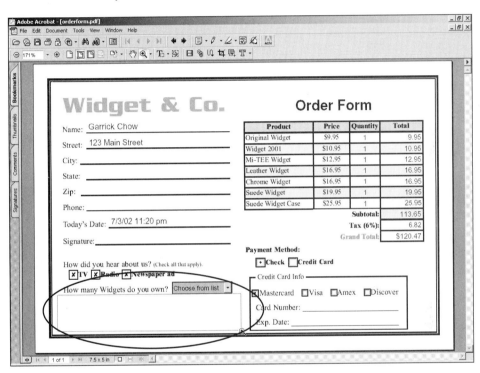

1. Click the **Fit in Window** button to see the whole page, and then use the **Zoom** tool to magnify the blank area in the lower-left-hand corner.

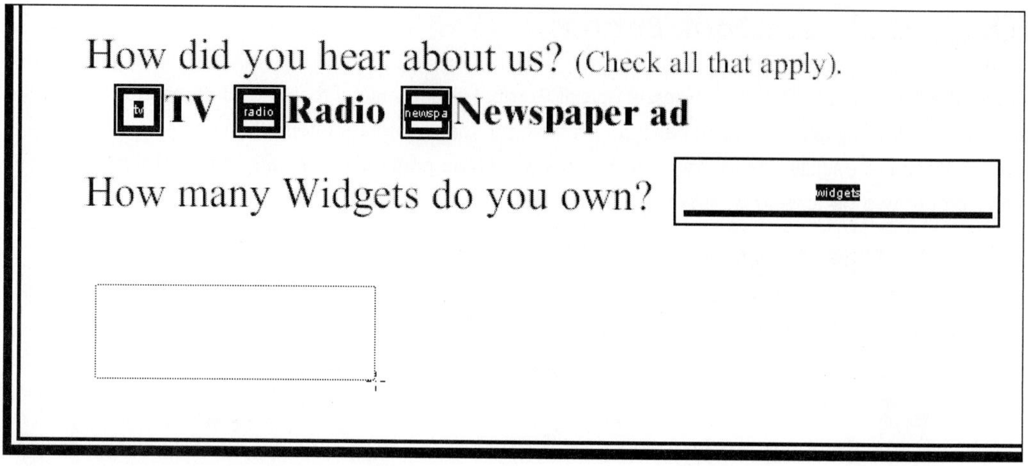

How did you hear about us? (Check all that apply).
☑TV ☐Radio ☐Newspaper ad

How many Widgets do you own?   widgets

2. Select the **Form** tool and draw a form field in the blank area. Use the picture above as a guide for the general size of the button. Remember you can always resize and reposition the form field later if necessary.

3. In the **Field Properties** dialog box, name this field **print**. Set its **Type** to **Button**.

Buttons can contain text, images, or both. In this exercise, you'll create simple text buttons. In Chapter 11, "Creating an Interactive Multimedia Presentation," you'll be working with buttons that contain images.

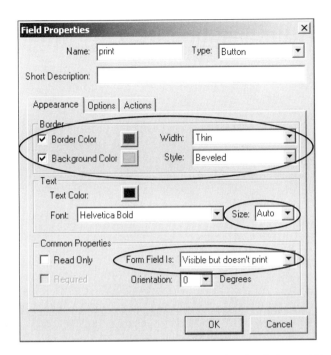

4. Click the **Appearance** tab. Make sure **Border Color** and **Background Color** are checked and select your own colors for both. Keep in mind that the text on the button is going to be black, so make sure you don't pick a background color that's too dark. Make sure the **Width** is set to **Thin**. Set the **Style** to **Beveled**. This will give the button a more three-dimensional look. Set the text **Size** to **Auto**. Under **Common Properties**, select **Visible but doesn't print** for **Form Field Is**. This is a great feature that will make the button appear on screen, but when the user prints the form, the button won't be on paper.

NOTE | Hidden but Printable Form Fields

Another choice for form field visibility is **Hidden but printable**. With this selection, the form field will be invisible on screen, but will be visible on paper if the end user prints the PDF. If you have a PDF document that you want a client to examine but not use, you could add a large form field that says **SAMPLE** and use this option. The PDF will appear normal onscreen, but if the client prints the document, the word **SAMPLE** will appear across the entire sheet. This is an alternative to completely disabling printing, which you'll learn to do in Chapter 10, "*Document Security*."

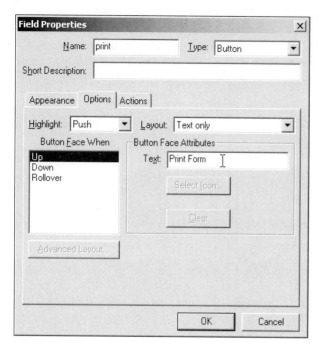

5. Click the **Options** tab. Here's where you'll determine whether this will be a text button or an image button, and how the button will react to clicking. For the **Highlight**, select **Push**. Now when it's clicked, the button will appear as though it's been pressed into the page. For **Layout**, select **Text only**, indicating that you don't want to use an image in this button. Under **Button Face When**, make sure **Up** is selected (you'll explore this option more in Chapter 11, "*Creating an Interactive Multimedia Presentation*"). Under **Button Face Attributes**, type **Print Form**. This is the text that will appear on the button. Click the **Actions** tab when you're done.

Next you must add the action to the button that will make it print the form when clicked. In the Actions tab, you can instruct the button to perform a specified action when a certain event occurs. Events are things the user of this form can do while using the form. Your choices are listed in the table that follows. In this case, you want the form to print when the user clicks the button, so the appropriate event is Mouse Up. Why Mouse Up instead of Mouse Down? Although most people don't realize it, a click is not completed until the mouse button is released. But think about it: How many times have you clicked down on a button, changed your mind, moved the cursor off the button, and then released the mouse? In almost all cases, Mouse Up, not Mouse Down, is the appropriate action event when you mean for the user to click a button.

Action Events	
Event	**Description**
Mouse Up	Action will occur when the user completes a click by pressing the mouse button down and releasing it.
Mouse Down	Action will occur as soon as the user presses the mouse button down.
Mouse Enter	Action will occur when the mouse cursor touches or enters into the form field.
Mouse Exit	Action will occur when the mouse cursor exits the form field.
On Focus	Action will occur either when the user clicks in the form field or tabs into the form field.
On Blur	Action will occur when the user clicks out of the form field or tabs away from it.

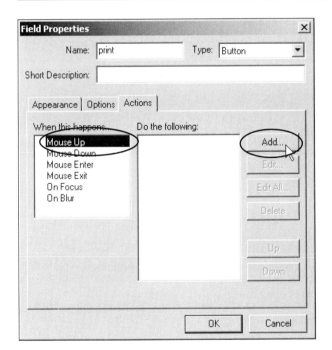

6. With **Mouse Up** selected, click **Add** to add an action to this event. The **Add an Action** dialog box will open.

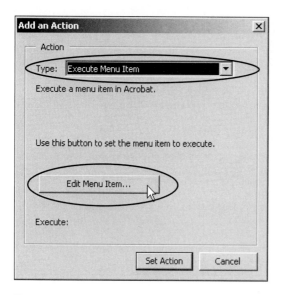

7. For the **Type of Action** choose **Execute Menu Item**. This is one of Acrobat's most powerful features. Execute Menu Item allows you to turn any Acrobat menu selection into an action. Click **Edit Menu Item**.

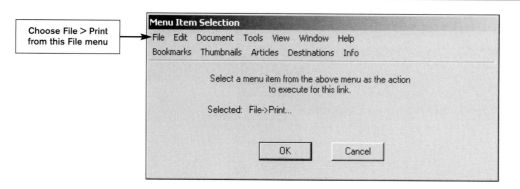

8. This step is different in Mac and Windows:

Windows: In the **Menu Item Selection** dialog box that opens, choose **File > Print** from the menu in the dialog box. Click **OK** after making your selection.

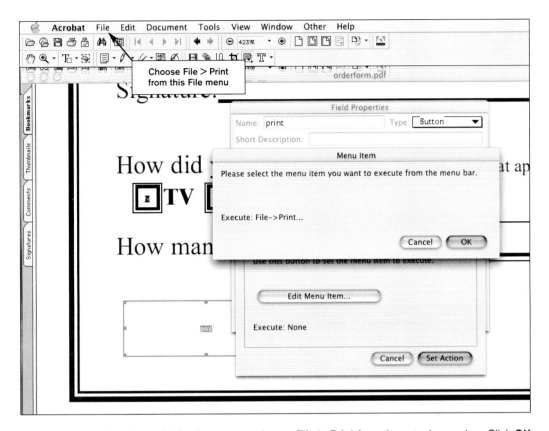

Mac: When the **Menu Item Dialog** box opens, choose **File > Print** from the actual menu bar. Click **OK** after making your selection.

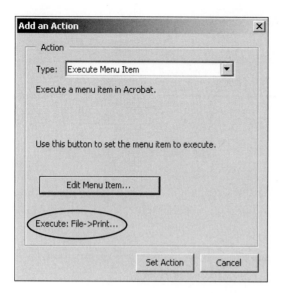

9. In the **Add an Action** dialog box, notice that the action has been listed at the bottom. Click **Set Action**. Click **OK** to close **Field Properties**.

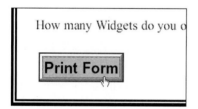

10. Select the **Hand** tool to check out your button. You've just made it super easy for someone to print a copy of this form. Click the button. (Notice that it appears to be pushed into the page.) Your **Print** dialog box should open up. Click **Cancel**, unless you really want to print a copy of this form right now.

Next you'll duplicate this button to maintain its basic appearance, but you'll change its assigned action to reset the entire form when clicked.

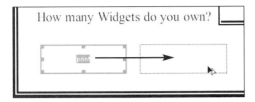

11. Select the **Form** tool and click once on the print field to highlight it. **Ctrl+click** (Windows) or **Option+click** (Mac) the field and drag it to the right. Remember you can press **Shift** to keep the duplicate field in line with the original, and remember to release the mouse button before releasing the keyboard keys. (Have I emphasized that point enough?)

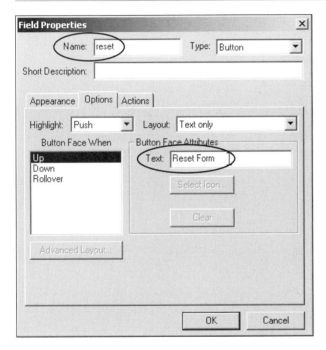

12. Double-click the duplicate field to open its **Field Properties** dialog box. Change the name of the field to **reset**. Under the **Options** tab, change the **Button Face Attributes** text to **Reset Form**.

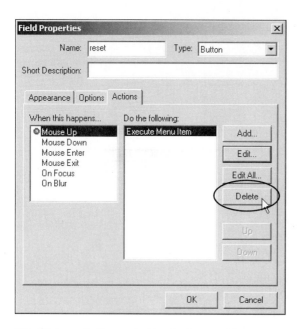

13. Click the **Actions** tab. You don't want this button to print, so under **Do the following:** click **Execute Menu Item**, and then click the **Delete** button to remove the **Execute Menu Item** action. Click the **Add** button.

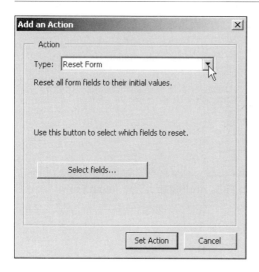

14. In **Add an Action**, choose **Reset Form** as the **Type**, and then click **Set Action**. Click **OK** to close the Field Properties dialog box.

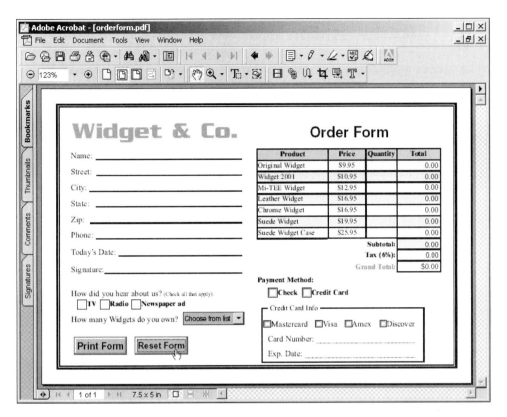

15. Select the **Hand** tool and click the **Fit in Window** button to test the Reset button. You should already have some fields filled out, but if not, take a moment to put some information into the fields. Click the **Reset** button to clear all the fields.

16. Save the file and close it.

NOTE | Setting the Form Field Tab Order

In most applications, when filling out a form or entering data into a table the Tab key is typically used to jump the cursor from field to field. The point is to make it unnecessary to click in each cell with the mouse before typing. Acrobat also allows you to press the Tab key when filling out PDF forms. The order in which the Tab key takes you from field to field is determined by the order in which the fields themselves are created. Therefore, you should try to create your form fields in the order that you think the end user might be filling out your form. If, however, you wish to change the tab order, you can do so by selecting the **Form** tool and choosing **Tool > Forms > Fields > Set Tab Order**.

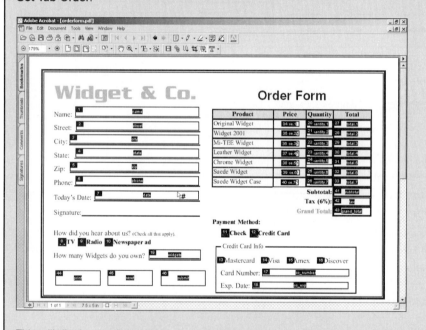

This will display numbers within all of the form fields in the PDF indicating the current tab order. The mouse cursor will become an arrow with a **#** sign next to it. To change the tab order (this is a *major* pain if you have lots of fields), you must click in each field, starting from the very first one, in the sequence in which you want the tab order to flow. Acrobat will automatically update the tab order as you click. Even if you only want to change the order of two fields somewhere in the middle of the sequence, you still have to start from the very first one. And to make things even more difficult, if you click outside a field while setting the tab order, Acrobat assumes that you're done, which is fine if you really are finished. But if you're not, you have to start all over again by choosing **Tool > Forms > Fields > Set Tab Order** and clicking from the first field again. So now you've been warned: Create your form fields in a logical order. Don't say I didn't warn you!

II. _____Sending Form Data over the Web

If you have a PDF form that's been created primarily for distribution over the World Wide Web, it makes sense that you should be able to process the form over the Web as well. Doing so can save your users the hassle of having to print out the form and mail or fax it in to you. As mentioned earlier in this chapter, receiving and processing a form over the Web usually requires a CGI script or some other type of form data handler, although there is an option to just have the completed form e-mailed to you. In this exercise you'll examine a form that has been prepared for electronic submission.

**Note:** At the time of publication of this book, electronic form submission is not running properly in Mac OS X. If you're on a Macintosh, please switch to OS 8.6–9.2 before continuing with this exercise.

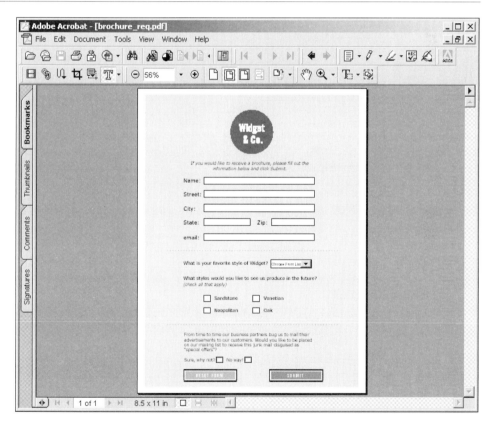

1. Open the file **brochure_req.pdf** from the **chap_08** folder. This is a form that has already been occupied with form fields for you. You'll examine the settings that have been applied to the Submit button at the bottom of the form.

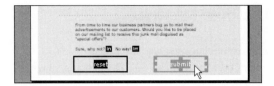

2. Select the **Form** tool to reveal the form fields. Double-click on the **Submit** field to examine its properties.

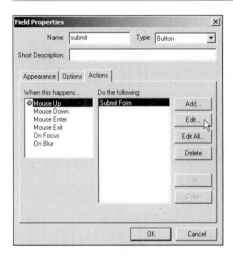

3. In the **Field Properties** dialog box, click the **Actions** tab. Notice that a **Submit Form** action has been added to the **Mouse Up** event. Next, you'll examine the settings of the **Submit Form** action. Select **Submit Form** and click **Edit**.

4. In the **Edit an Action** dialog box, click **Select URL**. This will open the **Submit Form Selections** dialog box.

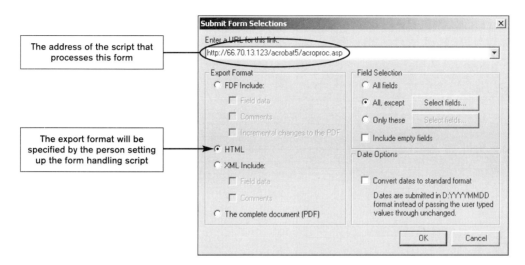

The address of the script that processes this form

The export format will be specified by the person setting up the form handling script

This dialog box determines how the form will be processed when the user clicks the Submit button. The choices you make here depend on how the person setting up the form handler on the Web server has determined to process the form data. The field under "Enter a URL for this link" shows the address of the server to which the form data will be sent. Under the Export Format section are the different ways the form data can be sent. Again, the method used will depend on how your Web developer prefers to receive the data.

Under Field Selection, you can determine which fields' data will be sent. In the Date Options area, checking the "Convert dates to standard format" check box will convert any dates listed in any form fields to a standard format of year/month/day, rather than using whatever format the user may have entered.

In the case of this particular form, the form data has been set to export as HTML. When the user clicks the Submit button, the data will be sent to the address shown at the top of the dialog box: http://66.70.13.123/acrobat5/acroproc.asp, which is an address that was provided by the script writer.

Next, you'll test this form by filling it out and sending it to the server for processing. You'll then receive an e-mail containing a summary of the information you entered. This section of the exercise requires that you to be connected to the Internet and have a working e-mail address.

Special thanks to Dave Clipper of CEI Design (http://ceidesign.com) for writing and hosting the script for this exercise.

5. Click **Cancel** to leave everything in the **Submit Form Selections** dialog box unchanged. Click **Cancel** two more times to close the remaining dialog boxes and return to the form.

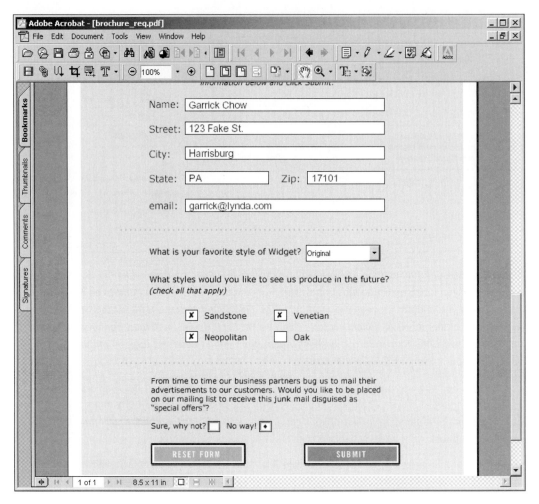

6. Select the **Hand** tool and fill out the form. This form data will not be collected in any way, but feel free to use phony information (except for your e-mail address). You need a valid e-mail address to receive the form data.

7. After you've filled out the form, click **Submit**.

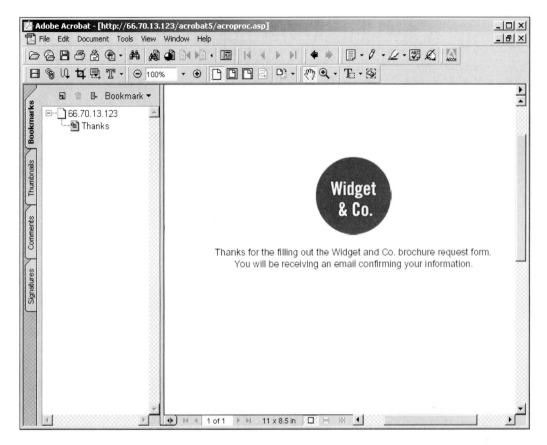

The form will be submitted to the server hosting the script. After a few moments, a new document will open confirming that your form data was received.

---

8. Close the confirmation page. You don't need to save it.

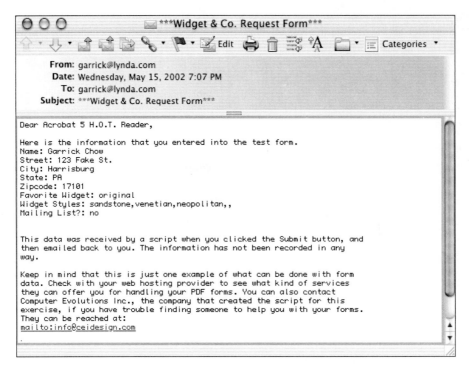

9. Wait a few minutes and check your e-mail. The e-mail you receive will display the data you entered into the form.

Keep in mind that this is just one of a multitude of options that are available for handling your form data over the Internet. Had this been a real form, the data you entered could have been entered into a database to automatically generate a list of customers who wished to receive a brochure.

MOVIE | forms.mov

To see the exercises from this chapter in action, check out **forms.mov** located in the **movies** folder on the Acrobat 5 **H•O•T CD-ROM**.

Phew, that was a lot of info! By now you should have a pretty good grasp of form fields and their abilities. Hopefully this chapter has inspired you to take a look at some of your own forms to see how you can make them more interactive. Take a well-deserved break. The next chapter will still be there when you're ready.

9.

Indexing and Searching PDFs

| Finding versus Searching |

| Preparing Your Files for Indexing | Creating an Index |

| Searching an Index | Searching Document Summary Information |

| Adding a Welcome Page |

chap_09

Acrobat 5
H•O•T CD-ROM

Is your hard drive cluttered with various PDF documents that you don't use very often but still want to keep? If so, Acrobat's Catalog feature is just what you need. Catalog is a "mini-application" that creates a searchable index from a collection of PDF documents.

There are numerous reasons to create a searchable index of your PDF files. For example, if you were distributing PDFs of product brochures on a CD-ROM, an index would make it easier for the users of your CD-ROM to find the information they're looking for. Instead of hunting through multiple files, they could perform a simple search to find all of the PDFs that mention a particular product.

If you have a large number of PDFs that you need to archive, creating an index will help you locate and retrieve content if you ever need those PDFs down the road.

In this chapter you'll first learn the difference between finding and searching in Acrobat. Then you'll create your own index of some collected files and search them for words and phrases. Finally, you'll learn techniques to help your users to search through your documents.

I. Finding versus Searching

Before you create an index, it's important to understand the difference between **finding** and **searching** in Acrobat. Finding is like the **Find** command used in many other applications. It allows you to locate a word or phrase within the particular document you're reading. **Search**, on the other hand, allows you to locate a word or phrase across a collection of documents. In this exercise, you will learn how to work with both the Find and Search features in Acrobat 5.

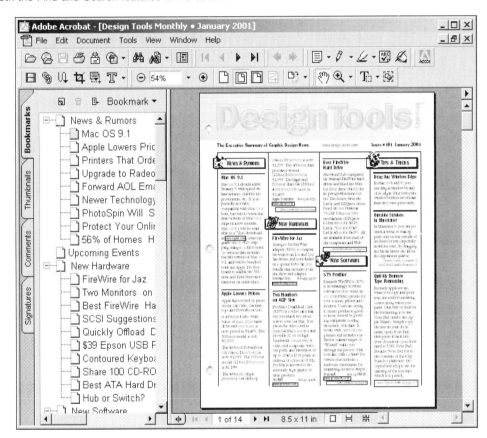

1. Copy the **chap_09** folder and files from the **H•O•T CD-ROM** to your hard drive.

2. Open **DTM_0101.pdf** from the **design_tools** folder in the **chap_09** folder on your hard drive.

Special thanks to Jay Nelson of Design Tools Monthly (www.design-tools.com) for donating a year's worth of his fantastic newsletters for use in this chapter. Design Tools Monthly is a collection of tips, tricks, and news published for and written by design industry specialists. You'll use this issue of Jay's newsletter to examine Acrobat's Find command.

3. Click the **Bookmarks** tab to close the Bookmarks pane. Click the **Fit Width** button to magnify the document for easier viewing.

The first goal of this exercise is to find out if this month's newsletter had any information about Acrobat. Using the Find feature, you can search the contents of this document for text relating to Acrobat.

4. In the Toolbar, click the **Find** button. Clicking the Find button opens the **Find** dialog box.

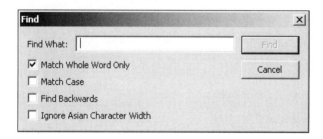

The Find dialog box is where you type the word or phrase that you're looking for.

Note: *If you want to find a phrase, do not place quotation marks around the phrase unless you want Acrobat to search for instances of the phrase that include quotation marks.*

NOTE | Find Options

There are four check boxes for special options, which are described in the following chart.

Find Options	
Option	**Description**
Match Whole Word Only	If checked, only the exact word you type will be found. If unchecked, all words that contain the word you type will be found. For example, if you uncheck it and type **pan**, you'll find words like **pancake**, **panel**, **company**, and **Ipanema.** The same applies to looking for phrases. With Match Whole Word Only unchecked, looking for **garbage can** would find the phrase **garbage canal** or **garbage candy**, if those phrases exist for some reason. (If you can use both words in a sentence, e-mail them to me.)
Match Case	If checked, you'll only find words that match the case of what you typed. When checked, searching for **Smith** will only return instances of **Smith.** If unchecked, you'll find both **Smith** and **smith**.
Find Backwards	If checked, the search will move backwards from the page you're currently viewing. If unchecked, the search will move forward.
Ignore Asian Character Widths	This option is only for the Japanese version of Acrobat. Just in case you're curious, it's for searching for full or half-width Kana characters.

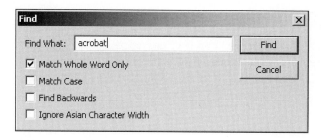

5. In the **Find What** field, type **acrobat**. Make sure **Match Whole Word Only** is checked because you're looking for just the word **acrobat**, not **acrobatic**, or **acrobatically**, etc. Everything else should be unchecked. Click **Find**.

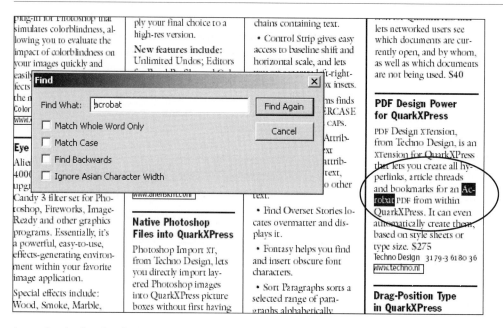

Immediately, Acrobat finds the first instance of "acrobat" on page 9. Notice that even though it's hyphenated, Acrobat was still able to locate it.

6. Click the **Find Again** button in the **Find** dialog box to look for the next instance of **acrobat**. The program will jump to page 14, where another instance of the word exists.

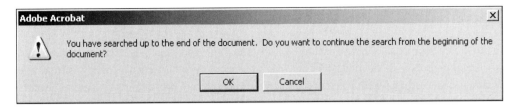

7. Click **Find Next** three more times. Acrobat will display a message telling you that it's reached the end of the document and asking whether you want to continue searching from the beginning. Because you started your search on page 1, there's no need to start again. Click **Cancel**.

8. Keep **DTM_0101.pdf** open for the next exercise.

If you wanted to find mentions of "acrobat" within the 11 other Design Tools newsletters, you'd have to open each one individually and click the Find button several times. There is a much easier way to search multiple documents; you can use Acrobat's Search command to hunt through all the documents at once. The bad news is that you can't just automatically search a collection of documents. The documents have to be indexed before they can be searched. To index a collection of documents, you'll learn to use a mini-application inside Acrobat called Catalog, which creates an index file for you. Next you'll use Catalog to create a searchable index for the 12 newsletters.

2. Preparing Your Files for Indexing

Before you create your index, it's important to take the time to prepare your files. Make sure all of your files are named properly with the **.pdf** extension. (See page **xx** of the Introduction if you're not sure how to view extensions in Windows.) Also make sure none of your files are named with any special characters such as spaces, hyphens, slashes, etc., as these may create problems when you index the files. If you don't know how to make your extensions visible, consult the Introduction of this book.

You also should take the time to fill out the Document Summary for each PDF, if the information hasn't already been created. In this exercise, you'll examine and edit the Document Summary for the newsletter you currently have open.

Note: At the time of publication of this edition, Catalog and the Search command are not available to Mac OS X users. To follow the exercises in this chapter, you must a version of OS 9 or earlier.

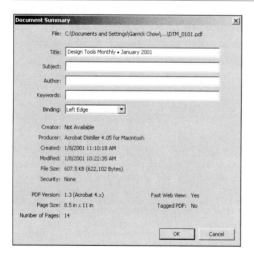

1. With **DTM_0101.pdf** still open, choose **File > Document Properties > Summary**. This will open the **Document Summary** dialog box. The Document Summary dialog box contains information about the creation and content of the PDF file.

The Acrobat Search command allows you to search the Title, Subject, Author, and Keywords of PDFs only if that information has been provided in the document. As you can see here, only the Title has been provided for this document. Next, you'll learn how to add some keywords to the summary. Keywords are words or phrases that you think someone might use when searching for this document. It's always a good idea to add a few relevant keywords to each document to help your users find the information they need. Try to anticipate what someone might type to search for the kind of content that's in your PDF.

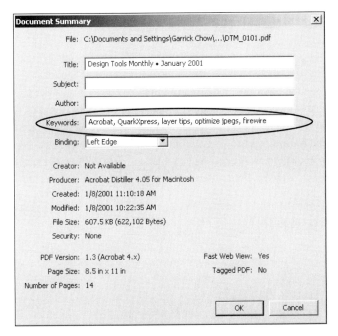

2. Click in the **Keywords** field and type, **Acrobat, QuarkXPress, layer tips, optimize jpegs, firewire.** (Keywords are not case-sensitive.) Each word or phrase should be separated by a comma. These are just some examples of keywords you could add.

Ideally, you would go through all 12 newsletters and create appropriate keywords for each of them, but for this chapter, you'll just be adding keywords to this issue. Later, you'll observe the results of adding these keywords to the Document Summary information.

3. Click **OK** to close the Document Summary dialog box.

4. Save and close **DTM_0101.pdf**.

When preparing your files for indexing, you should make sure that all of the PDF files are placed in one folder. It's okay to create subdirectories within the main folder, but keep in mind that once you index the main folder, you shouldn't change any of the files within it. Doing so will render your index obsolete, and you'll have to re-create it. In the following exercise, you'll be creating an index of the 12 Design Tools Monthly newsletters. They've already been placed into a single folder for you and named properly, so all you have to do is create the index.

3.————————————**Creating an Index**

If you've used previous versions of Acrobat, you might be familiar with Acrobat Catalog, a separate program that was installed with Acrobat. In Acrobat 5, Catalog is now included as part of the main Acrobat application and appears as a command under the Tools menu. Catalog is used to generate a complete searchable database of all the text in a collection of PDF documents. This database is referred to as an **index**, which must be saved and stored in the folder with its associated PDF documents. Before you use Catalog, you should always prepare your documents with summaries that contain as much information and as many keywords as needed, as you learned to do in the previous exercise. In this exercise, you will learn how to use the Catalog feature to create an index for a bunch of PDF documents.

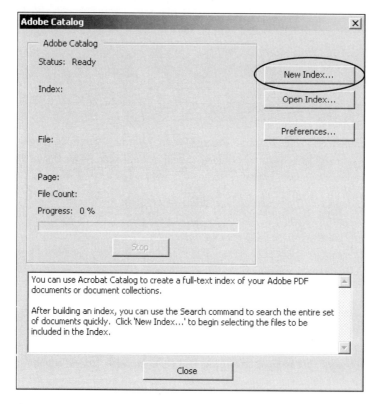

1. Choose **Tool > Catalog**. This will open the **Adobe Catalog** dialog box. Click the **New Index** button. The **New Index Definition** dialog box will open.

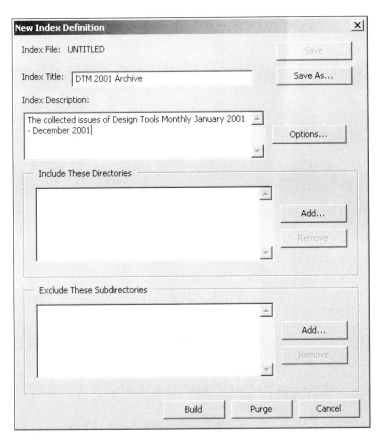

2. In the **Index Title** field, type, **DTM 2001 Archive**. Naming your index is important because it will appear in Acrobat's Search dialog box and will let the user know which index is being searched. If you don't name the index, it will have the generic name of **index**. In the **Index Description** field type, **The collected issues of Design Tools Monthly January 2001 - December 2001**. The Index Description is not a required field, but it does make it easier for the end user to figure out what documents are covered by this index.

3. Click the **Options** button to open the **Options** dialog box. Here you can view choices for searching and optimizing the index.

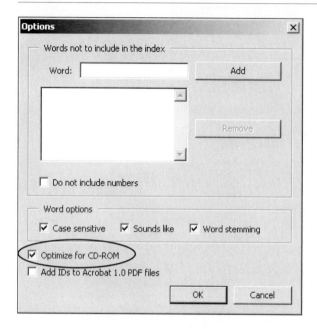

4. In the **Options** dialog box, check **Optimize for CD-ROM**. This will make searches of this index faster. Normally, when performing a search, if Acrobat comes across a document that has been altered since being indexed, Acrobat will display a dialog box asking if you want to continue, requiring you to click a button to continue your search. With Optimize for CD-ROM selected, this dialog box won't appear when this index is searched. Click **OK**. A chart that explains the Options dialog box is at the end of this exercise.

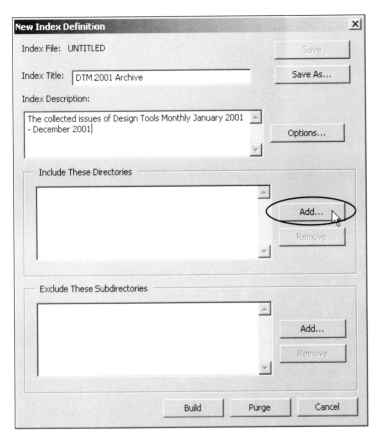

5. Now that you've named your file and chosen your options, you have to tell Catalog where the files to be indexed are located. Click **Add** under **Include These Directories**.

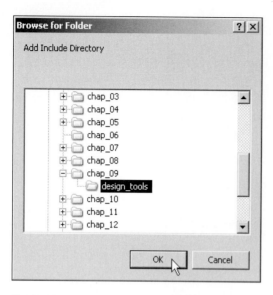

6. Windows: Navigate to the **chap_09** folder that you transferred to your hard drive and click on the **design_tools** folder to select it. Click **OK**.

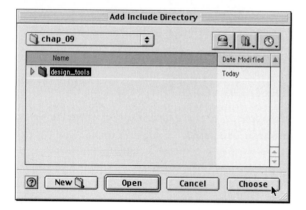

Macintosh: Navigate to the **chap_09** folder that you transferred to your hard drive and click on the **design_tools** folder to select it. Click **Choose**.

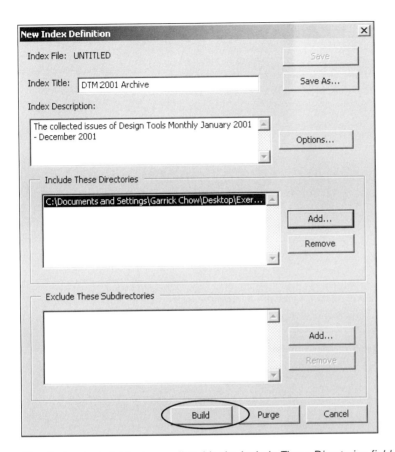

The design_tools folder is now listed in the Include These Directories field of the New Index Definition dialog box. By default, all folders within a selected folder are indexed. If you ever wish to exclude a subfolder from being indexed, click the Add button under Exclude These Subdirectories and select the folders you wish to exclude. Note that you only need to exclude folders that contain PDF files you don't want indexed. Folders that contain other files such as images or word processing files will be ignored by Catalog.

7. When you are ready to create the index file, click **Build** at the bottom of the dialog box.

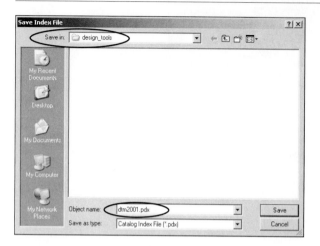

Acrobat will open a dialog box asking where you want to save the index file. It's very important that you save the index file into the same folder that contains the PDF documents you're indexing.

8. You should be in the **design_tools** folder, but if not, navigate to the **design_tools** folder in the **chap_09** folder on your hard drive and save this file as **dtm2001.pdx** (**.pdx** is the file extension for an Acrobat index). Click **Save**.

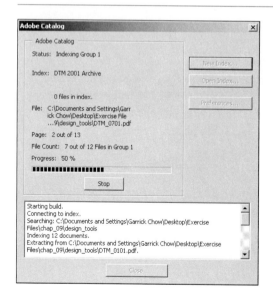

Acrobat Catalog will display a status window while the index is created.

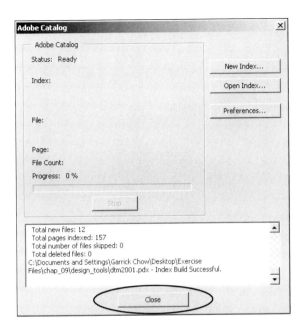

After a few moments, the Close button will become active; indicating that the index build is complete.

9. Click **Close**. You now have a searchable index. In the next exercise, you'll learn how to use Acrobat's Search command that will make use of the index you just created.

If you look inside the design_tools folder that you just indexed, you'll find the dtm2001.pdx file that was created, along with a folder called dtm2001. dtm2001 contains the various files that are needed for your index to function properly. Don't delete it.

Indexing Options Dialog Box

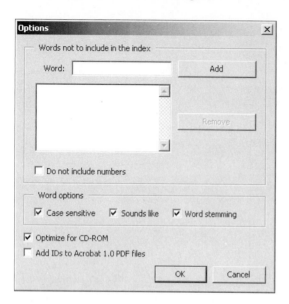

There are lots of settings inside the Options dialog box. This handy chart provides more detail about each setting.

Indexing Options	
Option	**Description**
Words not to include in the index	Here you can add words that you want Catalog to ignore. These words are known as **stopwords.** By default, Catalog indexes every single word in all of the documents, which results in a fairly large index file. Common stopwords are words such as **the, a, an, as, of**, etc. The more words you can exclude, the smaller and more efficient the index will be. Keep in mind though, that if you exclude words, some phrases will not be found. For instance, if you excluded the above words from the index, someone searching for the phrase **the Sheriff of Nottingham** would not find that phrase, because **the** and **of** were excluded from the index.
Do not include numbers	Catalog will ignore any numbers that it finds in the documents. If you believe no one will be searching your documents for specific numbers (phone numbers, addresses, etc.) you can check this option.

continues on next page

Indexing Options *continued*

Option	Description
Case sensitive	When checked, this enables the Match Case option in Search, allowing users to search for words or phrases with specified upper- and lower-case characters. Unchecking this option will result in a smaller index.
Sounds like	Checking this will enable the Sounds Like option in Search. This option attempts to find words based on their sound quality, but is not necessarily based on a rhyming scheme. Searching for **coat** will not yield a result of **boat.** This feature is mainly used to expand searches for proper names. Searching for **Garic** will find **Garrick**, searching for **John** will find **Jon.** Unchecking this option will result in a smaller index.
Word stemming	Checking this option will enable the Word Stemming option in Search. Searching for **run** will find **running, runner, runaway**, etc. Unchecking this option will result in a smaller index.
Optimize for CD-ROM	This feature arranges the files for quick access from a CD-ROM. Normally, if a user searches a file that has been modified after it has been indexed, Acrobat will warn the user that the document was changed. Checking Optimize for CD-ROM disables this warning. If you prefer to be warned if files have been altered, leave this option unchecked.
Add IDs to Acrobat 1.0 PDF files	Only check this if you have PDFs that were created with version 1 of Acrobat (I'd like to see that). Acrobat will add the necessary tags to ensure that these files will be compatible with current versions. If you do happen to have version 1 PDFs, your best bet is to open them with Acrobat 5 and choose Save As to save them as Acrobat 5 PDFs.

4. ——————————Searching an Index

Now that you've created an index, you'll learn how to load the index into the Search window and search for words and phrases. If you're familiar with using search engines on the World Wide Web, you'll find that searching in Acrobat is a very similar procedure, only with fewer ads for spy cameras and low-interest credit cards popping up behind your windows.

1. Click the **More Tools** arrow next to the **Search** button and choose **Expand This Button**. This will reveal all of the buttons associated with searching a PDF and make it easier to access these features.

2. Click the **Search** button. This will open the **Adobe Acrobat Search** dialog box.

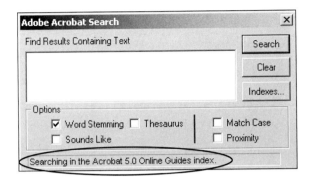

Before you can search an index, you have to tell Acrobat which index you want to search. If you've never searched an index with your copy of Acrobat before, the current default index is the Acrobat 5.0 Online Guides index. You need to load the Design Tools index created in the previous exercise.

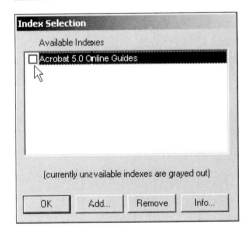

3. Click the **Indexes** button to open the **Index Selection** dialog box. By default, you'll find that the Acrobat 5.0 Online Guide is loaded. While it's possible to search multiple indexes at once, you only need to search your Design Tools index in this case, so **uncheck** the Acrobat 5.0 index.

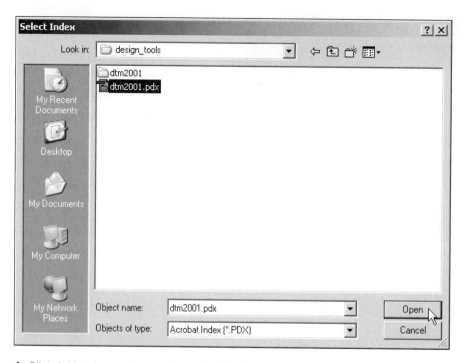

4. Click **Add** to browse for your index. Inside the **chap_09** folder, open the **design_tools** folder and select the file **dtm2001.pdx**. This is the index you created in the previous exercise. Click **Open**.

5. The **DTM 2001 Archive** is now listed and checked in the **Index Selection** dialog box. Click **OK**.

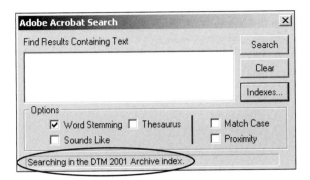

In these next steps, you'll learn some methods of searching an index and refining your searches to help you locate information more quickly. Note that this is different from using the Find command like you did at the beginning of the chapter. The Search command allows you to hunt through the entire indexed collection of documents. Let's say you wanted to find any documents that mentioned Adobe Photoshop 6.

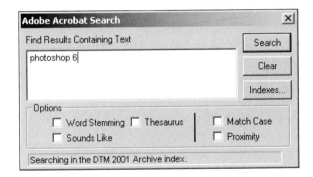

6. In the **Find Results Containing Text** field, type **photoshop 6**. Uncheck any of the Options, like Word Stemming, that may currently be selected. Click the **Search** button.

The text you type in the Search dialog box can be a word, phrase, or number. If a phrase includes a Boolean operator (explained at the end of this exercise in a note) you must include quotes around the phrase.

NOTE | Search Options

The following chart explains the search options available in the Adobe Acrobat Search dialog box.

Search Options	
Option	**Description**
Word Stemming	Finds documents containing words that contain the search word. Searching for **fun** will find words like **funny**, **funnel**, **fundamental**, **refund**, etc.
Thesaurus	Finds documents that contain words similar to the word that's being searched for. Searching for **type** will also find words like **sort** and **kind**. Applies only to single words, not phrases.
Match Case	Only finds documents that contain words that match the capitalization of the search word.
Proximity	Used when searching for two words or phrases. When checked, will only return results if the words or phrases are within 3 pages of each other. Acrobat will rank the relevancy of documents based on the proximity of the search words.

Acrobat displays the Search Results window and lists the 11 documents that contain "Photoshop 6" in order of relevancy. Relevancy is indicated by the circle to the left of each article, and it just so happens that Acrobat considers each of the 11 documents almost equally relevant.

7. Double-click the **February 2001** listing to view it. Acrobat opens the February newsletter and highlights the first instances of Photoshop 6. Feel free to click the **Fit Width** button if the text is too small for you to read. Close the **Search Results** window so that it doesn't obstruct your view of the page.

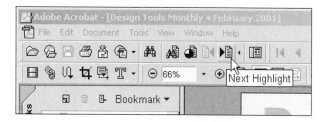

8. In the Toolbar, click the **Next Highlight** button to view the next occurrence of **Photoshop 6** in this document. Continue clicking the **Next Highlight** button. As you click, Acrobat will take you from instance to instance of the phrase, jumping from the end of the current document to the beginning of the next relevant document. (You don't have to click through all 11 documents if you don't want to.)

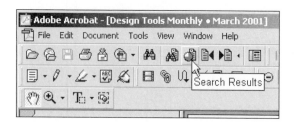

9. Click the **Search Results** button in the Toolbar to open the **Search Results** window again.

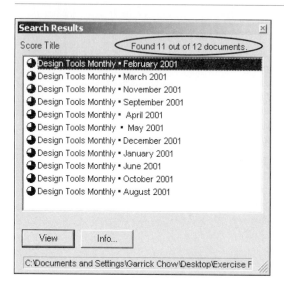

Since searching for Photoshop 6 yielded so many results, you'll refine your search to be more specific. Refining your search will allow you to search just the 11 files that resulted from your initial search.

10. Close the **Search Results** window and click the **Search** button to open the **Search** dialog box again.

This time you'll search for documents that contain Photoshop 6 and ImageReady.

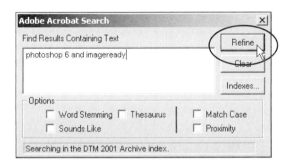

11. In the **Search** dialog box, type **photoshop 6 and imageready**. Hold down the **Ctrl** (Windows) or **Option** (Mac) key. Notice that this changes the Search button into the Refine button, allowing you to search the 11 documents you originally found. Click **Refine**.

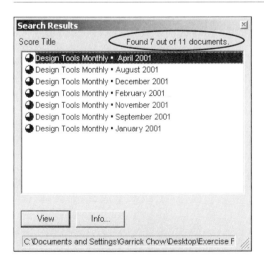

Acrobat finds that 7 out of the 11 documents contain both "photoshop 6" and "imageready." You can view the documents by double-clicking on them, just like before. Refining a search is a great way to narrow down your choices if you find that your first search yields too many results.

12. Close the **Search Results** window. Leave the file open for the next exercise, in which you will learn how to Search for Document Summary information.

NOTE | Boolean Operators

Boolean operators are named after George Boole (1815–1864) who invented the system of algebra upon which they are based. Hey, wake up! It's not that bad. In terms of searching, Boolean operators allow you to perform a search by combining two or more words or phrases and applying a positive, negative, or intersection attribute. The three Boolean terms used for searching in Acrobat are:

1. and (positive)

2. and not (negative)

3. or (intersection)

Searching for **bread and butter** will result in finding documents that contain both the word **bread** and the word **butter**. Searching for **bread and not butter**, will find all the documents that contain only the word **bread** and will exclude the documents containing the word **butter**. Searching for **bread or butter** will find documents that contain either the word **bread** or the word **butter**; the documents may contain both words, but they do not have to.

Note that if you want to find the exact phrase **bread and butter** (the three words in a row) you must use quotation marks around the phrase; otherwise Acrobat will treat the **and** as a Boolean term. And if you want to find separate instances of the three words, use a comma to separate each word as in: **bread, and, butter**.

5. ——————Searching Document Summary Information

In Exercise 2, you added information to the Document Summary dialog box of one of the newsletters. In the following steps, you'll learn how to search Document Summary info instead of searching for text. Searching the Document Summary information can be very useful if the author of the PDF file has taken the time to provide the information.

1. Choose **Edit** > **Preferences** > **General**.

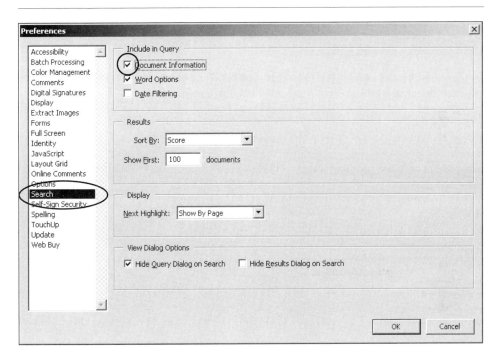

2. Select the **Search** category in the left column and click the check box next to **Document Information**. This will allow you to search the document summary information from the Search dialog box. Click **OK**.

3. Click the **Search** button in the Toolbar. Notice that the **Search** dialog box has expanded to include the **With Document Info** section, which allows you to further refine your search.

You only added Document Summary info to one document, dtm_0101.pdf, so typing any of the keywords you entered should result in finding just that one document.

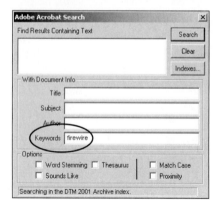

4. In the **Keywords** field, type **firewire**. Click **Search**. The file **dtm_0101.pdf** should open.

Any time a Search results in only one document being found, Acrobat bypasses displaying the Search Results window and instead just opens the document immediately. If you had added keywords to all of the documents, Search would have found all instances of "firewire" in the Document Summary information of all the files.

5. Close **dtm_0101.pdf**.

So now you know how to load an index into Acrobat so that it may be searched. But you can't rely on all of your end users knowing how to do this. In the next exercise you'll explore some methods for helping your users to search your PDFs.

6. ―――――――――Adding a Welcome Page

Now that you know how to prepare your documents for searching, and how to create and search an index, you have to consider that people using your PDF documents might not have had much Acrobat training and potentially know very little about navigating PDFs, let alone searching them. You can't expect all of your users to know how to load an index before they start searching it. In this exercise you'll learn to create and enhance a basic "welcome" document, which can be used to introduce your readers to your collection of documents. A welcome page is very helpful to show your readers how your documents are organized, and provide a helpful interface with which to search the documents.

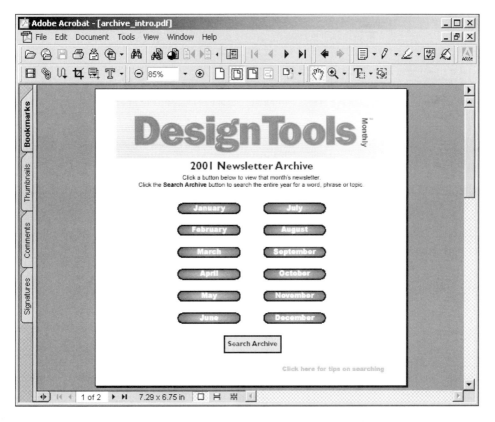

1. Open the file **archive_intro.pdf** from the **chap_09** folder. This will act as the welcome page for the collection of Design Tools Monthly newsletters. A copy of this welcome page needs to be copied and saved to the main **design_tools** folder for it to work. You will do this next.

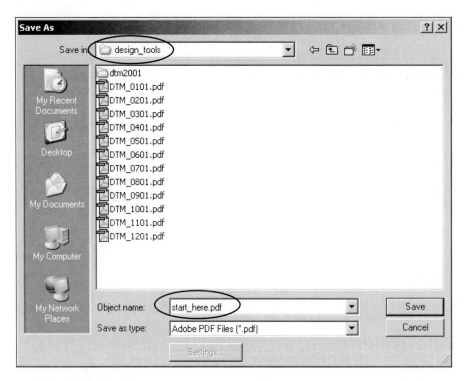

2. Choose **File > Save As** and navigate to the **design_tools** folder in **chap_09** folder. Rename this file **start_here.pdf**. By giving this file an instructional name in plain English, you're helping the reader find the welcome page. Click **Save**.

The welcome page instructs the reader to click the months below to access the newsletters, or to click the Search Archive button to search for a word, phrase, or topic. Neither of these actions is working yet—that's your job.

3. Using the **Hand** tool, click the text in the lower-right corner to view the **Tips for searching** page.

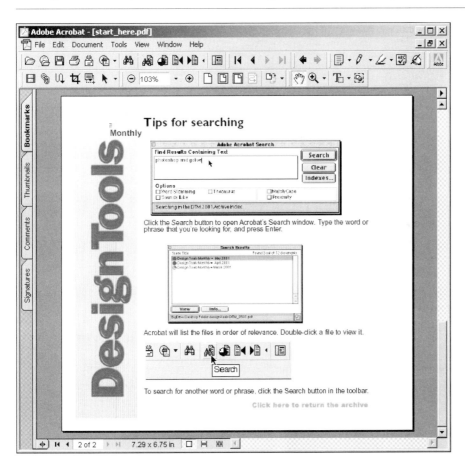

This page provides information on how to use Acrobat's search command. It's important to provide your users with basic information on searching if you expect them to use your index. This page doesn't go into the details of loading an index because you're going to make the index automatically load any time someone opens this page.

4. Click the text **Click here to return to the archive** in the lower-right-hand corner to return to the first page.

In the previous exercise, you learned to load an index yourself. In the following steps, you'll save the readers the trouble of mounting an index by automating this process for them.

5. Choose **File > Document Properties > Associated Index**. This will open the **Document Associated Index** dialog box.

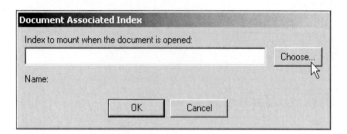

6. Windows: Click **Choose** to select the index.

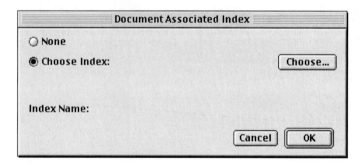

Mac: Click the **Choose Index** radio button and then click **Choose.**

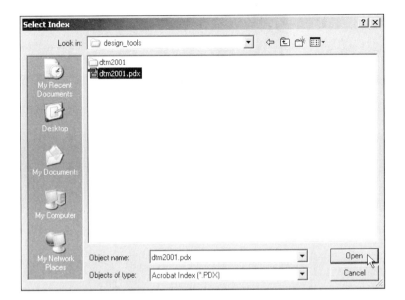

7. Select the **dtm2001.pdx** file in the **design_tools** folder. Click **Open**.

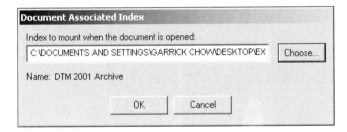

The DTM 2001 Archive is listed in the Document Associated Index dialog box.

8. Click **OK**. The index is now associated with this page and will load every time this welcome page is opened. You will test this a little later.

Next, you'll add a link around the Search Archive button on the page to make it a working button. In Chapter 3, "Working with Links," you learned how to create links to jump from one location to another. Here, you'll be creating a link and assigning it an action rather than a destination.

Note: *This welcome page was created with the intention of adding links to it in Acrobat. The Search Archive button was created in the program in which this page was authored. If you had a document to which you wanted to add a Search function but which lacked a pre-created Search button, you could use the form tool to create a button from scratch, just like the Print and Reset buttons you created in Chapter 8, "Forms."*

9. Select the **Link** tool and draw a link area around the **Search Archive** button near the bottom of the page.

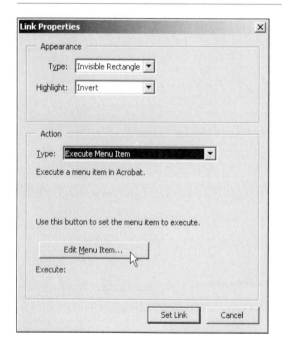

10. In the **Link Properties** dialog box that opens, make this an **Invisible Rectangle**. (There's already a border around the button, so there's no need for the link border to be visible as well.) Select a **Highlight** of your choice. For the **Type** of **Action** choose **Execute Menu Item**. Click the **Edit Menu Item** button.

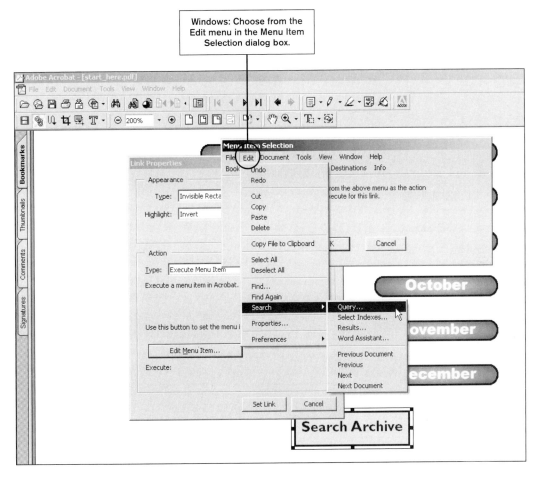

Windows: Choose from the Edit menu in the Menu Item Selection dialog box.

11. Windows: In the **Menu Item Selection** dialog box, choose **Edit > Search > Query**. This is the menu command for opening the **Search** dialog box.

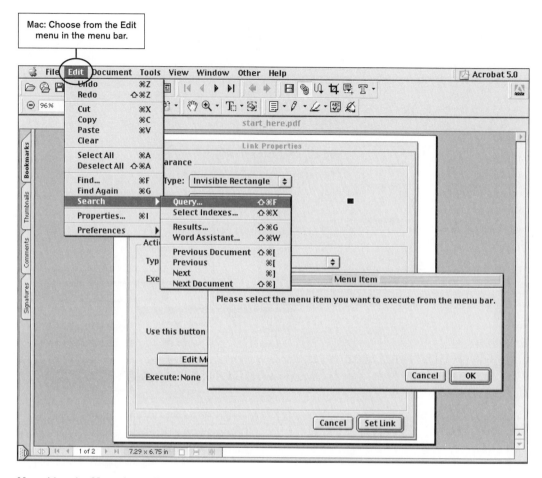

Mac: After the **Menu Item** dialog box opens, choose **Edit > Search > Query** from the main application menu bar.

12. Click **OK** in the **Menu Item** dialog box after you've selected **Query**. Click **Set Link** to close the **Link Properties** dialog box.

Now you'll test to see if the index has been properly associated with this page and if the Search button you just created works.

13. Save the file and close it. Keep Acrobat open.

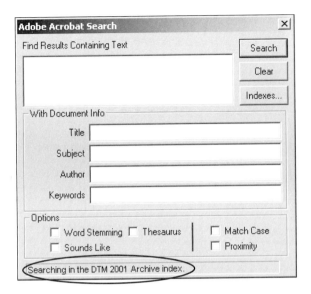

14. Click the **Search** button to open the **Search** dialog box. Notice that the **DTM 2001 Archive** is still loaded from your previous searches. You'll unload this index to see if opening the welcome page will reload it.

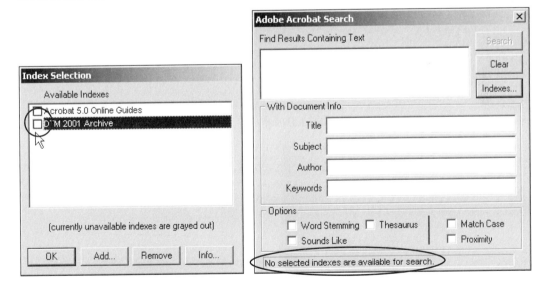

15. Click the **Indexes** button and uncheck the **DTM 2001 Archive**. Click **OK**. The **Search** dialog box indicates that there are no indexes loaded. Close the Search dialog box.

16. Open the **start_here.pdf** from the **design_tools** folder in the **chap_09** folder. By opening this file, the **DTM 2001 Archive** index should load automatically because you associated it with this document.

17. Click the **Search Archive** button at the bottom of the page. This opens the **Search** dialog box.

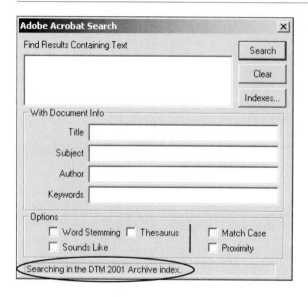

Notice that the DTM 2001 Archive index was loaded properly. Woo-hoo! See how easy you can make things for your users? Close the Search dialog box

The last thing you need to do is to add links to the month buttons on this page.

18. Select the **Link** tool and draw a rectangle around the **January** button.

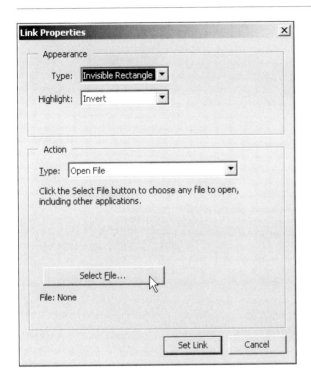

19. In **Link Properties**, choose **Invisible Rectangle**. For the **Type of Action** choose **Open File**. Click **Select File**.

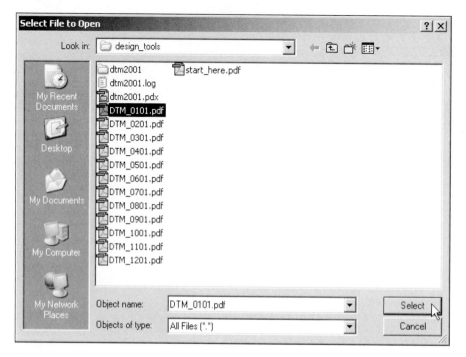

20. Browse to the **design_tools** folder in the **chap_09** folder and select **DTM_0101.pdf**. Click **Select** (Windows) or **Open** (Mac).

21. Click **Set Link** to close the **Link Properties** dialog box.

22. Save the file.

22. Test your link by selecting the **Hand** tool and clicking on the **January** button. The January issue of Design Tools Monthly should open. Click the **Go to Previous View** button to return to the welcome page.

If you feel you need the practice, go ahead and link the rest of the months to their proper newsletters. Remember that each file is named in this format: DTM_mmyy.pdf

23. Save and close the file when you're done.

MOVIE | welcomepage.mov

To learn more about adding a welcome page, check out **welcomepage.mov** located in the **movies** folder on the Acrobat 5 **H•O•T CD-ROM**.

With a completed welcome page and an indexed collection of documents, you're ready to copy the files to a CD-ROM for distribution. Remember that in a real-world situation you must keep indexed PDF files in their original folders. Don't create subdirectories or change the names of files after they've been indexed. The important thing is to be consistent in the way you save and name your files. Done properly, you'll find that indexing your PDF files is a great way to organize and store them for quick retrieval if they're ever needed later.

IO.

Document Security

Acrobat Standard Security	Changing Security Settings
Creating a User Profile	Digitally Signing PDFs
Validating Signatures	Acrobat Self-Sign Security
Adding a Signature Form Field

chap_10

Acrobat 5
H•O•T CD-ROM

As you've seen in the previous chapters, Acrobat allows you to add links, bookmarks, and form fields; edit text; move objects; extract images; and add comments. But what if you wanted to prevent someone with a copy of Acrobat from altering or extracting text or images from your documents? Document security allows you to protect and preserve the PDFs you've worked so hard to create.

In the first part of this chapter, you'll learn about Acrobat's standard security options that allow you to lock out certain functions of Acrobat on a document-by-document basis. In the second part of the chapter, you'll learn about digital signatures: what they are, how to create them, how to validate them, and how to create a form field to enable someone to sign a document.

Security can mean that your documents are protected from being changed, but it can also mean protecting your documents from being viewed by the wrong people or ensuring that no one else alters a document and blames the changes on you. In this chapter you'll learn how to prevent all of these bad things from happening.

I. ―――――――Acrobat Standard Security

When you need to add security to your PDF documents, you have two main choices: **Acrobat Standard Security** and **Acrobat Self-Sign Security**. Acrobat Standard Security allows you to place one security setting on a PDF that applies to everyone who uses the document. Acrobat Self-Sign Security, on the other hand, allows you to individualize the security settings on a single PDF to allow different users different levels of access. In this exercise, you'll explore Acrobat Standard Security.

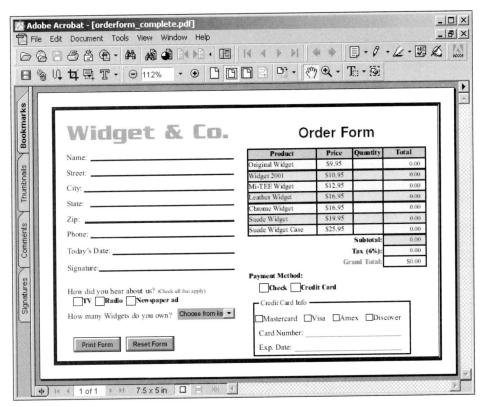

1. Copy the **chap_10** folder and files from the **H•O•T CD-ROM** to your hard drive. Open the file **orderform_complete.pdf** from the **chap_10** folder. This is a copy of the file you worked on in Chapter 8, *"Forms."* First, you'll see just how easy it is to change some things around on this form.

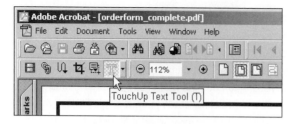

2. If necessary, zoom in on the ordering area of the form to view it at a larger size. Select the **TouchUp Text** tool from the Toolbar.

Product	Price	Qu
Original Widget	$9.95	
Widget 2001	$10.95	
Mi-TEE Widget	$12.95	

3. Click on the price for the **Original Widget** on the first line. An edit box appears around the price.

Product	Price	Q
Original Widget	$2.95	
Widget 2001	$10.95	
Mi-TEE Widget	$12.95	

4. Highlight the price and type **$2.95**.

See how the new price looks exactly like the other prices listed here? Anyone looking at this document would not suspect that the price had been altered.

5. Select **Edit > Undo Typing** to revert the price back to $9.95. (If Undo Typing is not available under the Edit menu, choose **File > Revert**).

To prevent anyone from altering the prices or any other aspects of the document, you'll add some standard security to this PDF.

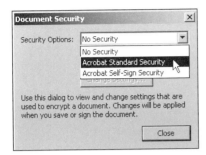

6. Choose **File > Document Security**. This will open the **Document Security** dialog box, where you can select the type of security you want to apply. From **Security Options** select **Acrobat Standard Security**, which will immediately open the **Standard Security** dialog box.

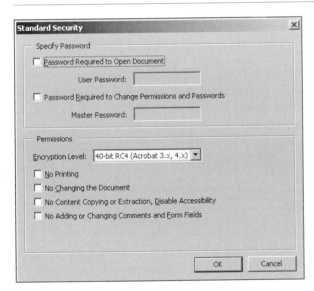

In the Standard Security dialog box you can determine the type of permissions you'll allow users to have for this document. It's broken down into two sections: Specify Password and Permissions.

Notice that you can select a password to open the document (User Password), as well as a Master Password that allows you to change permissions and security settings. Creating a User Password prevents unauthorized people from opening the document.

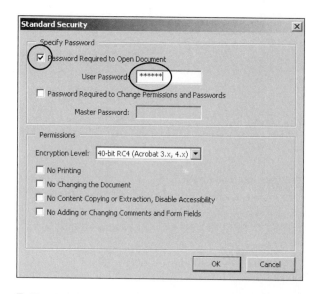

7. Check the box next to **Password Required to Open Document**. In the **User Password** field, type **apples** in lowercase. By setting a User Password, only the people who know the password will be able to open this document. (Feel free to choose your own password, but please don't forget it. I'd like to avoid writing *Hacking Acrobat 5 Hands-On-Training*!)

NOTE | Password Selection Guidelines

Here are some important points about passwords:

• Passwords are case sensitive. This can work to your benefit. By creating a password that comprises a series of uppercase and lowercase letters combined with numbers, you can make a password that's extremely difficult to guess. But be careful, because:

• If you forget your password, there's no way to open your document or to change the security settings. If you tend to forget passwords, you may want to keep one copy of your document without security on your computer, and apply security to another copy for distributing to others.

• Your passwords can have a maximum of 255 characters. Here's an example of a 255 character password:

5F4jdnak6hsjdnwpldnGDUhwVf5726wknd06heKmf90hwdheinfawbftwHSfhwqvzcsoxBNFD9
3j4kfpqkdJnct6jwsiKmbfe28910eodkcmKHDNWmjsofecjn2847dn5b4k8msweifn142jfwlmcB
Slkjfihebqpljdbciwnchtiemn7438jdkwplkmn1idksmHB632kdhew93nfjwk17mcgs07hnw76h13
5ndwqlkfnsHWEjExdheoalw2164

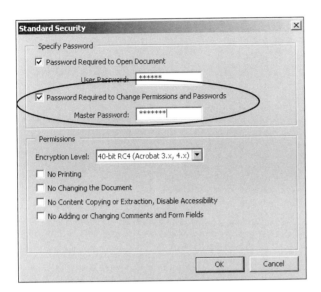

8. Check the box next to **Password Required to Change Permissions and Passwords**. In the **Master Password** field type **oranges**. The master password will unlock access to the document's security settings, allowing you to edit the setting or passwords.

Note: You must choose different passwords for the User and Master password fields.

Next you'll examine the Permissions area of this dialog box. The first thing you should select is the Encryption level. You can choose either 40-bit or 128-bit encryption. Either choice offers slightly different options throughout the rest of the Permissions section. Although128-bit encryption is more secure than 40-bit, keep in mind that 40-bit encryption is compatible with Acrobat versions 3.0 and up. 128-bit encryption, however, is only compatible with Acrobat 5 and Acrobat Reader 5. Users with earlier versions of Acrobat won't even be able to open the file.

9. If it's not already selected, choose **40-bit RC4 (Acrobat 3.x, 4.x)** as the **Encryption Level**.

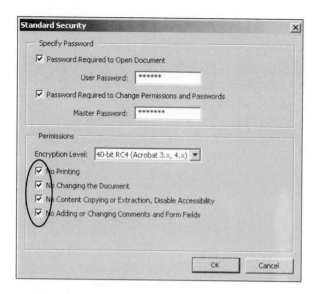

10. For the purposes of this exercise, check all four check boxes below the Encryption Level setting. While this is not a realistic security setting for this document, checking all four boxes will demonstrate just how secure your document can be. A chart that describes what each option in the Permissions section does is provided at the end of exercise 2.

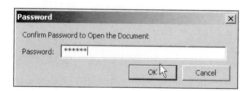

11. Click **OK**. Acrobat asks you to confirm the password to open the document. Type **apples** and click **OK**. Confirm the password to change security options by typing **oranges** and then click **OK**. Click **Close** to close the Document Security dialog box.

Now you'll test the security settings by closing the file and opening it again.

12. Choose **File > Save As**. Name the file **secure01.pdf** and save it in the **chap_10** folder on your hard drive. Close the file, keeping Acrobat open.

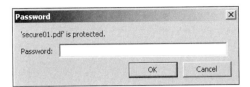

13. Open the file **secure01.pdf**. Acrobat informs you that the file is protected. Enter the user password, **apples**, and click **OK**. The document will open.

Note: The master password will also work to open a password-protected file, but it will also grant the user full access to the document. If you want ensure that your security permissions apply to the users, supply them only with the user password, and keep the master password secret.

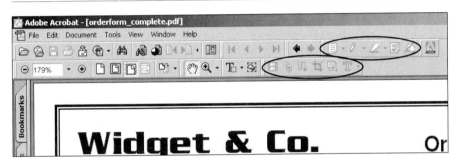

The order form can now be seen, but notice that because of the security settings you've chosen you can't do much more to this document than look at it. Observe that the Editing and Commenting tools are grayed out in the Toolbar. The Print command under the File menu is unavailable, as are most of the commands under the Document menu.

Perhaps most significantly, you can't click in any form fields to enter information. The current security settings prevent the user from filling out the form. The settings you chose are too extreme for this document, rendering the form useless. Next, you'll edit the security settings to make them more appropriate for this document.

2. _____Changing Security Settings

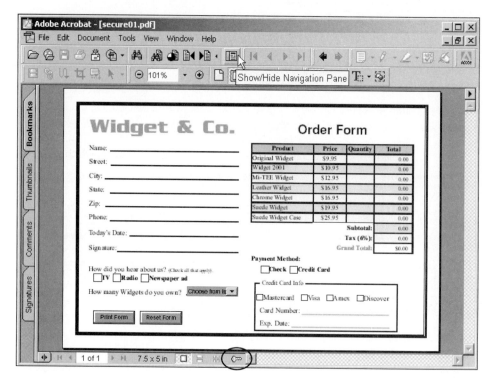

1. Because this document has had security added to it, a yellow key icon appears at the bottom of the document window. Click the **key** icon and choose **Document Security** from the pop-up menu. (This is an alternative to choosing **File > Document Security**.)

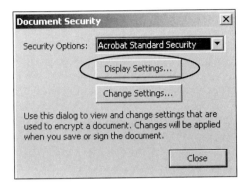

2. In the **Document Security** dialog box, click the **Display Settings** button, which will open a window that lists the status of all the security settings of the current document.

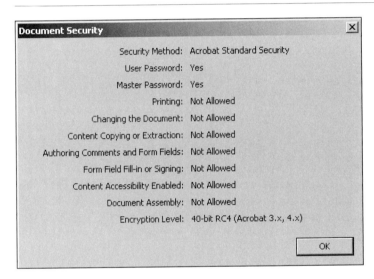

Display Settings is a quick way to check the security settings of any document, but you can't make any changes from here.

3. Click **OK** to close this window.

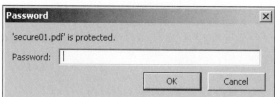

4. In the **Document Security** window, click **Change Settings**. Acrobat will prompt you for the master password. Type **oranges** and click **OK**. You'll be viewing the Standard Security window again.

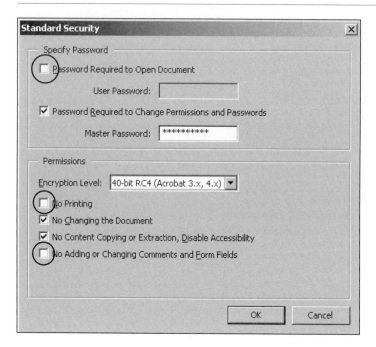

5. Uncheck **Password Required to Open Document**. Now anyone will be able to open the order form. You should always have a master password, however, because without one you might as well not set any security options—anyone could get to this dialog box to undo your settings. Uncheck **No Printing** and **No Adding or Changing Comments and Form Fields**. This will allow the users to fill out the form fields and print the form when they're done. By keeping the other two Permissions options checked, you're preventing users from being able to alter the document or to copy its contents. Click **OK**, and then click **Close** to close the Document Security window.

6. Save the file and close it, keeping Acrobat open.

7. Open **secure01.pdf** once more. Notice that you're no longer prompted to enter a password; the document simply opens normally. You can now make entries in the form fields, print the form, and even add comments, but you still don't have access to the Editing tools. You can now distribute this document to customers, confident that they won't be able to alter any of your content.

Next, you'll learn how to change the security options from the 40-bit encryption setting you've been working with to 128-bit encryption, which offers more robust security settings.

8. Click the **key** icon at the bottom of the document window and select **Document Security**.

9. Click the **Change Settings** button in the **Document Security** window and type **oranges** as the password.

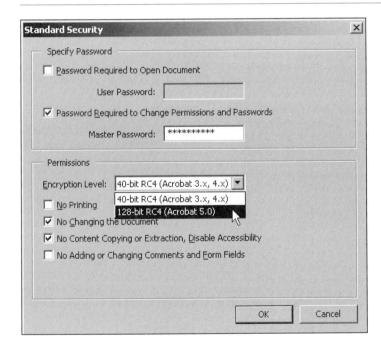

10. In the **Permissions** area of the **Standard Security** dialog box, choose **128-bit RC4 (Acrobat 5.0)** as the **Encryption Level**. This will change the Permissions options.

When you set your options with 40-bit encryption in the previous steps of this exercise, you allowed printing, filling in form fields, and adding comments. The 128-bit encryption option allows you to set the same permissions, but also enables you to customize them beyond the capabilities of 40-bit encryption.

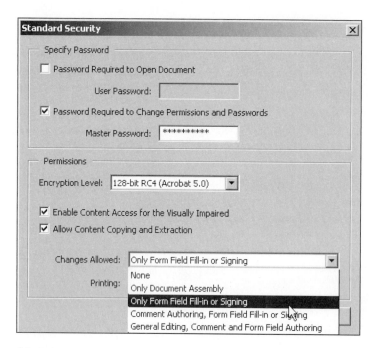

11. If they're checked, uncheck the two boxes under the **Encryption Level** setting. From the menu next to **Changes Allowed**, choose **Only Form Field Fill-in or Signing**. This will restrict the permissions to only allow users to fill in the form or to digitally sign it. They will not be able to make comments or alter the document in any other way. From the menu next to **Printing**, choose **Fully Allowed**. This will allow the users to print full-resolution copies of the PDF. Click **OK** to exit this dialog box. Close the Document Security window.

Warning: Only users who have Acrobat 5.0 and higher or Acrobat Reader 5.0 and higher will be able to open this file. Users with older versions of Acrobat will not be able to open the file, even if they have the master password.

12. Save the file and close it. Keep Acrobat open for the next exercise.

Encryption Permission Options

The chart that follows details the Permission options available under 128-bit encryption.

128-bit Encryption Permission Options	
Permission	**Description**
Enable Content Access for the Visually Impaired	When checked, enables the accessibility feature. This allows the document structure to be copied, which is a requirement of providing accessibility (see Chapter 15, *"Authoring PDF Files for Accessibility"*).
Allow Content Copying and Extraction	When checked, allows users to select and copy the contents of the document. Also enables extraction of images.
Changes Allowed	**None:** Prevents the user from making any changes to the file at all. **Only Document Assembly:** Allows users to insert, delete, and rotate pages, but does not allow extracting, replacing, or cropping pages. Bookmarks and thumbnails can still be created if this option is selected, but links, comments, and articles cannot. **Only Form Field Fill-in or Signing:** Users can fill in form fields and digitally sign PDFs, but cannot create new form fields, add comments, or change the document in any way. **Comment Authoring, Form Field Fill-In or Signing:** Same as the Only Form Field Fill-In or Signing selection, but allows users to add comments. **General Editing Comment and Form Field Authoring:** Enables all editing features.
Printing Allowed	**None:** Disables printing. File can only be viewed onscreen. **Low Resolution:** Allows the file to be printed, but rasterizes all fonts and images, resulting in a very low-quality print, unsuitable for publication. Reduces document resolution to 150dpi. This setting is useful for situations where the user may want to print your file to have a hard copy for proofing, but you want to protect your work from being duplicated. **Fully Allowed:** Allows high-resolution and postscript printing. The beauty of the three printing settings is that they allow you to send a full-resolution PDF to a client, but to limit its printing capability to None or Low Resolution. If you decide later to allow the document to be printed at its true resolution (after receiving payment, for instance) you can provide the user with the master password to change the print settings.

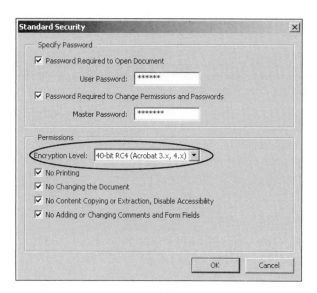

The chart that follows lists and explains the options available with 40-bit encryption.

40-bit Encryption Permission Options	
Permission	**When Checked**
No Printing	Prevents users from printing the PDF. The document can only be viewed onscreen.
No Changing the Document	Disables the Editing tools. Prevents the user from adding form fields, links, bookmarks, articles, and movies. Also prevents the user from changing text with the TouchUp Text tool or moving objects with the TouchUp Object tool. Comments can still be added to the PDF.
No Content Copying or Extraction, Disable Accessibility	Disables **Edit > Copy**, preventing users from copying text or images from the document. Disables **File > Export > Extract Images As**, preventing users from extracting images from the PDF. Also disables the Accessibility interface (see Chapter 15, *"Authoring PDF Files for Accessibility"*).
No Adding or Changing Comments or Form Fields	Prevents users from using the Comment tools and the Form tool. Users will not be able to fill in existing form fields.

Acrobat's Standard Security offers many options for setting permissions for your individual PDF files. In the next section, you'll learn how to use digital signatures to secure your documents, and you'll compare the differences between Standard Security and Self-Sign Security.

3. —————————Creating a User Profile

As you know, sending files in PDF format is a quick and convenient way to distribute documents for review and approval. However, for documents that require a signature for approval, many people still rely on signing the documents by hand and then returning them by mail, fax, or courier. Why print out a document just for the sake of signing it? With Acrobat 5, you can receive a PDF, digitally sign it, and then return it to the sender, without ever having to print a hard copy. Federal law and many states now consider digital signatures to be equivalent to handwritten signatures. So what is a digital signature, you may wonder?

When you digitally sign a document, you apply a unique user profile to the PDF file. This profile can then be authenticated by the person receiving the file to confirm that it was actually you who signed the document. Digital signatures are in fact more secure than those on paper documents because digital signatures allow you to verify the source of the endorsement. Therefore, before you can sign a document, you must first create a user profile.

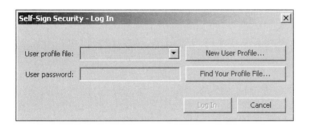

1. Currently, there are no documents open. **Choose Tools > Self-Sign Security > Log In**. This will open the **Self-Sign Security - Log In** dialog box. Click the **New User Profile** button to create your profile. This will open the **Create New User** dialog box.

When you create a user profile, you're generating two main components: a private key and a public key. You need the private key to sign documents. The private key remains on your computer, and accessing it requires a password. You give the public key, referred to as a "certificate," to anyone to whom you may send a signed document. The person receiving the signed PDF uses the public key to validate the authenticity of the signature created with the private key. This may sound complicated, but you'll soon see that Acrobat handles much of this process for you.

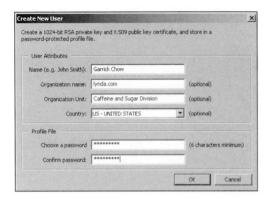

2. In the **Create a New User** dialog box, type your name in the **Name** field. Enter any of the optional information that applies to you. In the **Choose a password** field, type **woodchuck**. Type **woodchuck** once more in the **Confirm password** field. This is the password that will be used to access your profile information any time you want to sign a document. Click **OK**. This will create your profile file, which will need to be saved on your computer. Profile files are recognized by the **.apf** extension.

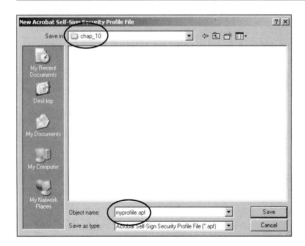

3. Acrobat will ask where you want to save your profile file. You can save your profile anywhere on your computer, but because you'll probably want to create a real profile with your own password later, name this file **myprofile.apf** and save it in the **chap_10** folder on your hard drive. You can delete myprofile.apf when you're done with this book.

Note: In real life, you can leave the default file name (yourname.apf). If a computer has multiple users, each user can create his or her own profile. Therefore, each profile should be uniquely named. Also, if you use Acrobat on more than one computer, you should copy your APF file onto each computer that you use. That way, you'll be able to access your certificate information whenever you want to digitally sign a document.

4. You may or may not see a dialog box indicating that you're now logged in. If you see the dialog box shown here, click **User Settings** to examine the properties of your profile. If you don't see this dialog box, someone has previously checked **Do not show this message again**. If this is the case, choose **Tools > Self-Sign Security > User Settings**. Either method will open the Self-Sign Security - User Settings dialog box.

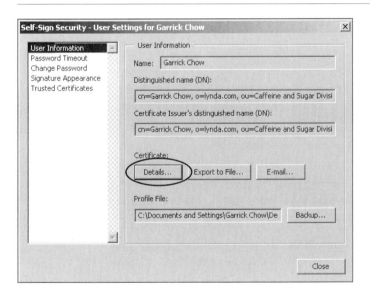

5. In the **Self-Sign Security - User Settings** dialog box, click **User Information** in the left column. This will display a bunch of information that's pretty much gibberish to most mere mortals like you and me. Click the **Details** button to view the **Certificate Attributes** window.

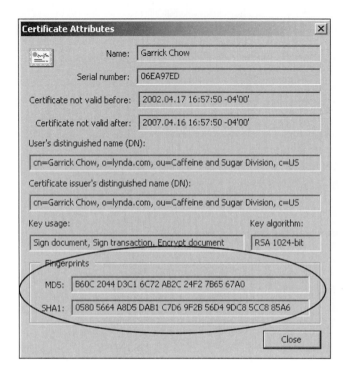

Observe the Fingerprints area. "Fingerprints" is an appropriate title because just as no two people have the same fingerprints, no two users will have the same Fingerprint sequences in their certificates. This is unique information that you will need to digitally sign a document.

When you digitally sign a PDF, you should provide your Fingerprint information to anyone who needs to verify that the signature is in fact yours. To do this, you export your certificate information as an FDF file (which you'll learn to do shortly) to send to your users by e-mail or on disk. After the users receive your certificate, they can then call you on the phone to confirm that the numbers they received match the numbers you sent. If the numbers match, they can add your certificate to their list of Trusted Certificates (which you'll also learn how to do shortly), and from that point on, any document you sign and send to them will automatically be validated as genuine. Without your certificate, users are unable to verify your signature. In the next few steps, you'll export your certificate information.

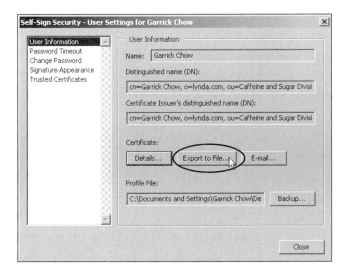

6. Close the Certificate Attributes window. In the **Self-Sign Security - User Settings** dialog box, click the **Export to File** button. This will export your public key as an FDF file.

Note: Alternatively, you could click the E-mail button to automatically attach the FDF file to an e-mail. Clicking the Export to File button, on the other hand, generates a stand-alone file that can be attached to an e-mail message or copied to a disk.

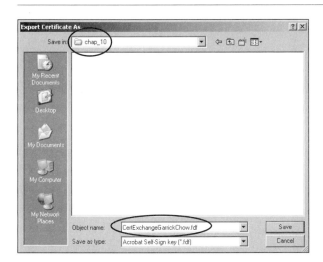

7. Leave the file's default name and save it in the **chap_10** folder. Although you could give the file any name you like, the CertExchange prefix lets you or another user immediately distinguish this file from other FDF files such as exported comments or form field data. You now have a copy of your public key ready for distribution to your users through e-mail or on disk.

After you save your certificate file, Acrobat will display an Export Certificate window listing the two fingerprint strings. These are the numbers contained in the certificate you just exported. After you send the FDF file to a user, it's best to call the recipient of the FDF and verbally confirm that the numbers match. This will foil anyone who might send your user a certificate claiming to be yours. (You can't be too careful these days.) The user can then add the certificate to his or her list of Trusted Certificates. This is analogous to e-mailing someone your shipping addresses and then calling to confirm that the correct information was received.

8. Click **OK** to close the Export Certificate window and then Click **Close** to close the Self-Sign Security - User Settings dialog box. Keep Acrobat open for the next exercise.

4. _____Digitally Signing PDFs

Now that you've created a user profile, you're ready to sign PDF documents should the need arise. In this short exercise, you'll learn how to sign a PDF and see what happens to it after it's been signed.

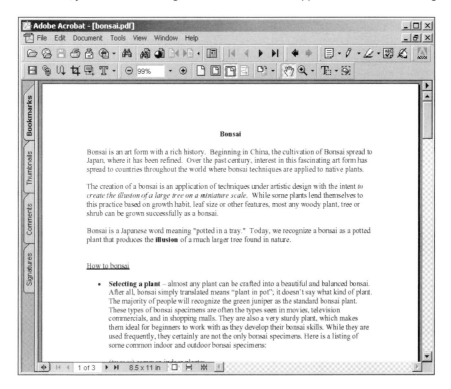

1. Open the file **bonsai.pdf** from the **chap_10** folder.

For this exercise, assume that you've approved this document and now need to digitally sign it.

2. From the Toolbar, select the **Digital Signature** tool. This tool allows you to draw a rectangle to determine how large or small you'd like your signature to appear on the document.

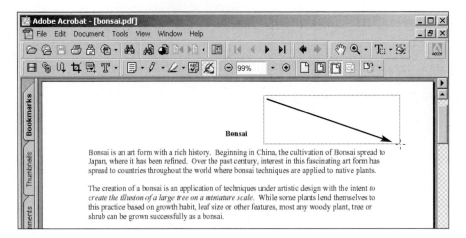

3. Use the Digital Signature tool to draw a rectangle in the upper right-hand corner of the document. You should still be logged in from the last exercise, so when you release the mouse, the **Self-Sign Security - Sign Document** dialog box will open.

Tip: If you happened to have quit Acrobat between the last exercise and this one, you'll get the Log In dialog box instead, prompting you to locate your User Profile File. If this is the case, make sure myprofile.apf (the file you saved in the chap_10 folder) is the User Profile file, and type "woodchuck" as the password. Click Log In.

4. In the **Sign Document** dialog box, confirm your password by typing **woodchuck** in the **Confirm Password** field. Don't click the **Save** button yet! Remember your password is the key to signing your documents. No one but you can sign a document with your signature unless they know your password.

5. You can also explain why you signed the document. Click the **Show Options** button. From the menu under **Reason for signing document**, choose **I am approving this document**. Notice you can also enter your contact information to make it easier for the user to find you and confirm your public key certificate information. Click **Save**. This will save the document with your signature. Note that if you want to keep an unsigned version of the document, you must first save a copy of the document before signing it.

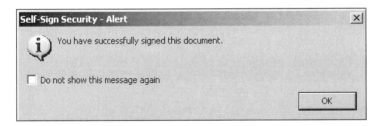

If you get a message saying that you've successfully signed the document, just click OK. As long as you remembered the password, there's really no way to unsuccessfully sign the document at this time.

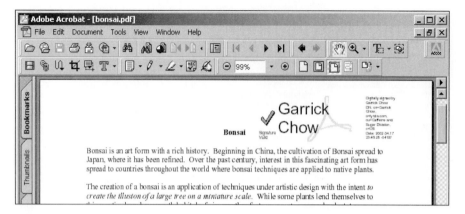

6. Your signature now appears on the document. The signature contains information such as the date and time the document was signed. The checkmark indicates that the signature is valid. Acrobat knows that the signature is valid because the creator of the signature (you) is currently logged in. If you were viewing a document signed by someone else, there would be a question mark next to the name, indicating that the signature had not yet been validated.

7. Click on the signature. The **Self-Sign Security - Validation Status** window will open and tell you that the signature is valid and that the document has not been altered since the signature was applied. One major advantage of working with digital signatures is that Acrobat can keep track of whether a document has been altered after it's been signed. Click the **Close** button.

You can't really get an idea of how to authenticate a signature when you're the one who signed this document. In the next exercise, you'll view a document that was signed by someone else and validate the signature to check for authenticity. You'll also further explore how a PDF document behaves once it's been signed.

8. Save **bonsai.pdf** and close it. Keep Acrobat open for the next exercise.

TIP | Customizing Your Signature

The default appearance of your digital signature is perfectly fine, but if you want to spice up your signature a bit, you can scan in your real longhand signature to use with your digital signature.

Begin by scanning your signature into an image editing program and save the image as a PDF (if you don't know how already, you'll be learning how to create PDFs in Chapter 12, "Acrobat Distiller").

In Acrobat, choose **Tools > Self-Sign Security > User Settings** and select the **Signature Appearance** category in the left column. Click the **New** button to create a new appearance for your signature.

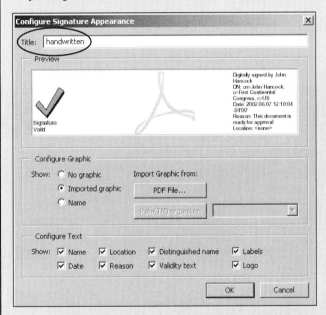

Give your signature appearance a title such as **handwritten**—anything that indicates that this is a longhand version of your signature. In the **Configure Graphic** section click the **Imported graphic** radio button. Click the **PDF File** button to find the PDF of your signature.

Note: If you don't have access to a scanner, you can use the **sample_signature.pdf** file in the **chap_10** folder if you'd like to try importing a PDF signature.

Click **OK** after you've located the signature.

continues on next page

TIP | Customizing Your Signature *continued*

Select the **Digital Signature** tool and draw an area for your signature just like you did in Exercise 4. In the **Sign Document** dialog box, type your password and click the **Show Options** button.

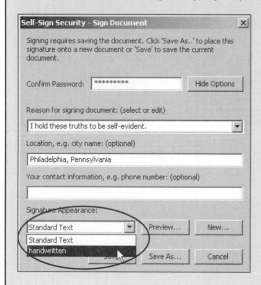

Select your handwritten signature from the **Signature Appearance** menu.

Your digital signature now includes an image of your handwritten signature. Spiffy!

5. ————————————Validating Signatures

In this exercise you'll learn how to authenticate a signature when you receive a digitally signed document.

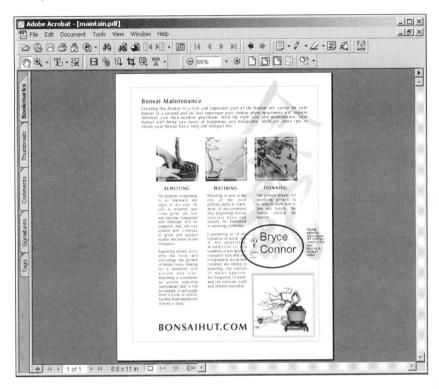

1. Open the file **maintain.pdf** in the **chap_10** folder. This document has been digitally signed. The question mark icon indicates that the signature has not yet been validated.

2. Click the signature to check its status. The **Validation Status** window appears. Acrobat cannot automatically validate this signature because it does not have the proper certificate. Click the **Verify Identity** button.

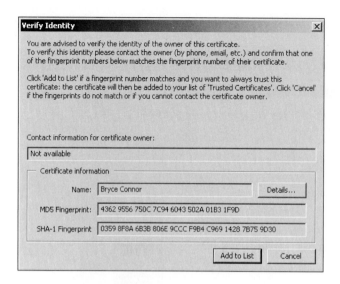

In the Verify Identity dialog box, Acrobat advises you to check with the owner of the certificate to see if his Fingerprint numbers match up with the numbers at the bottom of this dialog box. At this point, you would call or e-mail the owner to confirm the numbers. Pretend you called the owner and that the numbers checked out.

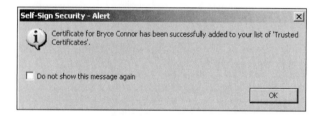

3. Click **Add to List**. Doing so adds this certificate to your Trusted Certificates list. This means that the next time you receive a signed document from this person, Acrobat will remember the certificate and you'll be able to validate the signature without calling the owner of the certificate. Click **OK** to close the Alert window (if it appeared).

4. Acrobat indicates that the signature is valid. Click **Close**.

5. Close this document.

Next, you'll open another PDF signed by the same person to see if Acrobat can authenticate the signature.

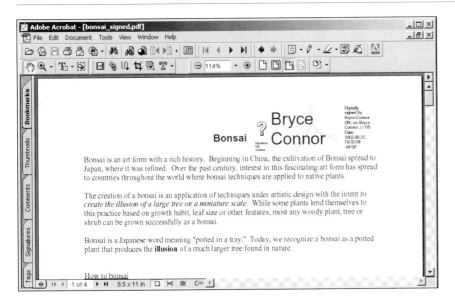

6. Open the file **bonsai_signed.pdf**. This document has been signed, but the signature has not yet been validated. Click on the signature. This makes Acrobat check the signature's certificate.

Because the certificate matches the one you have stored in Acrobat, the signature is determined to be valid.

---

7. Click **Close**, then close **bonsai_signed.pdf**.

As you can see, you can validate any signature as long as you confirm the authenticity of the certificate's Fingerprint string before adding it to your list of Trusted Certificates. In the next steps, you find out exactly where that list is located and learn how to add an FDF file to the list.

---

8. Choose **Tools > Self-Sign Security > User Settings**. This will open the User Settings dialog box for your user profile. From the left column, choose Trusted Certificates.

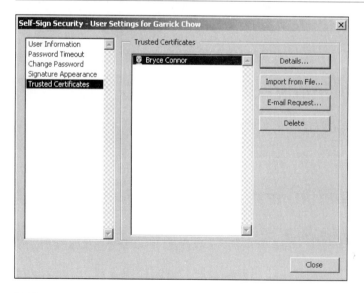

9. Here you can see the certificate you were just working with. Click the Details button.

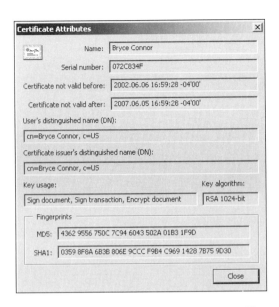

10. This window shows the details of this certificate, including the Fingerprint numbers. Click **Close**.

When you set up your profile earlier in this chapter, you learned how to export your public key information as an FDF file. This FDF file can be sent to any user for them to import into their list of Trusted Certificates. Next, you'll learn how to import an FDF file that I've created into your list of Trusted Certificates.

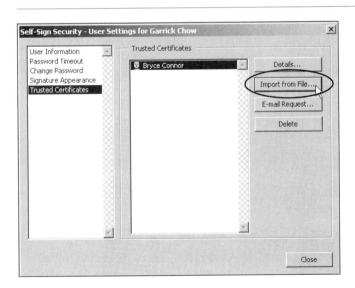

11. In the **User Settings** dialog box, click the **Import from File** button.

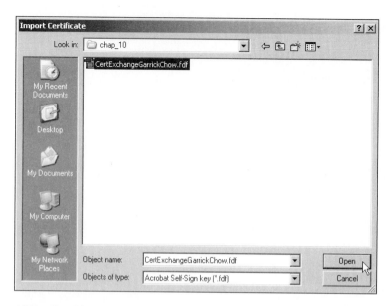

12. In the **chap_10** folder, open the file **CertExchangeGarrickChow.fdf**. This will open the **Verify Identity** window.

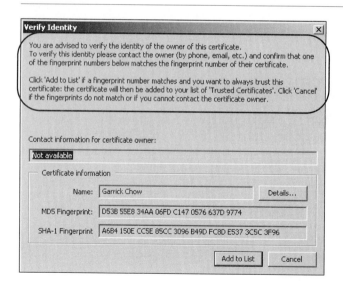

13. At this point you would call me to verify my Fingerprint numbers. But, um, my phone's been disconnected, so you'll just have to trust that this certificate really came from me. Click **Add to List**.

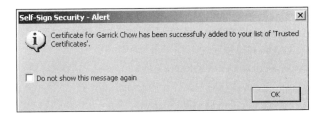

If you see the message above click OK.

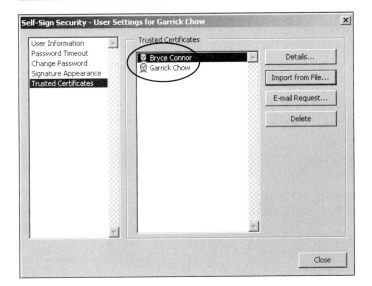

Hey, I look just like Bryce!

My public key has been added to your list of Trusted Certificates. Now you'll open a file I've signed to see if Acrobat can validate my signature.

14. Close the User Settings dialog box. Open the file **bonsai_garrick.pdf** from the **chap_10** folder.

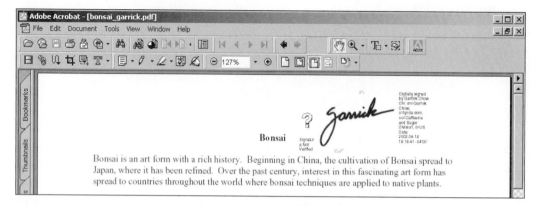

15. I've signed this document, but the question mark indicates that my signature has not been validated yet. Click my signature to have Acrobat authenticate it.

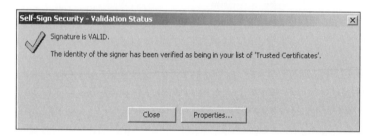

16. Because my signature is among the list of Trusted Certificates, Acrobat determines that the signature is valid. Click **Close**.

Now that this document has been signed and verified, pretend you were some unscrupulous person who wanted to alter this document but have me take the blame. After all, my signature is on it, right? Fortunately, Acrobat can determine if a document has been altered after it's been signed.

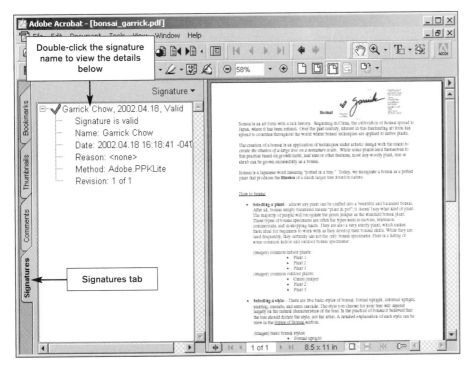

17. Click the **Signatures** tab in the Navigation pane. The Signatures pane lists all the signatures that appear within the document. Double-click my name to view the details of the signature. Everything here seems normal. Now you'll change the document slightly to see what happens.

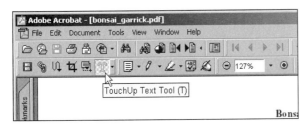

18. Select the **TouchUp Text** tool from the Toolbar.

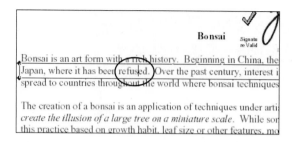

19. Click in the second line of the first paragraph. Change the word **refined** to **refused**. After you've made the change, select the **Hand** tool and click in a blank spot in the margin to deselect the text.

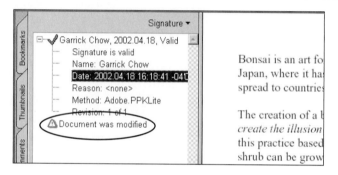

As soon as you make the change, an alert appears in the Signatures panel indicating that the document has been altered. This is helpful, but how are you supposed to know exactly what has been modified? Here's how to find out.

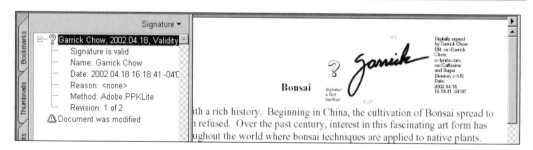

20. Save the file. Because this document is now different than the one I signed, the question mark appears next to my signature again.

When you sign a document, Acrobat takes a "snapshot" of the entire document and remembers it. If the document is altered after it's been signed, Acrobat can still remember what the document looked like at the time the snapshot was taken. This allows you to compare the current document with the one that was signed.

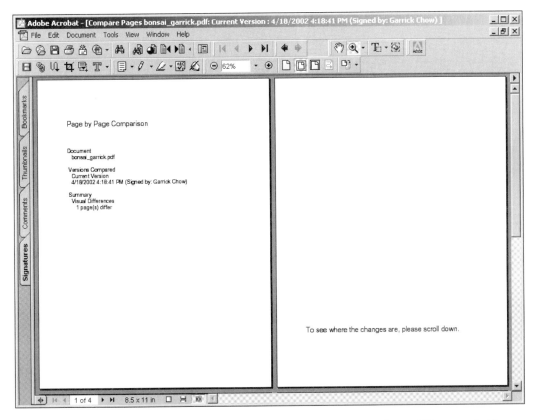

21. Choose **Tools > Digital Signatures > Compare Signed Version to Current Document**. After a moment, Acrobat will generate a brand new PDF containing a page-by-page comparison of the two versions of the document. Scroll down to view the page comparisons.

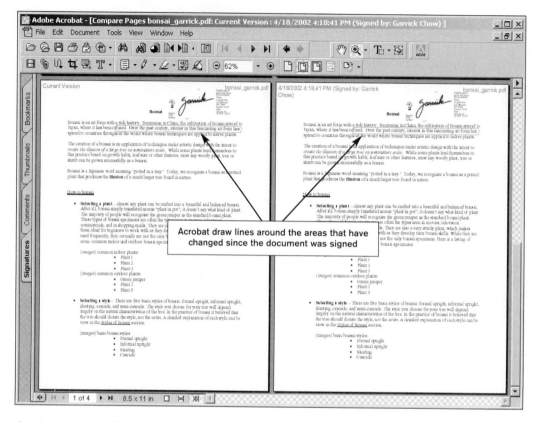

Acrobat has drawn lines around the area where a change has occurred.

22. After you've observed the changes, close this document without saving it. Close **bonsai_garrick.pdf** as well.

NOTE | Comparing Unsigned Documents

A document doesn't have to be signed before you can compare it to another version. If you just want to see what changes have occurred between two copies of the same document, choose **Tools > Compare >Two Documents**.

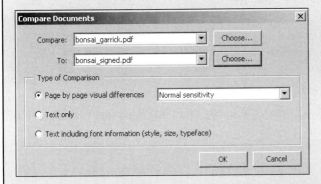

In the **Compare Documents** dialog box you can choose the two documents you want to compare and then select the type of comparison you wish to run. You can choose to view page-by-page visual differences, which is sort of like holding two transparencies up to the light to see if everything matches up. You can determine how sensitive you want Acrobat to be about the visual differences. Alternatively, you can choose to compare text only, or specify that you want to check the text for different font information. This last choice is useful for checking whether anyone has messed with your font choices or wording.

6. _____Acrobat Self-Sign Security

At the beginning of this chapter you learned how to set Acrobat Standard security, which allows you to control permissions for a PDF document. You learned how to apply a password to prevent unauthorized users from opening the PDF. Any user with the proper password can access a file protected by Standard Security. In this exercise, you'll apply Self-Sign Security to a PDF. Self-Sign Security uses your list of Trusted Certificates to control document access. Unlike Standard Security, Self-Sign Security ensures that only specific people can open a PDF. Even if a user has a password, he won't be able to open the PDF unless you've authorized his specific security certificate. Additionally, you can set different permissions for each user, meaning you can distribute a single PDF file to multiple users, but each user will have only the level of access that you have designated for him or her.

1. Open the file **bonsai_2.pdf** from the **chap_10** folder. You will apply Self-Sign Security to this file.

2. Chose **File > Document Security**. This will open the Document Security dialog box (where you set Standard Security at the beginning of the chapter). From the Security Options menu, choose **Acrobat Self-Sign Security**.

If you haven't quit Acrobat during this chapter, you should still be logged in and won't see the above dialog box. If you're not logged in, the Log In dialog box will appear. Enter the password "woodchuck" and click Log In. If you get a message confirming that you're logged in, click OK. Remember, it's possible for multiple people to have their user profiles saved on one computer, so if you quit Acrobat and restart it, you'll have to log in again to prove your identity.

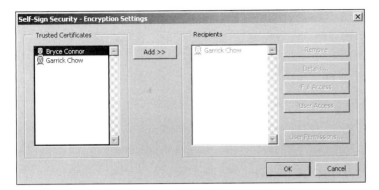

3. The **Self-Sign Security - Encryption Settings** dialog box opens. The left side of the dialog box displays all of your Trusted Certificates. Your own name appears in the Recipients list because you're currently logged in and Acrobat assumes that you trust yourself enough to have access to this file. To add a certificate to the recipients for this particular file, you simple simply select the certificate and click the **Add** button.

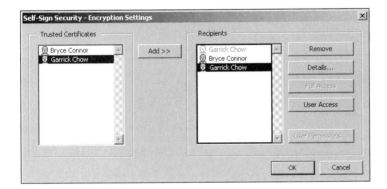

4. Select **Bryce Connor** and click **Add**. Select **Garrick Chow** and click **Add**. Both names now appear in your list of recipients.

The people whose names are listed under Recipients are the only ones who will be able to open this file. Each recipient can only open this file from a computer that has a copy of his security certificate (APF file). So even if the document is intercepted while being sent to a recipient, the file cannot be opened without access to one of the recipient's computers and the recipient's password.

By default, all recipients have Full Access to the PDF. Self-Sign Security gives you the benefit of being able to specify access permissions for each recipient. For instance, you can send a copy of the same PDF to both a colleague and a client, but you can give your colleague full access to edit and print the PDF while limiting the client to viewing the file onscreen only.

If you want to control permission for each user, simply select the recipient's name and click User Access.

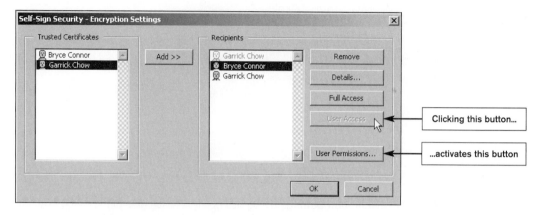

5. Select **Bryce Connor** from the Recipients list, and click **User Access**. This will make the User Permissions button available. Click **User Permissions**. The **User Permissions** dialog box will open.

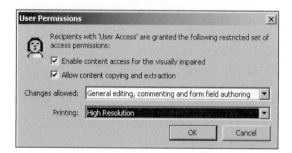

The User Permissions dialog box contains the same permissions settings that you observed for 128-bit Standard Security in the first exercise of this chapter. For this example, assume that you don't want this recipient to be able to print the PDF or to use its contents elsewhere.

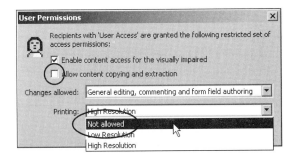

6. Uncheck **Allow content copying and extraction**. From the menu next to **Printing**, choose **Not Allowed**. Click **OK**.

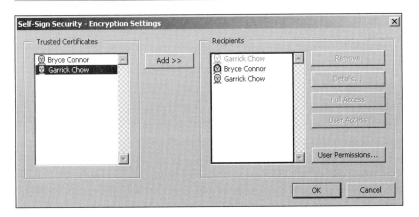

The image next to Bryce Connor has changed to reflect his User Access status. You can contact Adobe if you're outraged that the icon for Full Access appears to be male and the icon for User Access appears to be female. (Both, however, appear to be asleep.)

7. Click **OK**. Close the Document Security dialog box.

8. Save and close **bonsai_2.pdf**.

To test this file, you'll log out of Acrobat.

9. Choose **Tools > Self-Sign Security > Log Out [Your Name]**.

10. Open **bonsai_2.pdf** from the **chap_10** folder. The **Self-Sign Security - Log In** dialog box will appear, alerting you that you must first log in to access this document. Enter **woodchuck** for the user password. Click **OK** if you get a message saying that you're now logged in.

Tip: If you have access to another computer with a copy of Acrobat, you can experiment with this file to see how well Self-Sign Security works. Save bonsai_2.pdf to a disk and try to open it on a computer that doesn't have a copy of your User Profile. You won't be able to do it.

11. Close **bonsai_2.pdf**. Keep Acrobat open for the next exercise.

Acrobat Self-Sign Security gives you extreme flexibility in setting permissions for your documents. Self-Sign Security is also much more secure than Standard Security. This is because Self-Sign Security relies on each user's digital signature, which uses 1024-bit encryption. (For comparison, consider that most secure Web sites use 128-bit encryption.) But don't forget: Documents saved with Self-Sign Security can only be opened with Acrobat 5.

NOTE | Can My PDFs Be Any More Secure?

So you're still not convinced that your documents are as secure as they could be, huh? Well, you've pretty much taken Acrobat 5 to the limits of its security options, but if you're willing to invest more money (a *lot* more money), you could look into a program called Adobe Content Server. Adobe Content Server is a separate application that is used for creating and distributing PDF eBooks. With Content Server, you can "lock" a file onto a computer once it's been down-loaded, meaning that once a user downloads the file, that copy can only be opened from the computer that downloaded it. The user won't be able to copy the file and open it on another computer. You can also instruct a file to stop opening after a set amount of time has elapsed. You can even control how many times the user can print the file. The downside? At the time of publication, Adobe Content Server 2.11 costs $5,000. If that doesn't make you flinch, visit **http://www.adobe.com/products/contentserver/** for more information.

7. ————————Adding a Signature Form Field

Although you can create a signature at any location in your PDF, there will be times when you want
your users to sign your document in a specific spot. For their convenience, you can use the Form tool
to create an area designated for signatures. A **signature form field** allows users to simply click the
field to sign the document, rather than having to select the Digital Signature tool and drawing the signature box themselves.

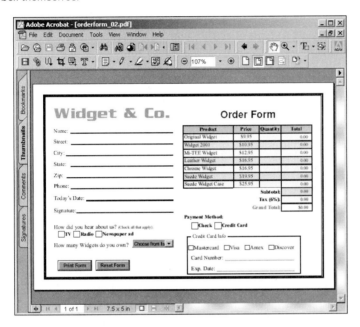

1. Open **orderform_02.pdf** from the **chap_10** folder.

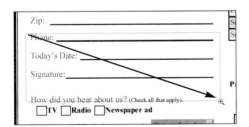

2. Use the **Zoom** tool to enlarge the area where the Signature field is located. It'll be easier
to work with this field at a larger magnification.

*First, you'll get rid of the line that's there for the signature. You'll be adding a box for the
digital signature, so there's no need to have the line as well.*

3. Select the **TouchUp Object** tool from the Toolbar by clicking the **More Tools** arrow next to the **TouchUp Text** tool.

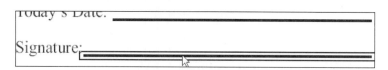

4. With the **TouchUp Object** tool, click the line next to **Signature** to select it. Press the **Delete** key to remove the line from the document.

Now you have a nice blank area for your signature form field.

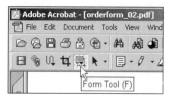

5. Select the **Form** tool from the toolbar. The other form fields on the document will appear.

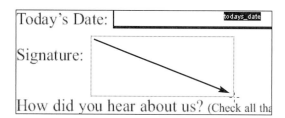

6. Draw a **form field** in the blank area next to **Signature**. Try to draw the form field a little taller than the other fields above it. This will give the digital signature enough room to appear at a reasonable size. When you release the mouse the **Field Properties** dialog box will open.

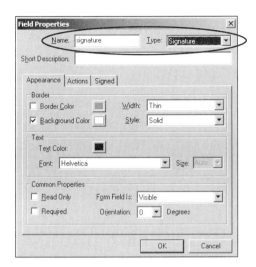

7. Name this field **signature**. For **Type**, choose **Signature**. Click the **Appearance** tab, if it's not already selected.

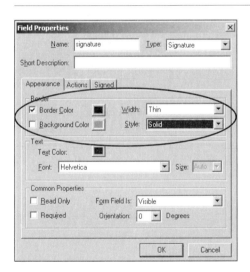

8. Check **Border Color** and select **black** for its color. If **Background Color** is checked, uncheck it. For **Width** choose **Thin** and for **Style** choose **Solid**. These selections will give you a black rectangle for the user's signature.

The other two available tabs in the signature Field Properties dialog box are Actions and Signed. You can associate different actions with the signature by going to the Actions tab, just like you did in Chapter 8, "Forms," when you assigned actions to the Print and Reset buttons. You can also specify certain actions by going to the Signed tab.

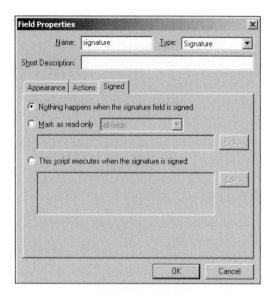

9. Clicked the **Signed** tab. The default selection here is **Nothing happens when the signature field is signed**. The second choice, **Mark as read-only**, will have Acrobat mark the other form fields as read-only once this document has been signed. This useful feature makes it more difficult for someone to alter the document once it's been signed. The third choice in this dialog box allows you to apply a custom JavaScript when the signature field is signed. For this exercise just leave everything the way it is. Click **OK**.

At this point you've finished setting up the signature field. Next, you'll test it. Of course, you wouldn't be signing your own signature field in real life, but you'll do so here to see how the signature field works.

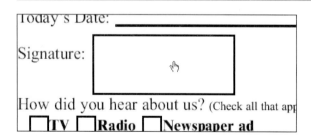

10. Select the **Hand** tool to test your field. Click inside the **signature** field.

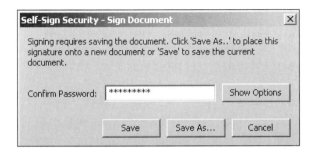

Note: If the dialog box on your screen looks different from the one in the screenshot above, you can click the Hide Options button.

---

11. You will be asked to confirm your password. Type **woodchuck**. (If you're prompted to log in, do so, and then confirm your password.) Click **Save**. If you get a message saying that you've successfully signed the document, click **OK**.

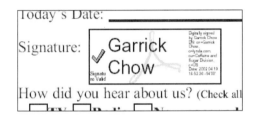

Your signature now appears in the signature field. Of course in real life you wouldn't be signing your own form, but you had to test it, right? That's really all there is to it. Once the signature field has been signed, the signature behaves like any other digital signature. All you did was provide a space for it.

Securing PDF documents was possible in earlier versions of Acrobat, but this feature just keeps getting better. Acrobat 5 is the first version to allow Self-Sign Security. Document security is also becoming more necessary as more and more people and organizations adopt the PDF standard. With more copies of Acrobat 5 out there, there are more people with the tools to mess around with your files. As a general rule, if you don't want your PDF altered in any way, apply security to it.

11.

Creating an Interactive Multimedia Presentation

Adding a Link Action	Creating and Duplicating Form Buttons
Rollover Buttons	Multiple-Action Buttons
Using Page Actions	Adding a Movie
Show/Hide Form Fields	Full Screen Mode

chap_11

Acrobat 5
H•O•T CD-ROM

Not too many people know this, but Acrobat is a wonderful tool for creating interactive multimedia presentations. Displaying a presentation created in Acrobat does not require that the full version of Acrobat be installed on the computer running the presentation. Any computer equipped with Adobe's free Acrobat Reader can run your presentation.

Acrobat's ability to display PDFs in Full Screen mode makes it an ideal presentation tool. Full Screen mode allows you to show your PDF without any of the Acrobat interface elements visible, so your audience sees only the PDF itself. Technically, any PDF displayed in Full Screen mode could be considered a presentation, but by adding a few buttons, form fields, and actions, you can create a presentation that really sets itself apart from your run-of-the-mill PDFs.

In this chapter you'll apply many of the skills you've learned throughout this book. You'll incorporate links, form buttons, page actions, sounds, and movies into your PDF. At the end you'll tie it all together by displaying the PDF in Full Screen mode.

1. _____Adding a Link Action

In this chapter you'll be finishing a partially completed presentation for **bonsaihut.com**. Depending on the purpose of your presentation, you may want to design it so that another user will be able to easily navigate it. In this exercise you'll add a link around an existing button on the first page that will start the presentation.

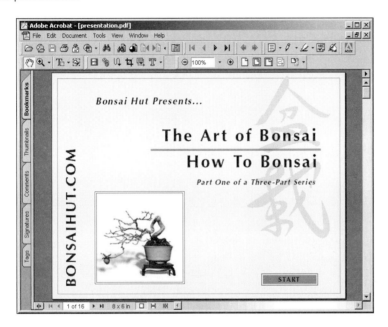

1. Copy the **chap_11** folder and files from the **H•O•T CD-ROM** to your hard drive. Open the file **presentation.pdf** from the **chap_11** folder on your hard drive. This is a partially completed PDF presentation. Take a moment to page through the document to familiarize yourself with its contents and appearance. You may want to select **Fit in Window** to get a better view. When you've finished browsing the PDF, return to the first page.

Tip: Although you'll be using a completed presentation in this chapter, in real life you will often be creating presentations from scratch. Because you'll be displaying your presentation on a computer or projecting it onto a screen, design your pages in landscape layout, meaning that the page is wider than it is tall.

Notice the Start button in the lower right-hand corner of page 1. Unlike the buttons you created from scratch with the Form tool in Chapter 8, "Forms," this button was created at the same time the rest of the document was generated, and is actually part of the document itself. On its own, the button does nothing—clicking it has no effect. You'll add an invisible link around the Start button that, when clicked, will take the user to the next page.

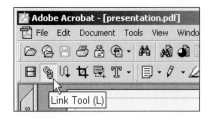

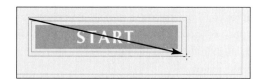

2. Select the **Link** tool and draw a rectangle around the **Start** button. The **Link Properties** dialog box will open.

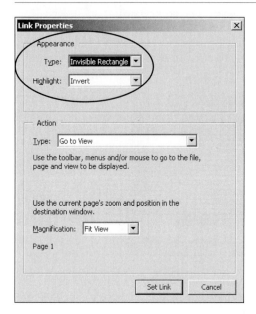

3. In **Link Properties**, set the Appearance **Type** to **Invisible Rectangle**. For **Highlight**, choose **Invert**.

The purpose of this link is to provide an easy way for the user to get to page 2 of the presentation. You could accomplish this by using a Go To View action like you did when you first learned about links in Chapter 3, "Working with Links," but for this exercise, you'll learn a simpler way: the Execute Menu Item action.

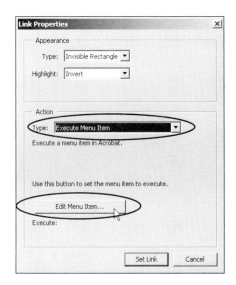

4. For the Action **Type**, choose **Execute Menu Item**. Click the **Edit Menu Item** button that appears.

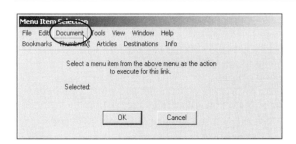

5. Windows: Choose **Document > Next Page** from the **Menu Item Selection** dialog box and click **OK**.

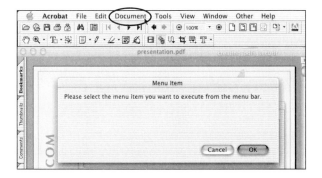

Macintosh: Choose **Document > Next Page** from the menu bar and click **OK** in the **Menu Item** dialog box.

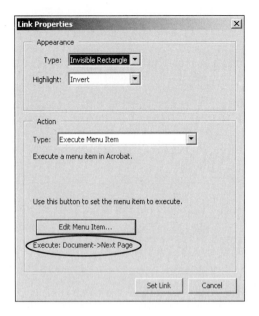

6. Your action is now listed at the bottom of the **Link Properties** dialog box. Click **Set Link**.

7. Select the **Hand** tool to test the link. Click the **Start** button (in actuality, you're clicking the invisible link area, but nobody needs to know that). You're immediately taken to page 2. Save the file and leave this document open for the next exercise.

In this exercise you placed a link over an existing object to take the reader to the next page of your presentation. In the next exercise, you'll learn how to create buttons that did not previously exist within the document. Why create buttons in a presentation, you ask? Think of it this way: After reading the first few chapters of this book, you should have no problem figuring out how to go from page to page in a PDF. But not everyone is going to know how to move from page to page as efficiently as you do. By placing buttons in the presentation, you're enabling all users to navigate it, whether or not they have experience with Acrobat.

2. —————————Creating and Duplicating Form Buttons

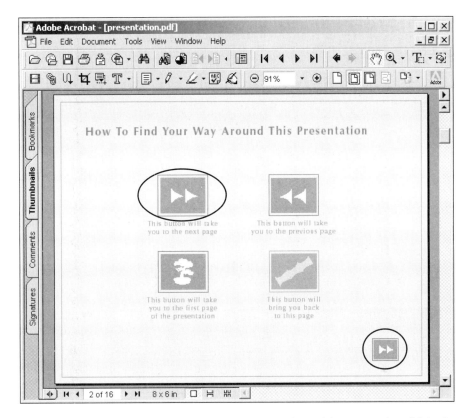

The information on page 2 instructs users how to navigate this presentation. Of the four buttons represented on this page, only one button, the next page button, currently appears within this document.

1. Click the **next page** button in the lower right-hand corner to advance to the next page. Notice that the button appears on this page as well. The button has been inserted into this document on every page but page 1 and page 16, eliminating the need for the user to scroll forward through the document. Return to page 2.

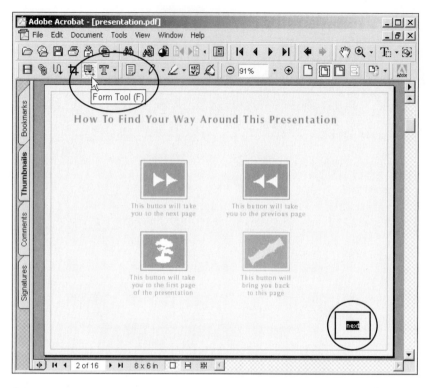

2. Select the **Form** tool from the Toolbar. Notice that the next page button in the lower right-hand corner is actually a form field. Unlike the Start button from the previous exercise, this button was created after the PDF was generated and was not part of the original document.

Tip: You may begin to wonder whether it's better to create buttons in your original document with the intention of adding a link around it in Acrobat, or whether it's better leave a blank area on the page and then use the Form tool to generate your buttons in Acrobat. There's no hard and fast rule, but you'll often find that it's much quicker to use the Form tool to create your buttons when you need to place the same button on multiple pages. As you'll see at the end of this exercise, once a Form button has been created on a page, it's a simple matter to duplicate it onto other pages. Links have no such capability, so if you want to create buttons while authoring your original document, you should just create the buttons that only appear once in the document (like the Start button on the first page of this presentation).

You will add the remaining three buttons to each page of the document. Don't worry—this isn't nearly as tedious as it sounds.

Before you begin, you will turn on Acrobat's layout grid. You can use the layout grid to help you maintain consistency in the size and alignment of your form fields.

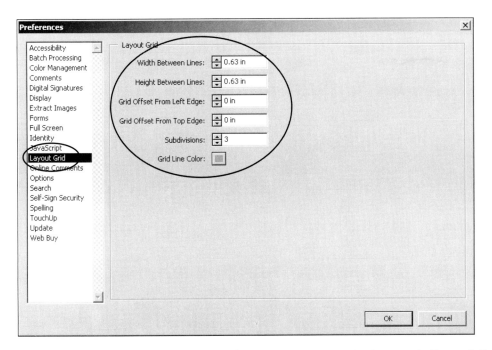

3. Choose **Edit > Preferences > General** (Mac OS X: **Acrobat > Preferences > General**). From the categories on the left side of the **Preferences** dialog box, choose **Layout Grid**. Set the **Width Between Lines** to **0.63 in** and **Height Between Lines** to **0.63 in** as well. **Grid Offset From Left Edge** and **Grid Offset From Top Edge** should both be set to **0** and **Subdivisions** should be set to **3**. Click **OK**.

Note: I experimented with different widths and height settings to determine the preferences for the layout grid that you just set. If you plan to use the layout grid for your own work, you too will have to experiment with several different settings before arriving at your own ideal grid widths and heights.

4. Choose **View > Grid** to display the grid lines. You can use the grid lines to visually size and align your form fields to intersecting points on the grid. For even more consistency, choose **View > Snap to Grid**. Snap to Grid makes it impossible to draw your fields anywhere outside the intersecting points of the grid.

Tip: If you find the grid lines too distracting in your own work, you can turn them off by choosing View > Grid. Your form fields will still snap to the grid points even if the lines are not visible. For the purposes of this exercise, however, keep the grid visible.

5. Select the **Form** tool from the Toolbar. If the **next** form field looks like it doesn't quite match up with the layout grid, single-click the field. This will make it snap to the nearest grid points.

Now you're ready to create your first form field button. You'll create the previous page button using the form tool and you'll learn how to place an image inside a form field. Placing an image inside a form field makes for a more visually interesting button—unlike the plain-text buttons you created in Chapter 8, "Forms."

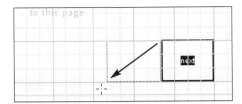

6. Place the **Form** tool slightly to the left of the upper left-corner of the **next** form field. Make sure your cursor is a crosshair and not a double-headed arrow. Draw a field to the left that's four squares wide by three squares tall. Use the picture above as a reference. When you release the mouse, the **Field Properties** dialog box will open.

 MOVIE | formbuttons.mov

To learn more about creating form buttons, check out **formbuttons.mov** located in the **movies** folder on the Acrobat 5 **H•O•T CD-ROM**.

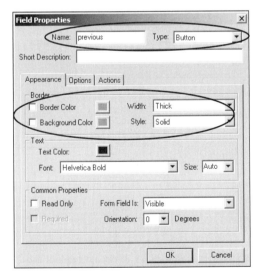

7. Name this field **previous** and set **Type** to **Button**. Under the **Appearance** tab, make sure **Border Color** and **Background Color** are both unchecked. Since you'll be adding a picture to this form field, there's no reason to have a border or background color. For the **Width** choose **Thick**. Thick is an arbitrary choice, but it does affect how the image in this field will be sized. You're selecting Thick here because the **next page** button is also set to Thick and you want your buttons to be consistent. Make sure **Style** is set to **Solid**. Click the **Options** tab.

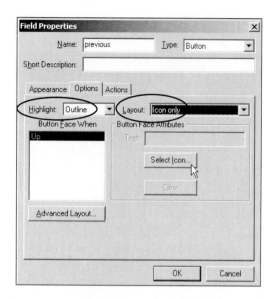

8. Under the **Options** tab, set the **Highlight** to **Outline**. This will make a dark outline appear momentarily around the button when it's clicked. From the **Layout** pop-up menu, select **Icon only**. This indicates that you only want to place an image in this field and do not want to provide any accompanying text. Now you're ready to select the icon for this button. Click **Select Icon**. The **Select Appearance** dialog box will open.

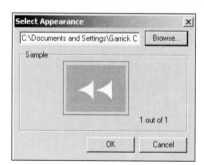

9. Click **Browse** to locate the image. Open the **Buttons** folder in the **chap_11** folder and select the **back.pdf** file. Click **OK** to return to the Field Properties dialog box.

Important Note: In order to place an image inside a form field, the image must be in PDF format. No other image format will be accepted. In this exercise, the images have been created for you. When creating your own images, remember to convert them to PDFs before attempting to insert them. (You'll learn to create PDFs in the next three chapters.)

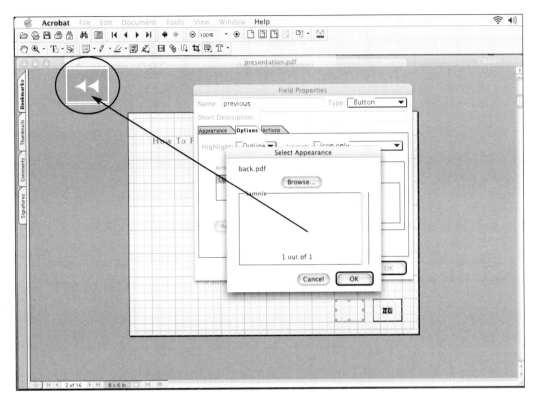

Note: *In Mac OS X you may encounter a glitch when selecting the back.pdf image. The preview of the PDF should appear in the Select Appearance dialog box, but may instead appear in the upper left-hand corner of your screen for some odd reason. This won't cause a problem with selecting the file though, so just click OK if this happens while you're working through the rest of this chapter.*

10. The **Field Properties** dialog box now displays the image you selected for the button. Click **OK** to exit Field Properties. Select the **Hand** tool to view your button.

The previous page button now appears on the page and should be the same size as the next page button. Clicking the previous page button will make the border appear around the button, but nothing else happens. You'll now add an action to this field that will take users to the previous page when they click the button.

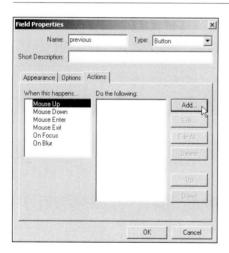

11. Select the **Form** tool and double-click the **previous** form field to open its **Field Properties** again. Click the **Actions** tab. In the Actions tab, under **When this happens...** select **Mouse Up**. (You worked with the Actions tab in Chapter 8, *"Forms,"* so this should be somewhat familiar.) Click **Add**. The **Add an Action** dialog box will open.

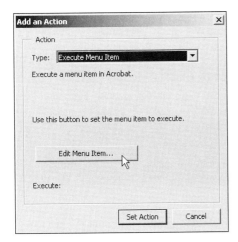

12. Select **Execute Menu Item** for the **Type** and click **Edit Menu Item**.

- **Windows:** From the **Menu Item Selection** dialog box, choose **Document > Previous Page.**
  Click **OK**.

- **Macintosh:** From the menu bar, choose **Document > Previous Page.** Click **OK**.

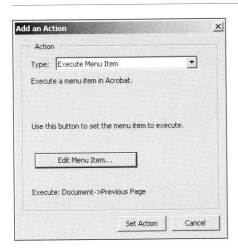

13. Click **Set Action** and **OK** to close the Field Properties dialog box.

14. Select the **Hand** tool and click the **previous page** button. You are immediately taken to page 1. Click the **Start** button there to return to page 2.

Now that you've successfully created the previous page button on page 2, you need to place it on the remaining pages of the presentation. If you're getting paid by the hour, this can offer an easy way to make some extra income. But for now, assume that you want to finish this exercise before the end of the month. Instead of manually recreating the button on every page, you'll duplicate it using a simple menu command.

15. Select the **Form** tool and single-click the **previous page** button to select it. Choose **Tools > Forms > Fields > Duplicate**. The **Duplicate Field** dialog box will open.

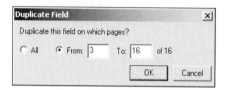

16. In the **Duplicate Fields** dialog box click the radio button next to **From**. Because you don't need the previous page button on the first page, and since it already exists on page 2, enter **3** to **16** as the range of pages. Click **OK**.

17. Select the **Hand** tool and click the **next page** button a few times. Notice that the previous page button now appears on pages 3 through 16. Click the **previous page** button on each page until you return to page 2 (or just scroll to page 2 if you get the idea).

18. Save the file and keep it open for the next exercise.

3. —————————Adding a Home Button

In this exercise, you'll use the same techniques you learned in the previous exercise to add a home button to this presentation. Additionally, you'll make this a **rollover button**, meaning that the button will provide visual feedback when the user's mouse enters the field.

You should still be on page 2 of the presentation, and the layout grid should still be visible.

1. Select the **Form** tool. Place the crosshair next to the upper left-hand corner of the **previous** form button and draw a new form field to the left that's four grid squares wide and three grid squares tall.

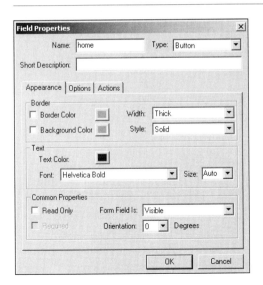

2. In the **Field Properties** dialog box that appears, name this field **home** and set **Type** to **Button**. Under the **Appearance** tab, make sure both **Border Color** and **Background Color** are unchecked. Set **Width** to **Thick** and **Style** to **Solid**. Click the **Options** tab.

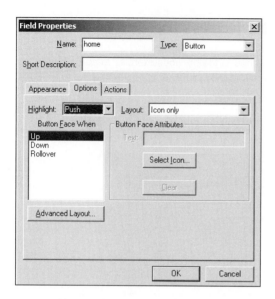

3. Set **Highlight** to **Push**. Selecting Push will make more options appear under the **Button Face When** area below the Highlight menu. Set **Layout** to **Icon only**. Make sure **Up** is selected. This means that you'll be selecting the icon that will appear in the form field when the button is not being clicked (known as its Up state). Click **Select Icon** to open the **Select Appearance** dialog box. Click **Browse** to find the image file.

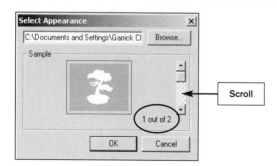

4. Locate the file **tree.pdf** in the **Buttons** folder in **chap_11** and select it. In the Select Appearance dialog box, notice that this is a two-page document. You can scroll to see that the second page contains a variation of the tree image. After you've seen both images, scroll to page **1 out of 2** and click **OK**.

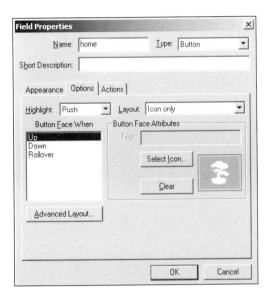

You've set the appearance of the button's Up state. Now you'll set the appearance for its Rollover state.

NOTE | Button Face Appearances

When Push is selected as the Highlight style for a form field button, you can add text and/or images for three different states. The chart below describes these different states.

States for Button Face Appearance	
Button State	**Description**
Up	Determines how the button will appear before the user clicks or rolls the mouse cursor over the field
Down	Determines how the button will appear when the user clicks on the field
Rollover	Determines how the button will appear when the user rolls the cursor into the field area

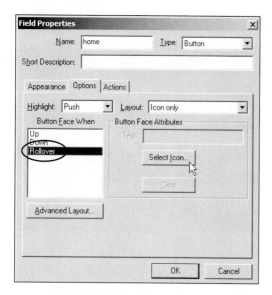

5. Under **Button Face When** select Rollover. Click **Select Icon**.

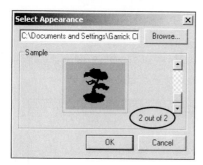

6. The **tree.pdf** image should still be in the **Select Appearance** dialog box. Scroll to page **2 out of 2** and click **OK**.

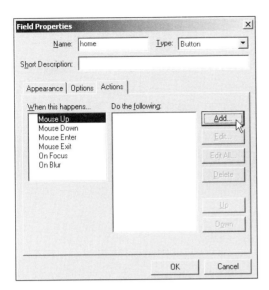

7. Before viewing your button, you'll add the appropriate action. Click the **Actions** tab. This button should return the user to the first page of the presentation. Select **Mouse Up** and click **Add** to select the action.

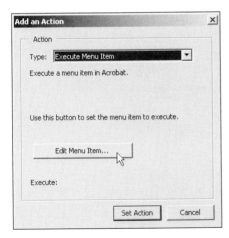

8. In the **Add an Action** dialog box, select **Execute Menu Item** for the **Type** and click **Edit Menu Item**.

   • **Windows:** From the **Menu Item Selection** dialog box, choose **Document > First Page**. Click **OK**.

   • **Macintosh:** From the menu bar, select **Document > First Page**. Click OK.

9. Click **Set Action** to close the Add an Action dialog box, and then click **OK** to exit the Field Properties dialog box.

10. Select the **Hand** tool to test your button. Place the Hand tool over the **tree** button. Notice that it changes into the second image as soon as your mouse enters the field area. Click the button. You are taken to page 1.

11. Return to page 2. You need to duplicate this button across the remaining pages.

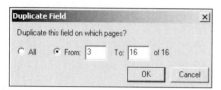

12. Select the **Form** tool and single-click the **home** form field. Choose **Tools > Forms > Fields > Duplicate**. In the **Duplicate Field** dialog box, click the radio button next to **From** and duplicate the button from page **3** to page **16**. Click **OK**.

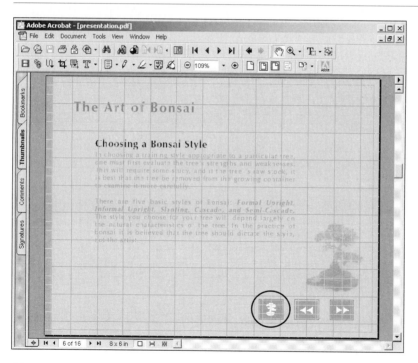

13. Select the **Hand** tool and click forward through the presentation. The **home** button should appear on each page.

14. Return to page 2. Save the file and keep it open for the next exercise.

4. _____Adding a Multiple-Action Button

So far, you've created two buttons in this presentation. Next, you'll add the final button. When clicked, the flute button will return the user to page 2, which is the help page for this document. In addition to adding an action that will bring the user to this page, you'll also learn to add an action that plays a sound when the button is clicked.

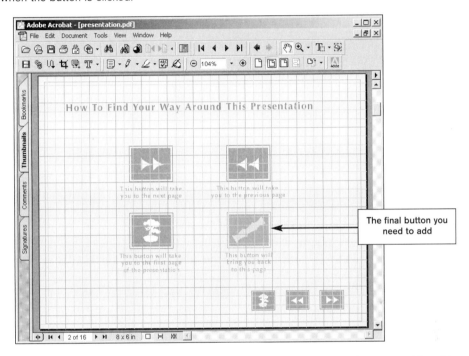

The final button you need to add

1. You should be on page 2. The flute button is supposed to return the user to this guide page. Therefore, there's no need to add that button to this page. Click forward to page **3**.

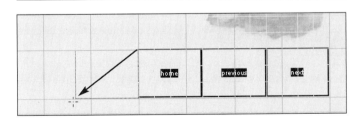

2. Select the **Form** tool. Place the crosshair next to the upper left-hand corner of the home form field. Draw down and to the left to create a field four grid squares wide by three grid squares tall (just like you did in the two previous exercises).

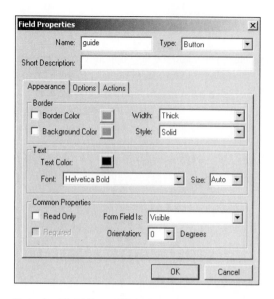

3. In the **Field Properties** dialog box, name this field **guide** and make sure **Type** is set to **Button**. Under the **Appearance** tab, make sure both **Border Color** and **Background Color** are unchecked. Set the **Width** to **Thick** and the **Style** to **Solid**. Click the **Options** tab.

4. For **Highlight**, select **Push**. For **Layout** choose **Icon only**. Under **Button Face When**, make sure **Up** is selected. Click **Select Icon**.

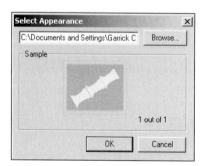

5. In the **Select Appearance** dialog box, browse for the file **flute_up.pdf** in the **Buttons** folder inside the **chap_11** folder. Click **OK** to return to the Field Properties dialog box.

6. Under **Button Face When** select **Rollover**. Click **Select Icon**.

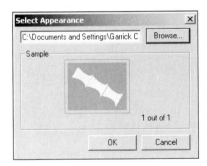

7. In the **Select Appearance** dialog box, browse for the file **flute_over.pdf**, located in the **Buttons** folder inside the **chap_11** folder. Click **OK** to return to Field Properties.

Note: In the previous exercise, both images for the home button were part of the same PDF file as a two-page document. In this example, two separate files are being used. It doesn't matter whether the images are all part of one PDF or if they're contained in individual files. As long as they're PDFs, you can have as many separate files as you like.

Now you'll add the action to the button that will take the user to page 2 (the help page) of the presentation. Unfortunately, there is no menu command to take the user to a specific page, so you won't be able to add an Execute Menu Item action like you did previously. Instead, you'll add a JavaScript action.

8. Click the **Actions** tab. Select **Mouse Up** and click **Add** to add your action.

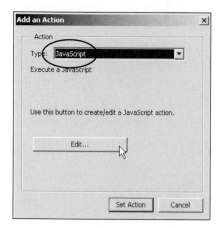

9. For the action **Type**, select **JavaScript**. Click **Edit**.

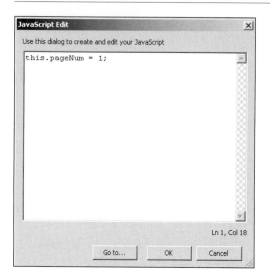

10. In the **JavaScript Edit** dialog box, type the following code exactly as it appears here:

   this.pageNum = 1;

Make sure you capitalize the N and include the spaces on either side of the =. This simple JavaScript instructs Acrobat to go to page 2 of the document (Acrobat considers the first page to be page 0; therefore, the second page is represented as 1 here). Remember to use this little snippet of code if you ever need to take the reader to a specific page of a PDF. Click OK after you've typed the code.

Note: *If you're interested in reading more (a lot more) about JavaScript, choose Help > Acrobat JavaScript Guide.*

11. In the **Add an Action** dialog box, click **Set Action**, then click **OK** to close Field Properties.

12. Thankfully, you won't need the grid anymore. Choose **View > Grid** to hide the layout grid. You can leave **Snap to Grid** selected for now.

13. Select the **Hand** tool to test your button. Roll over the button to see the image change. Click the button to be taken to page 2. If the button doesn't take you to page 2, go back and make sure that you entered the JavaScript properly.

14. Return to page **3**. Before you duplicate this button, you'll add an additional action that will play a sound when the button is clicked. One advantage of using form fields for your buttons is the ability to add multiple actions. Select the **Form** tool and double-click the **guide** form field (the flute button) to open its **Field Properties** again.

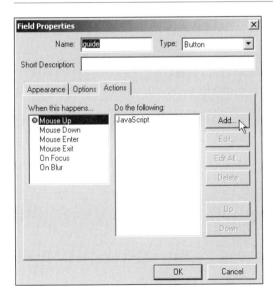

15. In the **Actions** tab, select **Mouse Up** and click **Add** to add another action.

16. In the **Add an Action** dialog box, choose **Sound** as the **Type**. Click **Select Sound**. Browse through the **Sounds** folder inside the **chap_11** folder and select the file **flute_quick.aif**. Click **Set Action**.

Note: When you add a sound to a PDF, Acrobat embeds the sound file into the PDF. This means that you don't have to include the sound file separately when you copy or distribute the PDF. It also means that the file size of the PDF will increase based on the size of the sound file.

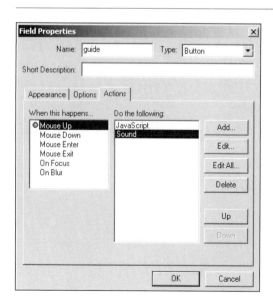

You now have two actions listed under the Actions tab for Mouse Up. Because you'll want this sound to play before the JavaScript executes, you'll change the order of the Actions.

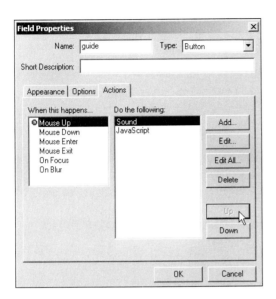

17. With **Sound** selected, click the **Up** button on the right of the **Field Properties** dialog box. Now the sound will begin to play before Acrobat jumps to page 2. You won't really notice much of a difference in this exercise, but if you ever have a form field with several actions applied, remember that actions execute in the order in which they're listed. Click **OK**.

18. Select the **Hand** tool. Click the **flute** button to test it. The sound should play and you should be taken to page 2.

You're finally ready to duplicate this button.

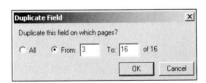

19. Return to page **3**, select the **Form** tool, and single-click the **guide** form field. Choose **Tools > Forms > Fields > Duplicate**. In the **Duplicate Field** dialog box, click the radio button next to **From** and duplicate the button from page **3** to page **16**. Click **OK**.

20. Select the **Hand** tool and page through the document to view your duplicated button. Return to page **3** when you're done. Save the file and keep it open for the next exercise.

NOTE | Sound File Formats

Of course, in order to add a sound file to your PDF, you have to acquire the sound from somewhere. You can create sounds by recording them directly on your computer with a microphone and sound editing software, or you can find sounds on the Internet. The two sound file formats that are accepted by Acrobat are AIFF and WAV. Apple's QuickTime Pro (**www.apple.com/quicktime**) can convert nearly any sound file into one of these two formats. Sounds can only be played if the computer running the PDF has a media player installed, such as QuickTime or Windows Media Player (**www.microsoft.com/mediaplayer**).

5. _____Playing a Sound with a Page Action

Another way to enhance your presentations is through the use of **Page Actions**. Page Actions allow you assign an action to a specific page, rather than to a form field, link area, or bookmark. You can specify whether you want the actions to occur when the page opens or when the page closes. In this exercise, you'll assign a page to play a sound when the page is opened.

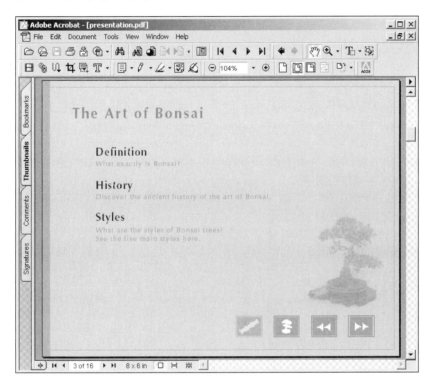

1. Go to page **3** of **presentation.pdf**. This page begins the section **The Art of Bonsai**. You'll add a short sound clip to this page that will play whenever this page is opened.

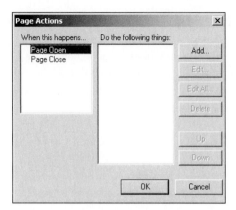

2. Choose **Document > Set Page Action**. This will open the **Page Actions** dialog box, which looks similar to the Actions tab in the form Field Properties dialog box you've been working with throughout this chapter. Here you can assign an action to either Page Open or Page Close. Just like adding actions to Form fields, you can assign multiple actions to either event. In this case, you'll just have the page play a sound when it opens.

3. With **Page Open** selected, click **Add**. In the **Add an Action** dialog box, select **Sound** as the **Type** of action and click **Select Sound**. From the **Sounds** folder inside the **chap_11** folder, select the file **flutes.wav**. Click **Set Action**.

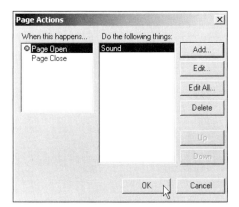

4. Back in the **Page Actions** dialog box, click **OK**.

5. Test your page action by clicking the **next page** button and clicking the **previous page** button to return to page 3. The sound plays. Lovely, isn't it?

Tip: Adding a page action to play a sound is a great way to spice up your presentation. If you have a long piece of music, for example, you could create an action to play the music starting from the first page. The music will continue to play as the users page through the document. Keep in mind, though, that the sound file is embedded, so a long piece of music will increase the overall file size of your PDF. This isn't really a problem if the presentation is being viewed from a CD-ROM, but it can make for a long download for someone accessing the PDF from the Web. Also, once a sound file begins to play, there is no way to stop it other than quitting Acrobat. (I don't know about you, but more than a few practical jokes involving loud sound effects spring to my mind right away.) Throughout the rest of this exercise, the sound you just added will play any time page 3 is opened. If this gets to be too annoying, go to page 3, choose Document > Set Page Action, and delete the page action.

6. ———————Adding a Movie

One of the most visually exciting elements you can add to your PDF is a movie. Everyone loves movies. With their ability to combine sound and video, movies are a great way to reinforce ideas or to demonstrate techniques that are difficult to describe. (See the movie understanding_the_intro_paragraph.mov if you don't understand this. Just kidding.) In this exercise, you'll add a short movie clip to this presentation.

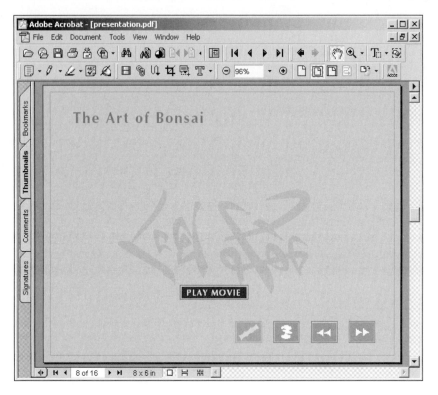

1. Go to page **8** of **presentation.pdf**. A blank space has been left on this page where you will place the movie that has been created for this presentation.

NOTE | Before You Continue with This Exercise...

Prior to you adding the movie to this page, it's important to understand some key points about incorporating video content into your PDFs. Before you can import video, you must have Apple QuickTime 3.0 or later installed on your system. Typically, Macintosh users will already have QuickTime installed as part of their operating system. Windows users must make sure they install QuickTime from Acrobat's CD-ROM (or the Acrobat **H•O•T CD-ROM**). Once you have QuickTime installed, you can import any type of file format supported by QuickTime, such as MOV, MPEG, SWF, and AVI.

In order for your audience to view the movie, they too must have QuickTime 3.0 or later installed on their systems. Otherwise, they will be unable to view the movie (they will be able to open and view the rest of the document, though). Note that while QuickTime can decode most movie files, it has trouble decoding some forms of AVIs. If you want to be sure that your movie is compatible across platforms, your best bet is to save the movie as either a QuickTime MOV file or an MPEG file. You can use programs like Adobe Premiere or Apple's free iMovie to convert your video footage into MOV files.

Also note that, unlike sound files, movie files are not embedded into the PDF when you add them to your document. Instead, a relative link is created between the PDF and the movie file. Therefore, when you distribute or copy the PDF, the movie file must accompany the PDF and the two files must maintain the same relative relationship.

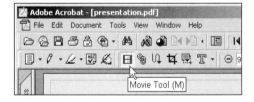

2. Select the **Movie** tool from the Toolbar. (It's grouped with the Editing tools and located to the left of the Link tool.)

3. Place the crosshair in the center of the two characters in the middle of the page, near the top of the characters (use the screenshot above as a guide). Click once. This will open the **Movie Properties** dialog box.

Note: Be sure that you just click once with the Movie tool—don't drag out a rectangle. Because it's unlikely that you'll drag the rectangle to the exact dimensions of the movie, you'll probably make the rectangle too large or too small, which can affect the appearance of the movie. Clicking with the Movie tool will import the movie in its native dimensions.

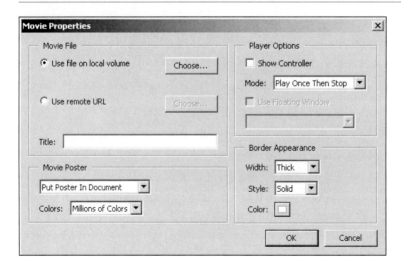

4. In the **Movie Properties** dialog box, click the radio button next to **Use file on local volume**. This tells Acrobat that you're going to be using a movie on your computer, rather then from a remote server. Click **Choose** to locate the file. Select the file **bonsai.mov** from the **movies** folder located inside the **chap_11** folder.

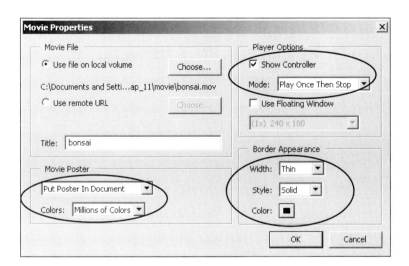

5. Back in the **Movie Properties** dialog box, select **Put Poster In Document** from the menu under **Movie Poster**. This will place the first frame of the movie onto the page to act as a placeholder and hotspot. From the **Colors** pop-up menu choose **Millions of Colors**. This will display the poster in 24-bit color, which will look better than just 256 colors. Under **Player Options**, check **Show Controller**. This will allow the user to start, pause, or scroll through the movie file. For **Mode**, choose **Play Once Then Stop**, which will make the movie play just once. Finally, under **Border Appearance**, choose **Thin** for **Width**, **Solid** for **Style**, and **Black** for **Color**. This will place a thin black border around the movie. Click **OK**.

Note: Refer to the chart at the end of this exercise for more information about the options in the Movie Properties dialog box.

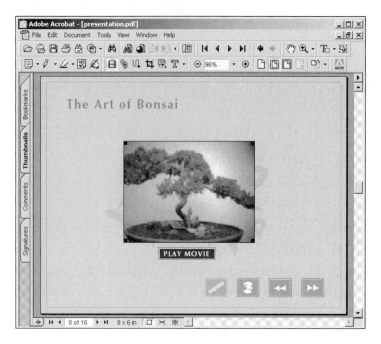

Because you checked Put Poster In Document, the first frame of the movie now appears on the page. At this point, if you'd like to adjust the position of the movie frame, you can click on it and drag it. Also, you could adjust the dimensions of the movie by dragging any of the corner handles, but you should avoid doing this unless you absolutely need to. The movie will maintain its correct aspect ratio when you drag its corners, but if you make the movie larger than its native size, it will look very pixelated when it plays. It's best to have your movie sized to your desired dimensions before bringing it into Acrobat.

6. Select the **Hand** tool to test the movie. When you place the Hand tool over the movie, the cursor will change into the Movie icon. Click the movie. Sit back and enjoying learning more about bonsai trees than you ever thought you would learn from a computer book.

Note: *While the movie is playing, the controller will show up at the bottom of the movie. If the controller overlaps the Play Movie button, simply select the Movie tool, click once on the movie to select it, and drag it up slightly.*

The author of this document anticipated that not everyone would know that clicking on a movie poster with the Hand tool will play the movie. You're going to add a link around the Play Movie button, so that anyone who can read English will know how to play the movie.

7. After the movie has finished playing, click anywhere outside of it to deselect it (which will also hide the controller). Also, choose **View > Snap to Grid** to turn that feature off. This will allow you to draw a more precise link area.

8. Select the **Link** tool and draw a link area around the **Play Movie** button.

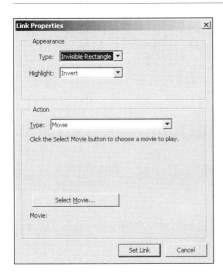

9. In the **Link Properties** dialog box, set the Appearance **Type** to **Invisible Rectangle** and the **Highlight** to **Invert**. For the Action **Type**, select **Movie**. Click the **Select Movie** button.

10. In the **Movie Action** dialog box, select **Play** from the menu next to **Select Operation**. Click **OK**.

NOTE | Movie Action Dialog Box Options

The chart below describes the movie actions offered in the Movie Action dialog box.

Movie Action Dialog Box Options	
Option	**Description**
Play	Plays the movie from the beginning
Stop	Stops the movie and sends the playback head back to the beginning of the movie
Pause	Stops the playback head wherever it happens to be in the movie
Resume	Restarts the movie from the point where the playback head was paused

---

11. Click **Set Link** to close the **Link Properties** dialog box.

12. Select the **Hand** tool and click the **Play Movie** button to test it.

13. If you feel like watching the bonsai movie again, go ahead. Otherwise, click outside the movie to stop it.

14. Save the file and keep it open for the next exercise.

Tip: *If you wanted to add buttons to stop, pause, and resume the movie, you could do so with the Form tool by drawing form field buttons and adding actions to them. This opens the possibilities to create your own controller artwork and custom interface, using the same techniques you've already learned in this chapter.*

Movie Properties Dialog Box Options

In this exercise, you learned how to insert a movie into your PDF. The chart on the follwing pages describes the various options that are available in the Movie Properties dialog box.

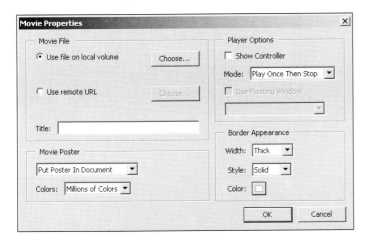

Movie Properties Dialog Box Options	
Item	**Description**
Movie Poster	**Don't Show Poster:** Does not place an image of the movie's first frame into the document. The movie area will not contain anything indicating that a movie is present in that location of the page. Choosing **256 colors** or **Millions of Colors** has no effect when this option is selected.
	Put Poster In Document: Places the first frame of the movie into the document. When this selection is chosen, you can use the **Colors** menu to choose to display this poster in either **256 colors** or **Millions of Colors**.
	Retrieve Poster From Movie: Also places the first frame of the movie into the document, but when this choice is selected, it uses the color depth used in the movie file itself. Choosing **256 colors** or **Millions of Colors** has no effect when this option is selected.

continues on next page

Movie Properties Dialog Box Options *continued*	
Item	**Description**
Player Options	**Show Controller:** When checked, displays the controller at the bottom of the movie while the movie is playing, allowing users to play, pause, stop, scroll, and adjust the movie's volume.
	Place Once, Then Stop: After the movie plays, it stops and closes.
	Play Once, Stay Open: After the movie plays, it stops but stays open on the last frame.
	Repeat Play: After the movie reaches the end, it loops back and plays from the beginning again. It continues to play until the user stops it manually.
	Back and Forth: After the movie reaches the end, it plays in reverse back to the beginning. When it reaches the beginning, it plays forward again and so on until the user stops the movie manually.
	Use Floating Window: When checked, the movie will open in its own window, separate from the document. The dimensions of the floating window can be chosen from the pop-up menu below this option.
Border Appearance	**Width:** Determines the thickness of the border around the movie. **Style:** You may select either a solid border or a dashed border. **Color:** Determines the color of the border.

7. _____Show/Hide Form Fields

Another action that can be added to form fields is the **Show/Hide Field** action. This action allows you to display or conceal certain fields to create a truly interactive experience. Showing and hiding fields is useful in a presentation where you might not want to display all of the information about a subject right away. For instance, you might pose a question to the audience and let them ponder it a moment before revealing the answer. In this exercise you'll add several Show/Hide Field actions to this presentation.

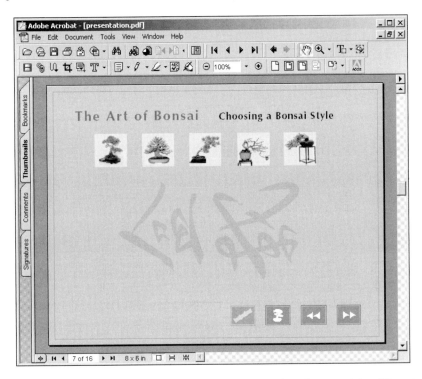

1. Go to page **7** of the presentation. This page contains pictures of the different styles of bonsai plants.

2. Place the mouse cursor over the first picture from the left. A larger version of the image suddenly appears below. When you move the mouse away, the image disappears. Roll the mouse over the next two images. Notice that they also trigger a larger image to appear below. You will add actions to the two remaining images.

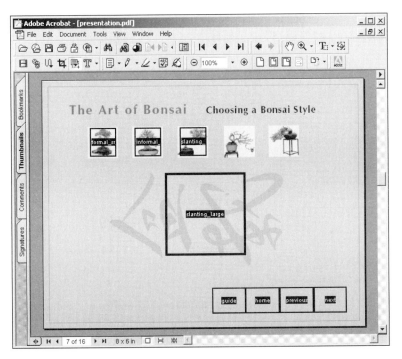

3. Select the **Form** tool from the Toolbar. This will reveal all of the form fields on the page. Notice the large form fields in the center of the page (there are three form fields there, but it's difficult to see them because they occupy the same space). These are the fields that contain the large versions of the images. The form fields over the smaller images are the fields that trigger the show/hide actions. Really, the best way to understand how this works is just to create a couple of them for yourself, so let's get to it.

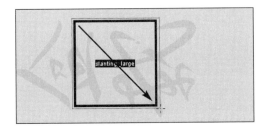

4. First, you'll create a form field to hold the large version of the next image. If Snap to Grid is still selected, choose **View > Snap to Grid** to deselect it. The grid coordinates don't fit with this exercise. With the **Form** tool, draw a form field in the same area as the other fields in the center of the page. You can draw the field slightly larger than the others to make it easier to work with. Just don't make it too large because images placed in form fields automatically scale themselves to fill the field, and you don't want your images to appear at sizes different from each other.

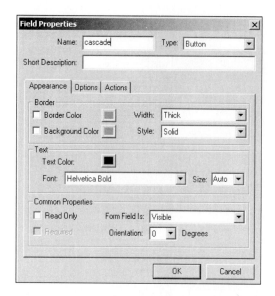

5. In **Field Properties**, name this field **cascade**, and set **Type** to **Button**. You're choosing Button in this case because the button form field allows you to place an image in the form field. The user won't actually be clicking this field like a normal button. Make sure **Border Color** and **Background Color** are unchecked, and that **Width** and **Style** are set to **Thick** and **Solid**, respectively. Click the **Options** tab.

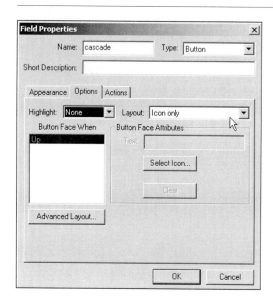

6. Under the **Options** tab, choose **None** for the **Highlight**. Select **Icon only** for **Layout**. Click **Select Icon**.

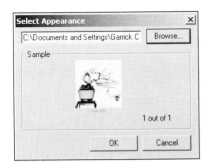

7. In the **Select Appearance** dialog box, click **Browse**. Locate and open the file **cascade.pdf** in the **Styles** folder inside the **chap_11** folder. Click **OK** to return to the **Field Properties** dialog box.

This field is now set up to display the image of the cascade-style bonsai tree. However, you don't want the image to be visible right away. You want to conceal the image first and only have it appear when the user rolls the mouse over the small version of the image. You'll learn to do this next.

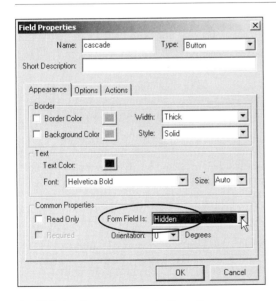

8. Click the **Appearance** tab. From the pop-up menu next to **Form Field Is**, choose **Hidden**. This will set the initial state of the field as Hidden. Click **OK**. Select the **Hand** tool. Notice there is no indication whatsoever that your form field exists. Next you'll add the field over the smaller image that will reveal the larger image.

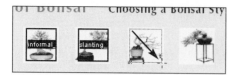

9. Select the **Form** tool and draw a field over the small version of the **cascade** style image. The field should cover most of the image.

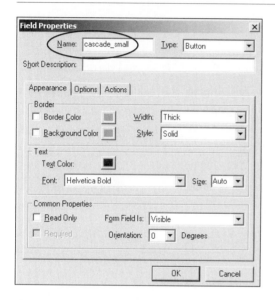

10. In the **Field Properties** dialog box, name this field **cascade_small** and set **Type** to **Button**. Make sure the menu next to **Form Field Is** is set to **Visible**.

In this case, you're selecting Button as the type of field because the Button field does not require the user to enter text or to make a selection from a list of items. The Button field is meant to be clicked or rolled over. This field will not contain any text or images. It is simply here to act as the trigger to reveal the larger cascade image.

11. Because the field will not have any content, you don't need to make any changes under the Options tab. Click the **Actions** tab.

First you'll add the action that will make the large image appear. To be consistent with the other images that have already been added to this page, you'll want the large cascade image to appear when the user's mouse touches the cascade_small field.

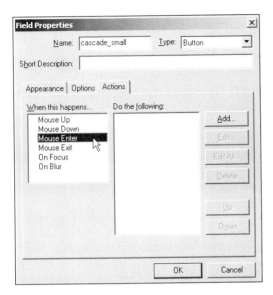

12. Under **When this happens...** select **Mouse Enter**. This will execute the specified action whenever the user's mouse enters the area occupied by this field. Click **Add** to select the action.

13. In the **Add an Action** dialog box, choose **Show/Hide Field** for **Type**. Click **Edit**. This will open the **Show/Hide Field** dialog box.

The Show/Hide Field dialog box lists every field contained within this PDF. You have to determine which field you want to show or hide. Because you're working on the Mouse Enter action right now, you'll want to show the cascade field.

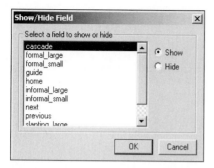

14. Click the radio button next to **Show**, and select **cascade** from the list of fields. This will cause the cascade field to appear whenever the user's mouse touches the cascade_small field. Click **OK**. Click **Set Action** to return to the Field Properties dialog box.

Now you'll set the action to hide the image when the user's mouse leaves the form field area.

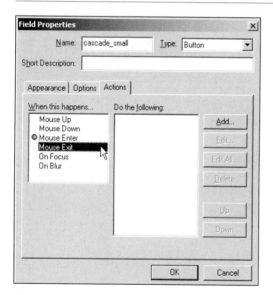

15. Select **Mouse Exit** from the **When this happens...** column and click **Add**.

16. Again, select **Show/Hide Field** as the **Type**, and click **Edit**. This time you want the cascade image to disappear when the user's mouse leave the area.

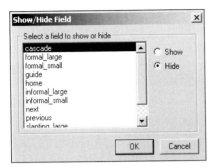

17. If it's not already selected, click the radio button next to **Hide**, and select **cascade** from the list of fields. Click **OK**. Click **Set Action**.

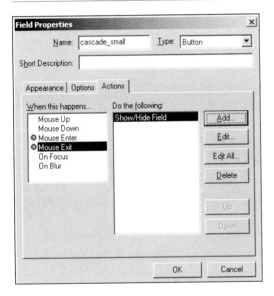

18. Click **OK** to close the **Field Properties** dialog box. Select the **Hand** tool to test your actions.

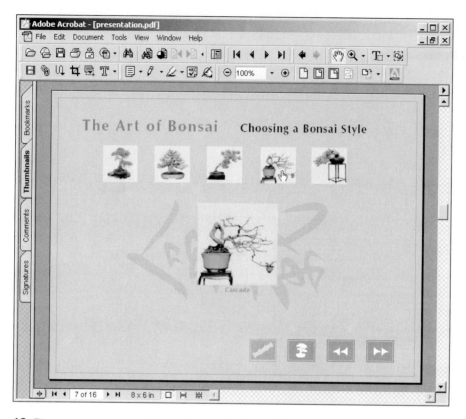

19. Place your cursor over the small cascade image. The large cascade image appears. Remove the mouse from over the small image and the large image disappears. Cool!

---

20. If you would like some more practice showing and hiding fields, the necessary final image has been provided to you to complete the last show/hide action on this page. Just follow Steps 3 through 18 of this exercise and substitute the word **cascade** with **semi_cascade**. The **semi_cascade.pdf** file is located in the **Styles** folder inside the **chap_11** folder.

---

21. Save the file and keep it open for the next exercise.

---

8. _____Displaying the Presentation in Full Screen Mode

You're finally ready to display your presentation. In this exercise you'll set up the presentation to display in **Full Screen mode**. Full Screen mode hides all the elements of the Acrobat interface and focuses attention solely on the document itself.

You can view any document in Full Screen mode at any time by choosing View > Full Screen. But rather than relying on the user of this document to know how to do that, you'll set up this presentation's Open Options to automatically enter Full Screen mode when the document is opened.

1. Choose **File > Document Properties > Open Options** to view the **Document Open Options** dialog box.

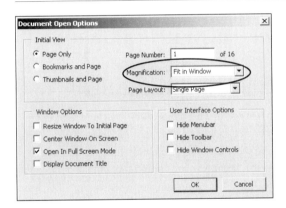

The choices you make in the Document Open Options dialog box determine how the document will act when it is first opened. The choices made here apply whether the document is viewed in Acrobat or Acrobat Reader, but you can only change these settings in the full version of Acrobat.

2. Under **Window Options**, check **Open In Full Screen Mode**. In the **Initial View** area, set **Magnification** to **Fit in Window**. This, combined with Full Screen mode, will size the presentation to fit on the screen at its largest possible size. Because Full Screen mode automatically hides all aspects of the Acrobat interface, there's no need to check any of the selections under User Interface Options. Click **OK**.

Note: *Refer to the chart at the end of this exercise for more information about the selections available in the Document Open Options dialog box.*

3. Save **presentation.pdf** and close it. Now you'll test the Open Options you just set by opening the document again.

4. Open **presentation.pdf** from the **chap_11** folder on your hard drive. The document opens in Full Screen mode. In Full Screen mode you don't have to worry about your audience staring at the Acrobat interface rather than your presentation. Notice there are no Acrobat interface elements available. To navigate through the presentation you can press the arrow keys on your keyboard or, better yet, click the Start button to proceed to the next page. Continue advancing your way through the presentation. All of the navigational elements you created in this chapter still function normally. Press **Esc** to exit Full Screen mode.

It's pretty easy to turn your PDF into a presentation, right? Next you'll examine some preferences that allow you to modify how the document behaves in Full Screen mode.

5. Choose **Edit > Preferences > General**. (Mac OS X: Choose **Acrobat > Preferences > General**.)

6. From the categories on the left of the **Preferences** dialog box, choose **Full Screen**. Under **Full Screen Navigation**, check the box next to **Advance on Any Click**. This will allow you to use the mouse to proceed through your presentation. From the menu next to **Default Transition**, select **Random Transition**. This will give you a sample of the various transitions that are available in Acrobat. Transitions determine how the pages will visually change from one to another. Click **OK**.

Note: *The preferences for Full Screen mode are identical in Acrobat and Acrobat Reader, but the choices you make only affect your copy of Acrobat. Unfortunately, you can't set the preferences of your users' computers through your Preferences dialog box.*

NOTE | Full Screen Mode Preferences

The chart below outlines the preferences you can set for Full Screen mode and what each does.

Full Screen Mode Preferences	
Item	Description
Advance Every X Seconds	Checking this option and entering a number will automatically advance the presentation to the next page after the proscribed number of seconds have elapsed. You can enter anywhere from 1 second to 32,767 seconds. (32,767 seconds is roughly 546 minutes or about 9 hours per page. That's one long presentation.)
Advance on Any Click	When checked, this option enables the user to go to the next page by clicking the mouse.
Loop After Last Page	When checked, the presentation will return to the first page after the user reaches the last page and chooses to advance.
Escape Key Exits	When checked, pressing the **Esc** key exits Full Screen mode. If you uncheck this option, the only other way to exit Full Screen mode is to press **Ctrl+L** (Windows) or **Cmd+L** (Mac).
Default Transition	Determines how the pages will changes from one to another as you advance through the presentation. The default action is **Replace**, which is identical to the **No Transition** choice.
Mouse Cursor	**Always Visible** keeps the Mouse Cursor visible on screen at all times. **Always Hidden** hides the mouse cursor in Full Screen mode and keeps it hidden until exiting Full Screen mode. **Hidden After Delay** hides the mouse cursor after a few seconds of inactivity. The cursor will reappear as soon as the mouse is moved.
Background Color	Allows you to choose the color that will fill in the parts of the screen that the document doesn't cover in Full Screen mode.

7. Save the **presentation.pdf** file and close it. Reopen it and click your mouse button. You should advance to each page with each click and you will see the various transition effects. Pretty cool, huh? Press **Esc** when you're done viewing the presentation.

The last thing you'll do here is add a page action to the final page of the presentation to automatically exit Full Screen mode. This is a good thing to do in case someone using your document isn't familiar enough with Acrobat to know to press Esc to exit Full Screen mode.

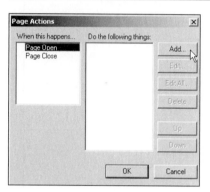

8. Go to page **16**. Choose **Document > Set Page Action**. In the **Page Actions** dialog box, select **Page Open** and click **Add**.

9. Choose **Execute Menu Item** as the **Type** of action and click **Edit Menu Item**.

- **Windows:** From the **Menu Item Selection** dialog box, select **View > Full Screen**. Click **OK**.

- **Macintosh:** From the menu bar, choose **View > Full Screen**. Click **OK**

10. Click **Set Action** to return to the **Page Actions** dialog box. Click **OK** to close it.

11. One more time: Save **presentations.pdf** and close it. Open it again and page forward to the last page. Upon reaching the last page you'll be returned to windowed mode, at which point you again have full access to Acrobat's interface elements.

12. When you're tired of staring at bonsai trees, save the file and close it.

Note: The Page Action you just set actually toggles the view between Full Screen and windowed mode. Therefore, if you're in windowed mode when opening page 16, you'll be switched to Full Screen.

Document Open Options

In this exercise you learned to set options that affect the way a PDF behaves when it is first opened. The chart on the following pages describes the various selections available in the Document Open Options dialog box.

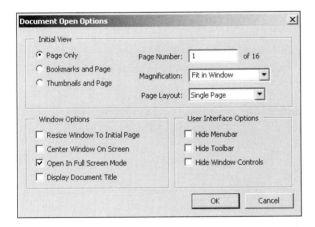

Document Open Options	
Item	**Description**
Page Only	Opens the document with the Navigation pane closed.
Bookmarks and Page	Opens the document with the Bookmarks pane open.
Thumbnails and Page	Opens the document with the Thumbnails pane open.
Page Number	Opens the document on the specified page. The default is page 1, but you can jump to any page of the document by entering its number here.
	continues on next page

Document Open Options *continued*	
Item	**Description**
Magnification	Determines the initial magnification level of the document when it's opened. The choices are the same magnification levels described in Chapter 2, *"Interface."*
Page Layout	Sets the document to open in either Single Page, Continuous Page, or Continuous Facing Page view (described in Chapter 2, *"Interface"*).
Window Options	This section of the Document Open Options allows you to choose any combination of the four choices it presents (listed below).
	Resize Window To Initial Page: Resizes the Acrobat window to match the size of the initial view you set. For instance, if you set the document to open at 75% magnification, the Acrobat window will resize to fit the page.
	Center Window On Screen: If the Acrobat window is less than the width and height of the monitor display, the window will be repositioned so that it appears directly in the center of the screen.
	Open In Full Screen Mode: Displays just the document with no Acrobat interface elements. Checking this selection essentially negates the effects of the other three choices under Window Options, as there will be no window visible in Full Screen mode.
	Display Document Title: Displays the document's title in the window's title bar (the title can be found by choosing File > Document Properties > Summary).

continues on next page

Document Open Options *continued*	
Item	**Description**
User Interface Options	Checking any of the three options below will hide the specified elements. These selections are useful if you want to conceal the Acrobat navigation elements, but don't want to enter Full Screen mode.
	Hide Menubar: Hides the menu bar (when the menu bar is hidden, pressing **F9** will bring it back).
	Hide Toolbar: Hides the Toolbar (when the Toolbar is hidden, pressing **F8** will bring it back).
	Hide Window Controls: Hides the Navigation pane, Status bar, and scrollbar. (To bring these elements back, you must return to the Document Open Options dialog box and uncheck Hide Window Controls.)

So that's it! You now have quite a range of Acrobat skills under your belt. The rest of the book shifts focus from using Acrobat to actually creating the PDFs that you'll enhance with Acrobat.

12.

Acrobat Distiller

| What's Distiller? | Viewing Job Option Differences |
| Customizing Job Settings | Creating PostScript Files |
| Distilling a PostScript File |
| Creating PDFs Directly from the Print Command |
| Watched Folders |

chap_12

Acrobat 5
H•O•T CD-ROM

You've been working with PDFs for 11 chapters now. It's finally time to find out where PDFs actually come from. (Hint: It's not the stork.)

In the following chapters you'll be exploring different methods of creating PDFs. You'll learn how to create PDFs directly from authoring applications, how to create PDFs from Acrobat itself, and, in this chapter, how to create PDFs using Acrobat Distiller. Acrobat Distiller is an application used only for the creation of PDFs.

My goal is to provide you with an understanding of Distiller that will enable you to prepare your PDFs for the Web and for general office use. If you need specific information on creating PDFs for high-end prepress output, there are many other books available on this topic, such as *Real-World PDF with Adobe Acrobat* by Anita Dennis (Peachpit Press). In this chapter, I will provide brief descriptions of the functions of Distiller that relate to prepress options, but unless you're a graphic designer working in the print or publishing industry, you don't have to worry about knowing every little detail about Distiller.

I. _____What's Distiller?

Acrobat Distiller is a separate application that was installed when you loaded Acrobat 5 onto your computer. **Distilling** a document used to be the only way to convert it into a PDF. As you'll soon see, there are now many other options available, but Distiller is still the number one choice of print professionals for generating PDFs because it provides the most control over how the PDF is created.

Distiller has only one job: to create PDFs. It can only create PDFs from two file formats: PostScript (PS) files, and Encapsulated PostScript (EPS) files. You'll learn more about these file formats and how to create them later in the chapter. For now, just keep in mind that these are the only formats that Distiller can handle. So before a document can be distilled, it must first be converted to a PS or EPS file. In this exercise you'll open Distiller and examine its interface and settings. Then you'll examine some PDFs that were generated with Distiller.

Acrobat Distiller is located inside the Distiller folder of the Acrobat application folder. You can open it by navigating to this folder, but it's much easier to access Distiller directly from the Acrobat menu bar.

1. From Acrobat, choose **Tools > Distiller**. This will open Acrobat Distiller.

Note for Mac OS X users: Distiller does not run natively in OS X. When you choose Tools > Distiller, Distiller will open in Classic mode. You can reboot in OS 8.6–9.x to follow along with the rest of this chapter as well.

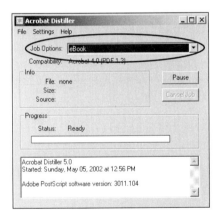

At the top of the Distiller window, you'll find the Job Options pop-up menu. This menu contains four choices: Screen, eBook, Print, and Press. Being able to distinguish between these four settings is essential to understanding Distiller. These settings affect the size and quality of your PDF files. When converting a file to PDF, it's important to first consider how the file will be used. Are you making the PDF for use on your Web site? Are you making the PDF for someone to print on his or her home printer? Choosing the proper Job Option will ensure that your PDF is best suited to the task for which it was created.

The most significant role of Job Options is to manage images and fonts. Individual Job Options handle images and fonts differently. Next you'll learn about the four Job Options settings, and then you'll examine some PDF files that have been created using these different settings.

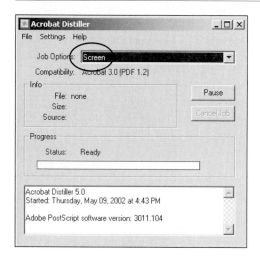

2. From the **Job Options** menu, select **Screen**. You'll use the Screen Job Option to examine the various settings that are available in Distiller.

The Screen setting is for creating PDFs that will be used primarily online—such as on a Web site. Because many people still have dial-up connections to the Internet, the Screen setting reduces the quality of the PDF to create the smallest possible file. You can examine the Job Options settings by selecting the Job Option then choosing Settings > Job Options.

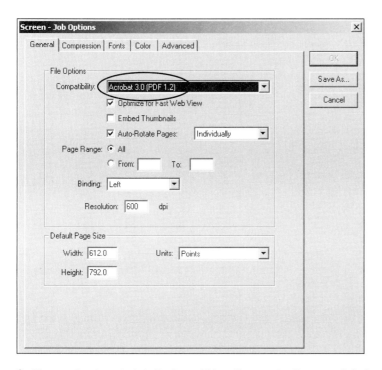

3. Choose **Settings > Job Options**. This will open the **Screen - Job Options** dialog box.

The Screen - Job Options dialog box contains five tabs, which in turn contain all the settings that can be changed to affect the quality and size of the PDF. Notice here in the General tab that the Compatibility menu has been set to Acrobat 3.0. Because this Job Option assumes that the PDF will be use largely on the Web, the Compatibility is set to make sure that the millions of people who haven't upgraded their copies of Acrobat or Acrobat Reader will still be able to view your document. In the following steps you'll be examining the settings in the Compression and Fonts tabs. They will be described in detail in the charts at the end of Exercise 3, "Customizing Jobs in Distiller." Because the settings in the Color and Advanced tab are used primarily for professional prepress work, you won't be learning about these settings here.

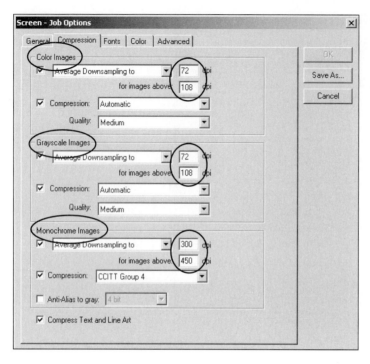

4. Click the **Compression** tab.

The settings under the Compression tab dictate how Distiller treats different types of images. Proper compression is essential to creating an efficient PDF. Fortunately, the default settings of the four Job Options are well-suited for the purpose of most documents. There are individual settings for color, grayscale, and monochrome images. While this may sound complicated and involved, there really isn't too much here that you need to concern yourself with. Simply stated, color and grayscale images distilled under the Screen Job Option are automatically converted to 72 dots per inch (dpi) if their resolutions are greater than 108dpi. Most monitors have a resolution of 72dpi. Images greater than 72dpi would be unnecessarily large in terms of file size, and the quality difference would be indistinguishable when viewing the image on a monitor anyway. However, if you were to print out a document distilled under these settings, the images would look very poor because of their low resolution. If you've ever printed out an image from a Web page, you know what I'm talking about. The settings for monochrome images (usually line art) are set to downgrade images to 300dpi if their resolutions are greater than 450dpi. Line art images—maps or diagrams for example—often need to look sharper than photographs, which is why they are set to downgrade at a higher resolution than color and grayscale images.

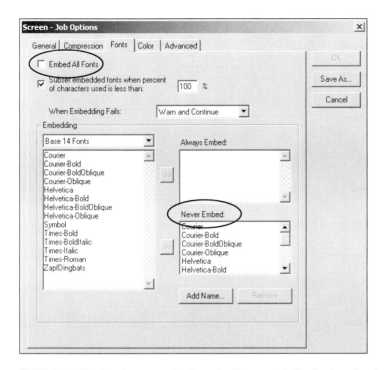

5. Click the **Fonts** tab to examine how the Screen Job Option handles font embedding.

The Fonts tab contains the settings that dictate whether a document's fonts will be embedded into the PDF. Notice that the Embed All Fonts check box is not selected in this Job Option. Embedding a document's fonts increases the overall file size of the PDF, and because this is the Screen setting, this option has been deselected to minimize the file size. When this document's fonts are not embedded, Acrobat will use font-substitution technology to select a font on the user's computer that will approximate the look of the original font. If you want to make sure that your PDF matches your original document exactly, however, you should choose a Job Option that embeds the fonts into the PDF.

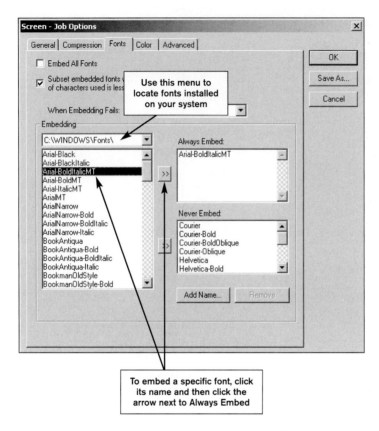

Use this menu to locate fonts installed on your system

To embed a specific font, click its name and then click the arrow next to Always Embed

If you wish to embed only a specific font from your document, but want to leave the rest of the fonts unembedded (if you wanted to embed the font used for your company logo, for instance), you can select the font from the list under the Embedding section and then add the font to the Always Embed list. Acrobat will let you select and embed any font on your system.

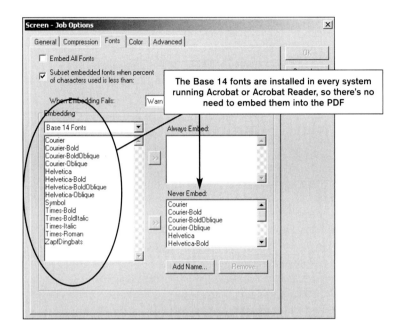

There are, however, some fonts that you most likely will never need to embed. The fonts listed in the Never Embed area here are known as the Base 14 fonts. These are the fonts that are installed whenever Acrobat or Acrobat Reader is loaded onto a computer. Therefore, there's usually no need to embed these fonts into your PDF, because, unless they've purposefully removed them, anyone viewing your PDF should already have these fonts installed on their systems. If you did want to embed one of the Base 14 fonts, though, you would simply click its name and click the arrow next to Always Embed.

Even if a rarer font is used in the document, Acrobat 5 does a fairly good job of finding fonts on the user's computer to match the original non-embedded font, but there will be some cases where the font substitution is noticeable. You'll examine some examples shortly.

The other two tabs in the Job Option dialog box, Color and Advanced, are only used when dealing with high-resolution professional printing, and don't need to be examined here. Even if you deal with a print shop that prefers you to send your documents in PDF format, they'll most likely tell you if any setting under Color or Advance needs to be altered when creating your PDF.

6. Click the **Cancel** button to close Screen - Job Options.

7. Keep Distiller open and return to Acrobat for the next exercise.

The three remaining Job Options are described in the chart below. If you'd like to see their settings, select the Job Option from the list in Distiller and then select Settings > Job Options to view the compression and font settings.

Job Option Settings	
Job Option	**Description**
eBook	The eBook option is new to Acrobat 5. It's similar to the Screen setting, but is set to be compatible with Acrobat 4 and higher. Under the eBook setting, fonts are embedded into the PDF and images are downgraded only to 150dpi, rather than 72dpi. PDFs created with the eBook setting are still used primarily onscreen, but because the eBook setting doesn't downgrade the image as much as the Screen setting does, you can get a fairly decent printout of the PDF on a home inkjet or laser printer. The images definitely won't be professional quality, but they'll look okay for general use. And because the fonts from the original document are embedded in the PDF, you can be sure that the user will see the document exactly as you intended it to appear. This results in a larger file, but if you want more accuracy than the Screen setting provides, eBook is an excellent choice.
	The eBook setting is also optimized to be used on portable eBook readers. You may have come across some of these eBook readers in your local computer/electronics store. In theory, you can load eBook PDFs onto these portable devices and read them on the device's screen. I say "in theory" because in every store I've ever been to, the eBook readers are either broken, out of batteries, or have been stolen. So I can't really say whether they work or not.
Print	The Print setting is used to create PDFs that will be viewed onscreen, but will also be printed on an inkjet or laser printer. Images are downgraded to 300dpi only if their resolution is greater than 450dpi. Fonts are embedded. This setting naturally produces larger file sizes than Screen and eBook. The PDFs it generates are compatible with Acrobat and Acrobat Reader 4 and higher.
Press	The Press setting produces the highest-quality PDFs at the largest file sizes. You'd only be likely to use this setting if you're a graphic designer preparing your PDF to be sent to a commercial printer. Acrobat embeds all fonts and keeps images below 450dpi at their intended resolution. Because of the large file size this setting generates, Press is not an appropriate setting for general-use PDFs. Even if you copy the file to a CD-ROM for distribution, it will still slow down Acrobat on older computers that are not fast enough to efficiently deal with the additional file information. If you've ever tried to scroll through a large PDF file only to wait while the images load on each page, you know what I mean.

2. _____Viewing Job Option Differences

Now that you're familiar with each Job Option, you'll take a look at four PDFs of the same document that were created with each of the Job Option settings.

1. Copy the **chap_12** folder and files from the **H•O•T CD-ROM** to your hard drive if you have not already done so.

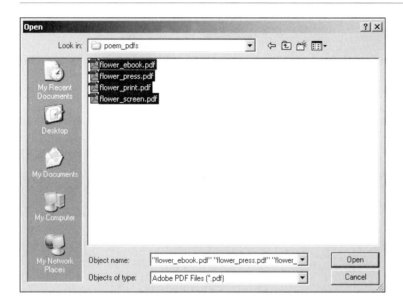

2. In Acrobat choose **File > Open** and navigate to the **poem_pdfs** folder inside the **chap_12** folder. Hold down the **Shift** key and click each of the four files to select them all. Click **Open**. Acrobat will open all four documents.

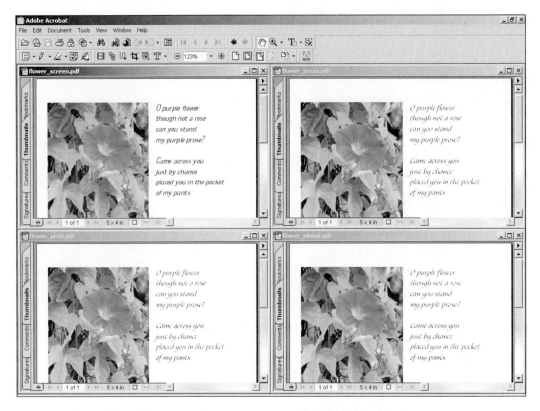

3. To view all the documents simultaneously, choose **Window > Tile > Horizontally**.

Note: The documents will not necessarily line up in the order shown in the screenshot above.

You're now viewing four versions of the same document. The name of each file tells you which Distiller Job Option was used to create it (flower_screen, flower_ebook, etc.). Unless you have a huge computer monitor, they probably all look about the same right now. You'll examine them more closely and observe the differences.

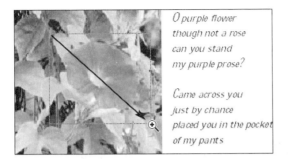

O purple flower
though not a rose
can you stand
my purple prose?

Came across you
just by chance
placed you in the pocket
of my pants

4. Select the **Zoom** tool from the Toolbar and draw a marquee around the flower in each of the four documents. Try to draw the marquee the same size for each one so that you'll be better able to compare the differences between the images.

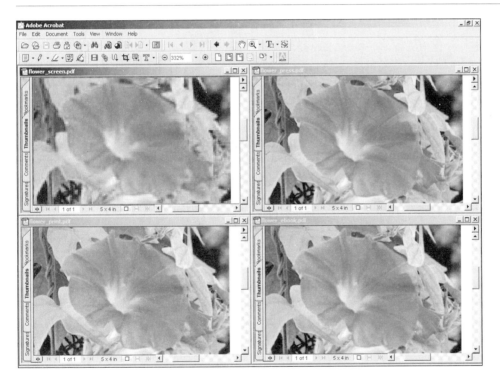

Right away, you should see that flower_screen looks the worst at higher magnifications. This image is set to 72dpi, which looks fine at magnification levels below 150% or so. But the image quality really starts to degrade between 250% and 300%. So while the Screen Job Option produces the smallest file, you can see that it compromises the quality of the image. Depending on your monitor size, you might have to zoom in even closer to see any major differences among eBook, Print, and Press.

5. Next, let's examine what each of the Job Option settings does to fonts. Select the **Hand** tool and drag each flower image to the left to bring the text on the page into view.

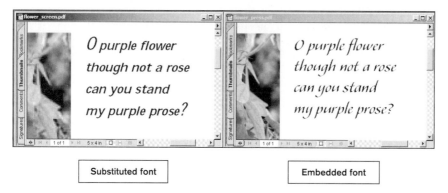

Substituted font   Embedded font

Again, the flower_screen document is the only one to show any obvious variation. The Screen Job Option is the only one that doesn't embed the original document's font into the PDF. When a font is not embedded, Acrobat substitutes another font in its place. In many cases, you might not even notice that a font had been subbed in, but because the font used here is so stylized, the difference is immediately obvious.

Next, you'll see how the text in each document holds up under magnification.

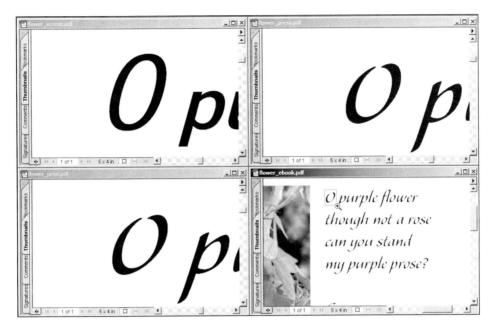

6. Select the **Zoom** tool and draw a marquee around the letter **O** in each of the four documents. Notice that even at the highest magnification setting of 1600%, the quality of the text is identical.

Many people try to gain quality for their PDF by choosing a higher Job Option setting than is needed. As you can see, there really is no difference among the quality of the text in each of the Job Option settings. The difference lies mostly in the quality of the images. So if you know that your document will be viewed mostly onscreen with the possibility that it may be printed out for general use, choose eBook. There's no need to overcompensate by choosing Press when eBook is all you need. In this case flower_press.pdf is more than 450KB larger than flower_ebook.pdf.

7. Close all four files and keep Acrobat open.

3. ─────────── Customizing Job Settings in Distiller

As you saw in the first exercise, each Job Option in Distiller has its own set of preferences. In this exercise you'll customize one of the Job Options.

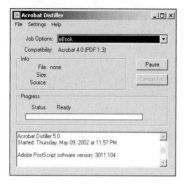

1. Return to Distiller. For **Job Options**, select **eBook**.

You learned earlier that the eBook setting downgrades higher-resolution images to 150dpi and embeds the document's fonts into the PDF. For this exercise, assume that you want to create a PDF that maintains the 150dpi setting for the images, but does not embed the fonts. You'll base your custom setting on the settings for the eBook Job Option.

2. Choose **Settings > Job Options** to open the **eBook─Job Options** dialog box.

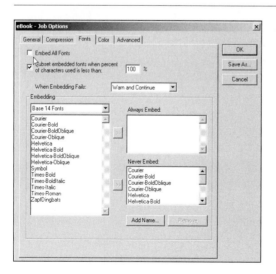

3. Click the **Fonts** tab and uncheck **Embed All Fonts**. You've now altered the default eBook settings. Click **OK**.

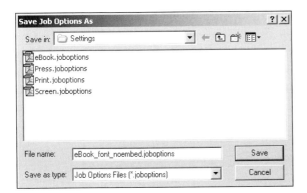

4. Acrobat doesn't let you save any changes to the default Job Options; you'll have to rename this Job Option that you just created. Click **Save As**. Distiller will prompt you to name and save this new Job Option in the **Settings** folder of the Acrobat application. This is where the other default Job Options are stored. Distiller has given your Job Option the name **eBook(1).joboptions**. Rename it **eBook_font_noembed.joboptions**. This is a more specific descriptive name that will help you identify this particular Job Option should you ever need it again. Click **Save** then **OK**.

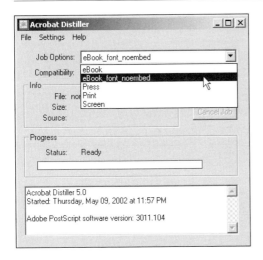

Your new Job Option is now listed in Distiller's Job Options menu. You can select this Job Option any time you want to create a PDF with images that look better than the Screen setting, but without embedded fonts.

Of course, being able to customize Distiller's Job Options does you no good if you don't have any PostScript files to work with. Without PostScript files, Distiller is pretty much useless. The next exercise walks you through the steps to turn your documents into PostScript files.

Job Options General, Compression, and Fonts Tabs

The charts that follow detail the options found in the Job Options dialog box. The settings for the General, Compression, and Fonts tabs are covered.

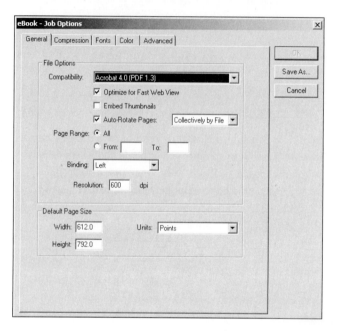

General Tab Settings	
Item	**Description**
Compatibility	You can choose from Acrobat 3, 4, or 5. For the Screen setting, 3 is chosen because it ensures that your document will be compatible with older versions of Acrobat. You would choose Acrobat 5, for instance, if you wanted to apply 128-bit encryption security to your document, which as you learned in Chapter 10, *"Document Security,"* is only compatible with Acrobat 5.
Optimize for Fast Web View	This is checked by default in all four Job Option settings and creates a smaller, faster-loading file than would be created if this option were not checked. It optimizes the PDF by removing repeating elements and providing pointers to the location of the element's first appearance. For example, if all of the document's pages use the same image in the background, there's no need for Acrobat to draw a new version of the image on each page. With Optimize for Fast Web View checked, Acrobat saves the image once, and then duplicates it on each page.

continues on next page

General Tab Settings *continued*

Item	Description
Optimize for Fast Web View *(continued)*	Optimize for Fast Web View also allows Web servers to **byte serve** the PDF, meaning that the PDF can be downloaded a page at a time so the user can start reading a page as soon as it's downloaded, even if the entire document hasn't been downloaded yet. This option also slightly compresses text and line art regardless of your settings in the Compression tab. Still, it's good to keep this option checked because the compression it applies is hardly noticeable onscreen or in print.
Embed Thumbnails	In Chapter 6, *"Modifying PDFs,"* you learned to embed thumbnails from the Thumbnails pane. Checking this option will generate the thumbnails for you when the PDF is created.
Auto-Rotate Pages	Choosing this option will automatically rotate pages based on the orientation of the text on the page. If you choose **Collectively by File**, Distiller will rotate the entire PDF based on the orientation of the majority of the text in the document. If you choose **Individually**, each page will be rotated based on the orientation of the majority of text on that particular page.
Page Range	Choosing **All** converts the entire file to a PDF. By clicking the radio button next to **From**, you can choose to convert just a range of pages.
Binding	This setting determines how the pages and thumbnails will display in Acrobat when viewed in **Continuous Facing** view. **Left** is the proper choice for all Western Languages.
Resolution	When creating a PDF, Distiller essentially behaves like a printer. Only instead of printing on paper, it prints a PDF file. As with a standard printer, you must set a resolution for the file it's printing. The default resolution for Screen and eBook is 600dpi, the most common resolution for laser printers. The Print setting has the resolution set to 1200dpi, while the Press setting has the resolution set to 2400dpi. When customizing your own settings, you should choose a resolution that matches the printer that will be printing the PDF. This resolution setting has no effect on the resolutions setting for images under the Compression tab.
Default Page Size	In previous versions of Distiller, this area appeared under the Advanced tab. The settings here have no effect on the PDF unless the boundaries of the document were not set in the original authoring application.

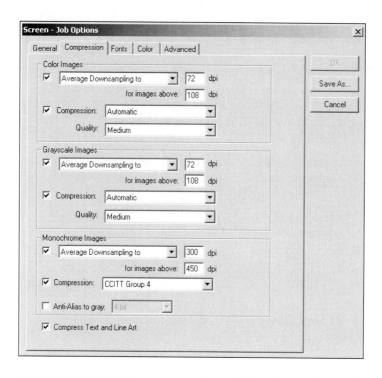

Compression Tab Settings	
Item	**Description**
Average Downsampling to; **Subsampling to**; **Bicubic Downsampling to**	The first choice under each section in the Compression tab is the type of downsampling that will be used. The Screen setting uses Average Downsampling, while the other three Job Options use Bicubic Downsampling. Bicubic Downsampling takes a longer time to distill, but produces better-looking images than Average Downsampling. Subsampling should only be used for images with large, single-color backgrounds; otherwise, images tend to look pretty bad. You're better off choosing either Average or Bicubic downsampling. Note that downsampling will only occur if the image is above the set threshold. For instance, in the Screen Job Option shown above, color and grayscale images will be downsampled to 72dpi only if they are greater than 108dpi.

continues on next page

Compression Tab Settings *continued*	
Item	**Description**
Compression	For each type of image, you can select the type of compression you want applied. For color and grayscale images, the choices are JPEG, ZIP, and Automatic. JPEG is best for photographic or continuous-tone images, while ZIP is best for images with large areas of solid colors. For the most part, Acrobat does a pretty good job of picking the proper compression so you should leave the compression setting to Automatic.
	The compression menu for Monochrome Images offers ZIP as well as CCITT compression, which is used for 1-bit black-and-white images. CCITT Group 4 is good for general-use monochrome images, while CCITT Group 3 is optimized for scanned documents such as faxes. In case you're ever on a computer geek trivia show, CCITT stands for **C**onsultative **C**ommittee for **I**nternational **T**elephone & **T**elegraph.
	The fourth Compression choice for monochrome images is Run Length, which is good for images with large areas of black or white. Generally though, CCITT 4 is the best for handling monochrome images.
Quality	Depending on which Compression setting you choose, the Quality menu will change to allow you to choose how much compression to apply to the image.
Anti-Alias to gray	Checking this box under the Monochrome Images settings will convert the anti-aliasing of images to levels of gray. You can select 2-, 4-, or 8-bit levels.
Compress Text and Line Art	Checked by default in all the Job Settings. This option applies ZIP compression to any vector images, resulting in a smaller file and no discernible degradation of the image. You should keep this checked.

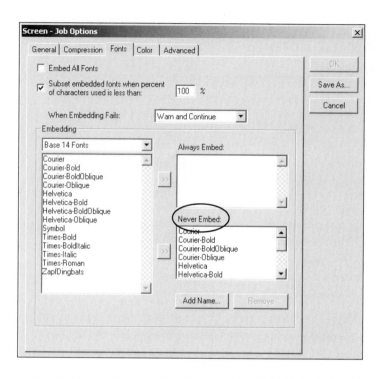

Fonts Tab Settings	
Item	**Description**
Embed All Fonts	Embeds all of the document's fonts into the document. If left unchecked, fonts will not be embedded (as in the Screen Job Option) and Acrobat will use a substitute font if the specified font is not found on the end user's computer. Note that some font manufacturers restrict font embedding, and embedding restricted fonts is considered a copyright violation. If in doubt, check with the font manufacturer first.
Subset embedded fonts when percent of characters used is less than:	When checked, Acrobat only embeds the characters used in the document (rather than the entire font set) if the percentage of characters used falls below the specified value. For example, if you choose 50%, and the document only contains the letters x, y, and z, then only those three letters are embedded. If, however, you choose 50%, but use the entire alphabet in the document, the entire font set would be embedded because more than 50 percent of it was used in the document.

continues on next page

Fonts Tab Settings *continued*

Item	Description
When Embedding Fails:	You can use this menu to determine what Distiller will do if something goes wrong during the distillation and fonts are unable to be embedded. You can choose from Ignore, Warn and Continue, and Cancel Job. If there's a font problem, and you've chosen Ignore, the distillation will continue without any notification of the problem. Warn and Continue will display a message alerting you of the problem and then continue with the distillation. Cancel Job will stop the Distillation if a font problem occurs.
Embedding	This section under the Fonts tabs contains the menus for determining which fonts to embed or not embed. The menu directly underneath Embedding displays the location of the all the fonts available for Distiller to embed.
Always Embed	You can choose to always embed a font whether you've checked Embed All Fonts or not. Do so by selecting the font or fonts from the list on the left and clicking the right-pointing arrow button to move the fonts into the Always Embed list. For example, If you have a logo that uses a specific font, you can choose to always embed that font to ensure that the logo always looks the same.
Never Embed	The fonts listed here by default are the Base 14 fonts, which every copy of Acrobat or Acrobat Reader installs on the user's system. Therefore, there is no need to embed these fonts because everyone viewing your document should already have them installed. You can add fonts to this list in the same manner that you add fonts to the Always Embed list.

NOTE | What Is a PostScript File?

PostScript is a programming language that was introduced by Adobe in 1985, intended to provide a device-independent language that could precisely describe a document's images, text, and layout. This PostScript file could then be printed on any printer that understood PostScript, without the need to have the authoring application, fonts, and original images provided. Many service bureaus and print shops still prefer clients to send documents as PostScript files for printing because the PostScript file contains all the necessary information to print the document out in exactly the way the client intends. Acrobat Distiller can be thought of as a PostScript printer, only instead of printing on paper, it prints electronically and produces a PDF file.

4.———————————**Creating PostScript Files**

There are many methods for creating PostScript Files. Although it is possible to create PostScript files without Acrobat, this exercise demonstrates how to create a PostScript file if Acrobat is installed on your computer. Because of the differences between Windows and Macintosh operating systems, this exercise is divided into separate sections for the two platforms. It does not include specific exercise files. What follows are general instructions on how to create a PostScript file from any application that prints. Note that some page layout applications such as QuarkXpress will require a few more steps than what's shown in this exercise. Specific page layout applications are covered in Chapter 14, *"Creating PDFs from Popular Applications."*

Steps for Creating PostScript Files in Windows

1. Open a document you wish to convert to a PDF. Make sure you've made any necessary changes or edits before you convert the file (you'll recall from Chapter 6, *"Modifying PDFs,"* that Acrobat has very limited editing capabilities, so it's better to make any changes before converting the file to a PDF). Choose **File > Print**.

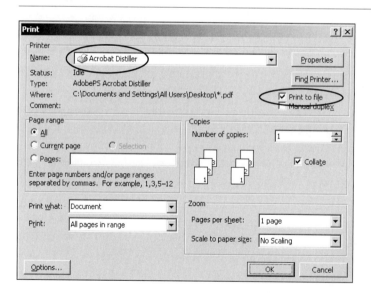

2. In the **Print** dialog box, choose **Acrobat Distiller** as the printer. Check the check box next to **Print to file**.

Note: *Choosing Print to file is the key to creating a PostScript file. If you don't check this box, a PDF file will be generated instead. Generating a PDF file this way will be covered later in this chapter.*

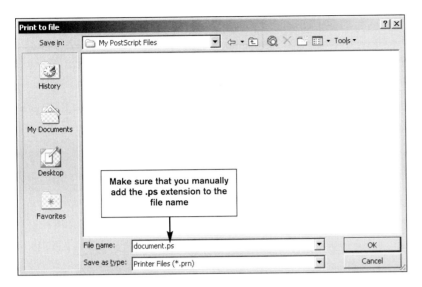

3. Click **OK**. You will be prompted to save this file. Name the file and include the **.ps** extension in the file name. This will ensure that Distiller recognizes the document as a PostScript file. If you don't add the .ps extension, Windows will give the file the extension of **.prn** (printer file format) instead. Although Distiller will usually accept files with this extension, it's better to name the file with **.ps** to make sure that you'll always be able to distill this file.

Note: In some applications, Windows will not accept your manual entry of .ps and will keep the .prn extension. If you encounter this problem, just leave the .prn extension in the file name and change it to .ps after the file has been generated.

4. Click **OK**. Your PostScript file will be created. Now all you have to do is drag it to Distiller to turn it into a PDF.

Note: If you encounter the above message after clicking OK, you'll need to make a quick change to your settings to ensure that Distiller will receive the proper fonts to create your PostScript file. Close this dialog box and click the Properties button in the Print dialog box. This will take you to the Printing Preferences dialog box.

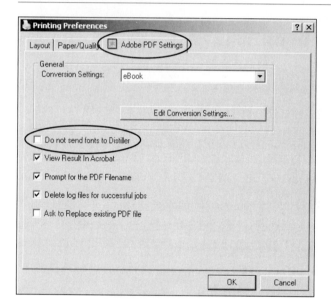

5. Click the **Adobe PDF Settings** tab and uncheck **Do not send fonts to Distiller**. Click **OK** and then click **OK** in the **Print** dialog box to generate the PostScript file.

Steps for Creating PostScript Files in Macintosh

Again, take note that these steps are for Mac OS 8.6–9.2 because Distiller is not an OS X native application. Also make sure that you have the most current Adobe PostScript printer driver by going to **www.adobe.com/support/downloads** and clicking on the Macintosh link under Printer Drivers.

1. From the **Apple** menu, select the **Chooser**.

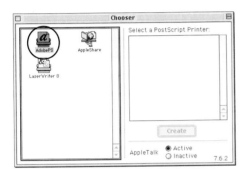

2. Select **AdobePS** as the printer driver. This driver was installed when you installed Acrobat on your system. There's no need to select a PostScript printer if any appear in the list on the right side of the Chooser. Close the Chooser.

3. In your authoring application, choose **File > Print**.

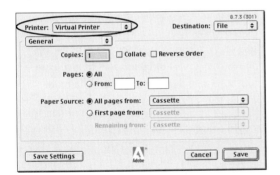

4. From the menu next to **Printer**, choose **Virtual Printer**. This is the printer that will create the PostScript file.

Note: If you've ever selected Virtual Printer in the past, the name of the printer here might have a number at the end, for example, Virtual Printer 2, Virtual Printer 6, etc. No matter; just select it anyway. You'll now have an icon on your desktop called Virtual Printer. This is created because the Mac OS needs to print to some sort of device and Virtual Printer is acting like, well, a virtual printer.

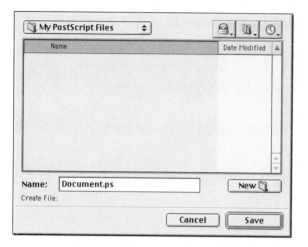

5. Click **Save**. Acrobat will prompt you to name the file. Make sure you keep the **.ps** extension in the name. Click **Save**. The PostScript file is generated.

That's pretty much PostScript file creation in a nutshell. In the following exercise, you'll use Distiller to convert a PostScript file into a PDF.

What Is an EPS File?

As you read earlier, Acrobat Distiller can convert PS and EPS files into PDFs. EPS stands for Encapsulated PostScript. EPS files are not usually intended to be displayed or printed by themselves, but instead are meant to be contained within larger documents. Unlike PostScript files, EPS files cannot contain multiple pages, so are not useful for printing long documents. However, EPS files can be useful because they can contain a preview image of the document so that computers or printers that can't read PostScript can at least display a representation (often a crude representation) of what the document is supposed to look like. EPS files are usually created directly from authoring applications with an Export command.

5. _____Distilling a PostScript File

Once you've converted your document into a PostScript file, turning it into a PDF is a piece of cake. Just drag the file to Distiller and the conversion begins. This exercise will walk you through the necessary steps, and also examine the security preferences you can set in Distiller.

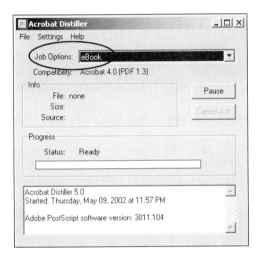

1. Acrobat Distiller should be open. From the **Job Options** menu select **eBook**. This will set the image in the PDF to 150dpi and also embed the font. The font used in this file is Helvetica, which should be on your computer unless you've purposely removed it.

Next, you'll change the security settings to prevent anyone from printing this PDF.

2. Choose **Settings > Security**.

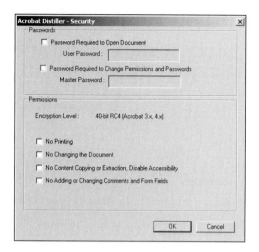

This dialog box should look familiar to you. It offers the same 40-bit encryption security settings that you worked with in Chapter 10, "Document Security." In fact, setting security preferences in Distiller is no different than setting security for a PDF in Acrobat. In Distiller, your security preferences are applied to the PDF as soon as it's created, while in Acrobat you have to open the PDF and then apply the security settings. Note also that Distiller does not offer 128-bit encryption security. If you want to apply this higher level of security, you have to open the PDF file in Acrobat and apply your preferred settings there.

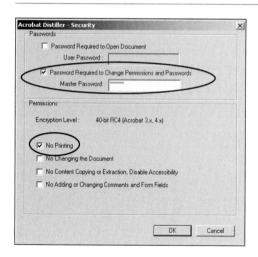

3. Check the box next to **Password Required to Change Permissions and Passwords**, and type **oranges** as the Master Password. In the **Permissions** section, check **No Printing**. Click **OK**. You'll be asked to confirm the Master Password. Type **oranges** and click **OK**.

Now you're ready to Distill the PostScript file.

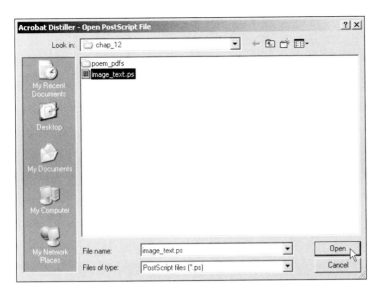

4. Choose **File > Open**. Select the file **image_text.ps** from the **chap_12** folder and click **Open**.

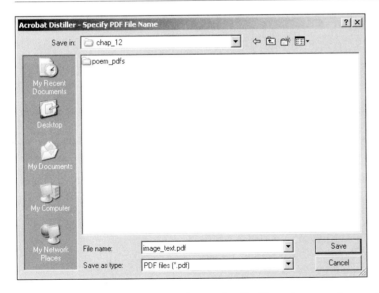

5. You'll be prompted to name and save the file. Keep the name **image_text.pdf** and save it in the **chap_12** folder. Click **Save**.

Tip: *You can also just drag a PostScript file directly into Distiller instead of choosing File > Open. The resulting PDF will be saved into the same folder as the PostScript file and will be given the same file name, but with the .pdf extension added to it.*

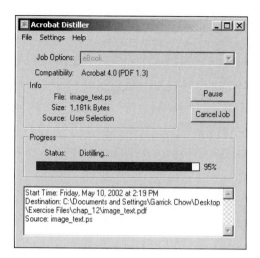

Distiller immediately begins to convert the file to a PDF.

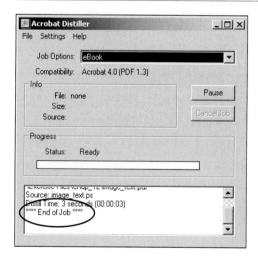

6. Once the distillation is complete (sounds like I'm writing a book on making your own moonshine), you'll see the message ****End of Job****. Close Distiller and return to Acrobat.

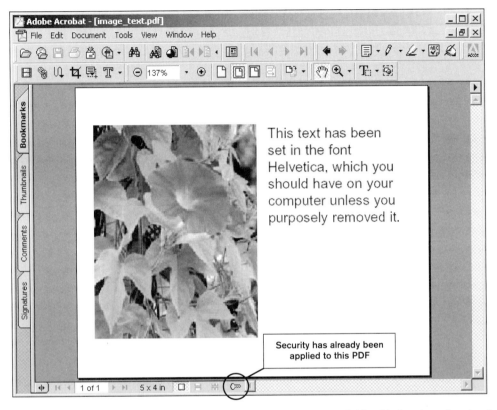

7. In Acrobat, open **image_text.pdf** that should be in the **chap_12** folder. Notice the yellow key icon in the Status bar, indicating that security has been applied to this document. If you look under the File menu, you'll see that the Print command is unavailable. Close **image_text.pdf**.

And that's how you turn a PostScript file into a PDF. It may seem like an involved process, but it really is the best way to control the size and quality of your PDFs. But it may not be your cup of tea to spend a lot of time tweaking PDFs for size and quality. In the following exercises and chapters, you'll explore other methods of creating PDFs and you'll understand the pros and cons of these various methods. Next, you'll learn how to turn your documents into PDFs without first having to convert them to PostScript files and without even having to open Distiller.

6. ————————Creating PDFs Directly from the Print Command

In this exercise you'll learn how to create a PDF directly from an application without having to turn the document into a PostScript file first. Now, before you start complaining about spending all that time learning to create a PostScript file, remember that there are times when it's better to create a PostScript file and then manually distill it (when you have several documents that need to be converted to PDFs, for example), and there are times when it's more convenient to just convert a document to a PDF directly from your authoring application. Even when you convert a document directly into a PDF, it's still converted into a PostScript file and distilled. The process just happens behind the scenes—as you'll see in the resulting PDF file.

This exercise, like the one on creating PostScript files, will be presented in general how-to terms rather than in relation to a specific application. Remember, as long as you can print from the application, you should be able to follow these steps to create your PDF. Again, the processes are different on Windows and Macintosh machines, so this exercise will be broken into two separate sections.

Steps for Creating PDFs in Windows

1. From your authoring application, choose **File > Print** to open the **Print** dialog box.

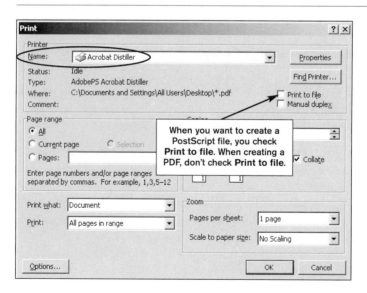

2. In the **Print** dialog box, choose **Acrobat Distiller** as the Printer. This is exactly what you did to create a PostScript file; the difference here is that you don't check **Print to file** in this case. Click the **Properties** button. This will open the **Acrobat Distiller Document Properties** dialog box.

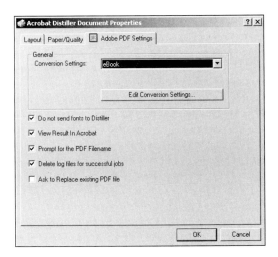

3. Click the **Adobe PDF Settings** tab. Look familiar? Next to Conversion Settings, you have access to the same Job Options settings that are available in Distiller, including any custom Job Options you may have created. (The **eBook_font_noembed** Job Option you created earlier will be in here, for example.)

4. Select whichever Conversion Setting is appropriate for the purpose of your PDF, and check any of the five check boxes that you want. The chart below describes the five choices. Click **OK** after making your selections.

Acrobat Distiller Document Properties Options	
Selection	**Description**
Do not send fonts to Distiller	This is not saying that you don't want to embed fonts. It simply means that instead of having to tell Distiller where the fonts for this document are located, Distiller will look for them itself. It's actually better to keep this option checked because Distiller can find all the necessary fonts much more efficiently itself.
View Result In Acrobat	With this option checked, your PDF will open in Acrobat as soon as it's created.
Prompt for the PDF Filename	Check this if you want Acrobat to ask you where you want the PDF saved and what you want to name it.
Delete log files for successful jobs	Every time Distiller creates a PDF, it creates a text file logging the progress of the job. By checking this option, you'll only see a log file if something goes wrong in the distillation process.
Ask to Replace existing PDF file	If you attempt to save a PDF file that has the same name as an existing PDF, you'll be asked if you want to replace the existing file.

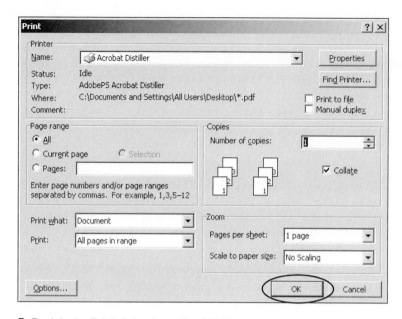

5. Back in the **Print** dialog box, click **OK**. If you checked the **Prompt for the PDF Filename** option, you will be asked to name and save the file. Wait a few moments (several moments if you're converting a large multipage document) while Acrobat creates a PostScript file and distills it in the background. If you checked **View Result In Acrobat**, the PDF will open in Acrobat when distillation is complete.

In Windows, the process you just learned is essentially a way to avoid opening Distiller. You have full access to the Distiller conversion settings in the Distiller Document Properties dialog box. Acrobat creates the PostScript file and distills it in the background, leaving you with just the completed PDF.

Steps for Creating PDFs in Macintosh

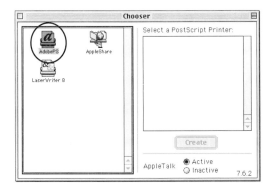

1. From the **Apple** menu, choose **File > Chooser** and select **AdobePS** as the printer driver (you only have to do this step if you've changed drivers since the last time you created a PostScript file). Close the Chooser when you're done.

2. From your authoring application, choose **File > Print**.

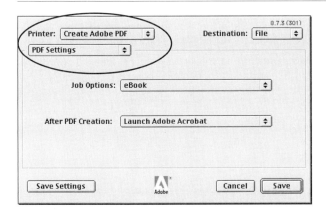

3. In the print dialog box that opens, select **Create Adobe PDF** as the **Printer**, and select **PDF Settings** from the menu below it. You don't have nearly as many options available here as your Windows counter-parts, but, hey, it's less stuff to worry about, right? From the **Job Options** menu you can select any of the four default Distiller Job Options, or any custom Job Options that you may have created. (Unlike the Windows Print dialog box, however, you cannot create any custom settings from this dialog box. If you wish to apply custom settings, you must create them in Distiller prior to choosing Print from your authoring application.) From the **After PDF Creation** menu, you can choose whether you want the PDF automatically opened in an Acrobat application or if you prefer not to immediately view the PDF.

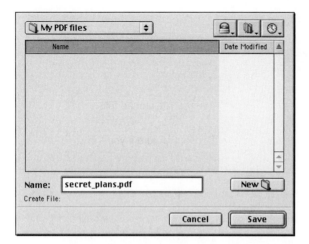

4. Once you've made your selections, click **Save**. You'll be prompted to name your PDF and to choose a location in which to save it. After clicking **Save** here, your document will be converted to a PostScript file and distilled in the background, and you'll have your PDF.

As you can see, there's nothing overly complicated about creating a PDF directly from the Print command of your authoring application. At this point you may really be wondering why you even bothered to learn how to create a PostScript file in the first place. As mentioned earlier, there will occasionally be times when it's more convenient to create the PostScript file first and distill it later. For instance, if you have multiple documents that need to be converted to PDFs, you can save them all as PostScript files and direct Distiller to convert them all into PDFs at once. You'll learn how to do this in the following exercise.

7. ───────────Watched Folders

Wouldn't it be nice if you could set up Distiller to always keep an eye a certain folder on your hard drive so that whenever you placed a PostScript file into this folder, Distiller would immediately spring into action and convert the file into a PDF? Doesn't that sound like a very leading, rhetorical question? In this exercise, you learn how to set up a **watched folder** in Distiller. A watched folder is nothing more than a folder that you tell Distiller to, well, watch. As soon as you place a PostScript file into this folder, Distiller will notice it and convert it to a PDF. This is a very convenient feature if you have multiple documents to convert to PDFs. All you have to do is save them as PostScript files and place them into the watched folder. Distiller will handle the rest.

1. If it's not already open, open Distiller.

2. Choose **Settings > Watched Folders** to open the **Acrobat Distiller - Watched Folders** dialog box.

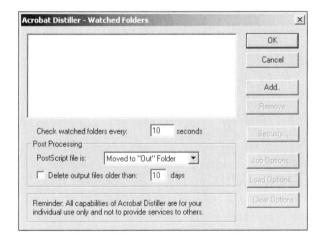

In this dialog box, you can choose any folders on your hard drive to act as watched folders.

Note: Although technically you could choose a folder on any computer in your company's network, Adobe has added a thoughtful reminder at the bottom of the dialog box, informing you that Acrobat Distiller capabilities are for your use only (you agreed to this when you installed the software and didn't read the licensing agreement). They frown upon people creating a watched folder on a network because then anyone who can create a PostScript file could drop a file in the watched folder to convert into a PDF, without ever having Acrobat installed on their system. So now that you know how to do it, don't do it.

3. Click the **Add** button to select a folder to watch.

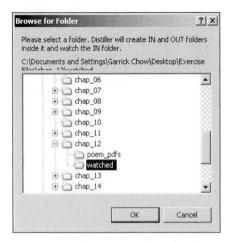

4. Select the folder called **watched** in the **chap_12** folder and click **OK**. This is an empty folder that's already been created for you. On Macintosh systems, you can create a new, empty folder after clicking **Add**, but on Windows machines the folder must exist before you click **Add**.

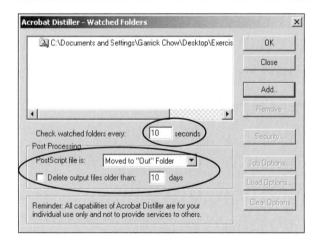

After you've selected the watched folder, you'll be returned to the Watched Folders dialog box. You can add as many watched folders here as you like. You could, for instance, create several watched folders based on specific applications. You could create a folder for PageMaker PS files, Illustrator PS files, etc., so that they'd be easier to find after they were distilled.

Notice here that the default setting is for Distiller to check the watched folder every 10 seconds. You can add any value between 1 and 1,000 seconds here. Under the Post Processing section you can decide what to do with the PostScript file after it's distilled. When you create a watched folder, Distiller automatically creates two folders in the watched folder called In and Out. You place your PostScript files into the In folder, Distiller distills them and then places them into the Out folder. You can choose to have Distiller move the used PostScript file into the Out folder, or just delete it right away. If you choose to keep the PostScript in the Out folder, you can then check "Delete output files older than" and then specify when to delete the PostScript file.

Next you'll specify which job settings you want to apply to your watched folder. The reason that you can add multiple watched folders is that you can apply different Job Options to each folder to truly automate the distillation process.

***Tip:** You can create multiple watched folders on your computer, each with a different job option applied to it. Once they're set up, all you have to do is drag your PostScript file to the appropriate watched folder to create your PDF.*

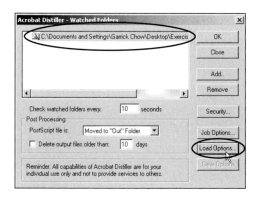

5. Select your watched folder from the window at the top of the dialog box and click **Load Options**.

6. You'll be prompted to select the Job Option you want applied to PostScript files placed in this folder. Select **eBook.joboptions** and click **Open**.

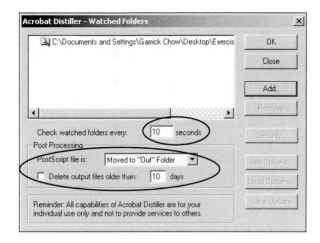

7. Make sure that **Check watched folders every** is set to **10** seconds and that PostScript files are set to be moved into the **Out** folder. Click **OK**.

Note: You can further customize your watched folder settings by clicking the Security button to apply security settings or by clicking the Job Options button to customize the Job Option applied to this folder.

8. Now you'll test your watched folder. Keep Distiller open, but move its window out of the way so that you can see your desktop. Distiller must be running in order to watch the folder.

9. From your desktop, open the **chap_12** folder and then open the **watched** folder in its own window. You should be able to see the contents of **chap_12** and **watched** simultaneously. Notice the In and Out folders that were created in the **watched** folder.

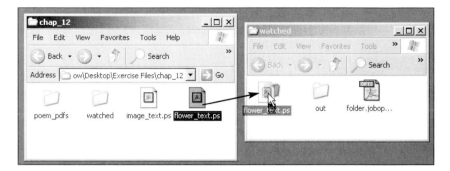

10. Drag **flower_text.ps** from the **chap_12** folder into the **In** folder. After a few seconds, Distiller will convert the file to a PDF. **Note:** If you minimized or hid Distiller, make it visible again so you can see it do its thing (although it will work whether or not you're watching it).

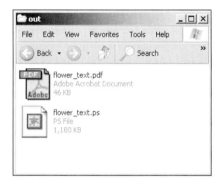

11. After Distiller finishes, open the **Out** folder and examine its contents. The PostScript file has been moved into this folder along with the brand new PDF. Cool!

12. You can now close any open windows.

13. If you wish to remove the watched folder, return to Distiller and select **Settings > Watched Folders**. Click on the watched folder here, and then click **Remove** then **OK**.

14. Quit Distiller and close any open PDFs.

Another chapter has come to a close. In the following chapters you'll continue to examine methods of creating PDFs. And while many of methods don't involve opening the Distiller application directly, remember that Distiller is often working behind the scenes. Without it, you'd have no PDFs.

I3.

Creating PDFs from Acrobat

| Open as Adobe PDF | Converting a Web Site into a PDF |

| Examining the Converted Web Site |

| Converting Scanned Documents to PDF |

chap_13

Acrobat 5
H•O•T CD-ROM

In the last chapter, you learned how to create PDFs using Acrobat Distiller, a process that allows you to manage the file size and quality of your PDFs. In this chapter you'll explore the benefits of creating PDFs directly within Acrobat.

While Distiller gives you great control over a PDF's file size and quality, using Acrobat directly to create PDFs has some advantages of its own. In this chapter, you'll first learn how to import image and text files as PDFs. Later you'll learn to convert a Web site into a PDF file. As well, you will learn how to convert scanned documents into searchable PDFs.

Note that while you'll be creating PDFs with Acrobat in this chapter, you're not actually creating content. That is, all of the documents that you convert into PDFs have to exist outside of Acrobat before they can be turned into PDFs. Acrobat is not a content creation tool; it can only work with existing files and documents.

I. _____Inserting PDF Documents

One of the choices you have to convert a file into a PDF from Acrobat is to choose **File > Open as Adobe PDF**. This command allows you to select an image or plain-text file to convert to a PDF.

1. Copy the **chap_13** folder and files from the **H•O•T CD-ROM** to your hard drive if you have not already done so. There should be no documents currently open in Acrobat. Choose **File > Open as Adobe PDF**.

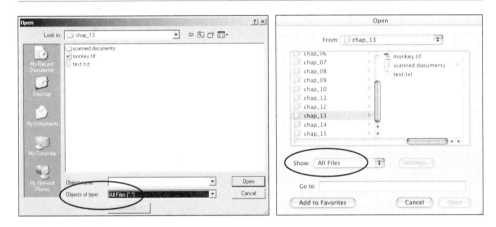

Windows   *Macintosh*

2. Make sure that you're set to look for **All Files** (see the screenshots above).

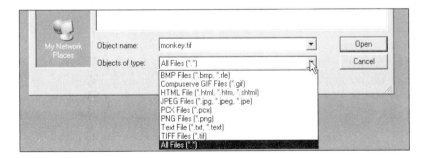

Tip: To see a list of the types of files Acrobat can convert into PDF, click the menu specifying the file type to open. Acrobat can open BMP, GIF, HTML, JPEG, PCX, PICT (Mac only), PNG, TXT, and TIFF files. Make sure you switch it back to All Files when you're done viewing the list.

3. Browse to the **chap_13** folder and open the file **monkey.tif**. This is an image file that Acrobat will convert into a PDF.

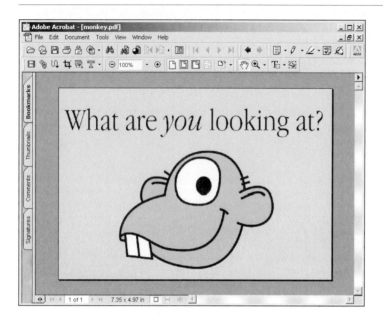

Acrobat will quickly convert this image file into a PDF, but it won't alter the original TIFF in any way. It simply creates a copy of this document as a PDF. After a moment, the image opens in Acrobat. You can click the Actual Size button in the Toolbar to view it at its default size. Although this is a very quick way to convert the image file into a PDF, you have no control over how the PDF is created. You have no way to set the resolution of the image or to embed fonts into the PDF. If you want to create a high-quality PDF from a TIFF, it would be better to use Distiller.

4. Select the **TouchUp Text** tool and click the text on the page. Notice that you're unable to highlight any of the text. That's because this is only an image of text, not real text. Because this PDF was created from an image file, Acrobat sees this entire PDF as one large image and does not recognize any text on the page. Still, it's a quick and convenient way to convert an image into PDF format, which, for instance, can be useful if you need to use an image in a form button, as you learned to do in Chapter 11, *"Creating an Interactive Multimedia Presentation"*. Later in this chapter you'll learn how to make Acrobat recognize text in an image.

5. Save this file in the **chap_13** folder and name it **monkey.pdf**. Close the file after you've saved it.

Next, you'll see how Acrobat handles converting a plain-text file into a PDF. Acrobat is unable to convert formatted text to PDF, so any text files that you wish to convert in Acrobat can only be plain TXT files.

6. Choose **File > Open** as Adobe PDF. Open the file **text.txt** from the **chap_13** folder.

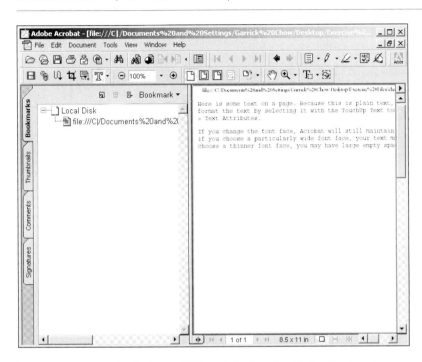

Acrobat converts this file into a PDF and displays it with the Bookmarks pane open.

7. Click the **Bookmarks** tab to close the Bookmarks pane. Because this originally was a plain-text file, no formatting was applied to the text and, once again, you have no control over the conversion settings. But because you converted a text file rather than an image file, you can now apply some formatting to the text. Next you'll use the **TouchUp Text** tool to format the text.

In most cases, you'll want to get rid of the header information that Acrobat automatically adds to a page of converted text.

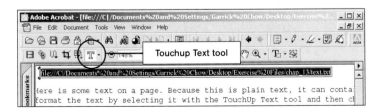

8. Select the **TouchUp Text** tool and highlight the header at the top of the page. Press the **Delete** key to remove the text.

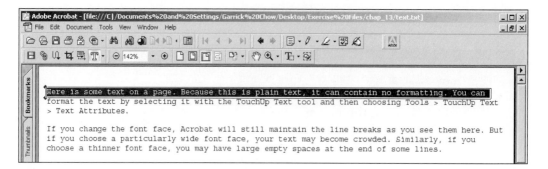

9. Now use the **TouchUp Text** tool to select the first line of text. You can reformat this text using the **Text Attributes** dialog box. Unfortunately, because Acrobat only lets you select a single line of text, you can only format one line at a time.

10. Choose **Tools** > **TouchUp Text** > **Text Attributes**.

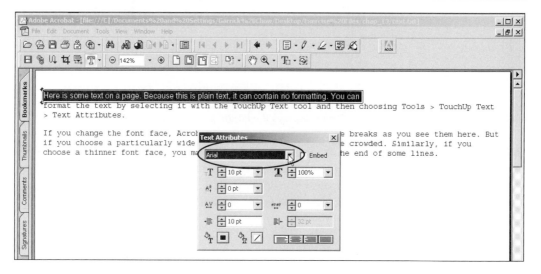

11. In the **Text Attributes** dialog box, select **Arial** from the font list. The text will immediately be formatted. Again, because Acrobat only recognizes single lines of text, the text does not reflow to compensate for the blank space at the end of the first line.

12. Keep the Text Attributes dialog box open and select the next line of text with the **TouchUp Text** tool. Change the font of this line to **Arial** as well. Select the remaining four lines of text and convert them all to Arial.

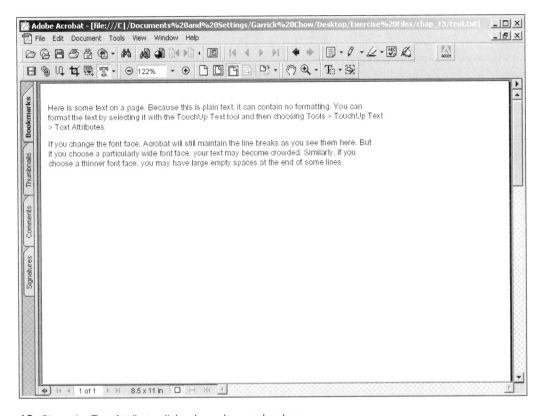

13. Close the Text Attribute dialog box when you're done.

14. Close the file without saving it. You won't need it for the next exercise.

As you can see, converting a text file to PDF with Acrobat offers you an element of control over the appearance of the text, but still severely limits your options. In general, you should only use the Open as Adobe PDF command if you're in a hurry to convert a file to a PDF. Otherwise, you're much better off using the techniques you learned in the previous chapter, which afford you many more choices in the creation of the PDF. In upcoming exercises, you'll see that there are more compelling reasons than speed to use Acrobat to create PDFs, such as capturing a Web site, or creating an editable text document from a scan.

2. _____Converting a Web Site into a PDF

Located directly above the Open as Adobe PDF command in the File menu is the Open Web Page command. Acrobat's ability to convert Web sites into PDFs is a popular feature among those who often have to travel and give presentations. When presenting a Web site to an audience, you must store all the necessary HTML files and images associated with the site, which sometimes amounts to dozens of separate files. When a site has been converted to PDF, however, all you need is the single PDF file. As long as you've converted all the necessary pages, the site's links will all still work and the site will behave just as it would online. In this exercise you'll convert the Bonsai Hut Web site into a PDF and examine the similarities and differences between a Web page and its PDF counterpart.

Special thanks to Dan Klain of **multimediawebs.com** for providing the server space for this exercise. Drop a line to **sales@multimediawebs.com** if you're looking for some of the most reasonably priced hosting packages around.

Before you convert the site into a PDF, you'll first examine the site from your Web browser. Make sure that you're connected to the Internet before continuing with this exercise.

1. Open **Internet Explorer** (or the Web browser of your choice).

2. Enter the Web address: **www.bonsaihut.com** to access the Bonsai Hut Web site. This is a fictitious company site that's been set up expressly for the purposes of this exercise. Once the site has been accessed, notice that the full URL of the site appears in the Address field of the browser (**http://www.bonsaihut.com**). This is the address you'll need to enter into Acrobat to download this site as a PDF. The easiest thing to do is to copy the address so that you can paste it into Acrobat later.

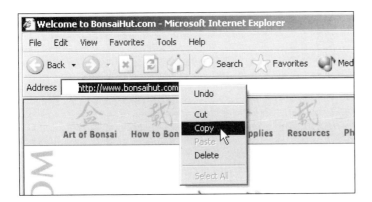

3. Highlight the URL and select **Edit > Copy**. Windows users can **right-click** to copy and Mac users can **Ctrl+click** to copy.

Now you'll further explore the site to examine some of the potential hurdles Acrobat may encounter when converting this site to a PDF.

4. Click the link for the **Art of Bonsai** in the upper left-hand corner of the page to go to that section of the site.

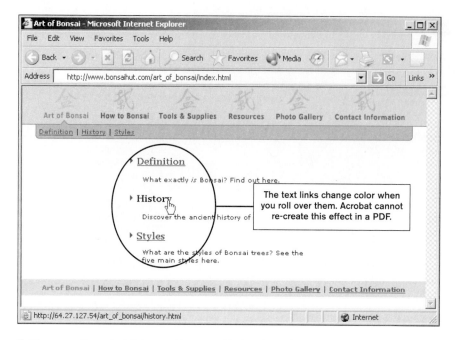

5. There are three text links on this page. Notice that when you roll your mouse over the text links, they change color. This is created with a Cascading Style Sheet, but, unfortunately, it's not an effect that Acrobat can re-create in a PDF. The links themselves will still function properly, but you won't see the colors change when you mouse over them.

Note: While Acrobat cannot maintain rollover effects, it can interpret most Cascading Style Sheets that control text appearance.

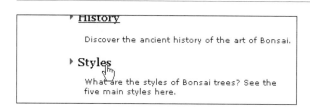

6. Click the link for **Styles** to go to the Bonsai Styles page.

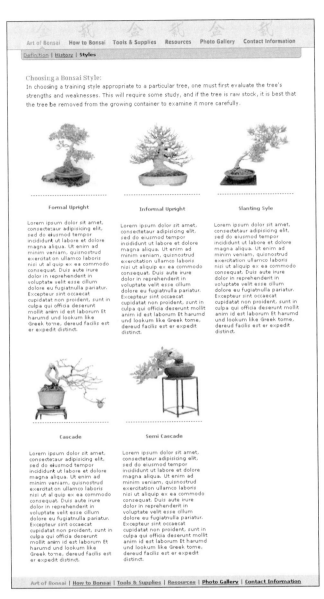

The Bonsai Styles page is a relatively tall page compared to other pages in this site. Unless you have a very large monitor, you most likely have to scroll to view this entire page. As you'll soon see, Acrobat has the ability to scale and rotate pages based on your preferences, but some pages may require two or more PDF pages to accurately represent them. After you convert this site to a PDF you'll see how Acrobat handles a tall page such as this.

7. Click the **Contact Information** link in the upper right-hand corner of the page. This will take you to the Contact page. Click the **Feedback** link. This will take you to a page containing a short form.

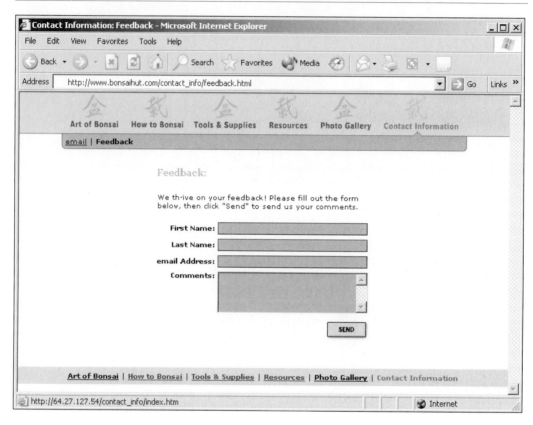

This form is in regular HTML. When Acrobat converts this site to PDF, it will also convert the form fields on this page into PDF format, saving you the work of going in and drawing form fields. You'll still have to tweak the form a little once it's in Acrobat, but at least the fields will have already been created.

8. Now take a few moments to browse around the rest of the site and familiarize yourself with its layout and content. It will be much more impressive to you if you actually recognize the site after you've turned it into a PDF.

9. When you're done browsing, close the browser and return to Acrobat.

NOTE | Downloading Web Pages in Acrobat

When downloading a Web site as a PDF, keep some of the following points in mind:

- Acrobat can download HTML, JPEG, and GIF files.

- Acrobat cannot display animated GIFs. If a Web page contains any animated GIFs, only the last frame of the animation will be downloaded. Acrobat is also unable to download Flash and QuickTime movies.

- Acrobat can download most standard HTML elements including tables, forms, background colors and images, and text formatted with size and color.

- Acrobat can also download pages contained in frames and framesets, but it will only download the default frameset once. Pages linked to from the frameset will be downloaded as separate pages and appear outside of the frameset.

- At the time of publication of this book, Acrobat will support some JavaScript.

- Acrobat does not support Java applets.

Always remember to check the PDF thoroughly after conversion to make sure that no vital sections are missing.

Now that you've examined the site, you'll set up your conversion preferences in Acrobat and turn the Bonsai Hut site into a single PDF file.

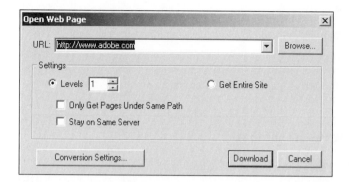

10. In Acrobat, choose **File > Open Web Page**. The **Open Web Page** dialog box will be displayed. If this is the first time you've used this feature, **http://www.adobe.com** will be the default URL. You'll fill in the Bonsai Hut URL momentarily. First, you'll take a look at the various options this dialog box contains.

Under the Settings section, you can choose how much of the site you want to download as a PDF. Some Web sites are very large, so you only want to download the section that you need. You can choose to download the site in its entirety or in levels.

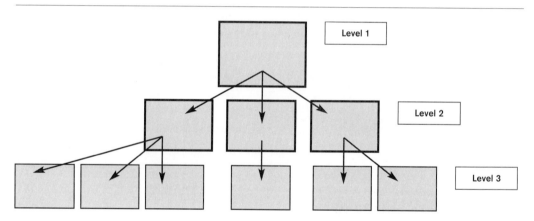

Levels refer to how the Web pages are linked together, starting from the first page of the site. If you choose to download the site by levels, bear in mind that the number of pages may increase significantly as you get farther down into the site, resulting in a very large download.

NOTE | Web Site Levels Downloading Options

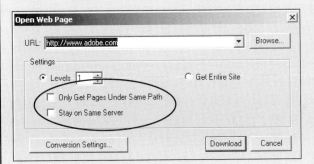

If you need to import only certain levels of the site into Acrobat, you can further control the download by checking **Only Get Pages Under Same Path** and/or **Stay on Same Server**. These selections are described in the chart below.

Options for Downloading Levels of a Web Site	
Option	**Description**
Only Get Pages Under Same Path	Acrobat will only download pages under the path that you enter for the URL and will not follow links outside of this path. For example, if you enter the URL as **http://www.bonsaihut.com/art_of_bonsai/**, Acrobat will only download files from the **art_of_bonsai** directory and will not download any pages outside of this directory.
Stay on Same Server	If the Web site you're downloading contains links to pages that are stored on servers other than the one hosting the initial URL you entered, checking this option will force Acrobat to download only pages stored on the first server.

Just keep in mind that some Web sites contain hundreds if not thousands of pages. Trying to download an entire site or even more than two levels of some sites could take forever and may even cause Acrobat to crash. Be sure that you know what you're downloading before you begin downloading it.

Because the Bonsai Hut Web site has been created as a relatively small site for the purposes of this exercise, you'll get to download the whole thing.

11. Check the radio button next to **Get Entire Site**. Notice that this disables the check boxes under the Levels radio button.

Next, you'll set some preferences to control how Acrobat will interpret the Web pages as they are converted to PDF.

12. Click the **Conversion Settings** button.

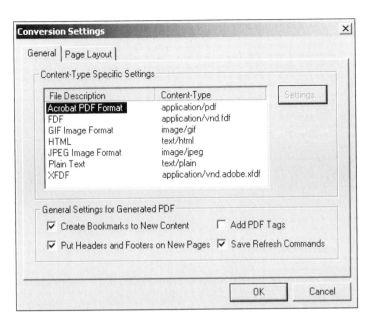

The Conversion Setting dialog box contains two tabs: General and Page Layout. The charts at the end of this exercise will explain the settings under both tabs. For now, you'll just examine the default settings and make a few adjustments to them.

Under the General Settings for Generated PDF, note that the default options automatically create bookmarks for each page and generate headers and footers on each page. You'll see the results of these selections after you convert the Bonsai Hut site into a PDF.

13. Click the **Page Layout** tab.

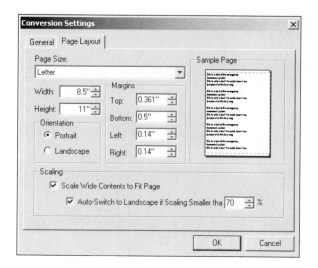

In the Page Layout area you can decide what size the PDF Web pages will be, how the pages will be oriented, and whether you want to scale large content to fit on the page. The default setting is to create letter-size pages in portrait orientation. If any Web pages are too wide to fit on the selected page size, Acrobat will scale down the contents to fit. If the page has to be scaled less than 70 percent, the page will be rotated into landscape orientation.

Because the Bonsai Hut Web site is mainly a horizontally designed site, you'll set the Orientation to Landscape. Later, you'll see how this affects taller pages.

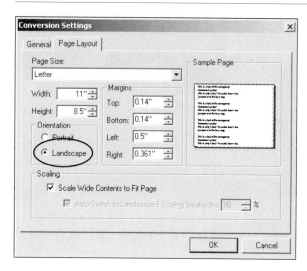

14. Windows: Click the radio button next to **Landscape**.

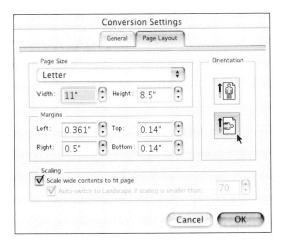

Macintosh: Click the **Landscape** button under **Orientation.**

*This will rotate the page. Click **OK**. You will be returned to the Open Web Page dialog box.*

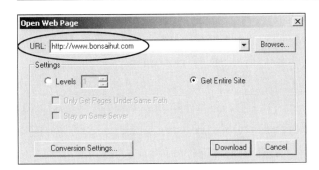

15. If you still have the URL copied from earlier in this exercise, **right-click** (Windows) or **Ctrl+click** (Mac) to paste the Bonsai Hut address into the **URL** field. Otherwise, just type **http://www.bonsaihut.com** into the **URL** field. Note that you must enter the full address when you want to download a site from the Web (that is, typing **www.bonsaihut.com** will not work).

16. Click **Download** to begin the conversion. You may receive a warning that downloading an entire site can be a potentially long process and may eat up a lot of your hard drive space. But I've already warned you about this and you don't have to worry about it for this exercise. Just click **Yes** to continue the download.

Acrobat will connect to the Internet and begin downloading the Bonsai Hut site. Depending on the speed of your Internet connection, this may take anywhere from a few seconds to several minutes.

Once Acrobat has downloaded a few pages, it will display the first page of the site and open the Bookmarks pane. Bookmarks will continue to appear as Acrobat follows links and downloads pages. Once the Bonsai History bookmark appears at the bottom of the list, the download will be complete.

17. Save this PDF as **bonsaihut.pdf** and place it in the **chap_13** folder on your hard drive. Keep it open for the next exercise.

Web Page Conversion Settings

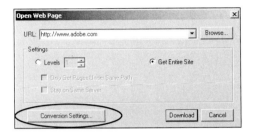

In this exercise you saw some of the settings that can be selected in the Open Web Page's Conversion Settings dialog box. The charts below detail the options in each area.

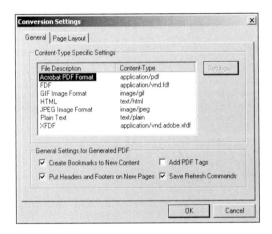

General Tab Settings	
Item	**Description**
Content-Type Specific Settings	This section lists the types of files Acrobat can convert. Only two of these file types have adjustable settings: HTML and Plain Text. Selecting either one will activate the Settings button to the right of the list. You can select HTML settings to control text and link colors, font faces, and whether you want Acrobat to include background colors or images in the download. The Plain Text settings control how regular text files will be converted to PDF.
Create Bookmarks to New Content	As you've already seen, checking this selection will make Acrobat generate bookmarks to each page it downloads.

continues on next page

General Tab Settings *continued*	
Item	**Description**
Put Headers and Footers on New Pages	When this is checked, Acrobat will create a header containing the page's title and a footer containing the page's URL and the date and time it was down-loaded. Knowing the date and time is useful if you want to use Acrobat to automatically download pages that have been updated on the site since your last download.
Save Refresh Commands (Windows)/ **Save Update Commands** (Mac)	When checked, Acrobat creates a list of all the URLs downloaded during this session. When you download the site again, Acrobat will update these pages if the online versions have changed. You can update a downloaded Web site by choosing **Tools > Web Capture > Refresh Pages**.
Add PDF Tags	When checked, Acrobat will add the necessary tags to allow the PDF to reflow within the document window. This is crucial to ensuring proper document accessibility. Accessibility is covered in depth in Chapter 15, *"Accessibility."*

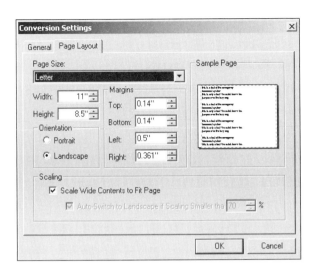

Page Layout Tab Settings	
Item	Description
Page Size	Controls the physical size of the document. If you wish to print out the site on standard U.S. paper, for example, you can choose Letter or Legal size from the menu under Page Size. The Width and Height settings can be individually altered if you wish to create a custom size for your PDF. Margins can also be set to custom settings if desired.
Orientation	Selecting Portrait sets the page vertically. Landscape sets the page horizontally.
Sample Page	Provides a thumbnail reflecting the choices made under the Page Size area.
Scale Wide Contents to Fit Page	If the contents of a Web page are too wide to display within the preferred page size, checking this selection will make Acrobat scale the page down to the size necessary to fit it on the page.
Auto-Switch to Landscape if Scaling Smaller than ...	If Acrobat has to scale the page to less than the determined minimum size (70% by default) the page will be rotated into landscape position, leaving the orientation of the other pages unchanged. This selection is unavailable if the page is already set to landscape orientation.

3. —————————Examining the Converted Web Site

This exercise will walk you through the new Bonsai Hut PDF you just created

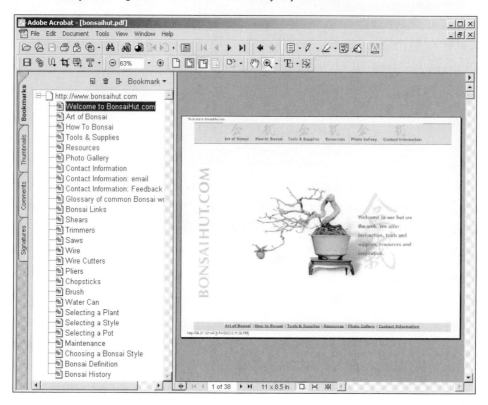

1. bonsaihut.pdf should currently be open to the first page. Click the **Fit in Window** button so that you can see the entire page.

2. Select the **Hand** tool and click a few of the bookmarks. The bookmark names were created from the title of each Web page. After you've clicked enough to see that they're behaving like normal bookmarks, return to the first page and click the **Bookmarks** tab to close the **Navigation** pane. This will give you more room to view the PDF itself.

Tip: If Fit in Window makes the PDF too large for you, click the Actual Size button.

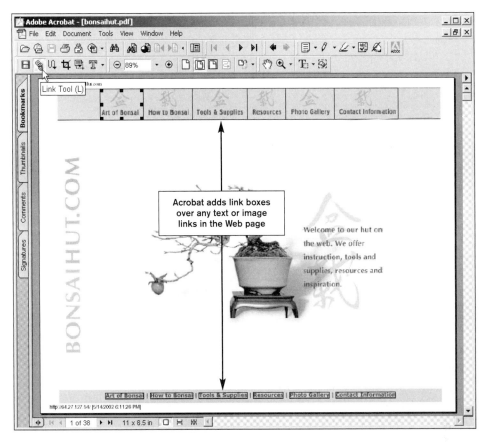

3. Select the **Link** tool from the Toolbar. This will reveal the links that Acrobat has placed on the page. Notice that Acrobat has added link areas to all of the items in the navigation bars at the top and bottom of the page.

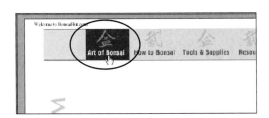

4. Select the **Hand** tool and click the **Art of Bonsai** link in the upper left-hand corner. When you click down on the mouse, you'll see that the Invert highlight has been applied to the link. When you release, you'll be jumped to the Art of Bonsai page.

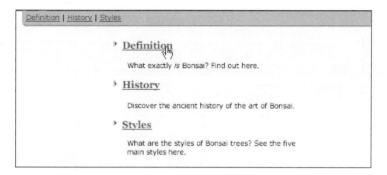

5. Place the mouse cursor over the **Definition** link. The links on this page have also been maintained, but notice that the text links no longer change color when the mouse is placed over them. This is one of the limitations in converting a Web page to PDF. Click the **Styles** link to go to that page.

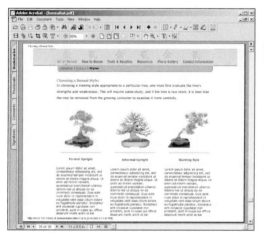 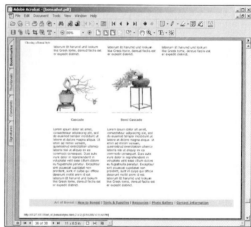

When you viewed this page on the Web, you had to scroll to see the entire page. Because of Acrobat's page size limitations, the Styles page now appears across two pages, making it difficult to read the columns of text (even if the text on this page wasn't just gibberish). Unfortunately, there's very little you can do to solve this problem other than designing your Web pages with the thought of converting them into PDFs in mind. Having a Web page span two PDF pages might not be as much of a problem if you only need to read the content of the page. Scrolling to the next page isn't that much of a hassle. It's only an issue if you're using this Web site as a presentation.

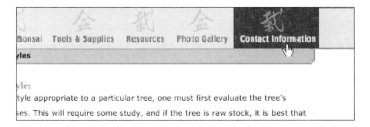

6. If necessary, scroll back to the first page of the Styles section and click the **Contact Information** link in the upper right-hand corner of the page. This will take you to the main Contact page. Once there, click the **Feedback** link.

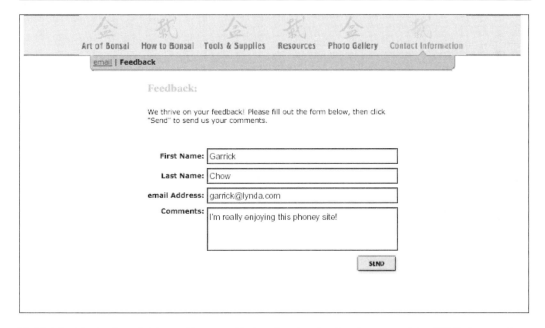

7. Click inside the form fields on this page. Notice that Acrobat has interpreted the HTML form and converted the fields into PDF form fields. Enter some information to test the fields.

While Acrobat did a great job creating the form fields, you most likely will still need to make some adjustments to them.

8. Select the **Form** tool to reveal the form fields on the page. Although the names of the fields are gibberish, you could still print out this form, but if you wanted to make the form work over the Internet, you'd have to change the names of the form fields so they could be interpreted by a form-handling script like the one you worked with in Chapter 8, "*Forms.*" You won't be submitting this form in this exercise, though, so you'll just leave the names as they are.

9. Select the **Hand** tool. Take a few moments to browse the rest of the PDF and examine its contents. Feel free to return to **www.bonsaihut.com** in your Web browser to compare the HTML site with the PDF version. When you're done browsing, save and close **bonsaihut.pdf** and keep Acrobat open for the next exercise.

As you can see, converting a Web site to a PDF is a pretty simple process. While there are limitations, the conversion produces a single PDF file, perfect for placing onto a disk or copying onto a laptop so that you can browse the site at any time.

Scanned Documents

Many companies are currently in the process of scanning multitudes of paper documents and converting them into PDFs. This is a great way to electronically archive documents, but, as you learned in the first exercise of this chapter, Acrobat is not able to recognize text that is part of an image. Without recognizable text, the documents cannot be indexed for search or even touched up with the TouchUp Text tool. This exercise discusses some of the OCR (**O**ptical **C**haracter **R**ecognition) options offered by Adobe to convert image PDFs into documents containing real editable text. You will work with a prescanned image. See the note "Scanning Documents in Acrobat" for information on properly scanning your documents for use in Acrobat.

Important: Exercise 4 deals with Acrobat's Paper Capture plug-in, which, at the time of publication of this book, is only available to Windows users. Paper Capture is OCR technology that was included in previous versions of Acrobat, but for some reason was left out of Acrobat 5 in its initial release. The Acrobat community raised enough of a stink that Adobe added this feature back into the Windows version of the software. If you purchased Acrobat 5 for Windows shortly after its release, you'll have to install the Paper Capture plug-in. If you recently purchased Acrobat 5 for Windows, it's already part of your application. If you're using Acrobat 5 on Macintosh, Adobe would like to cordially invite you to select **Tools > Paper Capture Online** and convert your PDFs through their Web site. You'll only be able to follow this exercise on a Windows machine. Mac users should still read through this exercise because the online paper capture option for Macintosh users will be covered at the end of this section.

NOTE | Scanning Documents in Acrobat

The ability to scan documents in Acrobat is a Windows-only feature. In Windows you can choose **File > Import > Scan** to access the scanner that's installed on your system. If you have a scanner with a sheet feeder, you can pretty much leave Acrobat unattended with a stack of documents that you'd like to convert to PDFs. On Macintosh systems, you have to first scan in your documents using an image-editing program before you can import them into Acrobat. Here are some tips for scanning documents that you intend to turn into PDFs with recognizable text:

- For most documents, scanning at 300dpi produces the best results.

- If a page has very small characters, try scanning at higher resolutions.

- Use your scanning software's brightness controls to make sure characters appear as clear and sharp as possible. Acrobat must be able to distinguish one letter from another in order to recognize text.

- Always use the cleanest version of the document you can find. A document that has been photocopied numerous times will be difficult to work with.

4.————————**Converting Scanned Documents to PDF**

In this exercise, you'll convert a scanned image of text from a TIFF into a PDF. You'll then use the Paper Capture plug-in to turn the scanned text into text that can be searched and edited.

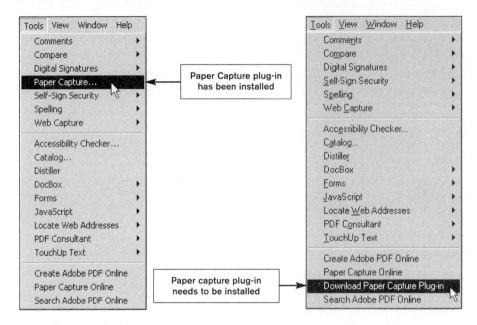

Note: Before starting this exercise, make sure that you have the Paper Capture plug-in installed in your copy of Acrobat. Click the Tools menu; if you see Paper Capture listed, you already have the plug-in installed. If you see Download Paper Capture Plug-in listed at the bottom of the menu, you'll need to install the plug-in before continuing with this exercise. The Paper Capture plug-in can be found in the "software" folder on the H•O•T CD-ROM, so you don't need to download the plug-in from Adobe's Web site.

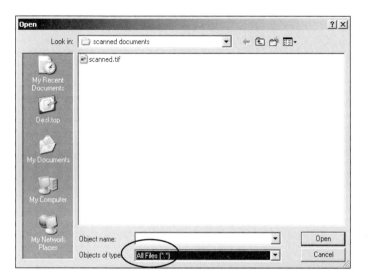

1. Choose **File > Open as Adobe PDF** (you used this function in Exercise 1). Select and open the file **scanned.tif** from the **scanned documents** folder located inside the **chap_13** folder. When selecting the image, make sure you're searching for all types of files. Acrobat will convert this TIFF into a PDF.

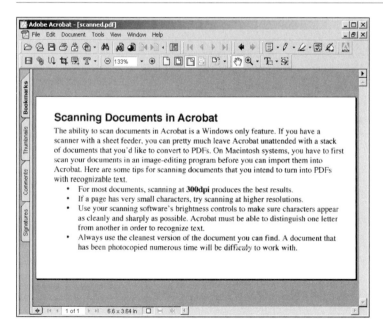

This document was printed on an inkjet printer and then scanned into Adobe Photoshop at 300dpi where it was then saved as a TIFF.

2. Select the **TouchUp Text** tool from the Toolbar and try to select some of the text on the page. Notice that you're unable to select any text at all, because as far as Acrobat is concerned, this is just a picture of text.

You'll next use the Paper Capture plug-in to make Acrobat recognize the shapes and squiggles on this document as actual text. When Acrobat converts scanned text into editable text, it selects a font that it considers to be the best match for what appears to be on the page. Understand that this will slightly alter the appearance of the text. If it's vital that your PDF documents match the font and appearance of the original document exactly, see the chart at the end of the exercise for other options

3. Choose **Tools > Paper Capture**. This will open the **Paper Capture Plug-in** dialog box.

Before you have Acrobat capture the text on this page, you'll set the preferences to make sure that Acrobat is looking for English words.

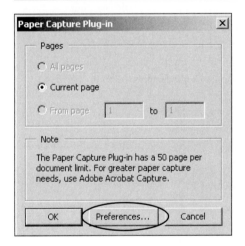

4. Click **Preferences**.

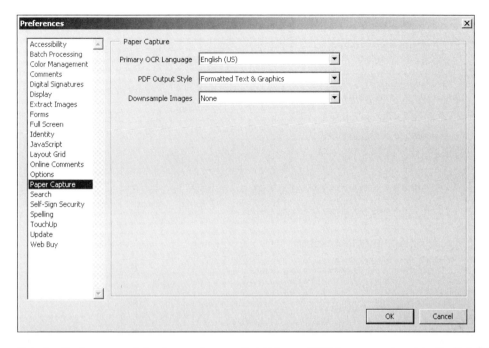

5. In the **Preferences** dialog box, make sure that **Primary OCR Language** is set to **English (US)**, **PDF Output Style** is set to **Formatted Text & Graphics**, and **Downsample Images** is set to **None**. Click **OK**. (The chart at the end of this exercise details the other options available in the Paper Capture Preferences dialog box.)

6. You're now ready to capture this page. Click **OK**.

The Paper Capture plug-in will do its thing ….

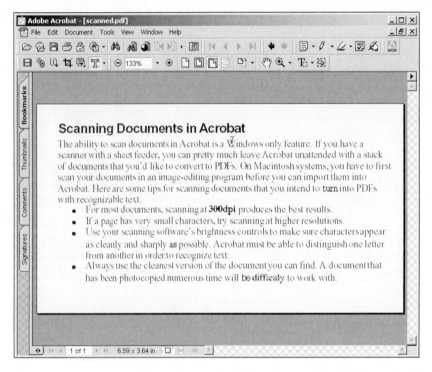

After a few moments, you'll see the results. This document now contains editable text. Notice that it looks slightly different than the original document because Acrobat chose a font that was similar in appearance to, but not exactly the same as, the original font. But there are a few things that need to be fixed. First, you'll check to make sure that Acrobat didn't misinterpret any words or letters in this document. You can do this by having Acrobat display "capture suspects," which are words that Acrobat suspects were incorrectly recognized.

7. Choose **Tools > TouchUp Text > Show Capture Suspects**. This will show you any of the words that Acrobat has doubts about.

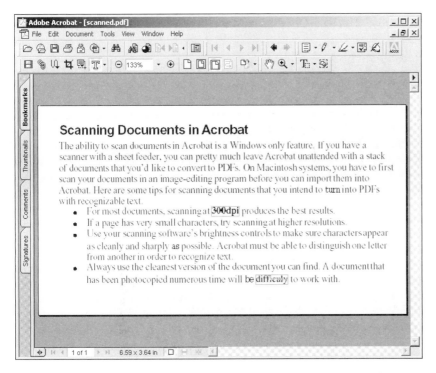

Acrobat has drawn red boxes around the words it suspects that it improperly recognized. The bold formatting on 300dpi most likely threw Acrobat off because the characters were crowded together. The word "difficult" was smudged, plus it was misspelled in the first place—both factors made it very difficult for Acrobat to properly recognize the word. Fortunately, now that you've made the text on this page editable, these two errors are easy to fix.

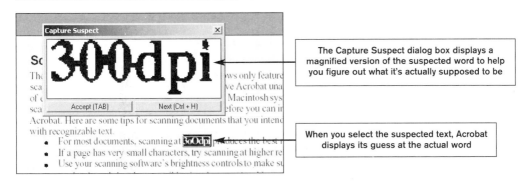

The Capture Suspect dialog box displays a magnified version of the suspected word to help you figure out what it's actually supposed to be

When you select the suspected text, Acrobat displays its guess at the actual word

8. With the **TouchUp Text** tool click on the first suspected word, **300dpi**. This will open the **Capture Suspect** dialog box. Acrobat will also highlight the suspected text and display its best guess at what the word should actually be. In this case Acrobat has come up with **3o0dpi**. Nice try, Acrobat.

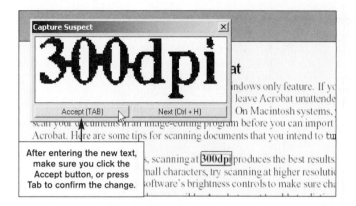

After entering the new text, make sure you click the Accept button, or press Tab to confirm the change.

9. To change the selected text, all you have to do is type. Enter **300dpi** and click **Accept** or press the **Tab** key. This will confirm your change and take you to the next suspected word.

Note: It's very important that you click Accept or press Tab before moving on to the next word. Otherwise, your change will not be confirmed and the text will revert back to its original appearance.

10. Change the next word to **difficult** and press the Tab key. You may need to add an extra space after **difficult** to prevent it from running into the neighboring word.

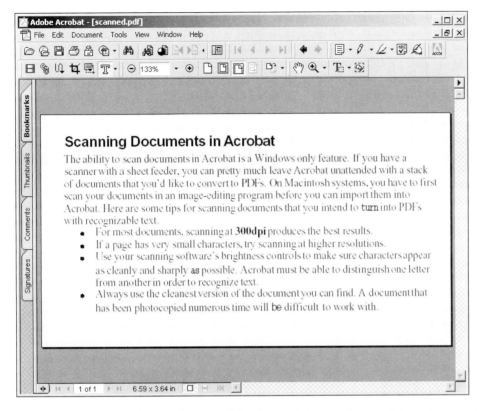

After pressing Tab, the Capture Suspect dialog box will close, indicating that you've corrected all of the suspect words. You have now successfully turned a scanned image into a document containing editable and searchable text. At this point you could continue to touch up text with the TouchUp Text tool, or index this document alongside other documents for archival purposes.

11. Save **scanned.pdf** and close the file.

NOTE | Adobe Acrobat Capture

The Paper Capture Plug-in can capture around 50 pages at a time. If you have to capture more than 50 pages, look into Adobe Acrobat Capture, which is a professional application created specifically for scanning large volumes of documents and converting them into search-able PDFs. It also features more sophisticated OCR and clean-up tools than Acrobat. Visit **www.adobe.com/products/acrcapture** for more information.

Paper Capture Settings

In the final exercise, you checked your OCR language settings before using the Paper Capture plug-in. The chart on the following pages describes the other options available in Paper Capture Preferences.

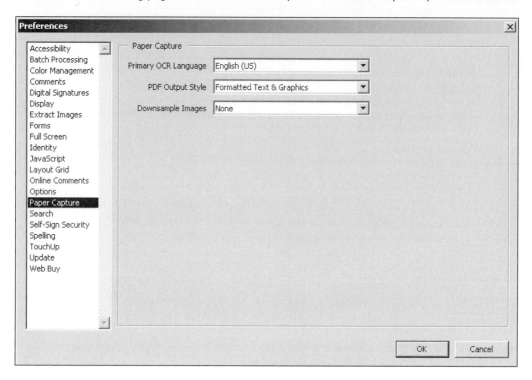

Paper Capture Preferences Settings

Item	Description
Primary OCR Language	Specifies which language you want the OCR to use when converting images to editable text.
PDF Output Style	The three settings under this menu determine whether Acrobat will alter the original scan of the image and, if so, how it will alter it. The three choices are:
	Formatted Text & Graphics: This is the option you used for Exercise 4. It replaces the scanned text with real fonts chosen to closely match the appearance of the original text. Depending on the quality of the scan, this may result in some words looking very different from the original (look closely at the captured document from this exercise and you'll notice that some words don't match the rest of the document). The fonts can be manually changed by selecting the text in question and choosing Tools > TouchUp Text > Text Attributes. But if you want the document to appear exactly as it was scanned, choose one of the other two options from the PDF Output Style menu (described below).
	Searchable Image (Exact): This option creates the searchable text as an invisible layer so that the original scanned file maintains its exact appearance. The document can be fully indexed, but there is no visible change to the document. This selection creates the largest file size of the three PDF Output Style options.
	Searchable Image (Compact): This is similar to the original selection, but it applies JPEG compression to the original image to make the file size smaller.
Downsample Images	The selections from this menu can be used to lower the resolution of any images contained within the file. Lower resolution reduces file size, but also creates lower-quality images. It's best to experiment with this setting to see how it affects your images and file size.

Online Paper Capture

When Adobe first released Acrobat 5 without the Paper Capture plug-in, the only option available for capturing pages with Acrobat was the Online Paper Capture. With this fee-based service, you opened scanned images in Acrobat and then connected to the Internet by choosing **Paper Capture Online** from the **Tools** menu. After registering with Adobe, you would upload your image, which would then be scanned by the OCR software running on Adobe's Web server. Finally, the file would be downloaded back into your computer and displayed in Acrobat. On a typical dial-up connection, this took *forever*. Once you received the file, you had the option of downloading it again from Acrobat's servers, but you only had 72 hours before the file would be erased.

Except for the fee, which Adobe has since eliminated, Online Paper Capture still works this way, and is still the only option for Macintosh Acrobat users. The steps for opening, capturing, and correcting a scanned file with Online Paper Capture are pretty much the same as described in Exercise 4, but instead of choosing **Tools > Paper Capture** to run the OCR software on the document, you instead choose **Tools > Paper Capture Online**. (More good news: This feature is not available in Mac OS X.)

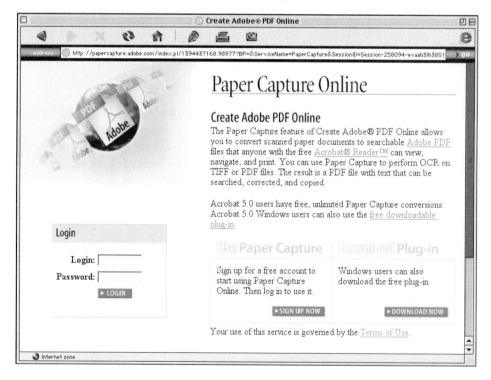

After choosing Paper Capture Online, you will be taken to Adobe's Web site where you need to create an account.

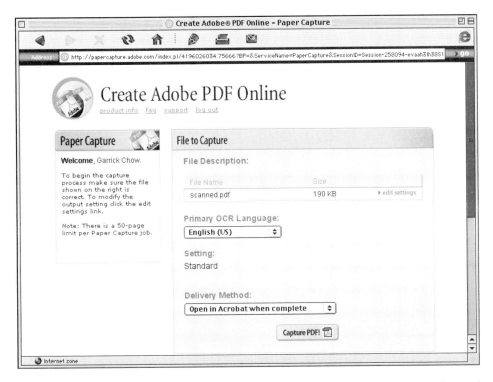

After you create an account and log in, you can choose your OCR language, conversion settings, and delivery method—you can have the captured PDF e-mailed to you, you can have Adobe e-mail you a link to the file, or you can have the file open in Acrobat as soon as it's ready. After making your selections, you can click the exuberantly labeled Capture PDF! button. Then you wait. And wait. Eventually the file will be converted. Once you receive the file, you use the Capture Suspects command as detailed in this exercise. Generally, the Online Paper Capture system works the same as the Paper Capture plug-in, but it would sure be nice to have the option of choosing between the two. If you want to see this feature returned to the Macintosh version of Acrobat, you can contact Adobe at **www.adobe.com/support/feature.html** and let the company know how you feel.

The purpose of this chapter was to demonstrate the abilities and limitations of the Acrobat application as a PDF creation tool. As you saw, the types of files that can be converted into PDF with Acrobat are limited at best. You'll often find that it's much better to create PDFs using Distiller or an application's Print command, as you learned in Chapter 12, "Acrobat Distiller." The main benefit of using Acrobat for creating PDFs is probably its ability to convert Web sites and images of text into PDFs. In the next chapter you'll learn how to create PDFs from specific applications.

14.

Creating PDFs from Popular Applications

| Microsoft Office | Adobe Photoshop 7 | Adobe Illustrator 10 |
| Adobe InDesign 2 | QuarkXPress 5 |

chap_14

Acrobat 5
H•O•T CD-ROM

As you saw in the Chapter 12, *"Acrobat Distiller,"* you can create PDFs from nearly any application that has a print command. But because of the growing popularity of the PDF format, many of these applications have incorporated the ability to bypass the print command and export PDFs directly. Obviously, most of Adobe's major applications such as Photoshop and Illustrator have long had the ability to generate PDFs. But other non-Adobe applications such as QuarkXPress have also included PDF exporting in their latest releases.

This chapter provides step-by-step instructions for creating PDFs from many of today's popular applications. Because PDFs are created for different purposes, these exercises provide just the basic steps to generate a PDF from the original application. Charts at the end of each exercise detail the specific options available for each application. Note that exporting PDFs directly from applications is usually used for creating general-use PDFs for the Web and office use. Professional printers almost always create their PDFs by distilling PostScript files, as you learned how to do in Chapter 12, *"Acrobat Distiller."*

Important Note: Example files have been provided for each exercise in this chapter, but you must have the specified application installed on your computer in order to follow along. The exercises also assume that you have a working knowledge of the application being used. You don't need to read these exercises in any particular order—in fact, you can just read the ones that will apply to your work. You should at least read through the first exercises on creating PDFs from Microsoft Office, however, because Chapter 15, *"Accessibility,"* will apply information from these exercises.

I. _____Microsoft Office (Windows Users)

When you install Acrobat 5, the installer scans your computer to see if you have a copy of Microsoft Office 98 or later on your system. If any of these versions of Office are found, the Acrobat installer will install a macro called PDFMaker into your copy of Office. Macros are sets of commands or tasks that have been programmed to be performed automatically. PDFMaker is a macro that gives you the ability to create PDFs directly from Word, Excel, and PowerPoint.

Note that in order for PDFMaker to be installed, you must have Office on your computer before installing Acrobat. If you install Office after Acrobat has been installed on your computer, you should remove Acrobat and then reinstall it if you want to use PDFMaker. Acrobat 5 for Macintosh did not ship with PDFMaker as part of the application, so Macintosh users must upgrade to Acrobat 5.05 in order to install PDFMaker into Office. The Acrobat 5.05 update Web page is located at **www.adobe.com/ products/acrobat/update.html**. The updaters for both Mac and Windows users can also be found in the "software" folder on **H•O•T CD-ROM**.

Although you'll be converting a Word document into a PDF in this exercise, the steps for creating PDFs from Excel and PowerPoint are essentially the same. Because the versions of PDFMaker differ greatly between the Windows and Macintosh platforms, this exercise relates to Windows users. Exercise 2 covers Microsoft Office for Macintosh users. If you are using a Macintosh, you may still want to read through the Windows exercise to see exactly how much is missing from the Macintosh PDFMaker.

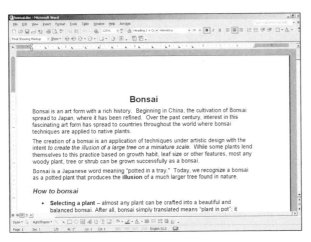

1. Copy the **chap_14** folder and files from the **H•O•T CD-ROM** to your hard drive. In **MS Word**, open the file **bonsai.doc** from the **chap_14** folder.

Before you convert this document to a PDF, you'll first examine how the document has been formatted. A properly formatted document makes it easy to automate the creation of elements such as bookmarks and links with PDFMaker.

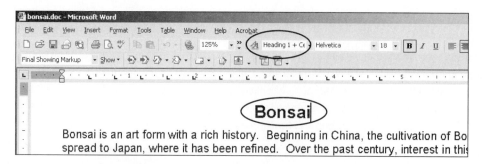

2. Click the cursor inside the title at the top of page **1**. If you look in your toolbar, you'll notice that the title has been formatted with the Heading 1 style. PDFMaker for Windows can convert headings and styles into Acrobat bookmarks.

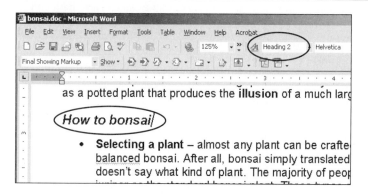

3. Scroll down and place your cursor in the line that reads **How to bonsai**. This has been set to Heading 2, and can also be converted into a bookmark by PDFMaker.

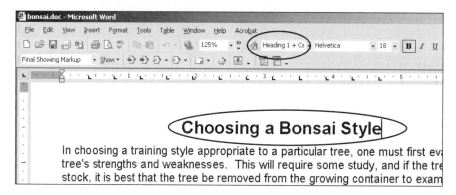

4. Go to page **4** and place your cursor in the title at the top of the page. This title has been formatted with a Heading 1 setting.

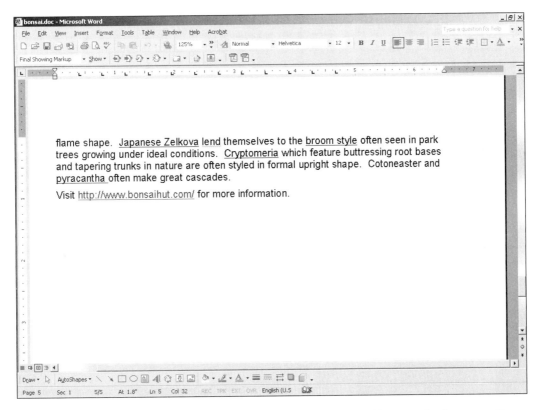

5. Scroll to the very end of the document. A hyperlink has been created here to take the user to the Bonsai Hut Web site. PDFMaker for Windows can convert this to an Acrobat link.

Next, you'll take a look at PDFMaker and the options you can choose from to create your PDF. As you'll see, PDFMaker gives you the same amount of control over your PDF as Acrobat Distiller, but PDFMaker also allows you to further enhance your PDFs directly from Office.

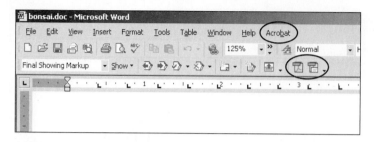

When PDFMaker is installed into Office, two buttons are added to the toolbars in Word, Excel, and PowerPoint, and an Acrobat menu appears in the menu bar. (If you don't see the buttons, choose View > Toolbars > PDFMaker 5.0.)

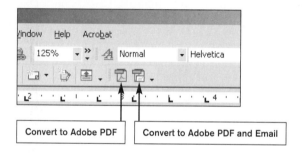

The two buttons are called Convert to Adobe PDF and Convert to Adobe PDF and Email, and they do exactly what their names imply.

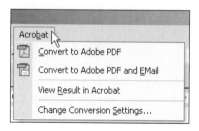

The Acrobat menu also contains the commands Convert to Adobe PDF and Convert to Adobe PDF and Email. It is also where you can choose to change the PDF conversion settings.

6. Choose **Acrobat > Change Conversion Settings**. This will open the PDFMaker dialog box.

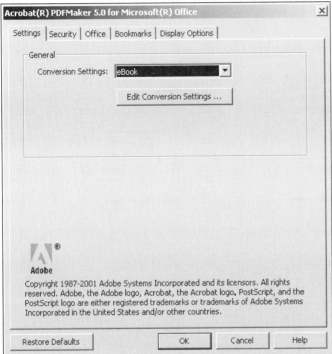

The PDFMaker dialog box contains five tabs, which in turn contain several options for PDF creation. The charts at the end of the exercise detail the various options. For now, you'll just examine a few settings.

The default tab, Settings, is where you have access to the same conversion settings that are available in Distiller. You can choose from Screen, eBook, Print, and Press, as well as any custom settings you may have previously created. But while these conversion settings are identical to the ones found in Distiller, they are completely independent. Any conversion settings currently set in Acrobat Distiller, whether Distiller is running or not, have no effect on the conversion settings you choose in PDFMaker.

7. Choose **eBook** for the **Conversion Settings** and then click the **Security** tab.

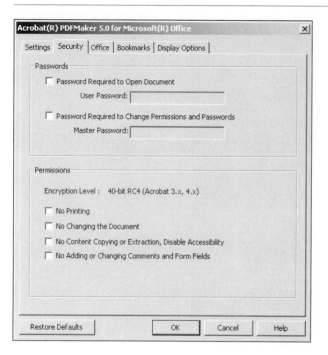

Under the Security tab, you can choose whether to apply security settings to the PDF. These are the same 40-bit encryption settings you worked with in Chapter 10, "Document Security." PDFMaker makes it convenient for you to make your selections here, rather than opening the PDF in Acrobat and then selecting security options. Note, however, that if you wish to set 128-bit security, you must open the PDF in Acrobat, because PDFMaker has no options for 128-bit security. Refer to Chapter 10 if you need a refresher on the security options.

8. You won't apply any security options here. Click the **Office** tab.

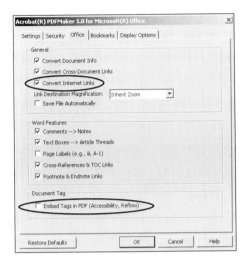

In the Office tab you can choose to preserve certain elements of your Word, Excel, or PowerPoint documents in their PDF versions. For instance you can choose to convert Word comments and Word links into Acrobat comments and links. For now, just make sure that Convert Internet Links is checked and Embed Tags in PDF is unchecked. You'll find out what these selections do momentarily.

9. Click the **Bookmarks** tab.

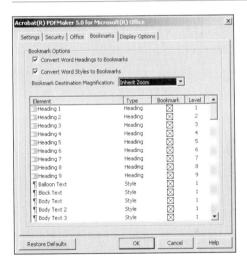

In the Bookmarks tab you can select the headings or styles that you want PDFMaker to turn into Acrobat bookmarks. For this reason, it's important that you format your Word documents properly with headings and styles rather than simply clicking the Bold and Italics buttons or increasing the text size manually. With properly created heading and styles, generating bookmarks is a snap.

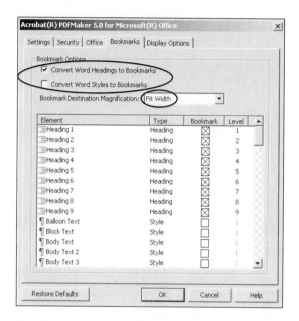

10. Check **Convert Word Heading to Bookmarks**. This will select all of the headings in the area below. Uncheck **Convert Word Styles to Bookmarks**. (This document doesn't use any styles, so it really doesn't matter whether this is checked or not.) Note that you could also select individual headings or styles by checking the box under the Bookmark column. The **Bookmark Destination Magnification** menu should already be set to **Fit Width**, but if it isn't, make sure you select Fit Width. This will allow the end user to see the entire width of the document page. Click the **Display Options** tab.

Under the Display Options tab, you can decide how you want the document to appear when it's opened, how links will appear, and which comments you want to include.

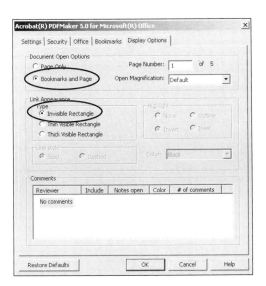

11. Under **Document Open Options**, select **Bookmarks and Page**, which will make the Bookmarks pane open as soon as the PDF is opened in Acrobat. Under **Link Appearance**, chose **Invisible Rectangle**. This will make any automatically generated link areas invisible in Acrobat. Click **OK** to return to the bonsai document.

Now that you've chosen your conversion settings, you're ready to create your PDF.

12. Choose **Acrobat > View Result in Acrobat**. This is not a necessary step, but it will save you some time by having the new PDF open automatically in Acrobat once it's been generated.

13. Click the **Convert to Adobe PDF** button or choose **Acrobat > Convert to Adobe PDF**.

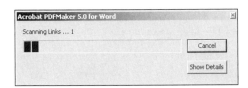

PDFMaker will begin converting the document; it will scan for headings to turn into bookmarks and links to turn into Acrobat links.

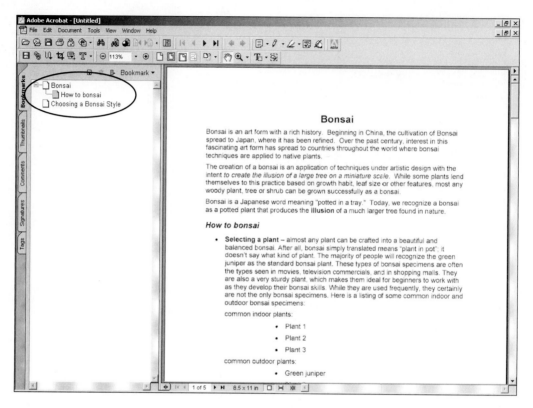

Once the conversion process is complete, the new PDF will open in Acrobat as an untitled document. Notice that the Bookmark pane is open and contains bookmarks created from the three headings from the bonsai document.

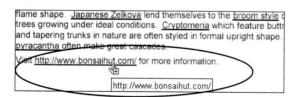

14. Click the **Last Page** button. Notice here that the link to **bonsaihut.com** has been created. If you select the **Link** tool, you'll be able to view the link area that PDFMaker generated.

From this point you could continue to work with this document like any other PDF. You could rearrange the bookmarks, create new links, touch up text, etc. PDFMaker has given you a nice head start on enhancing the PDF.

15. Save this file as **bonsai.pdf** and place it in the **chap_14** folder. Close the file once you've saved it.

PDFMaker Options (Windows Only)

The chart below describes the different options available in PDFMaker (for Windows only).

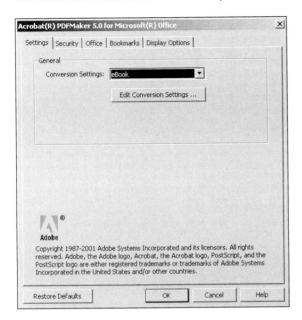

PDFMaker Options Tabs	
Item	**Description**
Settings	The selections here are identical to the conversion settings available in Distiller. Clicking the Edit Conversion Settings… button will allow you to create your own custom settings.
Security	Select options under this tab to apply 40-bit encryption security settings to your PDF. The options are identical to the 40-bit encryption options available in Acrobat. See Chapter 10, *"Document Security,"* for details.
Office	The options found here determine which elements from the document will be carried over into the PDF. See the Office Tab Options chart below.
Bookmarks	Under this tab you can choose which headings or styles PDFMaker should convert to Acrobat bookmarks. **Note:** The document must contain text formatted as Word headings or styles for this to work.
Display Options	Options under this tab determine how the PDF will appear when it's opened.

Office Tab Options

The following chart details the options found under the Office tab of PDFMaker.

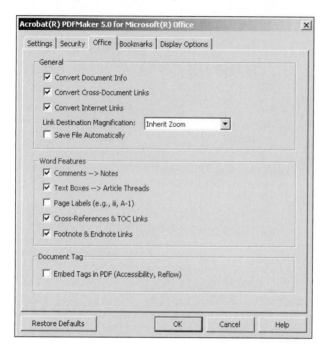

Office Tab Options	
Item	**Description**
Convert Document Info	Converts any stored information about the document's author and converts it into Acrobat Document Summary info. In Acrobat, choose **File > Document Properties > Summary** to view the document info.
Convert Cross-Document Links	Any links to other documents will be converted to links in the PDF file.
Convert Internet Links	Any links to Web sites will be converted to Web links in the PDF file.
Link Destination Magnification	This menu controls the magnification view of any links to PDF content.

continues on next page

	Office Tab Options *continued*	
Item	**Description**	
Save File Automatically	PDFMaker requires that your Office document is saved before converting it to PDF. Checking this option will bypass the dialog box asking you to save the file and do it for you automatically.	
Comments → Notes	Will convert any comments in the document to Acrobat comments. Acrobat comments were covered in Chapter 7, *"Commenting."*	
Text Boxes → Article Threads	Converts text boxes in Word to Acrobat article threads. Article threads were covered in Chapter 4, *"Creating and Editing Articles."*	
Page Labels	Transfers any unique numbering systems (such as i, ii, iii, etc.) over to the PDF file.	
Cross-References & TOC Links	If your document has taken advantage of Word's cross-reference or table of contents features, PDFMaker will convert these links into Acrobat links. Links were covered in Chapter 3, *"Working with Links."*	
Footnote & Endnote Links	Generates links from footnotes and endnotes to the actual notes in the document. For instance, if you had a footnote to an entry in the bibliography at the end of your document, PDFMaker would create a link from the footnote directly to the bibliography entry.	
Embed Tags in PDF (Accessibility, Reflow)	Adds PDF tags to your document to enable accessibility options. This topic will be covered in Chapter 15, *"Accessibility."*	

2. _____Microsoft Office (Macintosh Users)

If you're a Macintosh user and you've been reading the Windows PDFMaker exercise, prepare to be a little disappointed. To put it politely, compared to its Windows "equivalent," PDFMaker for the Mac sucks. While PDFMaker for Windows is a full-featured macro, offering lots of ways to automate and enhance PDF creation, PDFMaker for the Mac is little more than a conduit for Acrobat Distiller. There is no PDFMaker dialog box in which to create bookmarks, links, or security settings. In fact, using PDFMaker for the Mac is not that much different then choosing **File > Print** and selecting **Create Adobe PDF**, which was covered Chapter 12, *"Acrobat Distiller."* Don't forget that you can contact Adobe at **www.adobe.com/support/feature.html** to let them know how you feel about this.

Remember, you must be using Acrobat 5.05 and must have installed it after installing Office on your Mac. At the time of publication of this book, PDFMaker for the Mac was only available for Office 98 and 2001, so this exercise will feature screenshots from Office 2001 running in Mac OS 9.

Before converting your Office document to PDF, you must first open Acrobat Distiller and select your preferred conversion settings.

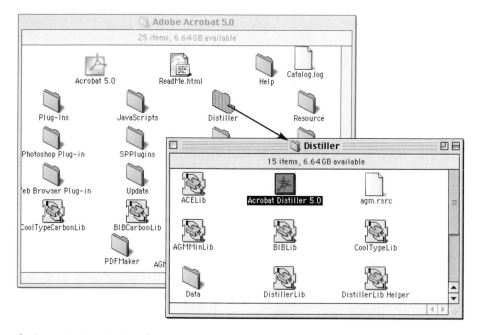

1. Open Acrobat Distiller. (It's located in the Acrobat application folder inside the folder called **Distiller**.) If you're running Acrobat, you can also choose **Tools > Distiller**.

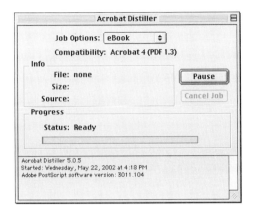

2. In Distiller you can select your preferred conversion settings. For this exercise, select **eBook**. At this point, you can either quit Distiller or keep it open; you can use PDFMaker whether or not Distiller is running. For this exercise, though, go ahead and quit Distiller.

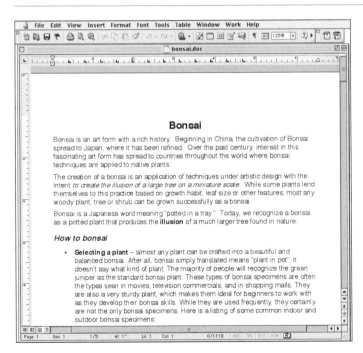

3. In **MS Word**, open **bonsai.doc** from the **chap_14** folder. You'll convert this into a PDF using PDFMaker.

As I mentioned in my rant earlier, PDFMaker on the Mac is not nearly the equivalent of its Windows counterpart. Like the Windows version, PDFMaker installs two buttons into the toolbars of Word, Excel, and PowerPoint. (If you don't see the buttons, choose View > Toolbars > Adobe Acrobat PDFMaker.)

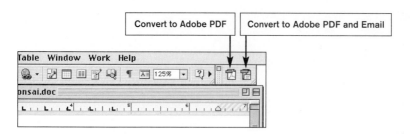

Clicking the Convert to Adobe PDF button will convert the document into a PDF based on the conversion settings you selected in Distiller. Clicking the Convert to Adobe PDF and Email button will do the same thing, but in addition to creating the PDF, it will open your default e-mail program and create a new mail document with the PDF as an attachment.

Unlike the Windows version of PDFMaker, the Mac version does not create an Acrobat menu in the menu bar. There are no options available to have PDFMaker automatically generate bookmarks, links, comments, security settings, or any other PDF enhancements. All you can do here is click one of the Convert to Adobe PDF buttons to create a PDF based on your current Distiller settings. So, that said....

4. Click the **Convert to Adobe PDF** button to create a PDF based on your current Distiller settings.

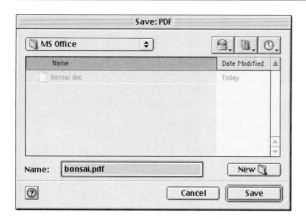

5. When prompted, name the file **bonsai.pdf** and place it in the **chap_14** folder. Click **Save**.

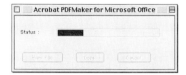

PDFMaker will begin converting the Word document into a PDF.

6. When the conversion is complete, click the **View File** button to open the file in Acrobat.

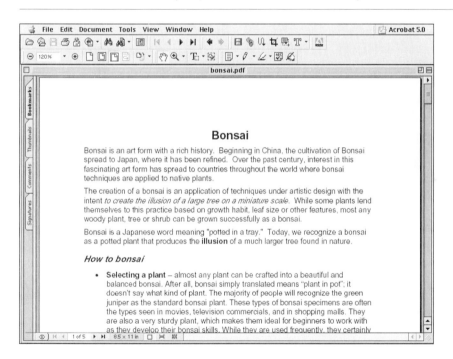

The new PDF opens in Acrobat. At this point you can work with this document like any other PDF— you can add bookmarks, links, articles, etc. But wouldn't it have been nice to have PDFMaker create some of these elements for you automatically?

7. Close this file. Go to **www.adobe.com/support/feature.html** and ask Adobe to please release a better version of PDFMaker for the Mac soon.

3.————————————Adobe Photoshop 7

This exercise will walk you through PDF creation from Photoshop 7. The process is identical on both Mac and Windows platforms, so only one set of instructions is provided. Note that these steps work for Photoshop 6 as well.

1. In **Photoshop**, open the file **ojai.psd** from the **chap_14** folder. In addition to the photograph, this image contains a text layer and a vector graphic layer.

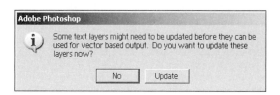

Note: If the above dialog box appears when you open ojai.psd, click Update.

2. To create a PDF from this image, select **File > Save As**.

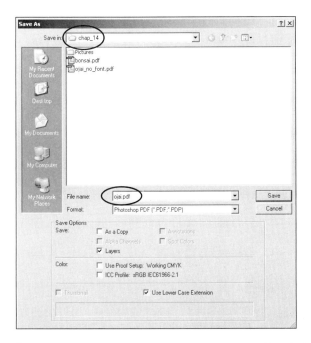

3. In the **Save As** dialog box, name the file **ojai.pdf** and place it in the **chap_14** folder. Set **Format** to **Photoshop PDF**. Click the **Save** button. This will open the **PDF Options** dialog box.

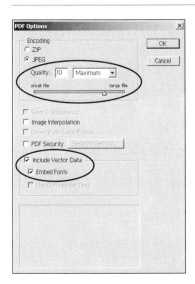

In this dialog box you can choose the type of compression to use on the image, its security settings, and whether or not to embed fonts.

4. Under **Encoding**, select **JPEG**, and set the **Quality** slider to **10** to produce a sharp image. Check the boxes next to **Include Vector Data** and **Embed Fonts**. This will ensure that your text will be nice and crisp in the PDF. Click **OK**.

Tip: To automatically apply security to the PDF, check the box next to PDF Security and click the Security Settings button. This will open a dialog box allowing you to apply either 40-bit or 128-bit security settings, exactly the same settings you worked with in Chapter 10, "Document Security." Security settings and Downgrade Color Profile are not available in Photoshop 6.

5. Switch to Acrobat and open the **ojai.pdf** file you just saved in the **chap_14** folder. Because you saved the PDF at a high quality and embedded the font, it looks identical to the original image.

6. Select the **Zoom** tool and draw a marquee around the **W** in **Welcome** to zoom in on the text.

Notice even at the highest magnification levels, the text remains crisp and sharp. Now as a comparison, you'll take a look at the same file, but without the embedded font.

7. Open **ojai_no_font.pdf** from the **chap_14** folder.

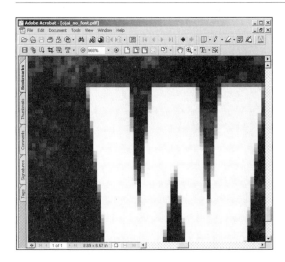

8. Initially, this file looks the same, but if you zoom in on the text again, you'll notice that it's jagged at high magnifications. On the other hand, without the embedded font, **ojai_no_font.pdf** is a slightly smaller file than **ojai.pdf**. It's ultimately up to you to decide whether embedded fonts or smaller file size is more important for your document.

9. Close any open files in Acrobat and Photoshop.

Photoshop PDF Options

The chart below details the options available in the PDF Options dialog box that appears when you export a PDF from Photoshop. Some of these items may be foreign to you if you're unfamiliar with certain aspects of Photoshop.

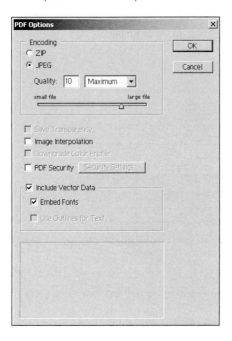

Photoshop PDF Options	
Item	**Description**
Encoding	Determines the compression method used on the PDF. ZIP compression is most effective for images containing large areas of single colors, while JPEG compression is better suited for photographic or continuous tone images. Selecting JPEG activates the Quality slider, allowing you to choose the level of JPEG compression you wish to apply.
Save Transparency	Preserves transparency when the file is opened in another application. Transparency is always preserved when the PDF file is opened in Photoshop.
	continues on next page

Photoshop PDF Options *continued*	
Item	**Description**
Image Interpolation	Checking this allows other applications to interpolate the image when resampling it to another size.
Downgrade Color Profile	If you selected ICC Profile (Windows) or Embed Color Profile (Mac) in the Save As dialog box, checking this option will downgrade the color profile from version 4 to version 2, which is useful if you plan to open the PDF in an application that doesn't support version 4. Not available in Photoshop 6.
PDF Security	Checking this box and clicking the Security Settings button enables you to apply 40-bit or 128-bit security settings to the PDF. See Chapter 10, *"Document Security,"* for a full description of the security settings. Not available in Photoshop 6.
Include Vector Data	Preserves vector graphics such as shapes and text as resolution-independent objects, providing smoother-looking output. Choosing **Embed Fonts** will include the font information in the PDF, ensuring that the end user will see the type exactly as you intended. **Use Outlines for Text** converts text to paths, which is useful if fonts cannot be embedded (some fonts are protected from being embedded) or if embedding the fonts produces overly large file sizes.

4. —————————Adobe Illustrator 10

This exercise walks you through the steps to create a PDF directly from Adobe Illustrator. Although the screenshots in this exercise were taken from Mac OS X, the steps are the same for Windows users, and also apply to Illustrator 9 for both platforms.

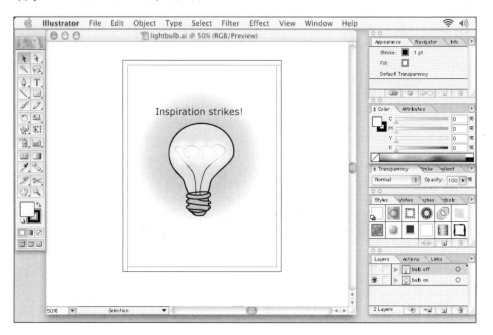

1. In **Illustrator**, open the file **lightbulb.ai** from the **chap_14** folder.

2. Select **File > Save As** to begin converting this file into a PDF.

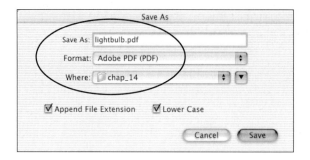

3. For **Format**, select **Adobe PDF**. Name the file **lightbulb.pdf** and save it in the **chap_14** folder. Click **Save**. This will open the **Adobe PDF Format Options** dialog box.

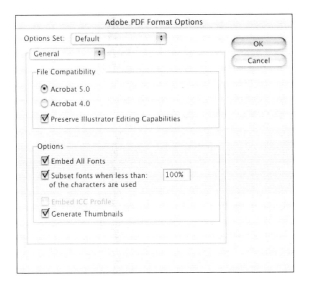

4. If it's not already selected, select **Default** from the **Options Set** menu. The Default setting makes the PDF Acrobat 5.0 compatible and embeds all fonts from the Illustrator file into the PDF. The chart at the end of this exercise details the options in this dialog box. Click **OK**. Acrobat will create the PDF.

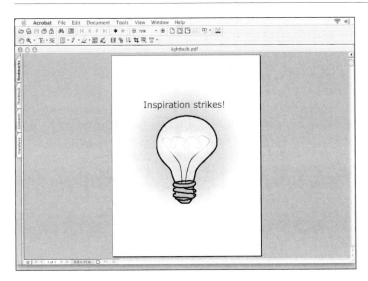

5. Switch to Acrobat and open **lightbulb.pdf** from the **chap_14** folder.

6. After you've viewed the file, close it and quit Illustrator.

Illustrator PDF Format Options

The chart below details the options available in Illustrator's PDF Format Options dialog box under the General settings.

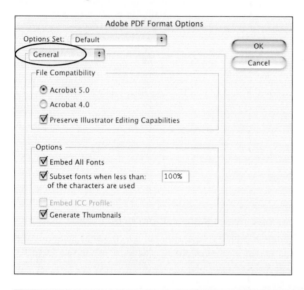

Illustrator PDF Format Options	
Item	**Description**
Options Set	This menu offers three choices: Default, Screen Optimized, and Custom. Selecting **Default** will set the dialog box to preset selections that are optimized for files that will be printed. **Screen Optimized** does not allow you to generate thumbnails and doesn't preserve Illustrator editing capabilities, meaning that the PDF will not be able to be altered in Illustrator. Changing any settings under File Compatibility or Options will automatically switch the Options Set menu to **Custom**.
File Compatibility	Determines whether the PDF will be compatible with Acrobat 4.0 and higher or only compatible with Acrobat 5.0. Choose Acrobat 5.0 to preserve transparency, text, and spot color data. Note that not all applications will be able to interpret this data, even though it is embedded in the PDF.

continues on next page

Illustrator PDF Format Options *continued*

Item	Description
Preserve Illustrator Editing Capabilities	Check this option if you want to open and edit the PDF in Illustrator.
Embed All Fonts	Embeds all the fonts from the Illustrator file into the PDF, ensuring that users without the specified font will still be able to open and print the file. Note that embedding fonts slightly increases the size of the PDF.
Subset fonts when ...	Determines when to embed fonts based on the percentage of the font's characters used in the document.
Embed ICC Profile	Creates a color-managed document.
Generate Thumbnails	Creates and embeds thumbnails into the PDF. You learned to manually embed thumbnails in Chapter 6, *"Modifying PDFs."*

NOTE | Compression Settings in Illustrator

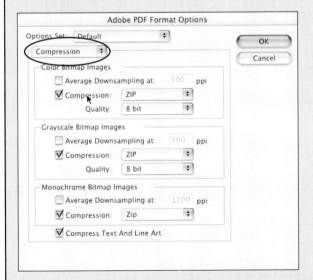

The options available under the **Compression** settings are identical to the compression settings found in Acrobat Distiller. See Chapter 12, *"Acrobat Distiller,"* for more information on compression settings.

5. —————————— Adobe InDesign 2

This exercise walks you through the steps to export a PDF from an Adobe InDesign layout. As you'll see, exporting PDFs from InDesign gives you the same amount of control over the PDF that Acrobat Distiller does. The conversion process is identical on Mac and Windows platforms.

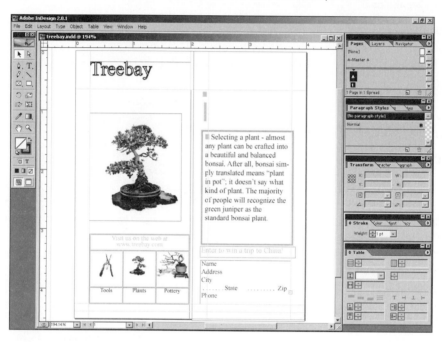

1. From **InDesign**, open **treebay.indd** from the **chap_14** folder.

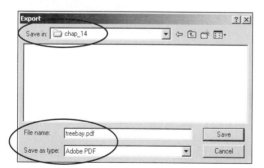

2. Choose **File > Export**. In the **Export** dialog box, navigate to the **chap_14** folder and name this file **treebay.pdf**. Save the file as **Adobe PDF**. Click **Save**. This will open the **Export PDF** dialog box.

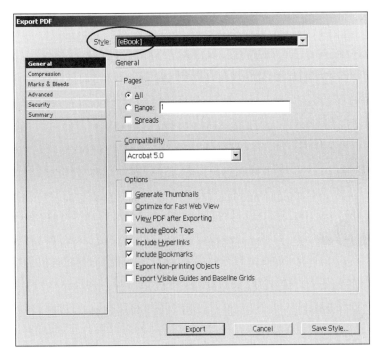

In the Export PDF dialog box, you'll find options that are nearly identical to those found in Acrobat Distiller. You can select from the categories on the left side of the dialog box to view the various options. The chart at the end of this exercise details the options found in the General category.

3. Select **eBook** from the **Style** menu at the top of the dialog box. This will automatically set your options to include eBook tags, hyperlinks, and bookmarks.

4. If you were working on your own project you could customize other settings at this point. For the purposes of this exercise, click **Export** to create the PDF.

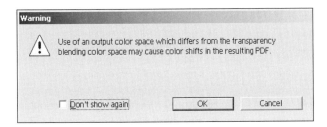

If you see a warning dialog box about the output color space, click OK to dismiss it.

5. Once the PDF has been created, close InDesign and switch to Acrobat. Open **treebay.pdf** from the **chap_14** folder.

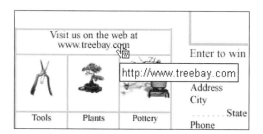

6. Place the **Hand** tool over the URL near the bottom of the page. Notice that InDesign has preserved the Web link. If you have a live Internet connection, clicking the link will take you to the Treebay Web site.

7. Close **treebay.pdf**.

InDesign Export PDF Options

The chart below details the options available under the General section of InDesign's Export PDF dialog box.

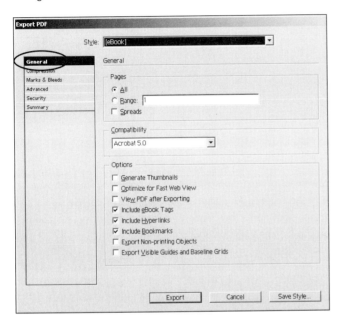

InDesign Export PDF General Options	
Item	**Description**
Style	This menu enables you to choose from eBook, Screen, Print, and Press settings. Choosing one of these four selections will alter the settings in the General, Compression, and Advanced categories. Any further changes made in any of the five categories will switch the Style menu to Custom.
Pages	In this area you can choose which pages you wish to convert to PDF. Selecting **All** will convert all the document's pages. To convert a range of pages, click the **Range** button and type in the page ranges separated by a hyphen. For example **2-7** will convert pages 2 through 7. You can also choose multiple ranges by using a comma, as in: 2-7, 14-20, 23-27. Selecting **Spreads** will export the pages as if they were bound or printed on the same sheet.

continues on next page

InDesign Export PDF General Options *continued*

Item	Description
Compatibility	Use this menu to choose whether the document will be compatible with Acrobat 4.0 and later or only with Acrobat 5.0. Selecting Acrobat 5.0 will preserve transparency, text, and spot colors in the document. Select Acrobat 5.0 if you might be opening the PDF in InDesign.
Options	The selections under the Options heading may be selected in any combination.
Generate Thumbnails	Will create and embed thumbnails into the PDF.
Optimize for Fast Web View	Reduces file size by reorganizing the file structure for page-at-a time downloading from Web servers. PDFs optimized for Fast Web View will load more quickly when downloaded from the Web. This option applies compression to text and line art, overriding selections made in the Compression category.
View PDF after Exporting	Will open the PDF in Acrobat as soon as it's created.
Include eBook Tags	"Tags" the PDF for Accessibility. This topic is covered in depth in Chapter 15, *"Accessibility."*
Include Hyperlinks	Converts InDesign hyperlinks, table of contents entries, and index entries into Acrobat links.
Include Bookmarks	Generates Acrobat bookmarks from table of contents entries and preserves the table of contents' structural hierarchy.
Export Non-printing Objects	Exports objects that have had the InDesign Non-printing option applied to them.
Export Visible Guides and Baseline Grids	Exports the baseline grid and guides, if currently visible. Guides and grids appear in the PDF in the same colors that were used in the InDesign document.

Of the other four categories in the Export PDF dialog box, **Marks & Bleeds** and **Advanced** are usually only used in professional printing scenarios. In most cases the person printing your document will specify these settings for you. The settings under the **Compression** category were covered in Chapter 12, *"Acrobat Distiller,"* while the **Security** settings provide the same 40-bit encryption settings covered in Chapter 10, *"Document Security."* The **Summary** category provides a run-down of the selections made in the Export PDF dialog box.

6. _____QuarkXPress 5

This exercise will teach you how to export PDFs directly from QuarkXPress 5. Unlike the Adobe products covered so far, QuarkXPress does not have built-in capabilities to create PDFs; instead, it uses Acrobat Distiller to generate PDFs. Therefore, you must have the full version of Acrobat installed on your computer if you wish to create PDFs from QuarkXpress.

The following steps are identical on Macintosh and Windows platforms, but do not apply to earlier versions of QuarkXPress. If you're a Macintosh user, you probably already know that QuarkXPress 5 is not compatible with Mac OS X.

Because QuarkXPress uses Acrobat Distiller to generate PDFs, you must first select your conversion settings in Distiller before you can create a PDF from QuarkXPress.

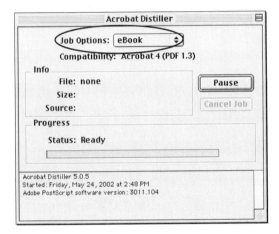

1. Open Acrobat Distiller. Choose **eBook** from the **Job Options** menu. (For your own work you would obviously select the Job Option that best suits your QuarkXPress document.) Once you've made your selection, quit Distiller. (It doesn't matter whether Distiller is running or not; QuarkXPress will open Distiller when it is needed).

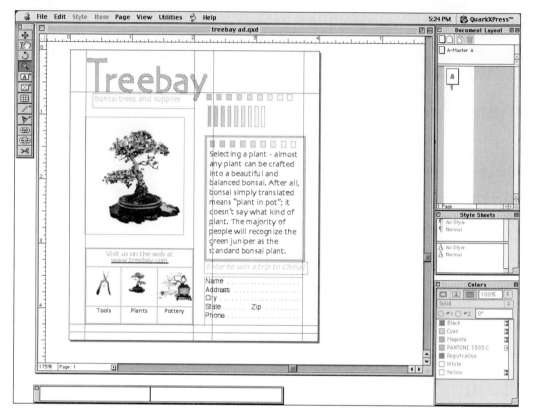

2. From **QuarkXPress 5**, open the file **treebay ad.qxd** from the **chap_14** folder. This document contains a link to the Treebay Web site. You will convert this document into a PDF.

3. Choose **File > Export > Document as PDF**.

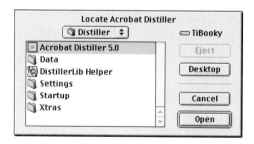

Note: If this is the first time you've exported a PDF from QuarkXPress, you'll be asked to locate your copy of Acrobat Distiller. Navigate to the Distiller application on your hard drive and then click Open. You will be prompted to select a name and location for the PDF.

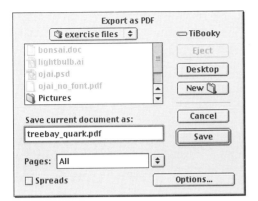

4. Navigate to the **chap_14** folder and name the file **treebay_quark.pdf**. Before you create the PDF, you'll examine some of the PDF settings. Click the **Options...** button.

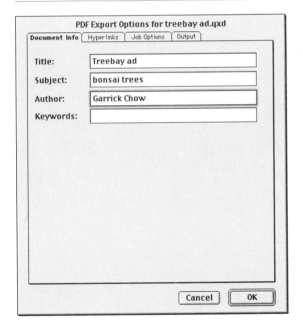

5. In the **PDF Export Options** dialog box, you can select from the four tabs at the top to customize your PDF conversion settings. Under the **Document Info** tab, type **Treebay ad** as the **Title**. In the **Subject** field, type **bonsai trees**. Enter your name in the **Author** field. This information will be available in the PDF's document summary page, which you'll take a look at shortly. Click the **Hyperlinks** tab.

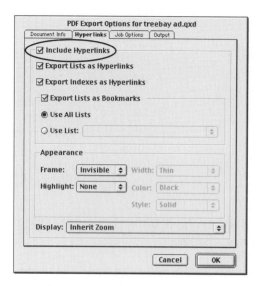

6. Under the **Hyperlinks** tab, make sure that **Include Hyperlinks** is checked. This will convert any hyperlinks into Acrobat links. Notice here that you also have the option of converting lists into bookmarks. This document doesn't contain any lists, so that option will have no effect. Click the **Job Options** tab.

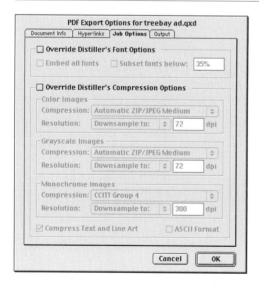

Under the Job Options tab you can choose to override Distiller's current Font and Compression settings. For this exercise you won't change anything here.

7. Click the **Output** tab.

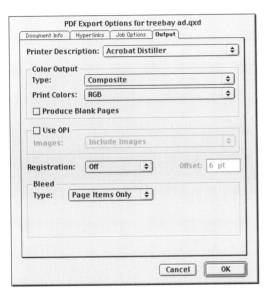

You would only need to be concerned about the selections under the Output tab if you were having this document professionally printed. The printer would advise you on any changes that needed to be made. Since you're only going to be viewing this document onscreen you don't need to make any changes.

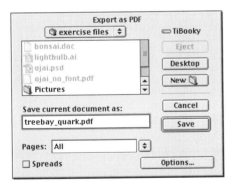

8. Click **OK** to return to the **Export as PDF** dialog box. Click **Save** to generate the PDF.

QuarkXPress will generate a PostScript file and then open Distiller to create the PDF. Once it's done, it will quit Distiller and you'll be returned to QuarkXPress.

9. Keep QuarkXPress open, but switch to Acrobat.

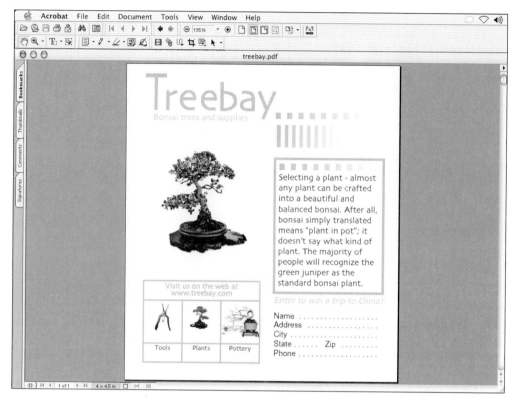

10. In Acrobat, open **treebay.pdf** from the **chap_14** folder. Now you'll see the results of the options you selected.

11. Place the **Hand** tool over the link near the bottom-left side of the page. Notice that the hyperlink here has been preserved. Clicking the link will take you to the Treebay Web site.

12. Choose **File > Document Properties > Summary**.

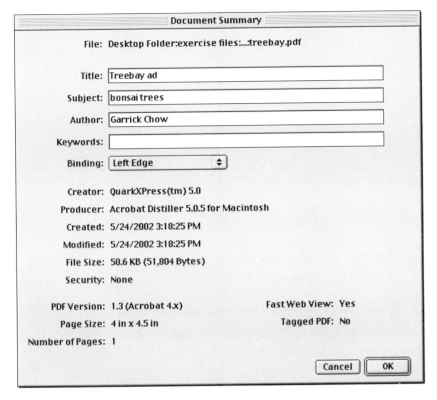

The Document Summary dialog box contains the information you added in QuarkXPress.

13. Click **OK** to close the Document Summary dialog box.

14. Close Acrobat and return to QuarkXPress. You'll next take a look at the PDF **Preferences** dialog box.

15. In QuarkXPress, choose **Edit > Preferences > Preferences**.

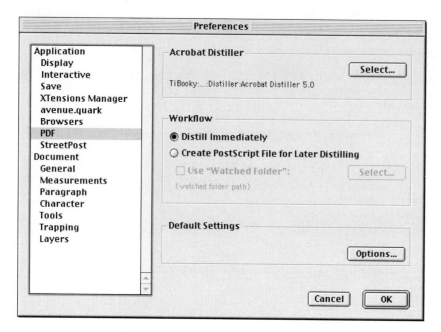

16. From the list of categories on the left of the **Preferences** dialog box, select **PDF**. See the following chart for the available options and what each does.

17. Click **OK** and quit QuarkXPress.

QuarkXPress PDF Preferences Options

The chart below describes the options in the QuarkXPress PDF Preferences dialog box.

QuarkXPress PDF Preferences Options	
Item	**Description**
Acrobat Distiller	Clicking the Select button here will allow you to locate the copy of Distiller you want QuarkXPress to use. This is useful if you move Distiller on your computer and QuarkXPress is no longer able to find it.
Workflow	The selections under this heading determine whether a PDF or a PostScript file will be generated.
Distill Immediately	QuarkXPress will create a PostScript file, immediately distill it to generate a PDF, and then delete the PostScript file.
Create PostScript File for Later Distilling	QuarkXPress will generate a PostScript file but will not distill it. You can then manually distill the file, or you can check Use "Watched Folder."
Use "Watched Folder":	If you've previously set up a watched folder (as you learned to do in Chapter 12, *"Acrobat Distiller"*), you can click the Select button here to have QuarkXPress place the PostScript file into the watched folder, where it will then be converted into a PDF.
Default Settings	Clicking the Options... button here is another way to access the same PDF Export Options dialog box that you worked with in this exercise.

One more chapter to go! In the last chapter you'll learn about Accessibility and what it means for you and your PDF documents.

I5.

Accessibility

Creating a Tagged PDF	Examining a Tagged PDF
Changing Reflow Order	Adding Alternate Text
Using the Accessibility Checker	The Make Accessible Plug-In
Accessibility Preferences

chap_15

Acrobat 5
H•O•T CD-ROM

The term **Accessibility** has been a buzzword for the past few years. When most people use the word accessible in relation to electronic media, they are usually referring to the act of making documents and Web pages usable by people with visual disabilities. While the visually impaired are a big part of the issue (and constitute a legal issue for government agencies), they represent just one aspect of the discussion. In a larger sense, accessibility is about creating documents that can be easily viewed and used by as many people as possible.

This chapter will cover various ways to make your PDFs accessible. You'll learn how to create "tagged" PDFs that contain information about the structure of your document. Users viewing tagged PDFs can "reflow" the PDFs so that text wraps and flows based on the dimensions of the device viewing the document, not on the original document's layout. Tagged PDFs also provide screen readers with the necessary information to ensure that your documents are read in the correct order to those with visual disabilities. Various other ways to make your PDFs accessible will be discussed in the exercises that follow.

Accessibility Overview

In this era of electronic media, there are dozens of ways to view Web pages, word processing documents, and PDF files. Some people work on huge 21-inch monitors while others work on palmtop computers. Most people enjoy good vision and take viewing text on computer screens for granted. Those with poor vision aren't so fortunate and must rely on screen readers, software that uses speech synthesis to read the contents of their monitors out loud. For a document to be truly accessible, everyone should be able to view the document, regardless of the quality of their vision or the size of their monitor. Ideally, your documents should be just as accessible to those viewing your PDF on a regular computer monitor as they are to those who are viewing your PDF on a palmtop computer or with the aid of a screen reader.

In this chapter, the first exercise will teach you how to create a tagged PDF file. Tagged PDFs enhance the reading experience on palmtop devices by allowing the content to reflow and fit the screen size. Tags also provide something called a logical structure tree, which dictates the order of the contents on the page. The logical structure tree not only ensures that paragraphs and sections of your document will be displayed in the proper order, but it also helps screen readers follow the proper flow of the text on the page. Without tags, it's possible that a screen reader might read paragraphs out of order.

If you have a document that you believe will be viewed on varying display sizes, you can create a tagged version of the document that can be reflowed. When a PDF document is reflowed, text size remains the same and stays at a reasonably legible level of magnification. Images, meanwhile, will scale to smaller sizes to accommodate the smaller viewing area. An illustration loses its effect if the user can only see a small corner of it.

Tip: For more information about screen readers for the visually disabled, check out the sites of some screen reader manufacturers such as Freedom Scientific (http://www.freedomscientific.com) and GW Micro (http://www.gwmicro.com). If you're curious about how these things work and you're using Windows 2000, Me or XP, you have a basic screen-reading utility called Narrator located in your Accessibility folder inside Accessories.

NOTE | What Is Section 508 and Why Does It Concern Me?

In 1998, Congress amended the Rehabilitation Act of 1973, Section 508, to require Federal agencies to make their electronic and information technologies accessible to people with disabilities. "Electronic and information technologies" include any devices used to share information electronically, including documents such as Web pages and PDFs, and hardware such as computers and information kiosks. Section 508 essentially gave the public the right to sue government agencies that did not comply with accessibility standards. By law, all government agencies were required to come into compliance with the Section 508 standards by June 21, 2001. This looming deadline caused many an agency to scramble frantically around January 2001 in a desperate attempt to get their documents up to standards. If you worked for a government agency at that time, you probably know what I'm talking about.

Creating tagged PDFs is crucial to making your PDFs conform to Section 508 of the 1973 Rehabilitation Act. But what if you don't work for a government agency? Should you concern yourself with accessibility? Yes, for a number of reasons. Even if you work for a private business, you don't want to risk alienating potential customers or clients by having documents that can't be accessed by the visually disabled. Also with many people now reading Web pages and other documents on palmtop devices, and even phones, you want your documents to be as accessible to as many devices as possible.

Of course, if you're just making a PDF for the guy down the hall to check out, you don't have to worry about making it accessible to the world. But if the audience for your PDF is the general populace, you should take the time to make sure that your document is accessible.

Check out **http://www.section508.gov/** for more information about Section 508.

I. —————————Creating a Tagged PDF

Tagged files can be generated from Adobe PageMaker 7.0, Adobe InDesign 2.0, and Microsoft Office for Windows (with PDFMaker installed). If your document was generated in a program other than these three, or if you no longer have the original file, you can still add tags to a PDF by using the Make Accessible plug-in in Acrobat. This plug-in will be examined later in this chapter.

In this exercise you'll use PDFMaker in Microsoft Word to create a tagged PDF file from a Word document, which you will then examine in Exercise 2. Only the Windows version of PDFMaker is capable of creating a tagged PDF file. If you're using a Macintosh or if you don't have Word, you won't be able to create the tagged PDF in this exercise, but you should still read through this chapter to understand how tags are created. When you move on to the second exercise, you'll be able to use a copy of the properly tagged PDF from the **chap_15** folder.

---

1. Copy the **chap_15** files and folders from the **H•O•T CD-ROM** to your hard drive.

---

2. Open **MS Word** 97, 2000, or XP. Make sure that **PDFMaker** is installed before continuing this exercise. See Exercise 1 of Chapter 14, *"Creating PDFs from Popular Applications,"* if you need a refresher on what PDFMaker is.

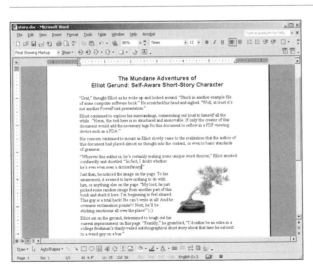

3. Open the file **story.doc** from the **chap_15** folder.

This single-page document contains a title, several paragraphs, and an image. As you're about to see, the process of creating a tagged PDF is nearly identical to the process you followed to create a non-tagged PDF in the previous chapter.

---

4. Choose **Acrobat > Change Conversion Settings** to open the PDFMaker settings dialog box.

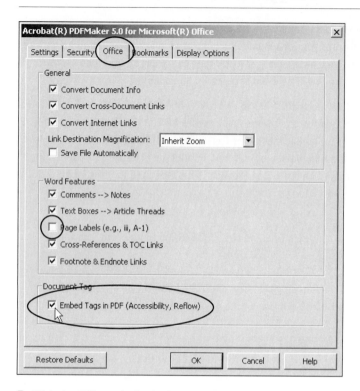

5. Click the **Office** tab. At the bottom of the dialog box, check **Embed Tags in PDF (Accessibility, Reflow)**. Also make sure that **Page Labels** is not checked. That's it! Now when you convert this document to a PDF, PDFMaker will add the necessary accessibility tags. Click **OK**.

6. Click the **Convert to Adobe PDF** button in the toolbar, or choose **Acrobat > Convert to Adobe PDF** from the menu bar. If PDFMaker displays a message saying that it needs to save the file before converting it, click **Yes**. When you're prompted to name the PDF, name it **story_tagged.pdf** and save it in the **chap_15** folder.

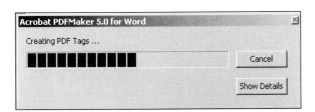

PDFMaker will convert the Word document into a PDF.

7. When it's finished, close Word and open Acrobat.

You've just created a tagged PDF. In the next exercise, you'll take a look at this PDF in Acrobat.

2. ———————Examining a Tagged PDF

If you were unable to follow along with the previous exercise, either because you are working on a Mac, or you don't have Microsoft Word, a pre-created PDF called **story_no_tags.pdf** as been provided for you so that you can still see how a tagged PDF behaves in Acrobat.

Before you examine the tagged PDF created in the last exercise, you'll take a look at a non-tagged version of the document.

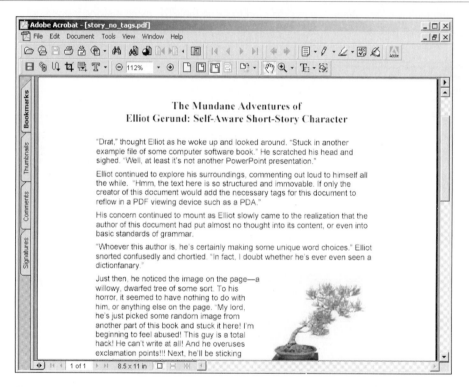

1. Open **story_no_tags.pdf** from the **chap_15** folder. Unlike the PDF you created in the last exercise, this version of the document has not had tags embedded into it, and it behaves pretty much like every other PDF you've worked with in this book. On a regular monitor, it's fairly easy to read the text on this page. The various magnification levels such as Fit Width and Fit Visible work fine to display the document at a reasonable viewing size.

Now let's mimic what this page might look like on a small palmtop device.

2. Click **Fit Width** and then press **F8** to temporarily hide the Toolbar (hiding the Toolbar will give you more screen space in which to view the document). Resize the document window to the approximate dimensions of the screenshot above. Suddenly it's not as easy to read this document, is it? Well, what if we increased the magnification level?

3. Choose **View > Actual Size** to display the document at 100%. The text becomes easier to read, but now you must scroll both vertically and horizontally to read the page. This isn't exactly conducive to easy reading. Some might even say that this document is not very "accessible" in a window this size.

As you can see, a normal-looking PDF has now become a hassle to read. Without tags, not only is this document inaccessible to audible screen readers; it's also inaccessible to people viewing the document on smaller devices. Next you'll examine this same document, but in tagged form.

4. Return the Acrobat window to its normal size and close **story_no_tags.pdf**.

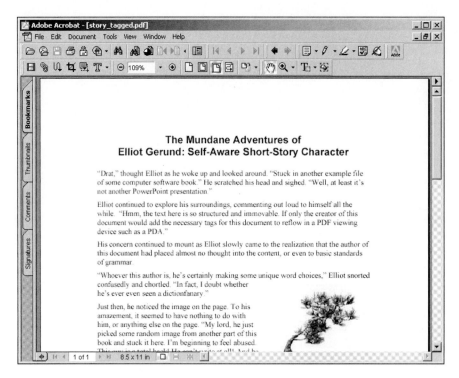

5. Open **story_tagged.pdf** from the **chap_15** folder. This is the PDF you created in the previous exercise. If you weren't able to create this PDF, you can use **story_tags.pdf** in the **chap_15** folder for this exercise. Press **F8** to bring back the Toolbar. Click the **Fit Width** button if it's not already selected.

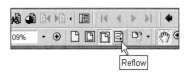

Notice in the toolbar that the Reflow button is available. This indicates that you're looking at a tagged document.

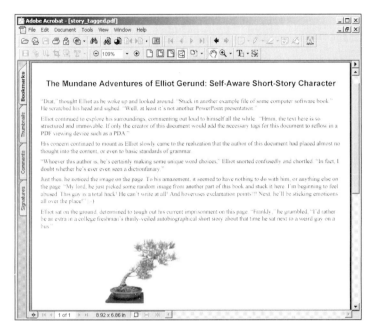

6. Click the **Reflow** button. The text now wraps to the boundaries of the document window and not to the original margins.

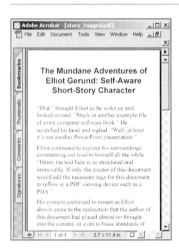

7. Press **F8** to hide the Toolbar and resize the document window back down to mimic a PDA display again. Notice that as you do so, the text remains at its current size and reflows within the window. Even with the window at this size, the text remains legible and you don't have to scroll both vertically and horizontally to read it.

8. Scroll down to the bottom of the document. Notice that the image, which was formerly aligned with the text, has now been moved to the bottom of the page. You might also notice that it has scaled down in size to fit within the document window.

Note: If you still find the text difficult to read at its current size, you can increase the magnification level by choosing View > Zoom In. The text will become larger, but it will never go beyond the boundaries of the document window and force you to scroll left and right to view an entire line.

Tip: If you can't really tell that the image has scaled down, make the document window even smaller. You should then be able to see how the text remains at the same size, but the image becomes smaller.

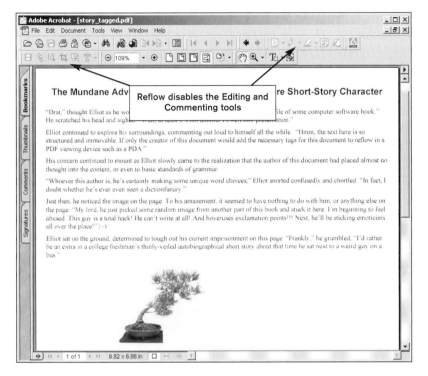

9. Return the window to its normal size and press **F8** to bring back the Toolbar. Note that the Reflow view does not alter or damage the PDF in any way—it's simply a method of viewing the document. But also note that the major difference between Reflow and other views is that Reflow disables the Editing and Commenting tools in Acrobat. If you select **Fit Width**, **Actual Size**, or **Fit in Window**, the document will again behave as a normal PDF.

10. Click **Fit in Window** to view the document in its original dimensions again. Keep the file open for the next exercise.

When you implement accessibility standards within your PDFs, it's not just the visually disabled who reap the benefits. You're also making your PDFs easier to read on the smaller screens of PDAs and eBook readers. The proliferation of palmtop devices has revolutionized the way information can be distributed. No longer are people tied to their 17-inch monitors sitting on their desks. Many people actually prefer reading Web pages and PDFs on these tiny devices. You know the people I'm talking about. You see them sitting in airports, casually squinting at their little screens. If you've ever downloaded Acrobat Reader for your palmtop device or tried reading your favorite Web sites on some of these devices, you know what a strain on the eyes this can cause. Creating a tagged PDF will allow these individuals to reflow your document within the confines of their screens, making the document much easier for them to read.

3. ————————Changing Reflow Order

There will occasionally be times when you'll want to reorder the flow of a tagged document so that certain elements don't become separated when the document is reflowed. For instance, you wouldn't want an image's caption to appear three paragraphs above it. In the last exercise you observed how the image in the **story_tagged.pdf** document had been relocated to the bottom of the page when the Reflow button was clicked. In this exercise, you'll use the TouchUp Order tool to adjust the order of the page's elements.

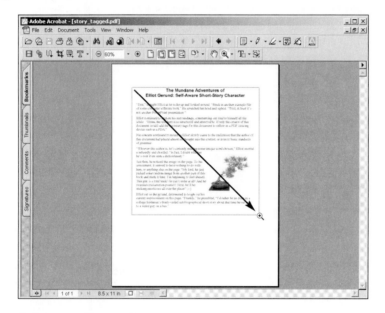

1. Select the **Zoom** tool and draw a marquee around all of the content on the page. This will magnify the text and image so that they'll be easier to work with.

2. From the Toolbar, click the triangle next to the **TouchUp Text** tool and select the **TouchUp Order** tool.

Note: The TouchUp Order tool cannot be selected if the document is in Reflow view.

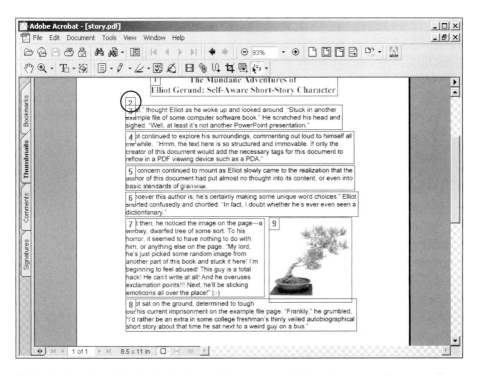

Selecting the TouchUp Order tool reveals boxes around the elements on the page. The numbers indicate the sequence in which they are currently set to display. Notice that sequence number 2 doesn't appear to be attached to any elements on the page. An important point to note is that when you create a tagged PDF, all elements are tagged. The area represented by sequence number 2 is an empty paragraph. The author of this document wanted to create some space between the title and the first paragraph, but instead of creating a paragraph style to do this, he simply pressed the Enter key. Empty paragraphs are considered to be content by PDFMaker and therefore receive tags just like any other content. And while empty paragraphs make little difference to someone reading this document, they can greatly slow down the screen readers used by visually disabled people. Each empty paragraph will be audibly noted before moving on to the next paragraph. You can imagine how annoying this would be to someone trying to get through your document. When creating documents in Word, make sure to eliminate empty paragraphs before creating a tagged PDF.

You'll now reorder the sequence numbers so that the image appears above the paragraph that is currently represented by sequence number 7. To use the TouchUp Object tool, you simply click each box in the order you want them to appear when the document is reflowed.

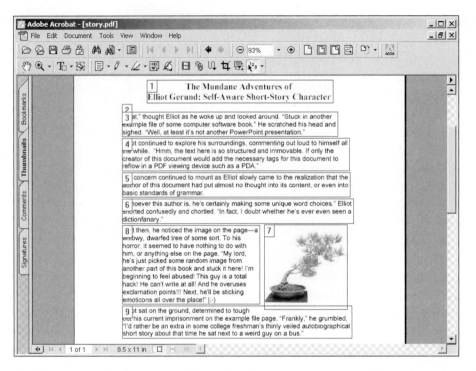

3. With the **TouchUp Order** tool, click the box with sequence number **1**. Then click **2**. (2 might be more difficult to click because of its small size. Make sure it turns red before you click it.) Continue clicking in order until after you've clicked number **6**. After number 6, click the image, which will then change to number **7**. You can stop at this point because everything else is already in order. Select the **Hand** tool to hide the sequence numbers. If you get the sequence out of order at any time, deselect the **TouchUp Order** tool by selecting any other tool and then reselect it to start again.

 MOVIE | reflow_order.mov

See the movie **reflow_order.mov** in the **chap_15 folder** if you have trouble with this step.

Now you'll check to make sure the image will appear in the proper location when this PDF is reflowed.

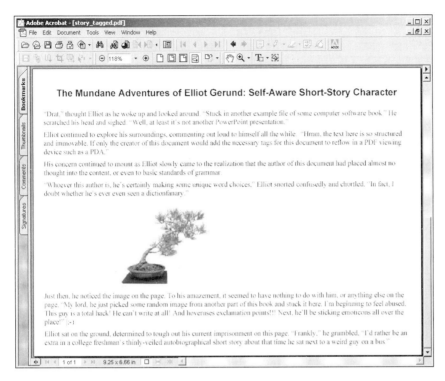

4. Click the **Reflow** button in the Toolbar. The image now appears within the body of the text, rather than at the end.

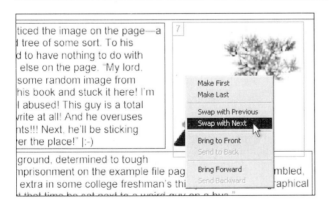

Tip: You can sometimes speed up the process of reordering the reflow sequence by right-clicking (Windows) or Ctrl+clicking (Mac) the sequence box and selecting a choice from the resulting menu.

5. Save the file and keep it open for the next exercise.

4. ——————————**Adding Alternate Text**

In this exercise you'll learn how to add alternate text to images in your tagged PDFs. Alternate text is very useful to visually disabled people and to people viewing your PDF on devices with limited graphic capabilities. Screen readers will read the alternate text to visually disabled people; without the alternate text, the screen reader is unable to describe an image, leaving your users to wonder what information the image contains.

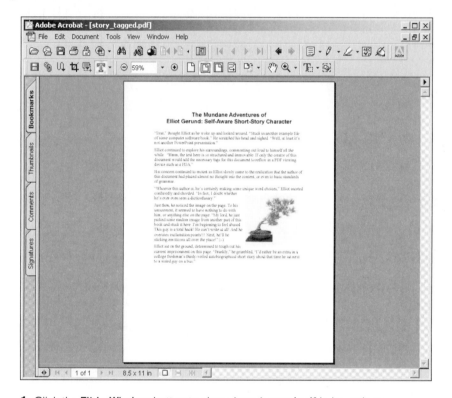

1. Click the **Fit in Window** button to view **story_tagged.pdf** in its entirety.

To add alternate text to an image, you need to use the Tags palette.

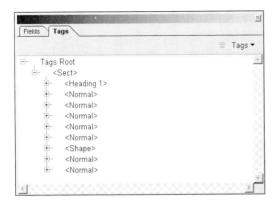

2. Choose **Window > Tags** to open the **Tags** palette. The Tags palette displays what's known as the **logical tree structure** of your document. Click the toggle buttons next to **Tags Root** and **<Sect>** to expand the tree. The logical tree structure is simply a visually representation of the various elements on the page and how they're ordered. The current structure reflects the order you set in the previous exercise.

Before continuing, you'll dock the Tags palette in the Navigation pane.

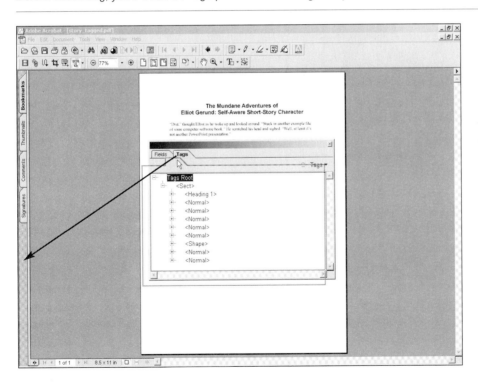

3. Drag the **Tags** tab next to the other tabs in the **Navigation** pane.

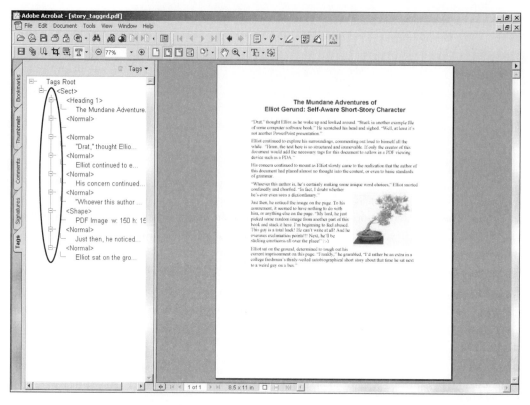

4. Once you've docked the Tags palette, expand it by clicking on the **Tags** tab. (If the Fields palette is still open, close it.) Click the toggle buttons next to each item in the Tags pane to expand it. Now you can see exactly which element each tag represents.

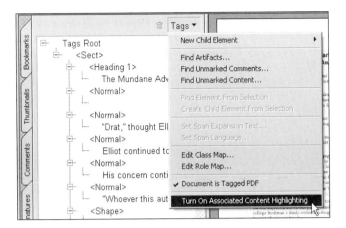

Tip: *If you ever have trouble telling which tag is associated with which element on your page, click the Tags contextual menu and select Turn On Associated Content Highlighting. Now when you click on a tag, a border will appear around the associated element on the page. With associated content highlighting turned on, however, you will not be able to pick any other items from the Tags contextual menu. If you chose to turn it on, you must turn off associated content highlighting before continuing with the next step.*

Now you'll add the alternate text to the image.

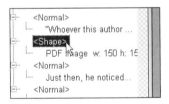

5. Click the **<Shape>** tag in the Tags pane to select it. This is the tag associated with the image.

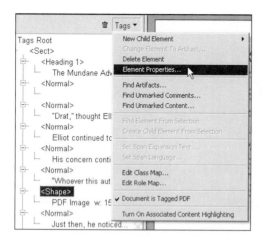

6. From the **Tags** contextual menu, select **Element Properties**. This will open the **Element Properties** dialog box.

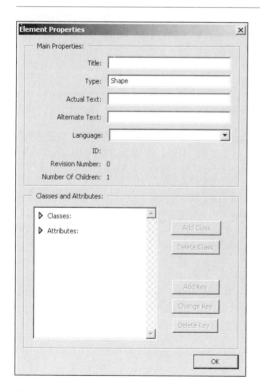

Alternate text should be as descriptive as possible without being overly wordy. Assume that the user cannot see the image at all. How would you describe it?

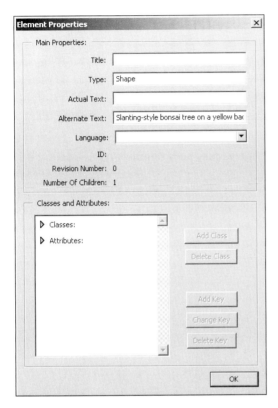

7. In the **Alternate Text** field, type **Slanting-style bonsai tree on a yellow background**. (Alternate text is not case sensitive.) Click **OK**.

There will be no visual change to the document, but with the alternate text now embedded in the PDF, screen readers will be able to read the description of the image to visually disabled people.

8. Close the **Tags** pane by clicking on the **Tags** tab. Save the file and keep it open for the next exercise.

5. ———————————Using the Accessibility Checker

Acrobat comes with a plug-in called the Accessibility Checker, which is a useful tool for examining your PDF and making sure that it meets accessibility standards. And it's a plug-in that (gasp!) actually works on both Mac and Windows platforms. In this exercise, you'll run the Accessibility Checker on the **story_tagged.pdf** file you've been working with to see if passes the tests. Then you'll run the checker on a non-tagged PDF to see what happens.

1. With **story_tagged.pdf** open, choose **Tools > Accessibility Checker**. This will open the **Accessibility Checker Options** dialog box.

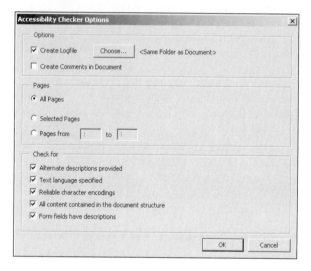

In this dialog box you can specify which check you want to run. The chart at the end of this exercise details the options available here.

2. Under **Options**, you can keep **Create Logfile** selected. This will generate a text file in the **chap_15** folder detailing the results of the Accessibility Check. Under **Check for**, make sure all of the options are selected. Click **OK**.

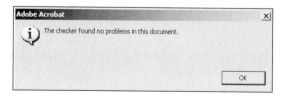

After a moment, Acrobat will give you the results of the check. This documents has no accessibility problems. Woo-hoo!

3. Click **OK**. Save **story_tagged.pdf** and close it.

Now you'll perform the Accessibility Check on the non-tagged version of this document to see what happens.

4. Open **story_no_tags.pdf** from **chap_15**.

5. Choose **Tools** > **Accessibility Checker**.

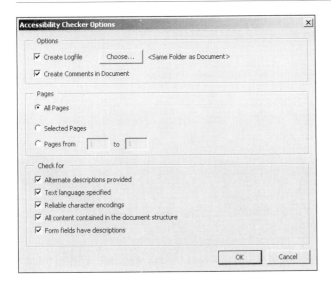

6. In the Accessibility Checker Options dialog box, check **Create Comments in Document**. This will make Acrobat place comments into the document at the exact location where it finds problems. Keep everything else the way it is. Click **OK**.

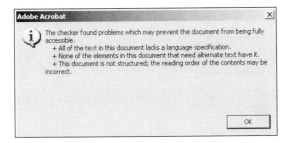

After a moment, Acrobat reports that it has found "problems which may prevent the document from being fully accessible." The specific problems will be addressed in the next exercise.

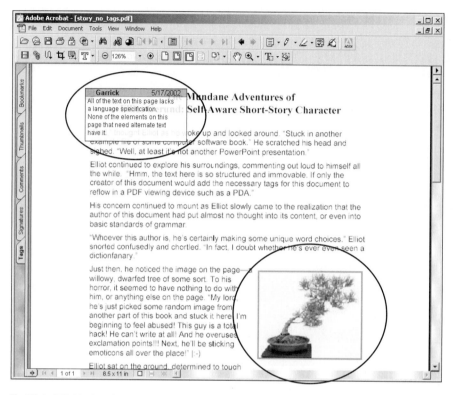

7. Click **OK**. Notice the comments that Acrobat has provided, identifying the problems spots of this document. The note in the upper left-hand corner tells you that the text on the page lacks a language specification and that none of the images on the page have alternate text.

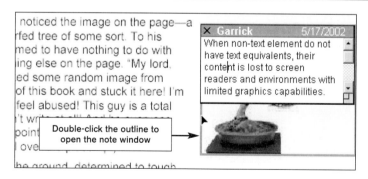

8. With the **Hand** tool, place the cursor over the edge of the colored border around the image, and double-click to open the note window. This note provides further information on why the Accessibility Checker considered the image to be inaccessible.

9. Save **story_no_tags.pdf** and keep it open for the next exercise.

In the following exercise, you'll use the Make Accessible plug-in on this document to, um, make the document accessible. Before you move on, read through the chart below, which details the choices available in the Accessibility Checker Options dialog box.

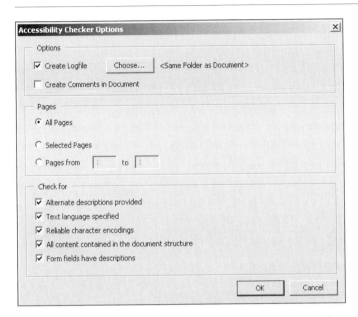

Accessibility Checker Options	
Option	**Description**
Create Logfile	Generates a text file that contains any messages that Acrobat displays concerning the document's performance in this specific Accessibility Check. By default, the log is stored in the same folder as the document, but you can select a different folder by clicking Choose.
Create Comments in Document	As you saw in the last exercise, this option generates comments at the specific locations where accessibility problems are found. Comments can be deleted by choosing **Tools > Comments > Delete All**.
Pages	This section allows you to select the page or range of pages on which you want to perform the check.

continues on next page

Accessibility Checker Options *continued*	
Option	**Description**
Check for	You can choose any combination of the options available under this section.
Alternate descriptions provided	Will check every image in the document to ensure that alternate text descriptions have been provided.
Text language specified	Checks to make sure that a language has been specified for the text. Note that screen readers currently can only have one language specified. The option is in anticipation of future readers that will be able to change languages.
Reliable character encodings	This checks to make sure that all characters in the documents have Unicode values. Unicode is a universal text format that is read by screen readers. When you tag a PDF, all text is converted to Unicode.
All content contained in the document structure	This selection checks to make sure none of the content in the document falls outside the tagged structure. For instance, comments are not part of the document structure and will not be read by screen readers.
Form fields have descriptions	If the document contains Acrobat form fields, this checks that each field has a description. Descriptions are added in the Short Descriptions area of the Field Properties. See Chapter 8, *"Forms,"* if you need a refresher.

6. _____The Make Accessible Plug-In

For untagged PDF documents that you wish to convert into tagged PDFs, your best choice is usually to go back to the original document in its native application and create a tagged PDF from there. If you no longer have the original document, you can use the free Make Accessible plug-in, which tags non-tagged PDFs. This plug-in can be downloaded from Adobe's Web site. Unfortunately, at the time of publication of this book, this plug-in was available to Windows users only. Macintosh users will not be able to follow along with this exercise, but should still read through the steps.

As you saw in the previous exercise, the Accessibility Checker found a number of compliancy problems with this document. In this exercise, you'll run the Make Accessible plug-in and then observe the corrections it makes.

Note: *Before continuing, make sure that you install the Make Accessible plug-in from the software folder on the H•O•T CD-ROM. You can also download the plug-in from Adobe's Web site at http://www.adobe.com/support/downloads/detail.jsp?ftpID=1161.*

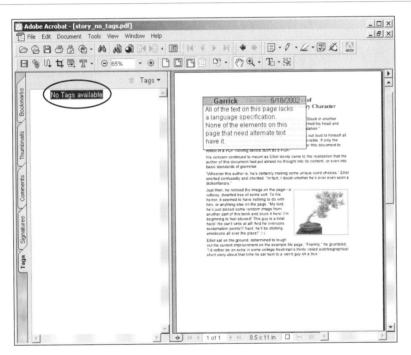

1. The file **story_no_tags.pdf** should still be open from the previous exercise. Click the **Tags** tab in the **Navigation** pane. Currently there are no tags available in this document. Opening the Tags pane is not a required step in using the Make Accessible plug-in. You're just opening it to observe the change after you use the plug-in.

2. Choose **Document > Make Accessible** to run the plug-in.

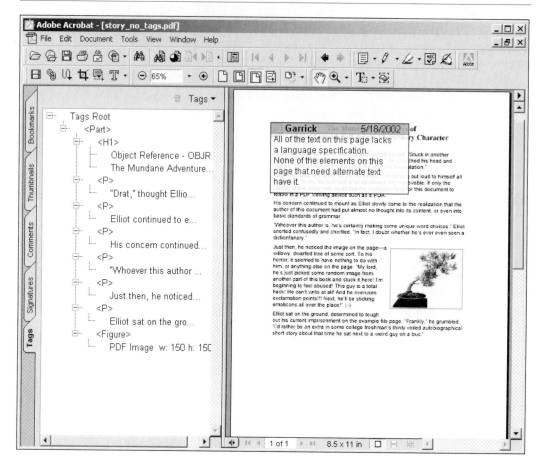

The procedure only takes a few seconds. When it's finished you'll find a logical tree structure in the Tags pane. You can click the toggle buttons next to the tags to expand the tree. As you can see, the Make Accessible plug-in has now fully tagged this document.

Now you'll see whether this document passes the Accessibility Checker's test.

3. Select **Tools > Accessibility Checker**.

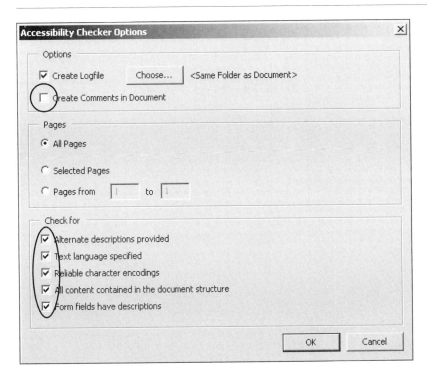

4. In the **Accessibility Checker Options** dialog box, uncheck **Create Comments in Document** if it's still checked. Also make sure that everything under **Check for** is also selected. Click **OK**.

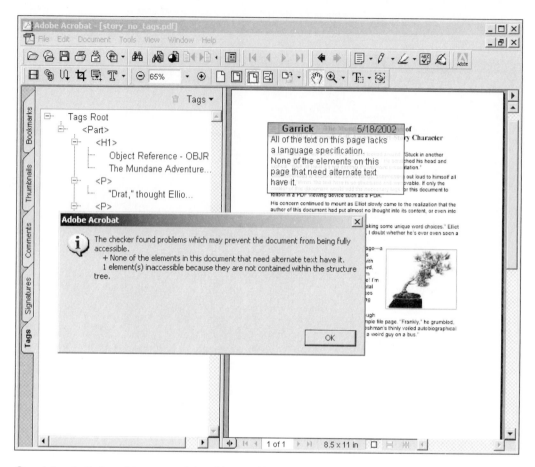

Oops! Acrobat's found two potential problems with accessibility. Looks like we forgot to add alternate text for the image on this page. Also notice that Acrobat has found elements that exist outside of the structure tree. In this case, the elements it's referring to are the comments left over from the previous Accessibility Check. Because comments are not part of the logical structure tree, screen readers do not recognize them.

Next, you'll remove the comments from this document and add alternate text to the image. Then you'll run the Accessibility Checker again.

5. Choose **Tools > Comments > Delete All** to remove the comments. Simple enough, right? Now to add the alternate text to the image's tag.

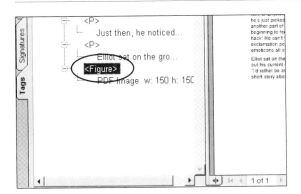

Take a look in the Tags pane. The tag associated with the image is the <Figure> tag.

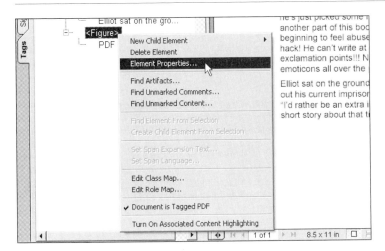

6. Right-click (Windows) the tag and choose **Element Properties** from the contextual menu.

Note: *Although Mac users are unable to run the Accessibility Checker, they can still add alternate text by Ctrl+clicking on image tags and choosing Element Properties.*

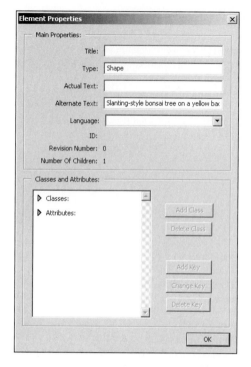

7. In the **Alternate Text** field, type **Slanting-style bonsai tree on a yellow background**. Click **OK**.

Now you'll run the Accessibility Checker one more time.

8. Choose **Tools > Accessibility Checker**.

9. Leave the same options checked that you selected previously and click **OK**.

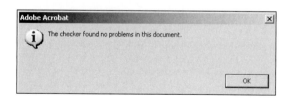

After a moment, you should get the message saying that the Accessibility Checker found no problems in the document.

10. Good job! Click **OK**. This document is just as accessible as the one you created from Word.

11. Click the **Tags** tab to close the Tags pane. Save the file and keep it open for the next exercise.

7. _____Accessibility Preferences

In this chapter you've learned to make PDF documents accessible to various devices and readers. Not too many people are aware of this, but Acrobat has some accessibility preferences of its own which can be used to make PDF documents easier to view for people with poor vision. For example, many PDF documents consist of black text on a white background. Now, most people have no trouble reading black on white, but for those who suffer from impaired vision or partial blindness, reading in this color scheme can be very difficult. In this exercise, you'll customize Acrobat's Accessibility preferences and examine the changes that you can make to the way Acrobat displays documents.

Note: *The preferences set in this exercise are identical to the ones that can be set in Acrobat Reader.*

1. The file **story_no_tags.pdf** should still be open from the previous exercise. If you weren't able to follow along with the previous exercise, open **story_tagged.pdf**. It doesn't really matter which one you select, as long as you have some sort of document open.

2. Choose **Edit > Preferences > General** (Mac OS X: Choose **Acrobat > Preferences > General**).

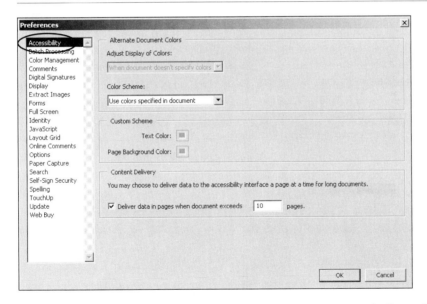

3. In the **Preferences** dialog box, select **Accessibility** from the top of the list on the left.

In the Accessibility preferences, you can set your own color schemes to make certain documents easier to read. This is a very useful feature for those who have color blindness or impaired vision.

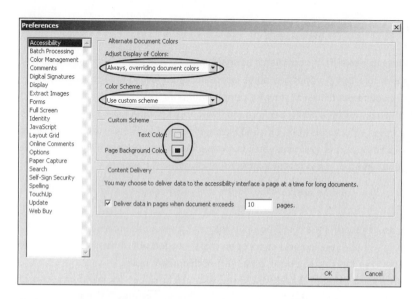

4. From the **Color Scheme** menu, select **Use custom scheme**. This will allow you to choose colors for text and for the page's background color. Choose bright green for the **Text Color** and black for the **Page Background Color**. From the **Adjust Display of Colors** menu at the top of the dialog box, select **Always, overriding document colors**. This ensures that PDFs will always display in this color scheme, no matter which colors the document itself specifies. Click **OK**.

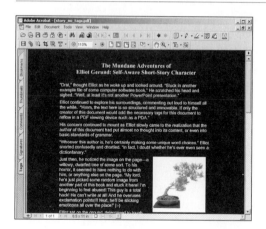

Your custom color scheme now overrides the colors in the PDF. It's great that anyone with Acrobat or Acrobat Reader can choose their own color schemes based on their own vision needs.

5. Choose **Edit > Preferences > General** (Mac OS X: Choose **Acrobat > Preferences > General**) to return to the Preferences dialog box.

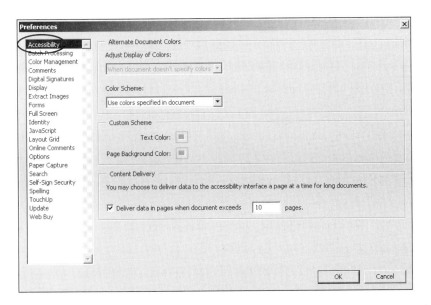

6. Under **Color Scheme**, select **Use colors specified in document** to return to the original settings. Click **OK**.

7. Close the file without saving.

Additional Color Scheme Setting (Windows Only)

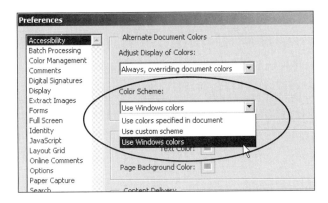

In Acrobat for Windows, the Color Scheme pop-up menu in the Preferences dialog box has one addition selection: **Use Windows colors**. Microsoft Windows 98, 2000, Me, and XP all have a Control Panel selection called **Accessibility Options**, where you can set high-contrast color schemes if you have trouble viewing the normal colors of the operating system.

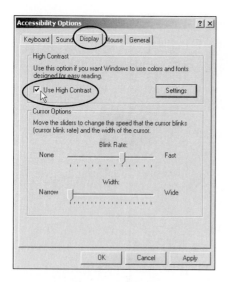

The Accessibility Options are located in the **Control Panel** folder on your Windows machine. Under the **Display** tab you can select **Use High Contrast** and then click the **Settings** button.

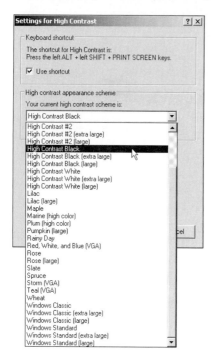

From the **Settings for High Contrast** dialog box, you can choose from a large selection of schemes that determine colors and text sizes.

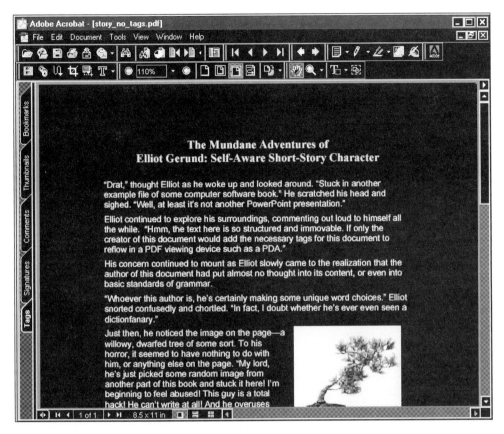

Once you've made your selection, the change affects your entire operating system. If you have **Use Windows colors** selected as your **Color Scheme** in Acrobat, Acrobat will display PDFs based on the color scheme you chose in Windows' Accessibilities Options.

Well that's it. The last chapter. If you've made it through the whole book, you know a whole bunch about Acrobat and PDFs now. Just don't let too many people know unless you want to become the person that everyone comes to when they have an Acrobat question. If you find yourself inundated by these people, calmly suggest to them that they find and purchase a brand-new copy of Acrobat 5 Hands-On Training.

Resources

H·O·T

Acrobat 5

These resources related to Acrobat and PDF production are intended to provide you with additional information and support. You might be surprised that we recommend training resources other than our own, but because Acrobat is used for numerous purposes—Web distribution, professional print work, document review—no one resource can cover the full range of its applications. There are a multitude of books written by experts in these fields that are worth looking into if you want to delve deeper into specific aspects of Acrobat. I also strongly encourage you to explore some of the Web forums listed here. If you've never participated in a Web forum, you may be amazed at the number of people who are willing to help you with Acrobat issues and answer your questions. Somewhere out there, someone has run into the same problem that you're having and may have already discovered a creative solution.

Books About Acrobat

Adobe Acrobat 5 PDF Bible
Author: Ted Padova
Publisher: Hungry Minds
ISBN: 0764535773

An excellent resource, particularly for more advanced Acrobat users who are interested in the nitty-gritty details of the application. Good coverage of JavaScripting.

Real World PDF with Adobe Acrobat
Author: Anita Dennis
Publisher: Peachpit Press
ISBN: 0201758946

Probably one of the best books available on using Acrobat to create documents for professional print production. If you've got a hankering to learn a lot about Distiller, this is the book to get.

Adobe Acrobat 5 Classroom in a Book
Author: Adobe
Publisher: Adobe Press
ISBN: 0201729377

A project-based book written and published by Adobe that covers a lot of Acrobat's popular features in a small amount of space.

CD-ROMs About Acrobat

Learning Acrobat 5
Author: Garrick Chow
Publisher: lynda.com
Time: 4 hours
http://www.lynda.com/products/videos/acro5cd/

If you liked the QuickTime movies in this book, try this CD-ROM: It has four hours' worth of movies to watch, covering most of the same topics as this book, in some cases in more depth. Hey, four hours of my mellifluous voice and winning personality? You can't lose!

Online Communities and Resources

Planet PDF
`http://www.planetpdf.com`

Dedicated to all things PDF. Here you'll find news, articles, reviews, and tutorials covering every aspect of Acrobat and the PDF format. Their discussion forum is loaded with experts and people with real-world experience who are more than happy to offer solutions or suggestions for your problems or questions.

PDF Zone
`http://www.pdfzone.com`

Devoted to providing news, interviews, and resources about all aspects of PDF. They also offer subscription services to individual e-mail lists that target specific areas of Acrobat and PDF creation and development.

Planet eBook
`http://www.planetebook.com`

A comprehensive Web site focused solely on eBook-related news and technologies.

Adobe Solutions for Accessibility
`http://www.adobe.com/products/acrobat/solutionsacc.html`

A listing of plug-ins, articles, and tutorials for creating accessible PDF documents.

Adobe Expert Center
`http://studio.adobe.com/expertcenter/acrobat/main.html`

Adobe's Web site for up-to-date Acrobat information. Contains tips and tutorials, guides and references, updates and plug-ins, technical support, and training resources.

Third Party Acrobat Plug-ins and Applications

The resources listed below are for non-Adobe products that add new features and functionality to Acrobat. Depending on your needs, the extra cost of these add-ons is usually worth the time you'll save once you have them installed.

PF-Print Merge
`http://www.pureforms.com/Products/PFPrintMerge/pfprintmerge.htm`

A program for automatically merging database records into PDF forms. Great for tedious repetitive tasks. You can download a trial version at the Web address above. Windows only.

BCL Magellan

`http://www.bcltechnologies.com/products/magellan/magellan.htm`

A plug-in for converting PDF documents into HTML. An extremely useful tool if you no longer have the original source files for your PDFs and need to repurpose their content to use for Web applications. Magellan preserves the original layout of documents including graphics, links, and bookmarks. You can download a demo version at the Web address above. Windows only.

Compose

`http://www.Infodata.com/compose.asp`

A powerful plug-in for batch processing PDFs. You can quickly generate, among other things, links, bookmarks, and tables of contents with this add-on. Visit the Web address above to see a full description and download a demo. Windows only.

Quite a Box of Tricks

`http://www.quite.com/box/`

As its name implies, this plug-in provides several useful tools for optimizing PDFs. To reduce the file size of your PDFs, you can use this plug-in to shrink images, scale pages, convert the PDF to grayscale, and remove form fields. There are several more features available as well. Download a demo version at the Web address above. Windows and Macintosh versions available.

ImageAlter

`http://apago.com/getprodpage.cgi?prodname=imageAlter`

This plug-in allows you to downsample and recompress images in your PDFs without having to redistill them. You can also create alternate images to speed up viewing time of large-resolution images. Download a trial version at the Web address above. Macintosh only.

ARTS Link Checker

`http://www.aroundtablesolution.com/arts_link_checker.asp`

A plug-in that checks your PDFs for dead or broken links. Has the ability to set all links to a specific color. Windows and Macintosh versions available.

ePublishstore.com

`http://www.epublishstore.com/`

A Web superstore of plug-ins. You can purchase nearly all of the products listed above here. Includes reviews and descriptions of the products.

B.

Troubleshooting

H•O•T

Acrobat 5

This appendix is the first place to check if you're having a problem with any of the exercises in this book. You might also want to check the book's Web site **http://www.lynda.com/ books/acro5hot/** to see if any errata have been posted. As a last resort, e-mail us with your problems— **acro5hot@lynda.com**. Due to the high volume of e-mail we receive, we cannot help you with your own Acrobat projects; our support covers only issues related to the exercises in this book. Please allow 72 hours for us respond to your message (longer over holidays or weekends). For tech support on general Acrobat questions, please contact Adobe **http://www.adobe.com/ support/products/acrobat.html** or join one of the discussion groups listed in Appendix A, "*Resources.*"

I can't find the toolbar you're referring to and/or my toolbar is in a different location than the one in the screenshot.

In Acrobat 5, the location of tools in the toolbar can be customized to suit your needs. Because toolbars can be dragged around to tailor the appearance of the Acrobat interface, the toolbars on your screen may not appear in the same locations as shown in the book. If you can't find a tool, or if you've accidentally closed a toolbar, choose **Window > Toolbars** and select the toolbar that you're looking for. See the "Customizing the Toolbar" sidebar in Chapter 2, "*Interface*," for more information.

I can't find the Bookmarks/Thumbnails/etc. tab in the Navigation pane.

All of the items usually found in the Navigation pane are listed under the **Window** menu. If you can't find a particular pane, you can easily get it back by selecting it under the Window menu. In most cases, the pane will appear as a floating palette that you can simply drag back into the Navigation pane to redock.

Acrobat's not letting me choose whether I want to open Web pages in my Web browser or in Acrobat. What gives?

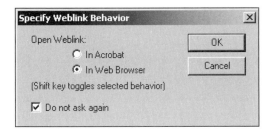

The **Specify Weblink Behavior** dialog box contains an option to *not* show the dialog box again once a selection has been made. **Do not ask again** is selected by default. If you want to make this dialog box reappear, choose **Edit > Preferences > Web Capture** (Mac OS X: **Acrobat > Preferences > Web Capture**) and click the **Reset Warning Dialogs to Default** button.

The New Bookmark button is missing from the Navigation pane.

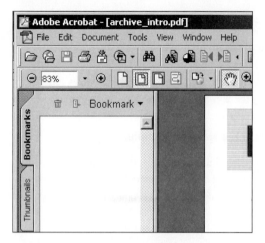

If you can't find the New Bookmark button, your Navigation pane is most likely too narrow.

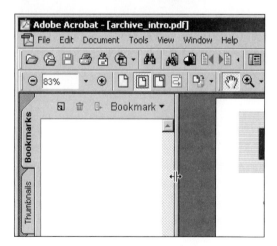

Widen the pane by dragging its border to the right. The button will appear.

I'm trying to insert additional pages into my PDF using the Document > Insert Pages command, but Acrobat isn't recognizing the file.

The only types of pages that can be inserted into a PDF using **Document > Insert Pages** are PDF pages. So before you try to sneak that request for a raise into your review, the request must be converted to a PDF.

You can quickly convert text files and many image formats to PDF by choosing **File > Open as Adobe PDF**.

I wanted to delete a form field radio button, but they all disappeared when I hit the Delete key.

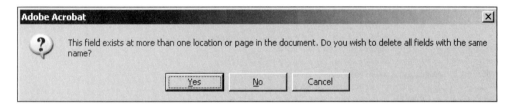

Whenever you attempt to delete a form field that shares its name with other fields, Acrobat will ask whether you want to delete just the field you selected or all of the fields with the same name. Make sure you click **No** if you want to delete only the selected field. Click **Yes** to remove all fields with that name.

My form fields aren't calculating correctly.

Acrobat performs form field calculations based on the order in which the calculation fields were created. To check the calculation order, have the **Form** tool selected and choose **Tools > Forms > Set Field Calculation Order**.

The Layout Grid isn't fitting my needs for sizing form fields.

Often the Layout Grid won't match the dimensions of the form fields you're trying to draw. You can adjust the Layout Grid settings by choosing **Edit > Preferences > General** (Mac OS X: **Acrobat > Preferences > General**). Select the **Layout Grid** category from the list on the left, and adjust the settings from there.

I included a movie in my PDF, but when I sent it to my client, the movie wasn't there.

Movie files are not embedded into PDF documents. When you use the Movie tool to place a movie file in your PDF, you must include the movie when you send the PDF file. The movie file must also remain in the same relative relationship with the PDF; i.e., don't place the movie into a subfolder after referencing it in the PDF.

I'm viewing a PDF in Full Screen mode, but I disabled the Esc key as the key for exiting Full Screen mode. How to I get back to the Acrobat interface?

To return to the Acrobat interface from Full Screen mode, press **Ctrl+L** (Windows) or **Cmd+L** (Mac).

I created a Watched Folder in Distiller, but when I drag files into the folder, nothing happens.

Disitller must be running in order to monitor a Watched Folder. Also, make sure that you're dragging your PostScript files into the folder called **In** inside the Watched Folder.

I'm trying to rotate my document with the Rotate View button, but each time I open the document, it switches back to its original orientation.

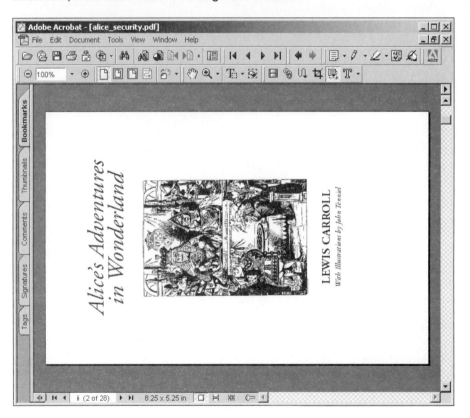

First, make sure that your monitor isn't lying on its side.

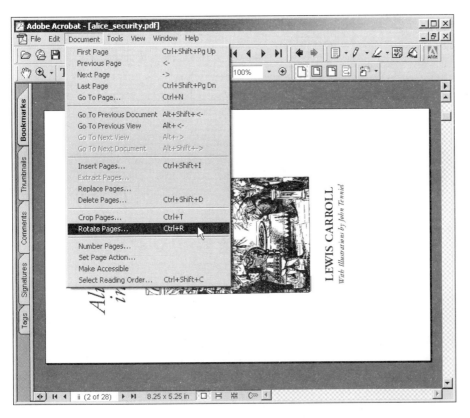

To rotate a page or pages of your PDF, you must use choose **Document > Rotate Pages**. Clicking the **Rotate View** button does indeed rotate the view of the entire document, but it doesn't tell the PDF to open this way every time.

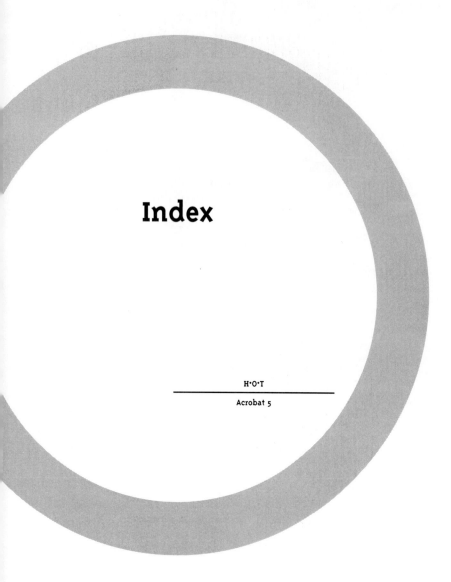

Index

H•O•T

Acrobat 5

B

CD-ROM LICENSE AGREEMENT

THIS SOFTWARE LICENSE AGREEMENT CONSTITUTES AN AGREEMENT BETWEEN YOU AND, LYNDA.COM, LLC. . YOU SHOULD CAREFULLY READ THE FOLLOWING TERMS AND CONDITIONS BEFORE OPENING THIS ENVELOPE. COPYING THIS SOFTWARE TO YOUR MACHINE, BREAKING THE SEAL, OR OTHERWISE RE-MOVING OR USING THE SOFTWARE INDICATES YOUR ACCEPTANCE OF THESE TERMS AND CONDITIONS. IF YOU DO NOT AGREE TO BE BOUND BY THE PROVISIONS OF THIS LICENSE AGREEMENT, YOU SHOULD PROMPTLY DELETE THE SOFTWARE FROM YOUR MACHINE.

TERMS AND CONDITIONS:

1. GRANT OF LICENSE. In consideration of payment of the License Fee, which was a part of the price you paid for this product, LICENSOR grants to you (the "Licensee") a non-exclusive right to use and display this copy of a Software program, along with any updates or upgrade releases of the Software for which you have paid (all parts and elements of the Software as well as the Software as a whole are hereinafter referred to as the "Software") on a single computer only (i.e., with a single CPU) at a single location, all as more particularly set forth and limited below. LICENSOR reserves all rights not expressly granted to you as Licensee in this License Agreement.

2. OWNERSHIP OF SOFTWARE. The license granted herein is not a sale of the original Software or of any copy of the Software. As Licensee, you own only the rights to use the Software as described herein and the magnetic or other physical media on which the Software is originally or subsequently recorded or fixed. LICENSOR retains title and owner-ship of the Software recorded on the original disk(s), as well as title and ownership of any subsequent copies of the Software irrespective of the form of media on or in which the Software is recorded or fixed. This license does not grant you any intellectual or other propri-etary or other rights of any nature what-soever in the Software.

3. USE RESTRICTIONS. As Licensee, you may use the Software only as expressly author-ized in this License Agreement under the terms of paragraph 4. You may phy-sically transfer the Software from one computer to another provided that the Software is used on only a single computer at any one time. You may not: (i) electronically transfer the Software from one computer to another over a network; (ii) make the Software available through a time-sharing service, network of computers, or other multiple user arrangement; (iii) distribute copies of the Software or related written materials to any third party, whether for sale or otherwise; (iv) modify, adapt, translate, reverse engineer, decompile, disassemble, or prepare any deriva-tive work based on the Software or any element thereof; (v) make or distribute, whether for sale or otherwise, any hard copy or printed version of any of the Software nor any portion thereof nor any work of yours containing the Software or any component thereof; (vi) use any of the Software nor any of its components in any other work.

8. THIS IS WHAT YOU CAN AND CANNOT DO WITH THE SOFTWARE. Even though in the preceding paragraph and elsewhere LICENSOR has restricted your use of the Software, the following is the only thing you can do with the Software and the various elements of the Software:DUCKS IN A ROW ARTWORK: THE ARTWORK CONTAINED ON THIS CD-ROM MAY NOT BE USED IN ANY MANNER WHATSOEVER OTHER THAN TO VIEW THE SAME ON YOUR COMPUTER, OR POST TO YOUR PERSONAL, NON-COMMER-CIAL WEB SITE FOR EDUCATIONAL PURPOSES ONLY. THIS MATERIAL IS SUBJECT TO ALL OF THE RESTRICTION PROVISIONS OF THIS SOFTWARE LICENSE. SPECIFI-CALLY BUT NOT IN LIMITATION OF THESE RESTRICTIONS, YOU MAY NOT DISTRIB-UTE, RESELL OR TRANSFER THIS PART OF THE SOFTWARE DESIGNATED AS "CLUTS" NOR ANY OF YOUR DESIGN OR OTHER WORK CONTAINING ANY OF THE SOFTWARE DESIGNATED AS "DUCKS IN A ROW ARTWORK" NOR ANY OF YOUR DESIGN OR OTHER WORK CONTAINING ANY SUCH "DUCKS IN A ROW ARTWORK," ALL AS MORE PARTICULARLY RESTRICTED IN THE WITHIN SOFTWARE LICENSE.

5. COPY RESTRICTIONS. The Software and accompanying written materials are protected under United States copyright laws. Unauthorized copying and/or distribution of the Software and/or the related written materials is expressly forbidden. You may be held legally responsi-ble for any copyright infringement that is caused, directly or indirectly, by your failure to abide by the terms of this License Agreement. Subject to the terms of this License Agreement and if the software is not otherwise copy protected, you may make one copy of the Software for backup purposes only. The copyright notice and any other proprietary notices which were included in the original Software must be reproduced and included on any such backup copy.

6. TRANSFER RESTRICTIONS. The license herein granted is personal to you, the Licensee. You may not transfer the Software nor any of its components or elements to anyone else, nor may you sell, lease, loan, sublicense, assign, or otherwise dispose of the Software nor any of its components or elements without the express written consent of LICENSOR, which con-sent may be granted or withheld at LICENSOR's sole discretion.

7. TERMINATION. The license herein granted hereby will remain in effect until terminated. This license will terminate automatically without further notice from LICENSOR in the event of the violation of any of the provisions hereof. As Licensee, you agree that upon such termina-tion you will promptly destroy any and all copies of the Software which remain in your posses-sion and, upon request, will certify to such destruction in writing to LICENSOR.

8. LIMITATION AND DISCLAIMER OF WARRANTIES. a) THE SOFTWARE AND RELATED WRITTEN MATERIALS, INCLUDING ANY INSTRUCTIONS FOR USE, ARE PROVIDED ON AN "AS IS" BASIS, WITHOUT WARRANTY OF ANY KIND, EXPRESS OR IMPLIED. THIS DISCLAIMER OF WARRANTY EXPRESSLY IN-CLUDES, BUT IS NOT LIMITED TO, ANY IMPLIED WARRANTIES OF MERCHANTABILITY AND/OR OF FIT-NESS FOR A PARTICULAR PURPOSE. NO WARRANTY OF ANY KIND IS MADE AS TO WHETHER OR NOT THIS SOFT-WARE INFRINGES UPON ANY RIGHTS OF ANY OTHER THIRD PARTIES. NO ORAL OR WRITTEN INFORMATION GIVEN BY LICEN-SOR, ITS SUPPLIERS, DISTRIBUTORS, DEALERS, EMPLOYEES, OR AGENTS, SHALL CREATE OR OTHERWISE ENLARGE THE SCOPE OF ANY WARRANTY HEREUNDER. LICENSEE ASSUMES THE ENTIRE RISK AS TO THE QUALITY AND THE PERFOR-

MANCE OF SUCH SOFTWARE. SHOULD THE SOFTWARE PROVE DEFECTIVE, YOU, AS LICENSEE (AND NOT LICENSOR, ITS SUPPLIERS, DISTRIBU-TORS, DEALERS OR AGENTS), ASSUME THE ENTIRE COST OF ALL NECESSARY CORRECTION, SERVIC-ING, OR REPAIR. b) LICENSOR warrants the disk(s) on which this copy of the Software is recorded or fixed to be free from defects in materials and workmanship, under normal use and service, for a period of ninety (90) days from the date of delivery as evidenced by a copy of the applicable receipt. LICENSOR hereby limits the duration of any implied warranties with respect to the disk(s) to the duration of the express warranty. This limited warranty shall not apply if the disk(s) have been damaged by unreasonable use, accident, negligence, or by any other causes unrelated to defective materials or workmanship. c) LICENSOR does not war-rant that the functions contained in the Software will be uninterrupted or error free and Licensee is encouraged to test the Software for Licensee's intended use prior to placing any reliance thereon. All risk of the use of the Software will be on you, as Licensee. d) THE LIM-ITED WARRANTY SET FORTH ABOVE GIVES YOU SPECIFIC LEGAL RIGHTS AND YOU MAY ALSO HAVE OTHER RIGHTS WHICH VARY FROM STATE TO STATE. SOME STATES DO NOT ALLOW THE LIMITATION OR EXCLUSION OF IMPLIED WARRANTIES OR OF INCIDENTAL OR CONSEQUENTIAL DAMAGES, SO THE LIMITATIONS AND EXCLUSIONS CONCERNING THE SOFTWARE AND RELATED WRITTEN MATERIALS SET FORTH ABOVE MAY NOT APPLY TO YOU.

9. LIMITATION OF REMEDIES. LICENSOR's entire liability and Licensee's exclusive remedy shall be the replacement of any disk(s) not meeting the limited warranty set forth in Section 8 above which is returned to LICENSOR with a copy of the applic-able receipt within the war-ranty period. Any replacement disk(s)will be warranted for the remainder of the original war-ranty period or thirty (30) days, whichever is longer.

10. LIMITATION OF LIABILITY. IN NO EVENT WILL LICENSOR, OR ANYONE ELSE INVOLVED IN THE CREATION, PRODUCTION, AND/OR DELIVERY OF THIS SOFTWARE PRODUCT BE LIABLE TO LICENSEE OR ANY OTHER PER-SON OR ENTITY FOR ANY DIRECT, INDIRECT, OR OTHER DAMAGES, INCLUDING, WITHOUT LIMITATION, ANY INTERRUPTION OF SERVICES, LOST PROFITS, LOST SAVINGS, LOSS OF DATA, OR ANY OTHER CONSEQUENTIAL, INCIDEN-TAL, SPECIAL, OR PUNITIVE DAMAGES, ARISING OUT OF THE PURCHASE, USE, INABILITY TO USE, OR OPERATION OF THE SOFTWARE, EVEN IF LICENSOR OR ANY AUTHORIZED LICENSOR DEALER HAS BEEN ADVISED OF THE POSSIBILITY OF SUCH DAMAGES. BY YOUR USE OF THE SOFTWARE, YOU ACKNOWLEDGE THAT THE LIMITATION OF LIABILITY SET FORTH IN THIS LICENSE WAS THE BASIS UPON WHICH THE SOFTWARE WAS OFFERED BY LICENSOR AND YOU ACKNOWLEDGE THAT THE PRICE OF THE SOFTWARE LICENSE WOULD BE HIGHER IN THE ABSENCE OF SUCH LIMITATION. SOME STATES DO NOT ALLOW THE LIMITATION OR EXCLUSION OF LIABILITY FOR INCIDENTAL OR CONSEQUENTIAL DAMAGES SO THE ABOVE LIMITATIONS AND EXCLUSIONS MAY NOT APPLY TO YOU.

11. UPDATES. LICENSOR, at its sole discretion, may periodically issue updates of the Software which you may receive upon request and payment of the applicable update fee in effect from time to time and in such event, all of the provisions of the within License Agreement shall apply to such updates.

12. EXPORT RESTRICTIONS. Licensee agrees not to export or re-export the Soft-ware and accompanying documentation (or any copies thereof) in violation of any applicable U.S. laws or regulations.

13. ENTIRE AGREEMENT. YOU, AS LICENSEE, ACKNOWLEDGE THAT: (i) YOU HAVE READ THIS ENTIRE AGREEMENT AND AGREE TO BE BOUND BY ITS TERMS AND CONDITIONS; (ii) THIS AGREEMENT IS THE COMPLETE AND EXCLUSIVE STATEMENT OF THE UNDERSTANDING BETWEEN THE PARTIES AND SUPERSEDES ANY AND ALL PRIOR ORAL OR WRITTEN COMMUNICATIONS RELATING TO THE SUBJECT MATTER HEREOF; AND (iii) THIS AGREEMENT MAY NOT BE MODIFIED, AMENDED, OR IN ANY WAY ALTERED EXCEPT BY A WRITING SIGNED BY BOTH YOURSELF AND AN OFFICER OR AUTHORIZED REPRESENTATIVE OF LICENSOR.

14. SEVERABILITY. In the event that any provision of this License Agreement is held to be illegal or otherwise unenforceable, such provision shall be deemed to have been deleted from this License Agreement while the remaining provisions of this License Agreement shall be unaffected and shall continue in full force and effect.

15. GOVERNING LAW. This License Agreement shall be governed by the laws of the State of California applicable to agreements wholly to be performed therein and of the United States of America, excluding that body of the law related to conflicts of law. This License Agreement shall not be governed by the United Nations Convention on Contracts for the International Sale of Goods, the application of which is expressly excluded. No waiver of any breach of the provisions of this License Agreement shall be deemed a waiver of any other breach of this License Agreement.

16. RESTRICTED RIGHTS LEGEND. Use, duplication, or disclosure by the Government is subject to restrictions as set forth in subparagraph (c)(1)(ii) of the Rights in Technical Data and Computer Software clause at 48 CFR § 252.227-7013 and DFARS § 252.227-7013 or subparagraphs (c) (1) and (c)(2) of the Commercial Computer Software-Restricted Rights at 48 CFR § 52.227.19, as applicable. Contractor/manufacturer: LICENSOR: LYNDA.COM, LLC, c/o PEACHPIT PRESS, 1249 Eighth Street, Berkeley, CA 94710.